Paradigm Shift in Language Planning and Policy

Contributions to the Sociology of Language

101

Editors
Joshua A. Fishman
Ofelia Garcia

De Gruyter Mouton

Paradigm Shift in Language Planning and Policy

Game-Theoretic Solutions

by
Ettien Koffi

De Gruyter Mouton

ISBN 978-1-934078-10-5
e-ISBN 978-1-934078-11-2
ISSN 1861-0676

Library of Congress Cataloging-in-Publication Data
A CIP catalog record for this book has been applied for at the Library of Congress.

Bibliographic information published by the Deutsche Nationalbibliothek
The Deutsche Nationalbibliothek lists this publication in the Deutsche Nationalbibliografie; detailed bibliographic data are available in the Internet at http://dnb.d-nb.de.

© 2012 Walter de Gruyter, Inc., Boston/Berlin

Cover image: sculpies/shutterstock
Typesetting: Apex CoVantage, LLC
Printing: Hubert & Co. GmbH & Co. KG, Göttingen
♾ Printed on acid-free paper

Printed in Germany

www.degruyter.com

To the teachers of CATA, the Anyi Literacy and Translation Center.

To Westwood Church, Saint Cloud, MN, and New Love in Church, Harrisburg, PA, for their sponsorship of the Anyi literacy and translation work.

To all those who give sacrificially to sponsor literacy classes in Anyi villages.

Acknowledgments

Writing a book such as this one can be construed as a cooperative game which involves many players. The list of the players who have contributed to this book is long but only a few of them will be acknowledged by name. First and foremost, I would like to acknowledge the significant role that the late Cathleen Petree, Senior Acquisitions Editor at Mouton de Gruyter, played. If it had not been for her, this book would never have seen the light of day. I would have continued presenting the ideas contained therewithin at conferences without ever assembling them into a book form. She nudged me into action with the following e-mail:

Dear Dr. Koffi,
As the senior acquisitions editor in linguistics/applied linguistics for Mouton de Gruyter in North America, I am attending AAAL next month. I noticed in the conference program that you will be offering a paper on "Paradigm Shift in Language Planning." This sounds like a great topic for a book. Have you thought about this possibility? If you are willing, I would enjoy speaking to you about it. What does your conference schedule look like? Do you have time for a coffee or drink? I will be in Denver from 3/20 to 3/25/09. I look forward to seeing you.

Subsequently, we met twice, had lunch together, and talked about the book. We exchanged several e-mails about my progress until one morning, much to my bewilderment, I received an e-mail about her passing. I'm sad that Ms. Petree is no longer with us to see the final product of the book that she nudged me into writing.

My gratitude goes to Kim Koffi, my wife, who read this book and made sure that non-linguists like her can read it and understand it. She asked for clarification, made corrections, and suggested less convoluted ways to communicate some ideas. Two of my colleagues in the English Department at Saint Cloud State University, Rhoda Fagerland and Jack Hibbard, have carefully read the entire document and made insightful comments and suggestions. I have greatly benefited from their expertise in editing. I'm especially indebted to them because their help came at a time when they were swamped with grading papers for their own courses.

Many veteran language planners in West Africa have helped me a great deal. Though they lack impressive academic credentials, they are full of common sense and practical solutions. I gained real life language planning experience when I was given oversight of language projects in Benin, Côte d'Ivoire, Ghana, and Togo. The six years that I spent in the language planning trenches showed me why my highvoluted "ivory tower" ideas about language planning were unimplementable. These seasoned language planners explained to me, not in words but through their deeds, that my theories were not doable because they failed to take account of logistical issues and "the human condition." If the solutions proposed in this book are implementable, it is due in a large part to the insights that I gleaned from them, and from my literacy and translation work among the Anyi people of Côte d'Ivoire. To all of them and to the many other people whose contributions to language planning have shaped my theory and practice, I say: *"Míın da amɔ ası kpáa,"* that is, "I lie you on the ground good," which is the Anyi way of saying "Thank You very much."

Preface

Paradigm Shift in Language Planning and Policy: Game-theoretic Solutions addresses the language planning conundrum that francophones and lusophones in Sub-Saharan Africa face. It proposes workable and implementable solutions by taking into account the fears, aspirations, influence, and positions of the stakeholders in the mother-tongue education debate that is going on in those countries. The following is a chapter-by-chapter preview of the book.

Chapter 1 diagnoses ten important impediments that have frustrated language planning efforts across Sub-Saharan Africa. The book starts with a diagnosis because, as De Mesquita (2009:31) puts it, "In predicting and engineering the future, part of getting things right is working out what stands in the way of this or that particular outcome."

Chapter 2 is devoted entirely to the inner workings of the Game theory. Since this theory is not widely known among linguists, a great deal of background information is provided. Two different models of the Game theory are used in tandem. Laitin's (1992) Repertoire Model explains why it would be optimal for most contemporary Africans to have a linguistic repertoire consisting of 3±1 languages. De Mesquita's (2009) Predictioneer's Model is used to predict the model of mother-tongue education planning that has the best chance of succeeding in francophone and lusophone Africa.

Chapters 3 and 4 apply the Game theory to the language games that were played in colonial Africa. Chapter 3 focuses on francophone and lusophone Africa while Chapter 4 deals with former Belgian, British, and German colonies. The game-theoretic calculations based on the influence, salience, and position of colonial authorities help explain why efforts toward mother-tongue education planning have stalled in former French and Portuguese colonies. When the weighted mean scores in these colonies are contrasted with those of former Belgian, British, and German colonies, it becomes clear why the latter are relatively better off using their mother tongues at school than the former.

Chapter 5 is a case study which applies Game-theoretic methodology to Côte d'Ivoire. This country was chosen for study for three reasons. First, Côte d'Ivoire has made far less progress in planning its indigenous languages than all its counterparts in Sub-Saharan Africa. Second, the ethnolinguistic landscape of the country is so complicated that if the proposed solutions can work there, chances are that they will work elsewhere in Africa. Third, I grew up in Côte d'Ivoire and have been collecting relevant sociolinguistic data on the country for more than a decade. As a result, I have reliable data to back up my claims.

Chapter 6 tackles the thorny issues of language of education planning in cosmopolitan African megacities. Laitin's Repertoire Model is used to classify megacities into three groups. Some cities are defined as ethnolinguistically homogeneous. Designing a language of education policy for such cities is relatively easy because city dwellers need to know only one language to communicate throughout the city. Some cities are categorized as having ethnolinguistic dominance, that is, an indigenous language is the dominant language of the city. Designing a mother-tongue education plan for schools in such megacities is challenging because of competing ethnolinguistic loyalties. However, these challenges pale in comparison with the last group of megacities that are characterized by ethnolinguistic equilibrium. These are megacities in which no indigenous language is dominant. Using Abidjan as a prototype of such megacities, I propose a model of language of education that is based on language family rather than on the demographic weight of the speech communities found in the magacity.

Chapter 7 shows how all the languages spoken in any given country can and should be planned: some for formal literacy, others for informal literacy. Cooper's (1996) methodology of *"Who plans what for whom, when, where, how, and why"* is used to suggest a fresh new approach to literacy planning in rural areas. This chapter draws from my many years of experience in rural literacy planning and sheds some light on the logistical problems that stand in the way of success. Furthermore, the Predictioneer's Model is used to compare and contrast four widely used approaches to adult literacy. The model that holds the most promise for rural areas in Sub-Saharan Africa is identified and discussed.

Chapter 8 deals with the economics of language and uses Côte d'Ivoire as a case study to show that planning multiple languages for use in schools is not more expensive than planning a single language. Two experiments reported by Bamgbose (2004:15) and Ladefoged (1992:811) show that this is economically feasible. In the first, it was shown that the cost of publishing in multiple African languages can be kept relatively low by creating a master document whose texts are translated into other languages while keeping the design, graphics, and layout the same. The second experiment showcases how Uganda has successfully taught six local languages in its schools. On the basis of these findings, I contend that 17 regional LWCs can be planned and taught in secondary schools in Côte d'Ivoire on a shoestring budget and for profit. Furthermore, I use enrollment data from 2010 to show that planning multiple languages can turn the vast linguistic resources of Côte d'Ivoire into a multimillion dollar economic bonanza.

Chapter 9, the final chapter, takes the view that language planning need not be only the responsibility of big government, big business, or deep-pocketed development agencies. I review historical data to show how individuals, through their personal efforts and sacrifices, have successfully planned languages. In the pantheon of illustrious language planners of past centuries, I chose to highlight the strategies used by St. Stefan for Komi, Eliezer Ben Yehuda for Hebrew, Samuel Ajayi Crowther for Yoruba, Johann Ludwig Krapf and Johann Rebmann for Swahili, Alexander Mackay for Luganda, Robert Moffat for Setswana, Alfred Saker for Duala, and Diedrich Westermann for Ewe. The study of these language planners shows that for language planning to be successful three of four indispensable ingredients – translation, lexicography, literacy, and newspapers in the local languages – must be present.

Finally, a word or two should be said about the use of certain terms and abbreviations in the book. Terms such "indigenous" and "illiterate" have acquired a negative connotation with some people, but not with others. I do not assign any negative meaning to these words when they are used in this book. I have used "ancestral," "local," "autochthonous," and "mother tongue" as synonyms for "indigenous." Similarly, I have substituted "pre-literate" and "non-literate" for "illiterate." Nevertheless, the terms "indigenous," and "illiterate" still appear in the book. Acronyms are unavoidable these days. A list of the ones used in the book is provided on page xvii to help readers identify them quickly.

Contents

Acknowledgments vii

Preface ix

Abbreviations xix

1 Ten deadly impediments to language planning in Africa
Introduction 1
   1.1 Excessive theorization 2
   1.2 The glorification of the LWC mode 4
   1.3 Faulty assessment of ethnolinguistic loyalty 6
   1.4 Elite hypocrisy 11
   1.5 Unaddressed parental concerns 14
   1.6 The low marketability of African languages. 16
   1.7 The "dependency" syndrome. 20
   1.8 The rigidity of mother-tongue acquisition models. 22
   1.9 The alleged prohibitive cost 27
   1.10 "Manisfesto syndrome" and the language plan of
        action for Africa 29
   1.11 Summary 33

2 The strategic Game theory and 3±1 language outcome
Introduction 35
   2.1 Correcting some misconceptions about the Game theory 36
   2.2 The universality of games. 37
   2.3 Modern Game theory. 39
   2.4 The working parables of the Game theory 53

2.5 Introducing the Predictioneer's Model 58
2.6 Summary.. 73

3 A Game-theoretic assessment of language of education
   policies in French and Portuguese colonies
Introduction 75
3.1 The Game theory and colonialism studies 76
3.2 The rationales for colonialism 77
3.3 Overview of French colonialism 87
3.4 A Game-theoretic analysis of players' preference 96
3.5 Overview of Portuguese colonialism 97
3.6 Implications for language planning in French
     and Portuguese colonies 104
3.7 Summary.. 106

4 A Game-theoretic assessment of language of education
   policies in Belgian, British, and German colonies
Introduction 109
4.1 The legacy of the pluralistic language ideology 109
4.2 Overview of British colonialism 110
4.3 Overview of Belgian colonies: Congo, Burundi, Rwanda ... 130
4.4 Overview of German colonies........................ 137
4.5 Summary.. 146

5 Case study: Rethinking mother-tongue education
   in Côte d'Ivoire
Introduction 147
5.1 Sociolinguistic survey of Côte d'Ivoire................. 147
5.2 The co-habitation of French and indigenous Ivorian languages... 153
5.3 Experimentation with TIM 159

5.4 Workable models of language of education 171

5.5 MM and the 3±1 language outcome 174

5.6 Personnel planning 176

5.7 Potential obstacles.................................. 177

5.8 Summary.. 179

6 Game-theoretic assessment of language of education
  policies in African megacities
Introduction 181

  6.1 Urbanization in Africa: Historical overview............... 181

  6.2 Colonial and post-colonial urbanization 184

  6.3 Rationale of the unprecedented urban growth............. 188

  6.4 Unemployment, underemployment and urbanization......... 189

  6.5 Assessing ethnolinguistic loyalty 190

  6.6 The ethnolinguistic profile of African megacities 193

  6.7 The ethnolinguistic occupation of urban spaces 194

  6.8 Urbanization and social network analysis 196

  6.9 Social network analysis in megacities.................... 198

  6.10 Language of education policy in megacities with linguistic
  homogeneity....................................... 201

  6.11 Language of education policy in megacities with ethnolinguistic
  dominance 202

  6.12 Language of education policy in megacities
  with ethnolinguistic dominance 204

  6.13 Language planning in cities with ethnolinguistic equilibrium ... 205

  6.14 Abidjan as a case study............................. 206

  6.15 The implementation of MM in Abidjan.................. 207

  6.16 Language endangerment in African megacities 209

  6.17 Summary... 209

7 Framework and rationale for literacy planning in rural Africa

Introduction 211

7.1 The state of adult literacy in Sub-Saharan Africa 211

7.2 A framework for literacy planning 214

7.3 How 223

7.4 Why 233

7.5 The quest for an optimal model of literacy planning 242

7.6 Summary 250

8 Planning multiple languages on a shoestring budget for profit

Introduction 251

8.1 An overview of the economics of language 252

8.2 Paradigm shift in language planning 255

8.3 Application to Côte d'Ivoire 259

8.4 A quick overview of MM 268

8.5 Overall cost comparisons and cost-benefit analyses 274

8.6 Language planning for all 280

8.7 Summary 283

9 Individual efforts in language planning

Introduction 285

9.1 Genre, organization, and selection 286

9.2 St. Stefan of Perm 287

9.3 Eliezer Ben Yehuda 290

9.4 The Reformation interlude 293

9.5 Samuel Ajayi Crowther 295

9.6 Europeans missionaries' language planning strategies in Africa ... 300

9.7 A comparison of the past and the present 305
9.8 Summary. 309

References. 311
Index. 325

Abbreviations

Aaa	American Anthropological Association
ACALAN	African Academic of Languages
AIM	Assimilationist Immersion Model
BMS	Baptist Missionary Society
CIA	Central Intelligence Agency
CMS	Church Missionary Society
DIM	Dual Immersion Model
FBO	Faith-based Organization
FEA	French Equatorial Africa
FESTAC	Festival of Black Arts and Culture
FIM	Full Immersion Model
FWA	French West Africa
GO	Governmental Organization
HDI	Human Development Index
IMF	International Monetary Fund
ISP	Interest Salience Position
LPAA	Language Plan of Action for Africa
LWC	Language of Wider Communication
MM	Maintenance Model
NGO	Non-governmental Organization
NLWC	National Language of Wider Communication
RLWC	Regional Language of Wider Communication
SIL	Summer Institute of Linguistics
TIM	Transitional Immersion Model
UBS	United Bible Societies
UNDP	United Nations Development Programme
UNESCO	United Nations Education Cultural Organization

Chapter 1
Ten deadly impediments to language planning in Africa

Introduction

Over the past 50 years, theorizing about language planning and policy has been very successful as evidenced by the sheer volume of books and scholarly journal articles devoted to the subject. Seminal works by early luminaries have enriched our understanding of the interface between politics, economics, sociolinguistics, and language planning. However, success in academia has not been accompanied by an equivalent level of success for most nation-states in need of language planning. This has led to the coining of the phrase "catastrophic success" to describe the chasm that exists between the theory and the practice of language planning. As a matter of fact, many indigenous African languages are not better off now than they were 50 years ago, despite more than half a century of sustained scholarship on language planning. The goal of this introductory chapter is to single out the ten deadliest impediments to successful language planning in Africa. Though the focus is on Africa, it is reasonable to believe, based on published articles and books, that these impediments are not idiosyncratic to Africa alone. The impediments in question are the following:

1.1 Excessive theorization
1.2 The glorification of the language of wider communication (LWC) model
1.3 Faulty assessment of ethnolinguistic loyalty
1.4 Elite hypocrisy
1.5 Unaddressed parental concerns
1.6 The low marketability of African languages
1.7 The "dependency" syndrome
1.8 The rigidity of mother-tongue acquisition models
1.9 The alleged prohibitive cost
1.10 The "manifesto" syndrome

The diagnoses made in this chapter will serve as the catalyst for a paradigm shift which will be developed fully in subsequent chapters where specific solutions will be proposed.

1.1 Excessive theorization

Myers-Scotton (2006:376) and Cooper (1996:41, 56–7) offer two diametrically different perspectives on why academic language planning has failed to achieve practical results. According to the former, it is ironic that language planning, a sub-discipline of Applied Linguistics, has thus far failed to find an implementable solution to language planning problems. She explains the failure as follows:

> Yet a third irony is that language policy and planning is a subject widely discussed and debated in numerous publications by academics from a wide variety of disciplines, such as sociology, anthropology, and linguistics, as well as language pedagogy. This flurry of interest in language policy was especially strong in the 1960s and 1970s following the independence of a number of new nations in Africa and Asia, amid idealism about the possibility of language planning along democratic lines ... Once again, language policy drew academic interest in the late twentieth century and receives even more today. Now, however, the reason seems to be more a set of problems than a set of opportunities. The irony of all this academic interest in language policy and planning is that the theories and analyses of academics do not seem to count much when policies are decided by governmental bodies – at least they **haven't had much impact in the past**. [Emphasis in the original]

A little over a decade into the language planning enterprise, Fishman (1974:98–9) warned about four "recurring doubts" that could derail it. He summarized these doubts as follows: 1) the recurring doubt about the gap between target plans and demonstrable attainments, 2) the recurring doubt about the vulnerability of language planning due to ever changing administrative structures and priorities, 3) the recurring doubt about excessive ideological pressure placed on linguists, and 4) the recurring doubt about the fallacies and limitations of the human mind and spirit. In spite of these serious reservations about the efficacy of language planning, Fishman encouraged practitioners to press on, telling them that "there is no need for language planning to feel crestfallen with respect to its own modest achievements to date." This exhortation was undoubtedly interpreted by many to mean that success in language planning need not be measured only by practical achievements. In other words, even if the achievements on the ground are modest, language planners can still claim victory at a scholarly level. As a result, no one seems particularly bothered by the fact that nearly 60 years of writing and publishing on the subject has not changed the reality in many African countries one iota. In this respect, language planners are not much different from their colleagues in theoretical linguistics who are not troubled at all if their insights do not help solve real life language situations. Pinker (1994:52) provides the following story to illustrate the huge divide between theory and practice in linguistics:

> One of the most fascinating syndromes recently came to light when the parents of a retarded girl with chatterbox syndrome in San Diego read an article about Chomsky's theories in a popular science magazine and called him at MIT, suggesting that their daughter might be of interest to him. Chomsky is a paper-and-pencil theoretician who wouldn't know Jabba the Hutt from Cookie Monster, so he suggested that the parents bring their child to the laboratory of the psycholinguist Ursala Bellugi in Lo Jolla.

The difference between academic language planning and theoretical linguistics is that, as this example illustrates, Chomsky was able to refer the woman to another specialist. Who does a theoretical language planner turn to when a language problem surfaces? No one, because language planning is meant to be a specialized area within Applied Linguistics that can solve language problems! In light of this reality, it is befitting to use the phrase "catastrophic success" in relation to language planning. Indeed, the successful cases that are often paraded in the literature cannot be credited to academic language planners. The historical factors that elevated Bahassa in Indonesia, Philippino in the Philippines, Malay in Malaysia, and Swahili in Tanzania predate contemporary scholarship on language planning by a century or more.

Unlike Myers-Scotton, who interprets excessive theorization as an impediment to successful language planning, Cooper (1996:41, 56–7) blames the lack of achievements on the absence of a robust theory of language planning. He contends that, because of these lacunae, individuals have engaged in language planning in a piecemeal fashion, without an overarching set of principles to guide them:

> As for being based on theory, we have yet to move beyond descriptive frameworks for the study of language planning. We have as yet no generally accepted language planning theory, if by theory we mean a set of logically interrelated, empirically testable propositions. ... Without a theory of language planning, we have no principled means of determining what variables should be included in descriptive, predictive, and explanatory studies of a given case. Each investigator must make this determination on a more or less ad-hoc basis. But ad-hoc studies serve as a preliminary step in the formulation of theories. ... In language planning we are still at the stage of

discovering behavioral regularities. Before we can discover regularities, we must first decide which variables it will be most useful to describe. Descriptive frameworks can help us to make such decisions.

Cooper's book, *Language Planning and Social Change*, is meant in part to address this deficiency by bringing practice in line with theory. However, there is little reason to be optimistic that this epistemological approach will bear any fruit. Contrary to Cooper's position, academic language planning has failed to change the reality on the ground not because practice has preceded theory but rather because excessive theorization has been done on the basis of scanty evidence. From an epistemological point view, Kaplan and Baldauf's book, *Language Planning: From Practice to Theory*, seems more reasonable because they are trying to build a theory on the basis of sixty years of accumulated experience. Though this is a laudable undertaking, it will be argued in 1.2 and in subsequent chapters that their book still falls short of providing fresh insights because it embraces the same hegemonic model of language planning. Such a model, it will be argued, ignores the real life challenges of ethnolinguistic behaviors in multilingual environments.

1.2 The glorification of the LWC model

The LWC model was alluded to in passing in the previous section. Now is the time to dwell on it a little longer and examine why it has been the favorite model for language planners. The LWC model can be described quite succinctly by the equation below:

One Nation = One Language

The rationale for this approach stems from the view that multilingualism is a liability, not an asset. This is the model that Kaplan (1998:424) proposed to the Philippines when he was an expatriate consultant at the request of the government:

Language policy is not, however, only concerned with lexical development. In the Philippines, for example, where the population speaks some 250 languages, *it was a political necessity to identify a national language.* [Emphasis added]

Kaplan is not the only scholar to espouse this view. Many of the leading experts believed until quite recently (and some still do) that the hegemonic approach was (is) the only viable solution to the multilingual dilemma that many countries are confronted with. For this reason, the LWC model was readily adopted because it was the one with which Western language planners were most acquainted because it had been in existence in Europe since the 17th century:

> Language planning has become part of modern nation-building because a noticeable trend in the modern world is to make language and nation synonymous. Deutsch (1968) has documented the tremendous increase within Europe during the last thousand years in what he calls 'full-fledged national language.' A millennium ago these numbered six: Latin, Greek, Hebrew, Arabic, Anglo-Saxon (i.e., Old English), Church Slavonic. By 1250 this number had increased to seventeen, a number that remained fairly stable until the beginning of the nineteenth century with, of course, changes in the actual languages, as Hebrew, Arabic, Low German, Catalan, and Norwegian either submerged or became inactive, and languages like English, Dutch, Polish, Magyar (i.e., Hungarian), and Turkish replaced the inventory. In the nineteenth century the total number of fully fledged national languages increased to thirty. According to Deutsch, it showed a further increase to fifty-three by 1937, and it has further increased since then. Each 'new' country wanted its own language, and language became a basic expression of nationalistic feeling, as we see in such examples as Finnish, Welsh, Norwegian, Romanian, Bulgarian, Ukrainian, Irish, Breton, Basque, Georgian, and Hebrew (Wardhaugh 2010:378).

In the 1940s, the Chinese vigorously defended the One Nation = One Language model in the name of national unity. Premier Chou En-lai[1] rationalized the official position of the Communist Party as follows:

> The diversity in dialects[2] has an unfavorable effect on the political, economic and cultural life of our people ... Without a common speech, we shall to a greater or lesser extent, meet with difficulties in our national reconstruction ... It is, therefore, an important political task to popularize vigorously the common speech with the Peking pronunciation as the standard (DeFrancis 1972:458, 462–3).

---

1 In a speech delivered on January 10, 1959.
2 DeFrancis (1972: 465) notes that the eight "dialects" are not orally mutually intelligible. However, they are mutually intelligible in writing because Chinese writing is logographic.

Some prominent Chinese linguists aligned themselves with the official position by putting forth the argument below:

> There is no nation which at one and the same time speaks several languages.[3] Another communist commentator explained the rationale of the Chinese' insistence as follows: There are some Western linguists who think there are several Chinese languages, because the differences among the Chinese dialects are rather large, to the point where the people who use these dialects cannot understand each other. This mistaken suggestion is from a political point of view very dangerous. Whoever says that there are several languages says in principle that there are several nations. To contend that there are several Chinese languages is to argue for the division of China into several states. ... Chinese is the language of the Chinese people. As everyone knows, a common language is one of the characteristics of a nation. Hence the common language of the Chinese nation is one of the fundamental marks of the Chinese nation (DeFrancis 1972:462).

With the Europeans and the Chinese firmly behind the LWC model, language planners sought to export it to Africa as the elixir that would cure its multilingual woes. To this day, advocates for the African Renaissance and some linguists are so enamored with it that they dream of imposing it at the continental level. They fathom Swahili as the pan-African language, Arabic as the regional LWC for North Africa, Hausa as the LWC for West Africa, and a Zulu-related language as the LWC for Southern Africa. It will be argued below that ethnolinguistic loyalty has been a formidable roadblock in the implementation of the LWC model in many parts of Africa. Recent survey data suggest that the hegemonic approach to language planning is no longer popular among Africans. Anyidoho and Dakubu (2008:146–147) report, for instance, that Ghanaians (including the majority of Akan speakers) oppose Akan being imposed as the national LWC on the rest of their countrymen and women.

1.3 Faulty assessment of ethnolinguistic loyalty

Under the indigenous national LWC model, hardly was any consideration given to ethnolinguistic loyalty in language planning. It was assumed that as soon as an indigenous LWC was decreed and imposed on the citizenry, they would gladly adopt it. In fact, leading African linguists such as

---

3 This quote is attributed to Stalin.

Bamgbose (1991:7) trivialized the correlation between multilingualism and divisiveness as a "convenient scapegoat" for inaction. He points to the intense social upheavals in Burundi, Madagascar, Rwanda, and Somalia, all of which are monolingual countries, to suggest that the ethnolinguistic identity card has been overplayed. Indeed, these cases underscore the fact that it is a fallacy to equate monolingualism with social cohesion, but it is nonetheless true that multilingualism can lead to divisiveness. The post-election conflicts that often flare up in Côte d'Ivoire, Kenya, Nigeria, and many other places in Africa are strong reminders that ethnicity and ethnic allegiances are still a hurdle in language planning. There are plenty of examples all over the world to prove this point, but let's content ourselves with the well-documented case of India where language planning in this multilingual state has led to various types of social conflicts. Dua (1996:2, 6) describes four types of language-related conflicts:

1. Language of wider communication versus national language
2. National language versus minority language
3. Majority language versus minority language
4. Majority language versus majority language

He contends that ethnolinguistic identity is prone to conflict in multilingual environments because it can be very easily "ideologized." "Ideologization," he argues, "serves as a rallying point for the speakers of a language." Furthermore, he warns that "[language] loyalty and pride can be ideologically cultivated and manipulated to produce either integration or separation." Examples of the latter are abundant in the literature. Secessionist discourse in Quebec on account of ethnolinguistic identity tells us that ethnolinguistic identity is not a joking matter in language planning. Biloa and Echu (2008:212) fear that promoting an indigenous Cameroonian language to the status of LWC on top of the uneasy relationship between English and French can aggravate the risk of a civil war. Most of the contributors to *Language and National Identity in Africa* express this fear for Africa in one way or another. Appleyard and Orwin (2008) correlate much of the turmoil in the Horn of Africa with multilingualism and ethnolinguistic identity. Suleiman (2006:51) warns that no heterogeneous society is free from identity-driven conflicts. Naturally, when everything is going well, ethnolinguistic identity remains dormant. However, it rears its head under conditions that lend themselves to social turmoil:

> We may also add here that identities come to the fore under conditions of stress, conflict and lack of security, which is often the case in national

identity at times of historical, social or political crisis. As Bauman states in a figurative turn of phrase, 'a battlefield is identity's natural home. Identity comes to life only in the tumult of battle; it falls asleep and silent the moment the noise of the battle dies down.'

Post-election violence in Côte d'Ivoire, Kenya, and Nigeria in recent years has shown clearly that ethnolinguistic loyalty is alive and well. No language planners in Africa can afford not to be vigilant about ethnolinguistic identity as a serious impediment to language planning. With increasing advocacy for minority rights and minority languages, any attempt to impose an indigenous national LWC on the rest of the citizenry is doomed to fail or lead to conflicts. Fortunately, some African countries have seen the handwriting on the wall and are in search of a new model. Mali is a case in point. Even though Bambara could legitimately be imposed as a national LWC because it is spoken by 40% of the population as their native language and another 40% as their second language, policymakers have distanced themselves from the LWC model and have selected 13 local languages as "national" languages[4] (Skattum 2008:99, 104).

Since independence, managing the various ethnolinguistic identities within the boundaries of independent African nations has been a nightmare for politicians. Truth be told, some are not blameless in this process. Many of them fan the flames of ethnicity for short-sighted political gains. The consensus, however, is that all over the continent, politicians see ethnic loyalty more as a liability than an asset because of its propensity for divisiveness. However, recent studies by Block (2006:39) and Omoniyi (2006:11–33) can help us understand identity better and capitalize on it to formulate successful language policies. The former has shown that identity is compositional and consists of the following components: ethnic, racial, national, gender, social class, language, and religious features. He also makes a useful distinction between "primordial identities" and "acquired identities." Primordial identity is conceived of as consisting of traits such as race, ethnicity, and nationality, which are passed down from one generation to the next. Acquired identities, on the other hand, are those traits that are not transferable: level of education, socio-economic status, employment, marital status, etc. Religious identity is hard to classify because it straddles both primordial and acquired identities. From Omoniyi's work we learn that identity is hierarchical. By combining the compositional nature

---

4 Ethnologue (2009:36) lists 56 indigenous languages for Mali. Estimates vary widely going from 20 all the way to 56 (Skattum 2008:104).

of identity and its hierarchical structure, it is possible to propose the following hierarchy for the purposes of language planning:

National identity > Ethnic Identity > Linguistic Identity > Religious Identity > Social Identity > Gender Identity > Racial Identity

National identity ranks highest in the hierarchy because language planning is first and foremost done for the benefits of citizens of specific nation-states. Ethnic identity comes in second place, higher than linguistic identity, because a group may lose its language and yet retain its ethnic identity. This is the case of many native Americans who, though they may no longer speak their ancestral languages, are still proud to be Dakotas, Ojibwes, Cherokees, etc. However, under normal circumstances, Wa Thiong'o (1986:15) argues, language, culture, and identity are inseparable because "culture is the collective memory bank of a people's experience in history. Culture is almost indistinguishable from language that makes possible its genesis, growth, banking, articulation, and indeed its transmission from one generation to the next." Fishman (1972:95) alluded to this in what he called "the value problem." Early on, he warned that the conflation between ethnic identity and linguistic identity would be a challenge to language planning:

> One of the difficulties frequently mentioned in connection with language planning is the value content within which language and language behavior are formed. According to this view, language planning is more difficult because it centrally impinges upon human values, emotions and habits than does planning with respect to production of tangible economic goods.

One is left scratching one's head as to why a warning such as this was not integrated into a comprehensive approach to language planning. Why was the national LWC the model of choice even though it was well-known that it could not work because of "the value problem"?

Ethnolinguistic identity has also been found to be gradable. A lexical item is said to be gradable if it can be modified by degree words such as "very" or "less," or by the comparative and/or superlative suffixes "-er" or "-est" (Fromkin et al. 2010:197). The adjective "hot," for example, is gradable because it can be modified by "very" and "less" as in "very hot" or "less hot." The claim that ethnolinguistic identity is gradable is very useful in language planning. It helps hypothesize a correlation between the level ethnolinguistic gradation and the anticipated outcomes in language planning. It will be shown below that the stronger an ethnolinguistic group feels about its identity, the less likely it will accept an imposed indigenous

LWC. The converse is also true, that is, if a group has a weak ethnolinguistic identity, it is more prone to accept an imposed local LWC to the detriment of, or in addition to, its native language. It has also been suggested that ethnolinguistic gradation correlates highly with ethnolinguistic loyalty, namely, the stronger the group's ethnolinguistic identity, the stronger its loyalty to its ancestral language. Strong ethnolinguistic loyalty is a double-edged sword in language planning. It can act as a facilitating agency or a deadly impediment. McLaughlin (2008:157–60) exemplifies this correlation with Pulaar and Seereer, two indigenous languages spoken in Senegal:

> Senegalese Pulaar speakers constitute about 23 per cent of the population, making them the largest minority language group in the country. However, their sense of belonging to a wider community of Fula speakers, and their strong sense of the role of language as a central marker of identity, have led them to be quite vigilant in maintaining their own language and keeping at bay the encroachment of Wolof in their communities. ... The Seereer, including speakers of Seerer-Siin and Cangin languages, have been the closest neighbors of the Wolof for centuries and have long spoken Wolof. ... Seerer speakers do not hold the same, often militant, prejudices against Wolof, although they are generally proud of their various languages. Possibly because they have been bilingual in various Seereer languages and Wolof for many centuries, compounded by the fact that they do not form a coherent linguistic group, the Seereer's concept of ethnic identity is not as centrality linked to language as it is for Haalpulaar.

In his Strategic Game theory, Laitin (1992:52) gives serious consideration to ethnolinguistic loyalty because of its consequential impact on language planning. He observes that "people can be mobilized to support terrorism, secession, or federalism in the name of language revival, in large part because of the psychological power of the sense of rootlessness that language loss imposes upon its speakers and their descendants." The recent literature on language and identity in Africa is helpful in understanding the role of ethnolinguistic loyalty and language planning. Marten and Kula (2008:298) suggest that a large number of Zambians who speak minority languages have a low ethnolinguistic loyalty. As a result, they are very willing to code-switch and "employ a number of different languages in different contexts." An indigenous LWC can be planned for groups such as these and for the Seereer because of their low ethnolinguistic loyalty. However, Appleyard and Orwin (2008:276–80) warn that such an indigenous LWC model would not work in Ethiopia because groups such as the Oromos and the Tigrinyas have a very strong ethnolinguistic loyalty. This realization has compelled the Ethiopian government to stop trying to force Amharic on the rest of the country. Instead, in 1994, a federalist form of government was adopted to accommodate the various strong ethnolinguistic egos. A similar solution ought to be adopted for language planning in Côte d'Ivoire, where McWhorter (2003:78) reports that the strong ethnolinguistic loyalties of the Anyi and the Baule cause them to see their languages as separate even though they can understand each other orally. Similarly, the imposition of a national LWC is less likely to work for Benin because of the strong ethnolinguistic loyalty of the Fons. They would not be inclined to accept any language except their own. Though the Fons and the Guns speak fairly mutually intelligible languages, the former have refused for more than a century to use the Gun Bible, alleging that the two languages are different from each other. After decades of trying to convince them otherwise, the Bible Society of Benin has relented and is translating the Bible into Fon. These examples underscore the fact that ethnolinguistic identity and loyalty should no longer be overlooked in language planning, because, as Essegbey (2009:129) notes, in Ghana, "the merest hint that one language might be more prestigious than another turns people against that language."

1.4 Elite hypocrisy

The previous sections have highlighted the fact that a multitude of non-linguistic factors can contribute to the success or failure of language planning. One of these paralinguistic factors is elite hypocrisy. This pattern of behavior is defined as a deliberate attempt by the elite of the country to sabotage language planning efforts by subverting them in one way or another. Laitin (1992:69, 113, 152) notes that this behavior has been attested to in India, Tunisia, and Catalonia. He describes it as follows:

> Often, although individuals vote for the promotion of a national language (showing diffuse support of it), in their personal lives they act in a way that subverts that vote. In many cases they enroll their children in schools where access to the former colonial language is ensured and, at the same time, demand equal favor for their vernacular. In the sardonic words of the Tunisian general secretary of secondary public education, "We do not cease to repeat 'Arabization, Arabization,' all the while sending our children to the schools of MUCF [French private system].

Skattum (2008:120, 121) reports a similar duplicitous behavior in Mali:

> Haïda's 2005 survey however shows that here as elsewhere, *speech and behavior do not necessarily go hand in hand*. When observing the parents' registration of their children in these seven schools, Haïdara found that *the monolingual French ('classic') schools all filled up first. Deprecatory remarks were overheard: 'I'm not enrolling my child in a Bambara school!'* or '*We have avoided the use of national languages once more this year'* (a school director reassuring a parent). In real life, *the more education a parent had, the more it turned out he preferred French for his children and this included the teachers themselves*. What this shows is that though *people may be in favour of national languages, they may not wish to gamble with the future of their own children in national education*. [Italics added for emphasis]

A number of observations can be made from these two quotes. First, the elite give lip service to language planning. They champion it for the whole country, yet they prefer for their own children to be educated in the ex-colonial language. Secondly, the elite are prepared to use every possible means to avoid subjecting their own children to mother-tongue education even though they may have fashioned the policy themselves, or may have helped fashion it. As the example from Mali shows, the elite do not hesitate to bribe their way out of sending their children to schools where the medium of instruction is the local language, if necessary. A school principal has used unconventional means to make sure that an educated parent's child is not put in a class where the mother tongue is the medium of instruction! Thirdly, there are several other hypocritical strategies that the educated elite use. Bamgbose (1991:117) reveals that policymakers try to exempt their children from mother-tongue education by writing language policies that are riddled with loopholes and escape clauses such as "when adequate arrangements have been made" or "whenever possible." Fourthly, in some instances language policies are formulated in such a way as to exempt metropolises on the grounds that such agglomerations are too linguistically diverse for the policies to be implementable. Another common loophole in language policy statements that the elite exploit to their advantage is the exemption given to private schools (religious or not). Such schools are not required to offer classes in the mother tongue on the grounds that some expatriate children may enroll there. Since more will be said about elite hypocrisy and lip-service in subsequent chapters, suffice it now to quote Simpson and Oyetade (2008:188) in order to underscore the private school exemption trick used by the elite in Nigeria:

1.4 Elite hypocrisy 13

> Although the ambitious intention was that children *everywhere* should receive their first three years of primary schooling in their mother tongue or the language of the local community, in practice this actually *happened only sporadically*, and more so in Yoruba, Hausa, and Igbo areas and *public schools* than in minority areas and *private education, which was set on providing all-English education from a very early age (primarily to satisfy the wishes of fee-paying parents that their children learn English well so as to be able to find better employment at a later age)*. [Italics added for emphasis]

Needless to say, this pattern of behavior has deeply hurt the cause of mother-tongue education in post-colonial Africa. The behavior of the elite speaks more loudly than their tiresome demonstrations of the alleged cognitive and intellectual benefits of early mother-tongue education. The duplicity of language planners has caused the elite who are not involved in the language industry to be skeptical, ambivalent, apathetic, or even hostile to the use of African languages in education. This, in turn, has hardened the resolve of parents against mother-tongue education in many French-speaking countries in Africa. Many pre-literate and semi-literate parents have grown cynical about the real motives behind the recent push for mother-tongue education in the early grades. Farmers and unskilled workers who live in rural or semi-rural areas see it as a cleverly designed conspiracy to keep their children at the bottom of the socio-economic ladder while the children of the elite are educated in languages that afford them socio-economic mobility. Who can blame them for their cynicism when one remembers that the language policies of the Bantu Education Act in South Africa were intentionally designed to achieve a similar result? If language planning is to succeed in contemporary Africa, the policies must be formulated in such a way that they apply fairly to all the citizenry, irrespective of whether they live in a megacity or in the most remote rural village, or whether their parents are educated or illiterate, rich or poor. The blueprint for such a policy will be discussed throughout this book to show how this new approach can be implemented.

In almost all these cases, there is a functional "linguistic separation of powers" which has resulted in a diglossia à la Fishman. The international lingua franca is also the colonial language, the official language, the language of elementary, secondary, and college level schooling; the administrative language, the language of the courts, the language of international business, the language of the formal sector of the economy: banking, services, telecommunication; of the armed forces, etc. In a nutshell, it is the language of upward social mobility. One cannot secure the job of one's dreams without mastering it.

However, contrary to the refrain in the sociolinguistic literature, knowledge of the international LWC is no longer confined to the elite. The term "elite closure" that Myers-Scotton introduced in the 1990s is now anachronistic. It may have been true a decade or so after the independence of most countries, but it is no longer applicable to contemporary Africa unless the definition of elite is stretched to include jobless college graduates. Not surprisingly, Bokamba (2008:103) has generously bestowed the label of elite to secondary school graduates! Even if this were so, Mazrui (2008:206) disproves that the label "elite" is stretched in describing the following situation in Kenya:

> Yet it would be wrong, at least in the case of Kenya, to regard English exclusively as a language of the elite. It may be an additional language of a minority of the country's population, but members of that minority are not necessarily members of the elite. Indeed, the slums of Nairobi – the capital city of Kenya – where I have had the opportunity to conduct research, are full of unemployed youth with an appreciable command of English.

In my previous employment as a linguistic consultant for a large international organization, I had the privilege of travelling to many countries and employing many people with an excellent command of French or English who did not belong to an elite class. Mazrui's assessment of the Kenyan situation is valid for scores of countries all over the continent. In general, there has been a steady increase in literacy levels all over Sub-Saharan Africa. As a result, there is an ever growing number of people who know the former colonial languages very well who cannot and should not be classified as elite without a severe distortion of contemporary sociolinguistic realities.

1.5 Unaddressed parental concerns

In the indigenous LWC model that has been in vogue since the 1960s, parental involvement in language planning is minimal. Of course, Kaplan (1998), Kaplan and Baldaulf (1997) and others make opinion surveys a central piece of their methodology. However, because an overwhelming majority of Africans are illiterate and/or live in rural areas, it goes without saying that their input in the language planning process and outcomes is negligible. It is therefore fair to assume that the national LWC model mostly seeks the opinion of educated city dwellers. This approach leaves out a large percentage of parents who are stakeholders in the language planning debate. However, Laitin (1992:119) is of the opinion that success or failure in language planning depends to a large extent on how parents' fears and aspirations for their children's future are addressed:

> The most important general finding of the game-theoretic analysis is that the "players" involved in state construction are different over the centuries, leading to differently constituted language games and different equilibrium outcomes. The nature of the postcolonial bureaucracy has made it a key independent player in African state building able to subvert the language goals of political leadership. Also, the involvement of the state in mass education has brought school administrators and parents into the arena of language policy, interests that state builders of earlier centuries never encountered. New players and newly unleashed interests have led to newly constituted games. The dynamic of these games has pushed many African states not toward rationalization but toward a 3±1 multilingual outcome.[5]

Recent language attitude surveys underscore clearly that parents in Nigeria are uneasy, opposed, or even hostile to mother-tongue education in primary schools. Simpson and Oeyetade (2008:192) quote a study by Iruafemi in which only 6% of Nigerian parents approved of an indigenous language as the medium of instruction, while 24% of parents favored English as the sole medium of education. They also report a study by Adegbija in which 77% of the respondents in Nigeria opposed replacing English with indigenous languages in elementary grades. Bado (2009:17) reports a study in which Ndebele and Shona parents in Zimbabwe prefer English as the only medium of education for their children. Parental involvement and support is critical for the success or failure of language planning, as has been well documented in other places in the world. Daniel (2003:5) reports that UNESCO was dismayed by the approval of Proposition 227 in California. The passage of 227 spelled doom for bilingual education:

> Many were outraged in 1998 when Californian voters, by a 61% majority, imposed English as the state's sole language in publicly-funded schools despite opposition from a coalition of civil liberties organizations. Approval by referendum of Proposition 227, as it was called, meant resident foreign born children, mostly Spanish-speaking, could no longer be taught in their own language. Instead, they would have an intensive one-year course in English and then enter the general school system. The move was watched closely nationwide because 3.4 million children in the United States either speak English badly or not at all.

---

5 The 3±1 formula will be explained thoroughly in Chapter 2.

After nearly a century of experimenting with mother-tongue education, Anyidoho and Dakubu (2008:149–150) report that Ghana switched to English as the only medium of instruction at all levels in 2002. The debates that have ensued are very telling about parental concerns and fears:

> The public continues to debate the issue. Ghanaian newspapers from time to time carry articles advocating either the maintenance of the policy or a change to local languages. Those who support maintenance reiterate the old arguments, that problems such as multiplicity of languages, inadequate resources to support their teaching and learning, classrooms with children from diverse linguistic backgrounds, etc., make the English medium a better option. *They also mention the huge social capital that fluency in English confers on individuals.* Their opponents stress that these drawbacks are the consequences of the *prevailing negative attitude towards local languages* and lack of attention to their development, rather than inherent to the policy. [Italics added for emphasis]

Essegbey (2009:129) reports that that decision has been overturned, but goes on to make the following comment: "While this policy has now been reversed, it serves as an illustration of the importance people place on English, often to the neglect of Ghanaian languages." Laitin (1992:123) mentions an editorial report in Lagos' *Daily Times* which underscores the fears of parents that mother-tongue education could hurt their children's chances for advancement: "The least luxury we can afford in the last decade of the twentieth century is an idealistic experiment in linguistic nationalism which could cut our children off from the main current of human development."

1.6 The low marketability of African languages

Sociolinguistic experiences all over the world indicate that all languages do not have equal market value; that is, some languages are more marketable than others. It is also a truism that the speakers of languages in the same geographical area know which languages are economically valuable to them and which ones are not. Thus, language consumers everywhere are savvy and know which language(s) rank(s) higher on the scale of importance and which rank(s) lower. This awareness that some languages are more desirable to acquire than one's own has been referred to as the *Language Marketability Hierarchy Hypothesis*. Illiterate people are probably more aware of the socio-economic value of language than many language professionals because the former are acutely aware of what they don't have, while the latter take literacy for granted. The reality of the socio-economic value of language is clearly understood by African parents, as seen in the following quote from Skattum (2008:119):

> Your language [French] is the language of money and regular salary. If a person has success, is it not a question of money? If you know French, you can travel and know the world, and nobody can fool you. With our language, you don't know anything.

High socio-economic ranking is not necessarily attached only to European languages. Speakers will generally learn any language that ranks higher than their own socio-economically. McWhorter (2003:275) provides an example of two African languages to illustrate the marketability hypothesis:

> In the conclusion of a much-discussed article in academic linguistics' signature journal *Language*, the eminent linguist Peter Ladefoged described a Dahalo-speaking father who was proud that his son now spoke only Swahili, because this was an index of his having moved beyond the confines of village life into material success beyond. 'Who am I to say that he was wrong?' writes Ladefoged. Certainly we cannot prefer that the son opt for poverty; he was most likely moving away from a context in which few Westerners, language revivalists or not, could even conceive of living if other options were available. This last point is crucial: even if the Dahalo speaker was seduced by attractions of city life and cash economy that in our eyes are of superficial value, we put ourselves in a tenuous position when we argue that the son should resist the very lifestyle that none of us, downsides fully acknowledged, would even consider giving up.

In the same country of Kenya, Mazrui (2008:205) provides us with the following pieces of information that allow us to rank Dahalo, Swahili, and English in relation to each other:

> Since independence, socio-economic advancement at the individual level and economic development at the national level have been pegged to the English language, both in policy and practice. There was a time when those aspiring to migrate from rural to the urban area would try to acquire Kiswahili to improve their chances of employment in the urban metropolis. But as both the Whiteley (1974) and Sure (1999) studies show, there is a growing demand for English even in the rural areas, and in several parts of the country rural dwellers who are proficient in Kiswahili are likely to have English in their repertoire.

Furthermore, Kanwangamalu (1997:245) notes that South African indigenous languages rank lower than Afrikaans and English: "Compared to English and Afrikaans, the status of African languages is relatively low. It does not take long for the language consumer to realize that education in an African language does not ensure one social mobility and better socio-economic life; and that those who can afford it, and among them policy-makers themselves, send their children to English-medium schools, and that when all is told, only education in English opens up doors to the outside world as well as to high-paying jobs." Mesthrie (2008:337) goes one step further and provides us with this sweeping ranking: "Despite the importance of tradition and despite the rhetorical challenges to colonialism, the colonial languages are inextricably linked to modernity." The cursory analysis in the preceding paragraphs lends incredible support to the language marketability hierarchy hypothesis. Armed with this information, one can rank all the languages spoken in a given country. Since the examples used in this section have dealt with Kenya, South Africa, and Mali, the following scales can be proposed for the languages in these three countries:

Kenya: English > Swahili > Dahalo > Indigenous languages
Mali: French > Bambara > Indigenous languages
South Africa: English > Afrikkans > Indigenous languages

For each country in Africa, one can proceed to a similar ranking of the languages. If the Language Marketability Hierarchy Hypothesis were used across the board to rank languages in Africa, all unbiased commentators would readily agree that the ex-colonial languages have the highest market value of all the languages spoken in Sub-Saharan Africa. This fact alone is a huge obstacle to language planning, especially to the kind of mother-tongue education advocated by UNESCO and most language planners in Africa. This has led Kamwangamalu (1997:238) to conclude that "many blacks in South Africa still perceive mother-tongue education as a lure to self-destruction." Skattum (2008:119) quotes a market-savvy Malian parent who sees no market value in sending his children to school to be educated in his mother tongue:

> It's French that's useful, that's what we've seen here in Dugukuna, because those of our children who have learnt it have become important people. But to this day, we haven't seen that any pupil who has studied Bambara has gained anything from it.

Kaplan (1998:421) has warned that language planning efforts fail because language plans are "couched in fairly altruistic terms," that is, the benefits of learning the language are tied to "a vague good in the distant future" or to a feel-good notion of preventing language endangerment. By all accounts, Africans had a very high level of instrumental motivation in the colonial era because European languages afforded them numerous opportunities for upward social mobility. Robertson (1995:314–5) describes these language-driven entrepreneurs as follows:

> In precolonial societies power and status were determined by age, family position, and ability, and in many societies by gender. ... The advent of European rule was to change all that, although this was not immediately evident. Thus, some rulers, when urged by missionaries to send their children to school, sent the children of their slaves, instead, considering that education was unimportant and that they could more easily control low-status educated persons. But in order to obtain even low positions in the colonial administration, Africans had to have a Western-style education. After World War I it was evident to all that the Europeans had prevailed and that the struggle for power was henceforth to be within the new system. Between the wars, the power of those precolonial gerontocracies that had survived the initial conquest was undermined by the newly educated Africans, who organized themselves into political parties, trade unions. ... The colonial presence created new opportunities for wages or self-employment: clerks, masons, domestic servants, miners, and other jobs most frequently filled by men.

As one combs through the long list of pronouncements on the value of mother-tongue education, one is hard pressed to find concrete ideas to make African languages marketable to their learners. I concur with Donnacha (2000:19) that "for language planning to be successful, the long-term viability of the community expected to support the language has to be taken into account. This calls for activities that promote the economic viability of the community: ensure they have access to services such as education, health and social welfare; develop the community's own sense of self-belief and esteem." Africans will not need to be convinced to be educated through their mother tongues if these languages afford them the same or similar opportunities for socio-economic advancement that the European languages give them. This point is aptly made by Cooper (1989:106). However, so long as the economic benefits of mother-tongue education are still shrouded in sentimentality or some nebulous ideological concept of "africanness," parents will continue to hesitate to enroll their children in schools that promote the mother tongue as the medium of instruction in the elementary grades.

1.7 The "dependency" syndrome

In post-colonial literature, the phrase "dependency syndrome" refers to a condition in which formerly colonized countries find themselves so conditioned that they rely completely on the ex-colonial powers for nearly everything they need for their development. Though the phrase is seldom used in sociolinguistics, its usage here to describe the state of corpus planning of African languages is appropriate. By most estimates, the continent boasts at least 2,000 languages. A great number of these languages are in desperate need of corpus planning. Without a decent description of the structures of these languages – phonetics, phonology, morphology, syntax, and vocabulary – language planning cannot take place. The elaboration of orthographies, reference grammars, dictionaries, primers, etc. is not possible without first reducing these languages to writing. However, to date, many African languages, even some that are spoken by hundreds of thousands of people, cannot be planned at all because they have not been studied at all or they have been inadequately studied. The bulk of these languages are found in countries which were under Direct Rule system of colonial administration, namely former French and Portuguese colonies (details are forthcoming in Chapter 3). For hundreds of these languages, the first steps towards mother-tongue education have not yet been taken. Native speakers of these languages are still waiting for expatriate missionaries to come and reduce their languages to writing. Many African governments have, as it were, outsourced corpus planning to Christian missionary organizations. There is nothing necessarily idiosyncratic about outsourcing corpus planning to churches. The Church has had a long and successful track record in corpus planning. Many of the European languages that are now sought after as international LWCs were first reduced to writing by Christian missionaries (Kaplan and Baldauf 1997: 228; Cooper 1989:126). In fact, an overwhelming number of African languages that have a literacy tradition owe it to Western missionaries, as will be discussed in Chapter 9. This is certainly the case for Akan, Ewe, Gun, and Swahili, to mention only a few. Since the 1930s, a well-organized and linguistically sophisticated missionary organization, SIL International (formerly known as the Summer Institute of Linguistics), has made its goal to translate the New Testament into as many languages as possible. For this reason, it has dispatched an army of more than 6,500 linguists to the four corners of the world (Svelmoe 2009:635). Many of these linguists are what Olson (2009:649) refers to as "ordinary working linguists," but a few, the cream of the crop, more than 300 men and women, have Ph.Ds in linguistics. Their contribution to the field of linguistics has been impressive. Olson mentions

1.7 The "dependency" syndrome

SIL International's involvement in more than 1,000 languages, its 13,000 entries of books, journals, book chapters, dissertations, its language analysis software, and its *Ethnologue*, a comprehensive and authoritative catalogue of languages, as tangible evidence of its presence in linguistics. In spite of the efforts by SIL International and similarly minded missionary organizations, more than 60% of African languages are still waiting to be provided with a writing system of the first time (Hasselbring 2006:2).

In the USA, the relationship between SIL International and what Dorbin (2009:623) calls "academic linguistics" has moved from cordial to tenuous over the years. The animosity that the American Anthropological Association (AAA) has harbored against SIL International is slowly spreading to academic linguistics as well. However, this is not the case in Africa, where both governments and academic linguists depend on this missionary linguistic organization for linguistic fieldwork. The African Academy of Languages (ACALAN)[6] acknowledges the significant contribution of SIL on its website and devotes a tab to it. There is no doubt that SIL International should be thanked profusely for its field linguistic services, but it must also be acknowledged that the relationship of exclusive dependency on an expatriate NGO (Non-governmental Organization) is unhealthy for several reasons. In some instances, a project is begun but is stopped for health reasons. In other cases, a young missionary falls in love with another missionary and gets married. In such cases, one of them must necessarily leave his/her post to join the new partner. There have been some instances, though very few, where a missionary goes on furlough and resigns. This means that the project that he/she started will sit idle for years until another trained missionary is found. Then there is always the threat of social upheavals and civil wars in the host country. When a situation such as this arises, the USA and other Western powers evacuate their citizens, and all the projects in the country come to a standstill.[7] These situations and many others should compel language professionals in Africa to lessen their dependency on SIL International. The Language Plan of Action for Africa[8] is doing precisely that by charging African universities with the following mission:

---

6 Retrieved from http://www.acalan.org/eng/accueil/accueil.php on May 14, 2010.
7 SIL International is trying to solve this problem by training more and more Africans. However, the number of well trained Africans for this purpose is too low for the moment.
8 Retrieved from http://www.bisharat.net/Documents/OAU-LPA-86.htm on May 02, 2010.

Aware that African universities, research institutes and other institutions concerned with the study and promotion of African languages have a unique role to play in strengthening the role these languages play in the daily lives of the African peoples, the need for these institutions to strike a proper balance in the future between the scientific study of the African languages and their actual use and practical promotion. In connection with the above, the need for each Member State to render its national universities and other research and related institutions a primary instrument for the practical promotion of African languages, as regards such critical promotional activities, as the compilation of technical and general dictionaries, the writing of textbooks on useful subjects, the training of teachers of language, translators, interpreters, broadcasters and journalists, the production of useful books and other types of literature, relevant to the lives of contemporary Africans and the up-dating of vocabulary in African languages.

Somehow I have the feeling that this call will go unheeded because the younger generation of African linguists is more interested in theoretical linguistics than the kind of field linguistics that yields results that are directly applicable to corpus planning. The drive towards theoretical linguistics has grown so strong that Larry Hyman in his plenary address at the 4th World Congress on African Linguistics/34th Annual Conference on African Linguistics in 2003 in Rutgers, New Jersey, felt compelled to entitle his keynote address, "Why describe African Languages?" Professor Hyman is one of the leading theoreticians in linguistics of this generation, and yet he feels the need for African linguists and Africanist linguists to go back to sound descriptive linguistic work. Though the number of linguistic programs is increasing all over the continent, and some have world-renown experts, the disdain for the kind of descriptive analyses necessary for corpus planning is an impediment that needs to be addressed seriously. It is unhealthy to outsource this aspect of language planning to SIL International. This linguistic dependency clearly means that as long as this organization has not described a language and provided it with an orthography, a dictionary, a reference grammar, a primer, etc. language planning has to wait. The lack of corpus planning in many African languages perpetuates the dominance of the national LWC model even though there is compelling ethnolinguistic evidence that this model is no longer viable.

1.8 The rigidity of mother-tongue acquisition models

The discussions in 1.6 may be misinterpreted to mean that African parents do not want their mother-tongues to be taught at school. Nothing could be further from the truth. Survey reports indicate clearly that they want their children to know their ancestral languages. Many equate losing proficiency in their language with losing their culture. So, they are looking to linguists to come up with a win-win formula that can help their children maintain proficiency in the mother tongue while acquiring proficiency in the ex-colonial language(s). Unfortunately, the solutions that have been proposed which are based on FIM and TIM have fallen significantly short of this expectation. Failure in this area is perhaps the most formidable obstacle to language planning in Africa. For now, the main stumbling blocks in the models of acquisition planning that have been proposed so far will be discussed. Chapters 2, 5 and 8 will pick up this discussion and propose a win-win formula that is likely to be acceptable to parents.

The labels to refer to the models of mother-tongue acquisition planning may have changed, but the practice has remained the same. In colonial times, the prevailing model among the Belgians, the British, and the Germans was FIM. It consisted in teaching African languages as the media of instruction throughout the six years of elementary school. In British colonies, parental complaints led to a change in the language of education policy. No longer were African languages used as the exclusive media of instruction in elementary school. Instead, these languages were used as media of instruction only during the first three years of elementary school. From the fourth year onward, the native language was progressively phased out while English took over. This has been referred to in the literature as TIM.[9] Wa Thiong'o (1986:11) describes his childhood experiences under both models of mother-tongue education:

> And then I went to school, a colonial school, and this harmony was broken. The language of my education was no longer the language of my culture. I first went to Kamaandura, a missionary run school, and then to another called Maanguuuũ run by nationalists grouped around the Giũkuũyuũ Independent and Karinga Schools Association. Our language of education was still Giũkuũyuũ. The very first time I was ever given an ovation for my writing was over a composition in Giũkuũyuũ. So for my first four years there was still harmony between the language of my formal education and that of the Limuru peasant community. It was after the declaration of a state of emergency over Kenya in 1952 that all the schools run by the patriotic nationalists were taken over by the colonial regime and were placed under District Education Boards chaired by Englishmen. English became the language of my

---

9 See 2.5.2 for an explanation of the various models of acquisition planning.

formal education. In Kenya, English became more than a language: it was *the* language, and all the others had to bow before it in deference.

This was also the prevailing model in Ghana (Anyidoho and Dakubu 2008:148), Nigeria (Simpson and Oyetade 2008:179), and in the Democratic Republic of Congo (Bokamba 2008a:103–4). There were, however, a few noteworthy exceptions like the use of Hausa as the medium of instruction for the whole six years of primary schooling. It is also worth noting that as far back as the 19th century, FIM was disavowed by Igbo chiefs who petitioned missionaries to stop using their native language as the medium of education for their children (Laitin 1992:122). Instead, they wanted their youngsters to be educated solely in English.

TIM received an unconditional endorsement by UNESCO in 1953 when a UNESCO "expert report" recommended it across the board for Africa and elsewhere:

> We must here lay down as a general principle what must have already been made apparent by our general approach to the problem: that in order to ease the burden on the child, the mother tongue should be used as the medium of instruction as far up the educational ladder as the conditions referred to on page 50 permit (in other words that the transfer to a second language, if necessary, should be deferred to as late a stage as possible); and that authorities should do everything in their power to *create* the conditions which will make for an ever-increasing extension of schooling in the mother tongue, and make the transition from mother tongue to second language as smooth and as psychologically harmless as possible.[10]

UNESCO (1953) officially endorsed TIM, and has since then been relentless in pressuring African governments to embrace it as THE mother-tongue education model (Bamgbose 2004:7). However, parental opposition to TIM has remained steadfast in francophone Africa. As a result, in 1987 UNESCO introduced a new model called *Pédagogie convergente* (Convergent pedagogy). It is used primarily in the French-speaking countries of Africa because "the historical dominance of the French language in the formal education systems ... has led to poor learning outcomes, teaching strategies that do not promote comprehension and the stunting of students' natural learning abilities." This new approach is described by Bühmann and Trudell (2008:9) as follows:

---

10 Retrieved from http://unesdoc.unesco.org/images/0000/000028/002897EB.pdf on April 27, 2010.

1.8 The rigidity of mother-tongue acquisition models 25

> In 1987, a new pedagogical approach called *Pédagogie convergente* (or 'Convergent pedagogy') was introduced on an experimental basis. ... The term convergence describes a pedagogy that emphasizes interactive learning and links teaching methods of the first and second languages. The child's mother tongue is used as the language of instruction throughout primary school and the second language is taught in such a way that the learners become functionally bilingual. The goals of this model are to improve school access and learning outcomes for students, to integrate the school into the social and cultural environment of the students, and to produce functionally bilingual learners. In *Pédagogie convergente* schools, students begin primary school in their first language, and they learn to read and write in it before starting to learn French. By the fifth and sixth grades, half of the teaching time is allocated to French and half to the national language. At this stage, students are expected to be able to learn subject content in each of the two languages. By the end of the six years of the primary school cycle, both languages are used equally as mediums of instruction. Students in *Pédagogie convergente* classrooms take the same primary school leaving exam as students in French-only classrooms, but they are also examined in subjects specific to *Pédagogie convergente*.

UNESCO claims this new approach has yielded miraculous results in Mali. On page 11 of a report entitled *Mother Tongue Matters*, the following claim is made:

> In 2000, the first student generation in the extended *Pédagogie convergente* programme reached seventh grade. Regional results for the entrance exam nationwide showed that these students performed better overall than students in French-only schools; *Pédagogie convergente* student achievement was an average of 16.23 points higher than that of French-only school students.

A similar upbeat assessment is found in Daniel (2003:4–7). However, the picture from Mali, a country where *Pédagogie convergente* has been used in rural areas for some years, is far from being rosy (Skattum 2008:120). Yet, Daniel (2003:1), writing on behalf of UNESCO, makes this astounding claim:

> Years of research have shown that children who begin their education in their mother tongue make a better start, and continue to perform better, than those for whom school starts with a new language. The same applies to adults seeking to become literate. This conclusion is now widely implemented, although we still hear of governments that insist on imposing a foreign language of instruction on young children, either in a mistaken attempt at modernity or to express the pre-eminence of a social dominant group.

The discrepancies between UNESCO's assessments and the reality on the ground are symptomatic of unproven claims about the merits of TIM as a good model of mother-tongue education. Some linguists are unimpressed by these self-congratulating reports. Fasold has expressed doubts about UNESCO's claims:[11]

> Thirty years and numerous studies after the publication of the UNESCO Report, the unanimous opinion seems to be that nobody knows whether using the mother tongue as the medium of instruction is better than using a second language or not. ... It seems that for every research that indicates that mother-tongue education is effective, there is another one that indicates that it is not. The consensus on this question of whether or not mother tongue education works is that 'we just don't know.'

Bender (2002:94–6) reports that bilingual education in English and Cherokee has not been successful in North Carolina. In 2010 I spent several months as a consultant for an Ojibwe revitalization project in central Minnesota, and I have come to the same conclusion as Bender. The school has implemented TIM for the past two decades, but there has been very little success. Students are not able to read, write, or converse in Ojibwe. Others have been skeptical about UNESCO's self-congratulatory assessments. However, many African linguists, including Dijté (2008:58, 62, 64, 67), Bokamba (2008a:103), and Bamgbose (1991:125)[12] have willingly accepted UNESCO's claims. The gullibility of leading African linguists vis-à-vis such claims gives some weight to Mesthrie's (2008:355) charge that African intellectuals have "too heavy a faith in language planning." Their unconditional support for language planning must be contrasted with the caution and dubitative approach taken by illiterate and semi-literate parents, as discussed in 1.5. In fact, many Malian parents are unconvinced by the merits of *Pédagogie convergente*. This is the reason why they do everything possible to avoid it, including bribing headmasters! Apart from Mali and Senegal where the Converging Pedagogy is being piloted in some rural areas, not

---

11 Quoted in Kamwangamalu (1997:241).
12 In the interest of transparency, it is worth noting that Professor Bamgbose is one of UNESCO's consultants. See the list of acknowledgment in *Education in a Multilingual World*. It should also be noted that UNESCO is a leading donor/partner of ACALAN, the implementation arm of the African Union's language policy. This information is found at ACALAN's website at http://www.acalan.org/eng/partenaires/partenaires.php.

many French-speaking countries are clamoring at UNESCO's doorsteps to implement the model in their schools. As long as mother tongue education is confined to rural areas, many parents will continue to believe that the elite is conspiring to keep their children from achieving success. Djite (2008:63) is sympathetic to their sentiment:

> It is therefore not surprising that many parents consider instruction in the local languages as a waste of time, and would rather like to see their children fluent in a European language. Many parents, for whom sending a child to school is a major investment, believe that they send their children to school to learn the official language (English, French or Portuguese), and that a policy forcing them to learn in the local language is only a ploy seeking to dumb down their children and maintain them at the bottom of the socio-economic scale.

Some Francophone policymakers are hesitant to embrace fully UNESCO's approach because of its rigidity. It has an-all-or-nothing mandate. It refuses to consider any other possibility except the use of the mother-tongue as a medium of instruction in elementary schools. UNESCO uses a strong-arm tactic against African governments and pressures them to adopt its prescriptive approach to mother-tongue education. Handman (2009:637) is critical of this language ideology which she finds to be too constraining:

> Although couched now in UNESCO-inflected language rights and freedom, this ideology can be just as burdensome as colonial language ideologies, particularly by insisting that local people maintain their languages in order to be 'authentic' members of an ethnolinguistic community.

In Chapter 8 MM will be proposed as a mother-tongue education model that is less ideologically driven and yet addresses parental concerns and meets their expectations. Language attitude surveys across much of Africa consistently show that between 60% and 70% of parents favor an acquisition model that allows both the mother tongue and the ex-colonial languages to be taught (Simpson and Oeyetade 2008:192 and Bado 2009:35).

1.9 The alleged prohibitive cost

Most cost-benefit analyses are based on the national LWC model. The mother-tongue education model that is used for such calculations is based on FIM or TIM. The cost projection analyses are those proposed by Thorburn (1972:517), Kaplan and Baldauf (1997:114) or Donnacha

(2000:13, 29). The cost modeling presented in these scenarios points to the fact that language planning is prohibitively expensive for African countries with fledgling economies. As of today, nobody has been able to give a ballpark figure of how much planning a language from the ground up would cost. All we know is that language planning is expensive and that the money to do it is needed in real time! When asked about the actual benefits that language planning brings, we hear hedges, such as "Benefits are slow to develop and hard to measure. Their worth often seems to be more to the individual than to society" (Kaplan and Baldauf 1997:139). If language is indeed a resource, as has been argued by Thorburn (1972:514), Vaillancourt (1981), Vaillancourt (2009), and many economists of language, then applied linguists have done a poor job in convincing African governments to invest in it. If it can be convincingly demonstrated to cash-strapped African governments that investing a certain amount of money will yield a good financial return on their investment, they will no doubt find the capital necessary to invest in it. Unfortunately, so far policymakers have not been told exactly how much money will be required to plan the languages in the country, how many jobs will be generated by the language industry, and how much the government stands to benefit monetarily from such an investment. The lack of clarity on this issue has been a serious impediment.

In many respects, the language planning community has been its own worst enemy by failing to propose a language planning model that is cost effective and doable. The cost projections, if there is any, are astronomical! It is therefore understandable that many African governments are ill-disposed to sink a lot of money into language planning when they are faced with mounting and urgent crises in healthcare, agriculture, education, and infrastructure. How can these governments afford the luxury of language planning while they are languishing under the weight of debt that Maathai (2009:89, 92, 93, 94) describes in the following terms:

> From 1970 to 2002, Africa received over half a trillion dollars in loans from the World Bank, the IMF, and individual wealthy nations, and paid back roughly the same amount. However, because of the interest on that debt, by 2002 $300 billion was still outstanding. Throughout this period, the international community continued to provide more loans to African states so that they could pay back the old ones. More recently some of these loans came with economic 'conditionalities' – requirements to curtail government spending, to open markets to foreign goods, and to restrict the money supply. These restrictions forced governments to slash budgets for health, education, and other essential services for their citizens.

Is it a sound education policy to engage in language planning when elementary and high schools are often overenrolled by twice or thrice their normal capacity because of demographic explosion? Which African government, no matter how willing or devoted to the cause of mother-tongue education, would invest in language planning while school and hospital buildings, bridges and roads are lying in a serious state of disrepair? Given the present economic plight of the continent, fair-minded individuals would be right in questioning the timeliness of such a colossal investment while urgent needs abound. Simpson and Oyetade (2008:197) are understanding towards Nigerian authorities for having put the issue of language planning on the back burner for the time being:

> Any promotion of the three major languages as national official languages on par with or replacing English in all official and formal domains will also need a massive, sustained investment of government funds, as high costs of maintaining genuine official multilingualism in countries such as Canada, Singapore, and Switzerland has shown. At the present point in time, this kind of major expenditure might seem to be something that Nigeria unfortunately cannot afford. Having suffered a drastic downturn in its economy since the 1980s, crippling the country's ability to innovate and develop new infrastructure on a national scale, now would not appear to be the time for experimentation with a new language policy poorly provided with financial support. Rather than see new national language policies fail or worse still intensify ethnic disharmony, it would seem that Nigeria is in fact realistically stuck with the inherited status quo for at least the immediate future, until the economy is rebuilt to a state where it could hypothetically bear the burden of a new national language initiative.

In Chapter 8 an affordable model of language planning will be proposed which gives policymakers realistic cost estimates of different models. The estimates for Côte d'Ivoire based on 2010 figures show that the country stands to earn more than $22 million annually if MM is adopted as the model of mother-tongue education. The realization that one can make a decent living studying and teaching African languages will without any doubt alleviate parental concerns about mother-tongue education and provide an antidote against the low marketability value of these languages (see 1.6).

1.10 "Manifesto syndrome" and the language plan of action for Africa

At its 22nd Ordinary Session, in Addis Ababa, from July 28–30, 1987, the Heads of State and Government of the Organization of African Unity signed a language policy document now called the Language Plan of Action for Africa (LPAA). Some articles of this declaration are quoted verbatim below because the LPAA is a document of continental importance that will be referred to again and again in several parts of this book. In order to understand the tone and tenor of this language policy declaration, a quick historical background is needed.

All may have started with a conference in 1962 entitled *A Conference of African Writers of English Expression.* This conference raised important questions about the very definition of "African literature." Some of the participants went so far as to question the "Africanness" of African literature that is not written in an African language (Wa Thiong'o 1986:5–6). Fifteen years later, when leading African writers met in Lagos for the Festival of Black Arts and Culture (FESTAC), they issued a strong call for Africa's "linguistic" independence (Bamgbose 1991:58). The LPAA came ten years after the Lagos Declaration and one year after Wa Thiong'o's seminal book, *Decolonizing the Mind.* He refers to 1986 as the year when self-questioning was at its height among the African elite. Two decades after political independence, the intelligentsia was itching for Africa's "linguistic" and "cultural" independence. The buzzword of the time was "authenticity" and its winning slogan seemed to be *"ad fuentes"* i.e., back to the sources/roots. In the name of "authenticity," some African political leaders and intellectuals traded their Western first names for 'authentic' African first names. Désiré Mobutu, the late president of Zaire (now the Democratic Republic of Congo) became Mobutu Sese Seko. In Togo, Etienne Eyadema became Gnassimgbe Eyadema, to mention only two. They also imposed "authentic" African first names on all their citizens. The authentication movement did not spare Western attire for both men and women. The suit and tie were traded for an "authentic" African attire for men, while women were being discouraged from wearing skirts. It is against this cultural backdrop that the following articles of the LPAA should be interpreted. The italicized words and phrases of the articles do not appear in the original. I have italicized them so as to comment on them later.

PART I: AIMS, OBJECTIVES AND PRINCIPLES

The aims and objectives of this Plan of Action are as follows:

> PART I, b. "To ensure that *all* languages within the boundaries of Member States are recognised and accepted as a source of mutual enrichment;"

1.10 "Manisfesto syndrome" and the language plan of action for Africa

PART I, c. "*To liberate* the African peoples from undue reliance on the utilisation of non-indigenous languages as the dominant, official languages of the state in favour of *the gradual take-over* of appropriate and *carefully selected* indigenous African languages in this domain;"

PART I, d. "To ensure that African languages, by appropriate legal provision and practical promotion, assume their rightful role as the means of official communication in the public affairs of each Member State, *in replacement of European languages*, which have hitherto played this role;"

PART I, e. "To encourage the increased use of African languages as vehicles of instruction *at all educational levels.*"

PART Ill: PROGRAMME OF ACTION (METHODS AND MEANS)

In order to fulfill the objectives set out in Part I, the African States solemnly subscribe to the following programme of action:

PART Ill: a. "At continental level and as a concrete expression and demonstration of the OAU's seriousness of purpose, the adoption without undue delay by the Organization of African Unity and the regional associations, organizations or institutions affiliated to it of *viable indigenous African languages as working languages*;"

PART Ill: f. "*The absolute necessity* that each Member State, as a matter of supreme practical importance, follows up the formulation of an appropriate national language policy with an adequate and *sustained allocation of the necessary financial and material resources*, to ensure that the language or languages prescribed as *official language(s) achieve(s)* a level of modernisation that meets the needs of administering a modern State;"

PART Ill: h. "In recognition that the formal national education system plays a key role in the practical use of any language, the need for each Member State to ensure that all *the sectors* (i.e. *primary, secondary and tertiary*) of the national education system, are pressed as appropriate in the service of the practical promotion of the indigenous language(s) selected and prescribed as (an) official language(s);"

PART Ill: i. "Aware that African universities, research institutes and other institutions concerned with the study and promotion of African languages have a unique role to play in strengthening the role these languages play in the daily lives of the African peoples, the need for these institutions to strike a proper balance in future between the scientific study of the African languages and their actual use and practical promotion."

An in-depth exegesis of the LPAA is not possible, lest it leads us to a wild goose chase. Suffice it to say for the moment that several phrases in the policy show clearly that the pan-African language document is an impediment to language planning. The first major obstacle is that the document openly advocates for the LWC model. This is seen in the phrase "*carefully selected indigenous African languages.*" The discussions in sections 1.2 and 1.5 have already shown that Africans are no longer in favor of imposed national LWCs. Another policy statement that is unpopular with most Africans is found in the phrases *"gradual take over"* and *"in replacement of European languages."* Both anecdotal and statistical evidence overwhelmingly show that most Africans want to be educated in ex-colonial languages. It is clear from the discussion in previous sections that the language policy statements contained in the LPAA are the work of language activists and the political and academic elite that have lost touch with the aspirations of the citizenry. Consequently, it is not at all surprising that the LPAA has failed for lack of popular support. Thirdly, the word *"liberate"* shows clearly and blatantly that the LPAA is an exercise in language activism. However, the average African does not share the sentiment that he/she needs to be "liberated" from the European languages; quite the contrary. There is indeed a widespread belief in Sub-Saharan Africa that European languages have "saved" Africans from ethnolinguistic conflicts. Simpson (2008:5) explains this paradoxical sentiment as follows:

> Large numbers of the territories created as colonies and which subsequently achieved independence had no widely dominant ethnic majorities, and often no language known by over 50 per cent of the population. Where there were sizeable ethnic groups which might have a regional importance (as, for example, in Nigeria, with Hausa, Igbo, and Yoruba groups), there was also a clear strong fear among other ethnic minorities of being dominated by larger groups, undermining the immediate possibility of selecting a combination of larger languages as official replacements for the ex-colonial language. Instead, smaller groups, which collectively might make up a significant amount of the nation's total population, frequently saw the ex-colonial language as a welcome guarantee of ethno-linguistic neutrality favoring no group over another and minimizing the potential of larger groups to accrue advantages for themselves through superior control of official and national languages. In many instances, the ex-colonial languages were therefore perceived as the only languages that could impartially hold an ethnically mixed population together and maintain the often rather fragile stability of newly independent states.

Finally, the phrase *"to encourage the increased use of African languages as vehicles of instruction at all educational levels"* is purely demagogical because it is well known to all that nearly all Sub-Saharan languages, including Swahili, are light years away from being used fully as media of instruction for all academic subjects in middle and high school, let alone in college (Bamgbose 2004). The discussion in 1.7 about outsourcing and linguistic dependency shows clearly that Africa is still many decades away from the kind of corpus planning that is necessary for this statement to be implementable. Alexander (2008:265) is right in using the word "grandiose" in describing the LPAA project that ACALAN is charged to implement. Demagogy and elite hypocrisy aside, it is impossible to read the LPAA without coming to the conclusion that it is a quintessential illustration of the "manifesto syndrome" that Bamgbose (1991:133) defines as a condition that leads to forceful pronouncement that cannot be implemented. Simpson (2008:4) sees such statements as "symbolic gestures not supported by concrete moves to give such languages new positions of authority and heightened use." Maathai (2009:16) calls declarations such as the LPAA "grandiose, attention-seeking projects" that African leaders are fond of. A kinder and gentler spin could be put on the LPAA so that it could be interpreted as an invitation for Africans to "dream big" about their languages. However, in dreaming big, we should remind ourselves that de Chateaubriand (1768–1848), a French political philosopher, warned that an ambition that one cannot afford is a crime.

1.11 Summary

In his article entitled "On the Futurology of Linguistic Development," Chaudenson (2008:177) laments the fact that it is hard to predict the future state of African languages. "The failure of futurology about language stems from the fact that," he contends, "these evolutions depend on numerous factors, almost none of which is in the proper domain of linguistics as traditionally practiced." However, with the ten deadly impediments discussed in this chapter, one no longer needs a crystal ball to see why language planning in Africa has failed and will continue to fail if corrective measures are not taken. The experience of the past 50 years tells us that if African countries keep on pursuing the language policies embodied in the LPAA document, their ancestral languages will be worse off in the future than they are right now because the hegemonic approach that it advocates is unimplementable. Its stated goal of replacing European languages with African languages is unpopular with parents and the larger segment of the citizenry. Furthermore, the insistence that only African languages be used as the medium of instruction in primary education is scientifically questionable. The model of language planning that has been in use since independence has failed to meet the linguistic expectation of African peoples. After half a century of an unsuccessful experimentation, a paradigm shift and a new model are needed. This new model is based on the Game theory and the 3±1 outcome. Alexander (2008:257) alludes to this model when he writes that "The realization that the ecology of languages had changed profoundly in the last quarter of the twentieth century and that most human beings have to become proficient in their mother tongue as well as in one or more international and regional languages to one degree or another is now widespread." The theoretical framework that will be used to show how the 3-Language Model can be successfully implemented in Sub-Saharan Africa is described in Chapter Two. Subsequent chapters will be devoted to show how MM can be implemented in many countries.

Chapter 2
The strategic Game theory and 3±1 language outcome

Introduction

The "catastrophic success" of contemporary language planning underscores the need for a new model of language planning. The paradigm shift that is being proposed in this book is firmly anchored in the *Game theory* which was originally designed as a theory in pure mathematics, but was later applied to economics by John von Neumann and Oskar Morgenstern. Since then the Game theory has been applied to political science, biology, computer science, and a host of other academic disciplines. Its successes in these fields have not sufficiently trickled down to applied linguistics, except for Laitin's 1992 book, *Language Repertoires and State Construction in Africa*, which unveils what the Game theory can offer language planners. Unfortunately, neither Laitin's book nor the Game theory has received the attention it deserves. This is a rather disappointing state of affairs because this theory holds much promise for language planning in Sub-Saharan Africa. In fact, it deals with all the ingredients that applied linguists pay or should pay attention to. Its strong and vibrant relationship with economics is an asset because language planners deal with cost-benefit analyses and economic forecasting. Its application by political scientists to conflict resolution around the globe can offer invaluable insights to language planners whose work in multilingual countries often leads to ethnolinguistic conflicts.

The primary goal of this chapter is to provide a comprehensive overview of the Game theory, of its key concepts and methodology, and to show how this theory is relevant to language planning. Core game theoretical concepts such as the *Prisoner's Dilemma*, the *Tragedy of the Commons*, and *Nash's Equilibrium* will be reinterpreted for the purposes of language planning respectively as the *Linguist's Dilemma*, the *Tragedy of Linguistic Commons*, and *Linguistic Equilibrium*. Undoubtedly, the most innovative but also the most controversial claim in this chapter is that Laitin's Repertoire Model can help plan most of the languages spoken in any given country. Traditional approaches have dismissed such an approach as unworkable. However, it will be argued here and in the rest of the book that the 3±1 language outcome makes this solution feasible and even desirable. De Mesquita

(2009) has developed a model of the Game theory in his book, *The Predictioneer's Game*, that is both understandable and easily applicable to language planning. The formula I × S × P / I × P that he uses to support his security risk assessment for governments and private companies will constitute the nuts and bolts of the analysis in this book. This formula helps to determine the influence (I), the degree of interest (S), and the position (P) of all the entities involved in the language game in Africa. The weighted mean score derived from these computations will help explain why the language policies of European colonists failed to meet the expectations of Africans. Used in tandem, Laitin and De Mesquita's models of Game theory are powerful tools that will lead to a workable mother-tongue education model for Côte d'Ivoire and other French-speaking countries on the continent that are in need of novel ideas in regards to language planning.

2.1 Correcting some misconceptions about the Game theory

In his evening plenary address at the 38th Annual Conference of African Linguistics in Gainesville, University of Florida, in 2007, Professor Eyamba Bokamba of the University of Illinois at Urbana-Champagne joked tongue-in-cheek about the Game theory. He quipped that "language is too serious a business to play games with." Professor Bokamba is not the only academic to make fun of the Game theory. Binmore (2007:36) remarks that "people sometimes think it frivolous to talk about human social problems as though they were mere games." However, this misconception can very easily be corrected by reminding everyone that the "Game theory is inspired by, but not necessarily *about*, games" (Poundstone 1992:64). In fact, Binmore sees an advantage in using the metaphor of games in addressing serious human problems because such an analogy helps everybody "to think dispassionately about the strategic issues that arise in games like Chess or Poker, without automatically rejecting a conclusion if it turns out to be unwelcome. But logic is the same wherever it applies." The charge that language is too serious a business for anyone to play games with does not hold water. In fact, this mindset has robbed language planning of valuable insights that could have lifted the discipline from the funk it has found itself in since its inception. The Game theory has been used to mediate political conflicts and wars. Game theoretic insights and strategies have been part of arms reduction talks and nuclear disarmament negotiations since the late 1940s (Poundstone 1992). According to De Mesquita (2009), the CIA takes very seriously game-theoretic predictions of security threats against the USA.

Even though we applied linguists believe that language planning is of great importance, it is foolhardy to think that it is weightier and more pressing than brokering peace in armed conflicts, reducing the nuclear stockpiles or threats, analyzing the pros and cons of transnational corporate mergers and acquisition, figuring out how to minimize climate change, stemming the severity of economic downturns, and devising strategic military plans for future wars. Game-theorists are hired by governments, banks, and security companies, or act as consultants for well-financed think-tanks that advise world leaders. Since powerful policy-makers and corporations take game-theoretic insights seriously, it is about time that applied linguists use its insights and methodology to tackle the recalcitrant language issues in Sub-Saharan Africa. The rest of the chapter is devoted to showing how it can be done.

2.2 The universality of games

Given the widespread misconception that exists in applied linguistics circles about the Game theory, it is worth noting again that the "Game theory is inspired by, but not necessarily *about* games." The theory is so named because its proponents believed that playing games reveals something unique about human nature, human decision-making processes, and human logic, irrespective of idiosyncratic characteristics such as nationality, culture, ethnicity, political affiliation, and religious beliefs. Game-theorists have collected games from hundreds of societies worldwide to validate their claims. In the process, they have also found that games are the most widespread form of entertainment in all human societies. They come in a variety of forms and shapes. Game theorists are interested in games, all types of games, because they believe that the strategies that one deploys when playing a game tell a lot about the person's reasoning abilities and his/her preferences. For instance, the answers that one provides to an enigma game such as the one below speak volumes about the players:[13]

> A man was crossing a river with his wife and mother. A giraffe appeared on the opposite bank. The man drew his gun on the beast, and the giraffe said, "If you shoot, your mother will die. If you don't shoot, your wife will die." What should the man do?

---

13 Poundstone (1992:1) credits this game to the Popo people of Benin, West Africa.

Catch-twenty-two games such as this one abound in African folklore. Likewise, ancient Middle Eastern societies seemed to have had a craving for games. They used enigma and riddles to make statements about a person's cognitive abilities and his/her dispositions. The prologue to the Book of Proverbs 1:2–6 reads as follows:

> For attaining wisdom and discipline; for understanding words of insight;[3] for acquiring a disciplined and prudent life, doing what is right and just and fair;[4] for giving prudence to the simple, knowledge and discretion to the young–[5] let the wise listen and add to their learning, and let the discerning get guidance–[6] for understanding proverbs and parables, the sayings and riddles of the wise.

These verses show that the Hebrew sages of bygone centuries equated finding the answers to riddles with wisdom, and urged parents to use them to instill commonsense into their children. Solomon, who ruled from 971–931 B.C and is credited by Jewish tradition to have written the book of Proverbs, was, according to his biographers, known all over the world for his wisdom because he was able to solve a serious legal dilemma:

> Now two prostitutes came to the king and stood before him.[17] One of them said, "My lord, this woman and I live in the same house. I had a baby while she was there with me.[18] The third day after my child was born, this woman also had a baby. We were alone; there was no one in the house but the two of us.[19] "During the night this woman's son died because she lay on him.[20] So she got up in the middle of the night and took my son from my side while I your servant was asleep. She put him by her breast and put her dead son by my breast.[21] The next morning, I got up to nurse my son– and he was dead! But when I looked at him closely in the morning light, I saw that it wasn't the son I had borne."[22] The other woman said, "No! The living one is my son; the dead one is yours." But the first one insisted, "No! The dead one is yours; the living one is mine." And so they argued before the king.[23] The king said, "This one says, 'My son is alive and your son is dead,' while that one says, 'No! Your son is dead and mine is alive.'"[24] Then the king said, "Bring me a sword." So they brought a sword for the king.[25] He then gave an order: "Cut the living child in two and give half to one and half to the other."[26] The woman whose son was alive was filled with compassion for her son and said to the king, "Please, my lord, give her the living baby! Don't kill him!" But the other said, "Neither I nor you shall have him. Cut him in two!'[27] Then the king gave his ruling: "Give the living baby to the first woman. Do not kill him; she is his mother."[28] When all Israel heard the verdict the king had given, they held the king in awe,

because they saw that he had wisdom from God to administer justice (1 Kings 3:16–28, *The New International Version*).

Binmore (2007:104–6), Osborne and Rubinstein (1994:186–7), and many other game-theorists have analyzed and reanalyzed this ancient dilemma tale to elucidate how complex decisions are made in situations involving conflicts. They concur that threats, though risky, are sometimes the best strategy out of a predicament. This solution is known in game-theoretic studies as "Solomon's Predicament." More will be said in 2.3.5 about using threats as a game-theoretic strategy to solve problems.

2.3 Modern Game theory

Some historians of the Game theory trace its origin back to 1713 when the British nobleman James Waldegrave (1684–1741) mentioned the phrase in a letter. However, others contend that ideas of the Game theory can be traced all the way to the Bible and the Talmud. The names of the Scottish philosopher, David Hume (1711–1776), the British mathematician, Bertrand Russell (1872–1970), and the French economist and mathematician, Antoine Augustin Cournot (1801–1877) have all been mentioned in connection with the Game theory. However, the Game theory, as it is used and applied today, is unanimously traced back to John von Neumann who was born in Austria in 1903, immigrated to the US at age 26, and breathed his last in 1957 (Poundstone 1992:10, 16–7). During his short terrestrial life of 54 years, von Neumann applied his mathematical genius to the study of games. He did many other incredible things such as laying the preparatory groundwork for computers, being a consulting mathematician and physicist at Los Alamos Nuclear Laboratory, and acting as a game-theoretical consultant at the RAND Corporation, a political and military think-tank based in California. It has become clear since von Neumann that playing games is not a trivial pastime. Understanding and accounting for the strategies that humans use when playing games calls for very sophisticated mathematical calculations. It took a scientist of the caliber of von Neumann to unlock the mathematical secrets behind games. His biographer, Poundstone (1992:12–32), writes that von Neumann was dubbed "the best brain in the world" because of his superior knowledge of mathematics, physics, chemistry, languages (Hungarian, German, English, French and classical Greek) and history. This title is not a small accolade, considering that Albert Einstein was his colleague and contemporary at Princeton University. Von Neumann was a child prodigy whose reputation in mathematics spread worldwide when he was only in his mid-twenties. He applied his great insights to launch a new kind of mathematics that Morgenstern describes in his foreword to Davis' book (1983:ix–x) as follows:

> Game theory is a new discipline that has aroused much interest because of its novel mathematical properties and its many applications to social, economic, and political problems. The theory is in a state of active development. It has begun to affect the social sciences over a broad spectrum. The reason that applications are becoming more numerous and are dealing with highly significant problems encountered by social scientists is due to the fact that the mathematical structure of the theory differs profoundly from previous attempts to provide mathematical foundations of social phenomena. These earlier efforts were oriented on the physical sciences and inspired by the tremendous success these have had over the centuries. *Yet social phenomena are different: people acting sometimes against each other, sometimes cooperatively with each other; they have different degrees of information about each other, their aspirations lead them to conflict or cooperation.* Inanimate nature shows none of these traits. Atoms, molecules, stars may coagulate, collide, and explode but they do not fight each other; nor do they collaborate. Consequently, it was dubious that the methods and concepts developed for the physical sciences would succeed in being applied to social problems. [Emphasis added]

Von Neumann's new brand of mathematics was squarely centered on human beings with all their complexities and unpredictability. Poundstone (1992:39) opines that a world-renowned mathematician like von Neumann would not have pursued the Game theory if his intuition had not told him that it was a field ripe for significant development. Though the mathematical foundations of the theory are austere and foreboding to novices like me, Poundstone (p. 42) hastens to add that the Game theory can be used by everybody:

> Fortunately for our purposes, the essential kernel of Game theory is easy to grasp, even for those with little background in – or tolerance for – mathematics. Game theory is founded on a very simple but powerful way of schematizing conflict, and this method can be illustrated by a few familiar childhood games.

Osborne and Rubinstein (1994:1–2) share the same view and note that game-theoretic insights are within the reach of everybody, not only seasoned mathematicians:

> Game theory uses mathematics to express its ideas formally. However, the game theoretical ideas that we discuss are not inherently mathematical; in

principle, a book could be written that had essentially the same content as this one and was devoid of mathematics.

Since I am not solidly grounded in high level mathematics, the version of the Game theory that appeals to me is the one that deals minimally with mathematic theory. Consequently, the discussions in this chapter and the applications in subsequent chapters will be free of complicated mathematical formulas. In fact the analyses in the entire book are based on one formula which is introduced and discussed in 2.5. I share Davis' (1983:50) concern that since "Game theory has its roots in human behavior, if the theory is not related to human behavior in some way, it will be sterile and meaningless except as pure mathematics."

2.3.1 The versatility and the appeal of the Game theory

The first noteworthy application of the Game theory outside of the realm of pure mathematics came when von Neumann teamed up with another Austrian-born Princeton University economics professor, Oskar Morgenstern. Together they wrote *Theory of Games and Economic Behavior*. Poundstone (1992:41) describes the book as "one of the most influential and least-read books of the twentieth century." The book is influential because it revolutionized economics by forging an alliance between mathematics and economics. This helped blaze new trails in applied mathematics and mathematical economics. According to Poundstone, the book is least read because its 641 pages are filled with mind-boggling mathematical formulas. Fortunately, some great minds have found ways of applying game-theoretic insights without the inscrutable trappings of mathematics. Since then the Game theory has yielded dividends by helping other disciplines such as political science and statistics make strides in economic forecasting and predicting electoral outcomes.

The greatest appeal of the Game theory is its versatility. It has been applied successfully to a wide range of issues: auctioneering, gambling, business mergers, electoral predictions, arms control, nuclear treaties, socio-political conflict resolutions, the assessment of security threats, evolutionary biology, military simulations, computerized modeling of climate change, demographic sampling, and opinion surveys. For Binmore (2007:1, 2), life circumstances to which the Game theory can be applied are limitless. He contends that "a game is being played whenever human beings interact." Game theorists have touted their successes all along. However, according to Binmore, it is only recently that the general population has taken notice. He explains why the successes of the Game theory are being noticed now:

> In spite of its theoretical successes, practical men of business used to dismiss Game theory as just one more ineffectual branch of social science, but they changed their minds more or less overnight after the American government decided to auction off the right to use various radio frequencies for use with cellular telephones. With no established experts to get in the way, the advice of game theorists proved decisive in determining the design of the rules of the auctioning games that were used. The result was that the American taxpayer made a profit of $20 billion – more than twice the orthodox prediction. Even more was made in a later British telecom auction for which I was responsible. We made a total of $35 billion in just one auction. In consequence, Newsweek magazine described me as the ruthless, poker-playing economist who destroyed the telecom industry!

De Mesquita (2009: xix, 137) cites declassified CIA documents which support his claim that 90% of his game-theoretic predictions have come to pass. The successes of de Mesquita's predictions have not gone unnoticed by foreign politicians and policy-makers. He reports that the governments of Muhammad Kaddafi and of the late Mobutu Sese Seko had called on him to help shape the outcomes of some political events. He declined their generous financial offers and reported the plot to the CIA, arguing that "no amount of money could have justified my intervention" (pp. 136–7). Since 1970, twelve game-theorists have won the Nobel Prize in Economics. In this decade alone, the Noble Prize in Economics has been awarded to five game-theoretical scholars.[14] With its credibility firmly established in mathematics, economics, political science, and statistics, it is my contention that the insights of the Game theory and its methodology can be profitably applied to language planning. This is what I will attempt to show in the remainder of this chapter.

2.3.2 The core concepts of Game theory

The main conceptual pillars on which the Game theory rests can be captured by the pentagon below:

---

14 Retrieved from http://lcm.csa.iisc.ernet.in/gametheory/nobel.html on July 12, 2011.

2.3 Modern Game theory 43

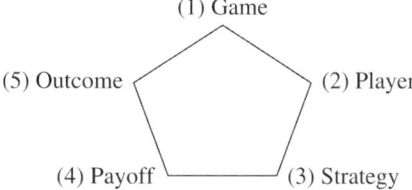

Figure 2.1. The Representation of Core Concepts

These concepts will be discussed separately according to the numerical order prefixed to them. Davis (1983:5–6) gives us a summary that will serve as the launching pad of our analysis of these key ingredients. The main words have been highlighted to draw attention to them. They are not bolded in the original text.

> In a **game** there will be **players** (at least two), and each will pick **a strategy** (make a decision). As a result of this joint choice – and possibly chance, a disinterested player – the result will be a reward or punishment for each player: **the payoff**. Because everyone's strategy affects **the outcome**, a player must worry about what everyone else does and knows that everybody else is worrying about him or her.

2.3.3 Definitions and classification of games

Games have probably existed as long as human beings have lived together in society. Moreover, in any given community, there are myriads of games. So, to avoid being bogged down by endless typologies, let's use Binmore's (2007:1) broad definition and classification of games:

> … Courting is one of the many different kinds of game we play in real life. Drivers maneuvering in heavy traffic are playing a driving game. Bargain-hunters bidding on eBay are playing an auctioning game. A firm and a union negotiating next year's wages are playing a bargaining game. When opposing candidates choose their platform in an election, they are playing a political game. The owner of a grocery store deciding today's price for corn flakes is playing an economic game. In brief, a game is being played whenever human beings interact.

As can be seen from this definition, Game theorists use games as a metaphor to gain a better understanding of the strategies that people employ to make choices on how to navigate through life. After nearly half a century of analyzing games, an incredible amount of insights has been gathered about human nature. This, in turn, has made it possible to theorize about games and the behavior patterns of those who play them. These findings and insights have endowed the Game theory with both descriptive and predictive powers. It has been used to describe historical events and to predict upcoming events with an amazing rate of success. Tremendous progress has been made in the area of game-theoretic simulations and experimentations since 1983. De Mesquita (2009) has taken full advantage of these advances to improve the accuracy of his game-theoretic predictions. His Predictioneer's Model is the main staple that we will depend on to propose MM as the best mother-tongue education model for many African countries.

2.3.4 Focus on players

Once a situation has been labeled a "game," then that particular game must meet the 1) the minimal number of players criterion. This requirement is met if the game is played by at least two players. This minimalist criterion has led to the sub-classification of games according to the number of players. Some games are labeled "two-person games" because they have only two players. Games of more than two players are known as "n-person games." The complexity of a game increases exponentially in direct proportion to the number of players. Some game-theoretic models set the number of players low so that they can control the variables better. However, the Predictioneer's Model that is being used in this book does not limit the number of players. In the language planning game in 5.4, there are as many as 56 players.

Rationality and logic are two additional criteria that players must have. All the players involved in a game must be rational; that is, according to Osborne and Rubinstein (1994:4), "They must be aware of alternatives available to them, they must be cognizant of unknowns, they must have clear preferences, and they must be able to choose their actions deliberately after some process of optimization." Players are logical if they meet the criteria set forth by Poundstone (1992:44):

> Game theory is about *perfectly logical players interested only in winning*. When you credit your opponent(s) with rationality and desire to win, and play so as to encourage the best outcome for yourself, then the game is open to the analysis of Game theory. Perfect rationality, like perfect anything, is fiction. There's no such thing as a perfect straight line. This didn't stop Euclid from developing a useful system of geometry. So it was with von

Neumann and his perfectly rational players. You can think of the players of Game theory as being something like perfect logicians you hear about in logic puzzles, or even as being computer programs rather than human beings. The players are assumed to have perfect understanding of the rules and perfect memory of past moves. At all points in the game they are aware of all possible logical ramifications of their moves and their opponents' moves. [Italics in the original]

The fourth requirement that players must fulfill is that they must have the desire to win. This is an important prerequisite because it eliminates make-believe games (also called trivial games) from consideration. Suppose a burly dad is wrestling with his five-year old child and the child wins. Even though the father and his child are playing a wrestling game, this is not the sort of game that game theorists are interested in analyzing because it fails the crucial test of "desire to win." Games that are worth analyzing are those in which the players will do everything within their power to advance their personal interests, whatever those interests may be. In fact, the player's self-interest and his/her desire to win at all costs is one of the quintessential assumptions in all game theoretical analyses. As a result, De Mesquita (2009:12–3) observes that game-theorists have come to view people as cold, calculating, and ruthless when they play real games.

Game theorists add a fifth constraint on players by specifying that they must be endowed with human attributes. Note, however, that this constraint does not say that a player must be a real human being. All it says is that all those involved in a game must have human-like attributes, namely rationality, logic, and the desire to win. The humanness requirement does not preclude computers, government agencies, clubs, associations, corporations, sports teams, etc., from qualifying as players so long as it is understood that such entities are used metonymically and that behind the label are true human beings. For instance, if a human being plays a game against a computer, the computer qualifies as a real player because the programmers transferred onto it their own rationality, their own logic, and their own desire to win.

2.3.5 Focus on strategies

When players get together to play a game, not only do they have their eyes set on the payoff (see 2.3.6), but they also have their minds set on the strategies that they intend to use. Davis (1983:xiv) describes how players strategize: "In a game, each player must assess the extent to which his or her goals match or clash with the goals of others, and decide whether to cooperate or compete with all or some of them. It is this blending of players' mutual and conflicting interests that make Game theory fascinating." A little later, on page 7, he proposes a more rigorous definition of the term "strategy" as "the complete plan of action that describes what a player will do under all possible circumstances. In ordinary usage a strategy is considered to be something clever, but nothing like that is intended here. There are poor strategies, just as there are good strategies." Poundstone (1992:48) also underscores the importance of the concept of strategy, noting that "in Game theory, strategy is an important idea, and it has a more precise meaning than it usually does. ... A strategy is a much more specific plan. It is a complete description of a particular way to play a game, no matter what the other player(s) does and no matter how long the game lasts. A strategy must prescribe actions so thoroughly that you never have to make a decision in following it."

Some strategies are orthodox, but others are not. Orthodox strategies are not risky because the player plays by the book. However, unorthodox strategies are risky. They include bluffing, an attempt to convince one's opponent that one may have certain attitudes or capabilities, whether one really has them or not (Davis 1983:99). Cheating, deception, lying, breaking promises are commonly used strategies, though such behaviors may be morally reprehensible. De Mesquita (2009:12) is of the opinion that John Nash won the Nobel Prize in economics because he was able to come up with the mathematical formula that helps factor in risky strategies in economic games:

> By the early 1950s, the mathematician John Nash, the subject of *A Beautiful Mind* and winner of the 1994 Nobel Prize in Economics, invented a different kind of Game theory. He drew attention to the propensity people have not to cooperate with one another. Poker players and diplomats use polite terms, like 'bluffing,' for what ordinary people mean when that say someone is a liar. In noncooperative games, promises are kept when a player decides it's in her interest to do what she promised. When promises and interests differ, people renege, they break their word, they cheat, they do whatever they think will benefit them most. Of course, they know that bluffing and cheating can be costly. Therefore, they take prospective costs as well as benefits into account. In fact, raising costs is one way, albeit a difficult and painful way, of encouraging people to be truthful.

A recent example from the world of sports will illustrate the notion of payoff associated with the use of risky strategies. In the 2010 soccer World Cup quarter finals, Ghana was playing against Uruguay. There was a draw after ninety minutes of regular play. Thirty minutes of extra time was added. In the very last seconds of the game, Ghana's striker kicked the ball that would have been their qualifying goal. A Uruguayan defender pushed the ball back with his two hands. This was an extremely risky strategy. Batting the ball away with one's hands is a major offense for which he received a red card and was kicked out of the game. The Ghanaian team was awarded a penalty kick. According to soccer statistics, 75% of penalty kicks are converted into goals. However, the best Ghanaian striker missed. Eventually, Ghana lost the game and failed to qualify while Uruguay moved on to the semi-finals. This was a risky strategy which resulted in a huge payoff for the Uruguayan national team.

In real games, when people's backs are against the wall, they resort to unorthodox strategies and risky moves. Threats are a commonly used risky strategy that players use. Davis (1983:101, 102) sees threats as risky for the following reason:

> A threat is a statement that you will act in a certain way under certain conditions. ... It is a self-imposed restriction that is not binding; you can always change your mind. The purpose of a threat is to change someone's behavior: to make that person do something he or she would not do otherwise. If the treat is carried out, it will presumably be to the detriment of the party that is threatened, but often it is also to the disadvantage of the party making the threat. A threat is effective only to the extent that it is plausible. The greater the price the party making the threat must pay to carry it out, the less plausible the threat. ... Often both players are in a position to threaten. In a bargaining game, for example, both the buyer and the seller can refuse to complete the sale unless the price is right.

Some risky strategies fail, others succeed. In the Ghanaian example, and in the Solomon example mentioned in 2.2, the risky strategies prevailed. Another strategy that is used in real life economic games is called "side payment," a euphemism for bribery. Davis (1983:105) notes that "in some games it is possible for one player to affect the actions of another by offering a side payment, a payment made 'under the table.' The figure skating scandals during the 2002 Olympic Games in Utah indicate clearly that players use all kinds of strategies to win, no matter how risky they are, if they think that they can get away with it. The controversy involved how the French and Russian referees conspire to deprive the Canadian skaters from the gold medal.[15] It will be shown in various parts of this book that players

---

15 Retrieved from http://www.youtube.com/watch?v=yQww4LzujqE on July 3rd, 2010.

in Sub-Saharan Africa try to affect the outcome of the language planning game by using risky strategies.

2.3.6 Focus on payoffs

Game theorists pay close attention to the nature of the payoff because there is a correlation between the desire to win and the value of the payoff. All real games must have payoffs. A game without payoff is not a real game and falls outside the purview of game theorists. Payoffs come in a variety of ways. Some rewards are psychological, others are material. Some include both. Winning a gold medal during the Olympics is intensely psychological because the recipient of the award stands for his/her country or the cause that he/she represents. It is also material because he/she can feel the gold medal around the neck. He/she can trade it for cash.

Game theorists have used the concept of payoff to introduce a binary classification of games. Some games are known as "zero-sum games" because the winner takes all and the loser gains nothing at all. Zero-sum games are universally competitive games in the sense that players are competing to win the prize. Games of this type abound around us: sport games, parlor games, casino games, board games, and various types of competitions that the entertainment industry throws our way. Game theoretic analyses of such games in real life or in experiments have revealed the sad but true condition of human beings, that is, they enjoy the psychological reward of winning and do not care much about the sentiments of the loser (Poundstone 1992:175). I have a friend who is ordinarily a compassionate person but she does not hesitate to rub it in and gloat whenever she beats her opponent(s) in a board game. The opposite of zero-sum games is "non-zero-sum games." In such games, the players are not competing against each other to win the payoff. Instead, they are working cooperatively. However, games can get complicated. In non-zero-sum games, some players can form a coalition, and turn against another person in the hope that they will share the payoff by excluding the person who is not in the coalition. For this reason, Davis (1983:75, 81) argues that non-zero-sum games are more complex and more challenging since "there is no universally accepted solution; that is, there is no single strategy that is clearly preferable to others, nor is there a single, clear-cut predictable outcome. As a rule, we will have to be content with something less than the unequivocal solutions we obtained for zero-sum games." It will be argued in Chapters 3 and 4 that Europeans played the two types of language games in Africa. The French and the Portuguese played a zero-sum/competitive game, while the Belgians, the British, and the Germans played a non-zero-sum/ cooperative language game with their subjects. This has led to two different language planning results in Sub-Saharan Africa. However, since both games offer the same payoff, ultimately the end result of both games is the same, namely that the mastery of European languages affords a greater payoff than the mastery of African languages.

2.3.7 Focus on outcomes

The fifth and last key ingredient in game theoretical analyses is "outcome." If there is no outcome, the game may go on and on, ad infinitum. For some games, the outcome is clear. Such is the case of zero-sum games. There must be a winner, and there must be a loser. But, in non-zero-sum games with n-person players, sometimes the outcome is not very clear because coalitions can be formed when the players' interests converge, and disbanded when their interests conflict. In such cases, Davis (1983:xv) observes that analysts "often settle for outcomes that are more stable, enforceable, or equitable than others." In game theoretic jargon, such outcomes are known as "Nash's Equilibrium." This outcome is named after John Nash because of his significant contribution to n-person coalitional games.

The short biographical sketch that Poundstone (1992:96–97) gives of Nash tells us that he was child prodigy, like his predecessor von Neumann. He received his Ph.D. in mathematics from Princeton University under the eminent mathematician Albert Tucker, the inventor of the *Prisoner's Dilemma* (to be discussed in 2.4). Nash taught mathematics at the Massachusetts Institute of Technology while serving, like many noted Princeton mathematicians and game-theorists before him, as a consultant for the RAND Corporation. He was awarded the Nobel Prize in Economics in 1994 for designing the mathematical equations that solved the conundrum of assigning equilibrium points in non-zero-sum games of three players or more. It is in recognition for this contribution that the equilibrium outcome was named after him. Osborne and Rubinstein (1994:14) define Nash's Equilibrium as follows:

> The most commonly used solution concept in Game theory is that of Nash equilibrium. This notion captures a steady state of the play or a strategic game in which each player holds the correct expectation about the other player's behavior and acts rationally. It does not attempt to examine the process by which a steady state is reached. ... Briefly, no player can profitably deviate, given the actions of the other players.

Fortunately, Poundstone (1992:98) gives us a more accessible definition of Nash Equilibrium, namely, the "outcomes where the players have no regrets. If everybody is happy with the way they played, then the outcome is an equilibrium point." Davis (1983: 14) completes the picture when he says that Nash Equilibrium is "a stable outcome of a game associated with a pair of strategies. It is considered stable because a player unilaterally picking a new strategy is hurt by the change." Phrases such as "the players have no regrets," "everybody is happy with the way they played," and "stable outcome" are the operative words in achieving equilibrium in a game. This notion of equilibrium is very useful for planning languages in a multilingual country, as explained below.

2.3.8 Summary of games and application to language planning

Much of the preceding information related to the core concepts in the Game theory can be summarized as follows:

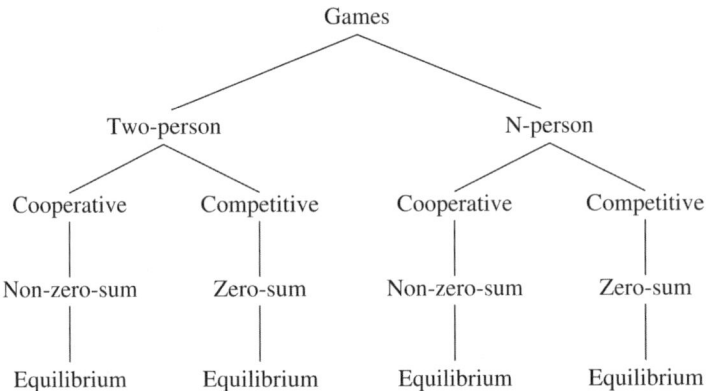

Figure 2.2. Summary of Key Concepts

Now, the most important questions for which we need to provide answers are the following: Is language planning a game? If it is, what kind of a game is it? The answer to the first question is a resounding "yes." It is a game in the sense of the Game theory. First and foremost, the Game theory is interested in situations and issues that are prone to conflicts. Poundstone (1992:6) describes its penchant for conflicts as follows:

> Game theory is a study of conflict between thoughtful and potentially deceitful opponents. This may make it sound like Game theory is a branch

of psychology rather than mathematics. Not so: because the players are assumed to be perfectly rational, Game theory admits precise analysis. Game theory is therefore a rigorous branch of mathematical logic that underlies real conflicts among (not always rational) humans. Most great advances in science come when a person of insight recognizes common elements in seemingly unrelated contexts. This describes the genesis of Game theory. Von Neumann recognized that parlor games pose elemental conflicts. It was these conflicts, normally obscured by the window dressing of cards and chessmen and dice, that occupied von Neumann. He perceived similar conflicts in economics, politics, daily life, and war. As von Neumann used the term, a 'game' is a conflict situation where one must make a choice knowing that others are making choices too, and the outcome of the conflict will be determined in some prescribed way by all the choices made.

If conflict is the main staple of the Game theory, then language planning is definitely a game because Dua (1996:13) has illustrated it with the four types of conflicts in India mentioned in 1.3. This is the reason why he was enthusiastic at the prospect of applying the Game theory to language planning:

> It has been suggested and in some measure substantiated that Game theory has great potential in analyzing the dynamics of political linguistics and modeling conflicts between state and society and between region and centre (Laitin 1987). At the same time it is essential to extend the Game theory model if we are to understand language conflicts and language retention in a society as complex and multilingual as that of India (Laitin 1989).

Previous attempts at language planning can be described game-theoretically as a two-person, zero-sum game. This simply means that, under such a framework, all minority indigenous languages of the country count as one player while the dominant national LWC counts as a player all by itself. The dominant strategy in such cases is to convince or coerce the rest of the citizenry to accept the dominant LWC at the detriment of their own languages. Where this attempt has been successful, as is the case in the Philippines, Malaysia, Indonesia, Kenya, and Tanzania, the result has been that the national LWC and its speakers are the winners, and all the other languages and their speakers are the losers. Given the nature of the language game that has been played so far, it is not surprising that of the more than one hundred highly multilingual countries in the world, only these five are presented as "success" stories. In all the others, language planning has stalled.

The kind of language planning game that will be advocated in this book qualifies as an n-person, non-zero-sum game. In other words, it is a cooperative game in which all the ethnolinguistic groups in the country will be winners because their languages will be planned. The expected outcome in this new language planning game is *linguistic equilibrium*. This equilibrium is achieved in a multilingual environment when the speakers of indigenous languages feel linguistically secure and know that the acquisition of additional languages is not detrimental to their native tongue. Following Laitin (1992:117–9), this outcome is described as 3±1 where all the speakers of the various languages are winners because their mother tongue is planned. Four operational spheres of language planning are envisioned under Laitin's Repertoire Model: the local language level, the regional language level, the national language level, and the international language level. The logical outcomes for the linguistic repertoires of citizens in such a multilingual country will vary, but in general, some people will have to know four languages, some three languages, and some two languages, if they wish to benefit from the socio-economic advantages offered by their countries. The 3±1 outcome is an umbrella formula which can be deconstructed as follows:

Table 2.1. Language Outcomes

No.	Deconstructed Formula	Repertoire Outcome
1.	1 + 1 + 1 + 1	4 languages
2.	1 (–1) + 1 + 1	3 languages
3.	1 (–1) (–1) + 1	2 languages

The "+1" in the deconstructed formula represents the local language and the international LWC. Both of them remain constant in all the equations because for linguistic equilibrium to be achieved, speakers have to be bilingual and biliterate in the local language and the official language(s) of their country. For most of Sub-Saharan Africa, this means that the citizen must know how to speak, read, and write in his/her indigenous language and English, French, Portuguese, or Spanish. The "–1" in the formula can be interpreted to mean "same as." Some Africans, depending on where they live and the particular sociolinguistic configuration of their country, may need to learn two additional languages to improve their sociolinguistic lot in life. This happens for speakers of very small minority languages whose native language is different from the regional LWC, and whose regional language is different from the national LWC (if there is one). However, for citizens whose native language is the same as their regional language, they will only need to add the national LWC (if there is one). Citizens whose native language is the same as the regional language and the same as the national language won't need to learn any additional language to operate fully nationally. However, they will need to know an ex-colonial language to operate both nationally and internationally. These logical possibilities can be represented by embedded concentric circles in which the first outlying circle represents the international LWC, the second circle the national LWC, the third circle, the regional LWC, and the innermost circle, the native language:

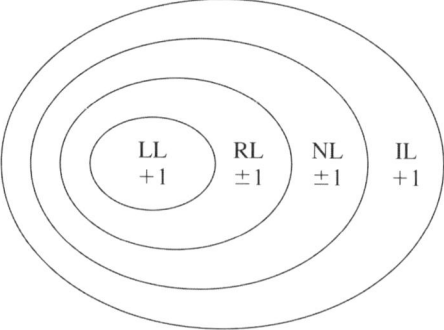

Figure 2.3. Outcome Circles
Legend: LL = Local Language, RL = Regional Language, NL = National Language, IL = International Language

The language planning model that is proposed in this book categorically rejects linguistic outcomes such as 2−1 or 1+0. In the first case, the model describes cases where citizens who have grown up bilingual lose the mastery of their ancestral languages while shifting to the international LWC. Such a language shift usually takes place in cosmopolitan megacities. Solutions are proposed in Chapter 6 that are intended to reverse this tendency. The 1+0 outcome is likely to happen in the context of interethnic marriages where the couple decides to use the international LWC as a "neutral" in raising their children. The acquisition planning model discussed in Chapter 8 ensures that all citizens are bilingual and biliterate in an indigenous language and the international LWC by the time they graduate from high school.

2.4 The working parables of the Game theory

Many of the insights that game theorists have gathered have come directly from simulating the Prisoner's Dilemma and applying it to real life situations.

Poundstone (1992:8–9) credits Albert Tucker (see section 2.3.7) for having "discovered" the Prisoner's Dilemma. Here is how he portrays the theoretical significance of this discovery:

> The prisoner's dilemma is a universal concept. Theorists now realize that prisoner's dilemmas occur in biology, psychology, sociology, economics, and law. The prisoner's dilemma is apt to turn up everywhere a conflict of interest exists – and the conflict need not be between sentient beings. Study of the prisoner's dilemma has great power for explaining why animal and human societies are organized as they are. It is one of the great ideas of the twentieth century, simple enough for anyone to grasp and of fundamental importance. ... The prisoner's dilemma has become one of the premier philosophical and scientific issues of our time. It is tied to our very survival.

For Poundstone (1992:123), "Discovering the prisoner's dilemma is something like discovering air. It has always been with us, and people have always noticed it – more or less." The universality, the versatility, and the applicability of the Prisoner's Dilemma have been recognized by virtually all game theorists. Slightly different versions exist, but the following is the most widespread:

> *Two suspects are arrested by the police. The police have insufficient evidence for a conviction, and, having separated both prisoners, visit each of them to offer the same deal. If one testifies (defects from the other) for the prosecution against the other and the other remains silent (cooperates with the other), the betrayer goes free and the silent accomplice receives the full 10-year sentence. If both remain silent, both prisoners are sentenced to only six months in jail for a minor charge. If each betrays the other, each receives a five-year sentence. Each prisoner must choose to betray the other or to remain silent. Each one is assured that the other would not know about the betrayal before the end of the investigation. How should the prisoners act?*

Various experimentations and simulations have been done with the Prisoner's Dilemma. The three most important findings after myriads of such studies are as follows:

1. People have a competitive impulse (Poundstone 1992:123, 174, 175).
2. People normally look out for their own interests (Poundstone 1992:123, 174, 175; de Mesquita (2009:12–3).
3. Uncooperative play is the hallmark of the prisoner's dilemma (Davis 1983:128).

These findings are very significant in understanding normal human behavior. These game-theoretic insights have been used over and over to draw valuable evidence in criminal cases. The Prisoner's Dilemma can help explain why language planning is prone to conflicts all over the world. It also validates the claim made in 1.3, that for ethnolinguistic reasons, people are less likely to give up their mother tongue for a rival indigenous language. Furthermore, they are more likely to be uncooperative when an indigenous language is imposed on them. This is reminiscent of Essegbey's (2009:129) quote in 1.3, namely that in the competition among languages in Ghana, "the merest hint that one language might be more prestigious than another turns people against that language." These insights from the Prisoner's Dilemma help explain why the hegemonic model of language planning has failed in many parts of the world.

The second game-theoretic parable that can be used to explain the failure of language planning is the "Tragedy of the Commons." In 1968, microbiology expert and professor of ecology, Garrett Hardin, wrote an essay which he entitled the "Tragedy of the Commons." Since then, this essay has been used by game theorists to highlight the role of the individual in ecological disasters and other man-made disasters, including language death and endangerment:[16]

> *Visualize a pasture as a system that is open to everyone. The carrying capacity of this pasture is 10 animals. Ten herdsmen are each grazing an animal to fatten up for market. In other words, the 10 animals are now consuming all the grass that the pasture can produce. Harry (one of the herdsmen) will add one more animal to the pasture if he can make a profit. He subtracts the original cost of the new animal from the expected sales price of the fattened animal and then considers the cost of the food. Adding one more animal will mean less food for each of the present animals, but since Harry only has only 1/10 of the herd, he has to pay only 1/10 of the cost. Harry decides to exploit the commons and the other herdsmen, so he adds an animal and takes a profit. Shrinking profit margins force the other herdsmen either to go out of business or continue the exploitation by adding more animals. This process of mutual exploitation continues until overgrazing and erosion destroy the pasture system, and all the herdsmen are driven out of business.*

---

16 Poundstone (1992:125–6) discusses the "Free Rider Dilemma," which is in every respect similar to the Tragedy of the Commons. Retrieved from www.dieoff.org/page109.htmsiness on July 3, 2010.

2.4.1 A linguistic re-interpretation of the tragedy of the commons

The insights of the Prisoner's Dilemma have been applied to many situations. Laitin (1992) used some aspects of it in formulating his Strategic Game theory, especially the Repertoire Model. I also rely on some of these findings in this book. However, I find myself agreeing more with Binmore (2007:19, 159) that "The paradox-of-rationality phase in the history of Game theory is just about over." I also concur with him that the parable of *Tragedy of the Commons* is more applicable to the language planning situations in Africa. In fact, the *Tragedy of the Commons* is more compelling and more directly applicable to language planning than the Prisoner's Dilemma. Therefore, it is the former that is reinterpreted here as the *Tragedy of the Linguistic Commons*:

> *Visualize a multilingual country where dozens and dozens of indigenous languages are spoken by the local population. Imagine also a village in this country where 10 families live. Since time immemorial, these ten families have passed on their local language to the next generation, thus ensuring the survival their language for generations. Now, Harry and Henrietta (a couple) in the village see the wind of progress and modernization blowing and decide to send their children to school where the ex-colonial language is the language of instruction at all levels of education. Their children are successful at school and master the ex-colonial language. The only drawback is that Harry and Henrietta's children no longer master the indigenous language as they should. What's more, their grandchildren "understand the language but cannot speak it." At first, some villagers resent this attitude but, seeing the material success of Harry and Henrietta's children and grandchildren, soon the remaining nine families follow suit by sending their own children to school with the same predictable outcome. If this pattern is allowed to continue, the ability to communicate in the ancestral language will erode to the point of no return. Language loss, and even death, looms in the horizon.*

This parable depicts accurately the fate of many indigenous languages in Africa. Some local languages are further along on the road to linguistic self-destruction, others have barely begun. Overall, Brenzinger (2007) does not paint a rosy picture for minority languages in North Africa, neither does Blench (2007) for West Africa, nor Connell (2007) for Central Africa. Brenzinger (2007), again, indicates that he has reasons for concern in South Eastern Africa. Language planners and revivalists are faced with an ethical dilemma as they strive to prevent language endangerment and breathe new life into languages that are on the path toward morbidity. Do they blame

2.4 The working parables of the Game theory   57

Harry and Henrietta, and the entire community for that matter, for shifting their linguistic allegiance? Are people to be persuaded or shamed into maintaining their native tongues at all costs even if they do not see any payoffs for keeping them? Are linguists interested in the language saving business so that they can make a name for themselves in the scholarly arena? The dilemma presented by this parable and the questions surrounding the motives of the players were the subject of an academic debate that pitted Ken Hale, Michael Krauss, Lucille Watahomigie, Akira Yamamoto, Colette Craig, Laverne Masayesva, and Nora England against Peter Ladefoged in 1992. Ladefoged accused the language revivalists of using "appeals to our emotions, not to our reason" in their effort to save languages. For him, "in this changing world, the task of the linguist is to lay out the facts concerning a given linguistic situation." However, Hale (1992:36) makes a compelling case that when a language dies, it is not only a language that dies, but it is an intellectual loss for humanity: "In this circumstance, there is a certain tragedy for the human purpose. The loss of local languages, and of the cultural systems that they express, has meant irretrievable loss of diverse and interesting intellectual wealth." Krauss (1992:8) appeals to linguists "to work responsibly both for the future of our science and for the future of our languages, not so much for reward according to the fashion of the day, but for the sake of posterity." He challenges linguists to follow the example of biologists, who have created as many as 300 organizations "engaged in education, publicity, research, lobbying, monitoring, and in activism for the survival of animal species. What do we have for languages?"

The main difference between advocating for animal species and advocating for human languages is that the former is not disappearing out of their own volition, whereas languages are disappearing, in many cases, because human beings endowed with reason and economic and political sense deliberately choose the language that offers more payoffs to them than their local language. If community members have decided for whatever reason, usually for socio-economic mobility, to forego their ancestral language, who are linguists to convince them otherwise? Whose interest do linguists have at heart: their own scientific interest or a genuine interest in the welfare of the community? This raises moral and ethical dilemmas that Ladefoged faced and for which he refused to take sides but only to fulfill "the task of the linguist":

> Last summer I was working on Dahalo, a rapidly dying Cushitic language, spoken by a few hundred people in a rural district of Kenya. I asked one of our consultants whether his teen-aged sons spoke Dahalo. 'No,' he said.

'They can still hear it, but they cannot speak it. They speak only Swahili.' He was smiling when he said it, and did not regret it. He was proud that his sons had been to school, and knew things that he did not. Who am I to say that he was wrong?

My contention in this book is that an attractive language of education policy can be formulated using the Game theory so that people like Harry and Henrietta and the other members of their community can be fully bilingual and biliterate in their local language and in the ex-colonial language. Moreover, some who choose to study the local language can make as much money or more money than those who operate in the ex-colonial language.

2.5 Introducing the Predictioneer's Model

The game-theoretic methodology that will be used in this book has been greatly influenced by De Mesquita (2009). His approach is adopted here for several reasons. First, its mathematical basis is simple and straightforward. It is summed up by following formula:

$$\text{Weighted mean} = \frac{I \times S \times P}{I \times S}^{17}$$

The letters **I**, **S**, and **P** stand for "Influence," "Salience," and "Position" respectively. Tables such as the ones in sections 2.6 through 2.6.5 are used to display the results. First, the I × S × P product of each player are displayed individually in the I × S × P column. The same is done for the I × S product. The last row in the table displays the sums of all I × S × P and I × S values. The weighted mean gives us the most likely outcome for the game being played. The weighted mean score corresponds to the language policy that the different constituencies agree on.

---

17 De Mesquita (2009) uses the phrase "weighted mean." However, the chair of the Statistics Department at Saint Cloud State University has informed me that among statisticians, the most accurate phrase is "weighted percentage" since the values are expressed in percentage point. I keep the phrase "weighted mean" because it is used more frequently than "weighted percentage."

2.5 Introducing the Predictioneer's Model 59

The second reason for the appeal of the Predictioneer's Model lies in the fact that, unlike other game-theoretical books that lean too heavily towards business and economic applications, De Mesquita's can handle a wide variety of topics. He applies his model to historical events such as the Greek Peloponnesian War of 431–404 B.C., or to explain why the Catholic Church lost its political and economic hegemony in Europe from 1122 to 1648. He also applied it to account for why Spain "discovered" America. He used his computational game-theoretic model to predict, on the basis of available evidence, on which month World War 1 was most likely to have started. The same approach was used to predict why De Mesquita thought that former President Bill Clinton's healthcare package would pass. However, this prediction did not play out and the fiasco cost him his clients and his reputation. The humiliation caused by this debacle forced him to rework his calculations and to include more variables. Since then, he has applied his new and improved model to current world affairs such as the North Korean nuclear disarmament talks, the discussions about the Iranian nuclear ambitions, and the USA-Pakistani coalitions in the fight against Al Qaida and the Taliban. In a very daring move, he has used his model to predict the outcomes of the impending US withdrawal from Iraq.

The final reason why the Predictioneer's Model is appealing is that its methodology is falsifiable and applicable to language planning. De Mesquita has used it to train novice undergraduate and graduate students at New York University where he teaches political economics courses. He has shown in his book how he takes students from knowing nothing about the Game theory to helping them make predictions about world affairs. De Mesquita (2009:52–3) provides simple step-by-step directions on how to use his $I \times S \times P$ methodology:

1. Identify every individual with a meaningful interest in trying to influence the outcome. Don't just pay attention to the final decision makers.
2. Estimate as accurately as possible with available information what policy each of the players identified in point 1 is advocating when they talk in private to each other – that is, what do they say they want. This is equivalent to **P** in the formula.
3. Approximate how big an issue this is for each of the players – that is, how salient it is to them. Are they so concerned that they would drop whatever they're doing to address this problem when it comes up, or are they likely to want to postpone discussions while they deal with more pressing matters? This is equivalent to **S** in the formula.

4. Relative to all of the other players, how influential can each player be in persuading others to change their position on the issue? This is equivalent to **I** in the formula.

He also provides the rationale for assigning various numerical values from 0 to 100 points on the Position scale, the Salience scale, and the Influence scales:

> Models talk in numbers. So, part of my job is to turn sentences into numbers so that the computer can crunch away. Numbers have big advantages over words – and not just for computers. Most importantly, numbers are clear; words are vague. It is essential to turn information into numerical values, and in fact it's not especially hard to do.

2.5.1 The identification of players

Table 2.2 provides a fairly comprehensive list of the players of the language game in colonial Africa. European powers have been grouped differently because their language policies often differed greatly. In some cases, there were just subtle nuances among them. The justification for grouping French and Portuguese players together will be provided in Chapter 3. Chapter 4 will explain why Belgian, British, and German colonial officers, missionaries, and teachers are grouped together. During the early stages of colonial enterprise, Europeans brought people from Asia to serve as petty bureaucrats, bookkeepers, managers, railroad workers, etc. In French-speaking areas, Middle Easterners, mostly Lebanese, constituted the bulk of the non-white expatriate community. The Portuguese colonies were the exception. For reasons that will be fully discussed later, Portugal sent its citizens to Africa to fill middle management positions. Between the white colonizers and the mass of colonized Sub-Saharan Africans was a small but important segment of the population which consisted of people of mixed ancestry. Their number and influence varied from area to area, but generally they had privileges and opportunities that other Africans did not have. As for the Africans themselves, important distinctions must be made among them so as to fully understand their role in the language game. Chapters 3 and 4 will provide a deeper analysis of the role that Africans played. Suffice it for now to say that once Africans realized the socio-economic advantages of knowing European languages, they did their very best to earn as much language capital as possible. However, not all Africans could have access to European languages. In general, Africans in the hinterland had no access, or a very restricted access to these languages.

2.5 Introducing the Predictioneer's Model 61

Table 2.2. Identification of Players

No.	Players
1.	French/Portuguese Catholic missionaries
2.	British Protestant missionaries
3.	Belgian missionaries
4.	German missionaries
5.	French and Portuguese teachers in lower elementary
6.	French and Portuguese teachers in upper elementary
7.	British teachers in lower elementary
8.	British teachers in upper elementary
9.	Belgian and German teachers in lower elementary
10.	Belgian and German teachers in upper elementary
11.	French/Portuguese colonial administrators
12.	British colonial administrators in Islamic areas
13.	British colonial administrators in other areas
14.	Belgian/German colonial administrators
15.	French and Portuguese business operators
16.	British business operators
17.	Belgian and German business operators
18.	Euro-Africans in French /Portuguese colonies
19.	Euro-Africans in British colonies
20.	Expatriates in French/Portuguese colonies
21.	Expatriates in British colonies
22.	Assimilated Africans in French/Portuguese colonies
23.	African political elite in French/Portuguese colonies
24.	African political elite in British colonies
25.	African political elite in Belgian colonies
26.	African educated/employees in French/Portuguese colonies
27.	African educated/employees in British colonies
28.	African missionaries in English colonies
29.	African missionaries in Belgian and German colonies

(*Continued*)

Table 2.2. Identification of Players (*Cont.*)

No.	Players
30.	African WWI and WWII vets in French and Portuguese colonies
31.	African WWI and WWII vets in British colonies
32.	African chiefs in French/Portuguese colonies
33.	African chiefs in British colonies
34.	African chiefs in Belgian and German colonies
35.	African chiefs' sons in French/Portuguese colonies
36.	African chiefs' sons in British colonies
37.	African manual workers in urban settings in French/Portuguese colonies
38.	African manual workers in urban settings in British colonies
39.	African manual workers in urban settings in Belgian and German colonies
40.	African uneducated/rural/farmers in French and Portuguese colonies
41.	African uneducated/rural/farmers in British colonies
42.	African uneducated/rural/farmers in Belgian and German colonies

One major advantage offered by the Predictioneer's Model is that it allows for a large number of players. Other models would have a very hard time handling such a large number of players, but the Predictioneer's Model can handle an amazingly large number of players. In 5.4 the model handles 56 players. The only problem is that the longer the list of players, the larger the numbers that will have to be crunched. Fortunately, software programs such as Excel exist to assist in this task.

2.5.2 Describing and applying the Position (P) scale

The Position scale has to do with where people stand on a particular issue. Extreme positions for or against an issue are often held. Between the two extremes are intermediate positions. In this excerpt, de Mesquita (2009:53) explains how to rate P scales:

> Pick an issue that is important to your family or friends. It doesn't have to be about world affairs; it could be about where to have dinner, or what movie to see, or whatever else leads to disagreements. The easiest sort of issue to do as a first try is what I call a beauty contest. Say you and some

2.5 Introducing the Predictioneer's Model 63

friends are trying to choose between two movies. Anyone who really truly wants to see *The Sound of Music* (or fill in whatever first-run movie might grab your fancy) gets a value of 100, and anyone really committed to seeing *A Clockwork Orange* (another great old film) gets a 0. Then you should be able to rate how strongly each friend leans toward one movie or the other. Any who are truly indifferent get a 50; anyone leaning slightly toward *A Clockwork Orange* might be close to 50, say at 40 or 45, and so on. You or the "expert" you are interviewing needs to calibrate their strength of feeling as accurately as possible. This way, movie preferences are turned into one value for each chooser – that is, each family member and/or friend involved in shaping the decision. The process is exactly the same, although the choices may be more complex, whether deciding what movie to see or addressing North Korea's nuclear choices. Sure, the stakes differ, but once the essential facts are extracted, the process of turning stated objectives into a predicated outcome is the same.

The *"Position"* in the context of this chapter is the language of education policy adopted by the European powers in their African colonies. They could have chosen from among the five language of education policies listed in Table 2.3:

Table 2.3. Position Matrix

No.	Position Scale Matrix	Position Scale
1.	**Assimilationist Immersion Model (AIM):** Exclusive use of European languages in primary school	100
2.	**Language Maintenance Model (MM):** Disproportionate use of European and indigenous languages in primary school, 80–70/30–20 time share	75 (not implemented)
3.	**Dual Immersion Model (DIM):** Balanced (50/50) use of colonial and indigenous languages throughout primary school	50 (not implemented)
4.	**Transitional Immersion Model (TIM):** Split use of indigenous languages in lower primary and European languages in upper primary school.	25
5.	**Full Immersion Model (FIM):** Exclusive use of indigenous languages in primary school	0

These five policies will be encountered in several portions of the book where they will undergo extended explanations and illustrations. For now, suffice it for me to highlight their main characteristics. The definitions and the taxonomy are inspired by Lessow-Hurley's (2000:16). AIM encouraged proficiency only in the European languages. No African language was used as a medium of instruction at school. AIM was implemented by the French and the Portuguese. In fact, African languages were banned from formal education in those colonies. The next model is MM. It was never implemented in Africa. If it had been, it would have recommended that the European languages be used as the media of instruction in all academic subjects but that African languages be taught as academic subjects. DIM also was never implemented. Its implementation would have meant that European languages and African languages would have been used equally as media of instruction for all academic subjects. So, each classroom would have two teachers. One who may teach math, history, and social studies in a European language while, the other would teach biology, chemistry, writing in an African language. TIM was a model in which students were introduced to literacy in their own ancestral languages during lower primary school. All academic subjects were taught in the students' mother tongue, a regional LWC, or a national LWC. From fourth grade upward, the colonial language took over as the medium of instruction in all academic subjects. The African language assumed a lesser role because it became taught only as an academic subject. From 1922 onward, the British became the advocates of TIM because African parents grew impatient with FIM. The proponents of FIM used African languages only throughout elementary school. By and large, the Belgians and the Germans were the only colonists to have been successful in implementing FIM. Wa Thiong'o's educational experiences reported in 1.8 illustrate the use of FIM in British colonies before they switched to TIM.

For the purposes of the weighted mean calculations that will be done later in 2.5.4, numerical values have been assigned to each of these five positions. The extreme position of total assimilation of Africans to the language of education policy of the French and the Portuguese is rated at 100. The other extreme position of not teaching Africans the European languages at school is rated at 0. The intermediary position of TIM is rated at 25, while DIM and MM are rated 50 and 75 respectively. The weighted mean calculations in 2.5.4 will tell us which one of these five models of language of education would have worked best in colonial Africa if advice of a game theorist had been sought. The same line of reasoning will be used to predict the best mother-tongue education model for Côte d'Ivoire and other Sub-Saharan African countries that were colonized by the French and the Portuguese.

2.5 Introducing the Predictioneer's Model 65

2.5.3 Describing and applying the Salience (S) scale

The Predictioneer's Model first identifies and lists all the players. Secondly, it identifies the various positions and rates them. Thirdly, it determines the level of interest, or their commitment to the position that they hold. De Mesquita (2009:53) uses the term *Salience* **(S)** to describe and measure their level of interest. The methodology for assessing and assigning numerical values to salience is described as follows:

> Now estimate how eager each friend or family member – each player – is to weigh in on the decision. If you think a family member will drop what he or she is doing to discuss the movie to see, rate that person's "salience" close to 100 (no one is ever really at 100). The less focused you think someone is on the movie choice, the lower the salience score. If a family member is the sort who would say, "Look, I'll go to whatever movie you choose, but I don't have time to get involved in picking which one," that's somewhere around 10. On the other hand, if you think a friend will say, "I'm busy right now but call me back in ten minutes," that's pretty high salience. "Call me back in an hour" is lower, and "Call me back next week" is much lower. With a bit of effort, it shouldn't be that hard to calibrate how important the movie decision they have to make (not compared to each other, mind you, but compared to other things they need to do or deal with).

In the context of the language game in colonial Africa, salience is understood as the measurement of **the level of interest** in using or not using European languages as media of instruction in colonial schools. A high level of interest is rated at 95 because De Mesquita does not believe that anybody ever reaches 100% of interest on any given issue. On the issue of whether or not to use a European language as the sole language of instruction in colonial times, even the most ardent supporters of linguistic assimilation wondered if it was the right course of action in French and Portuguese colonies. So, in order to leave room for doubt, the salience score of the diehard supporter of the use of a European language in school is rated at 95. Similarly, the salience of the diehard opponent of teaching a European language to Africans is rated at 10.[18] Here too, there is historical evidence that even the Belgians and the Germans who were ardent supporters of the exclusive use of indigenous languages in education second-guessed their approach and tried to make changes to it between 1905 and 1913. The

---

18 The lowest salience score assigned in De Mesquita (2009:233) is 10.

salience is rated at 75 for people who did not have any choice but learned European languages because that was the language policy decreed by colonial authorities. This rating applies to Africans in French and Portuguese colonies. European missionaries in these colonies are included in this group because they preferred to train Africans to read and write in their own languages. The rating of 50 is given to educated Africans in English-speaking countries who are torn between the European language and their own languages. It is also given to British colonial officers in non-Islamic areas of Africa. The rating of 25 is given to Africans in settings where the European language is not needed to get a job. This applies to most people in Belgian and German colonies. It also applies to uneducated Africans in urban settings who get menial jobs that do not require proficiency in any European languages. Table 2.4 summarizes all the salience ratings of all the players of the language game played in colonial Africa.

Table 2.4. Salience Scale Matrix

No.	Salience Scale Matrix	Salience Matrix
1.	High interest in European languages	95
2.	Moderate interest in European languages	75
3.	Average interest in European languages	50
4.	Low interest in European languages	25
5.	No interest in European languages	10

2.5.4 Describing and applying the Influence (I) scale

After identifying and listing players, after determining their position on a specific issue and measuring it, and after ascertaining the level of interest of players and assigning it numerical values, the last step in the Predictioneer's Model is determining the level of influence that players have in relation to each other. Numerical values are assigned to the influence that each player has. It is well known that in society people do not have the same influence; that is, they do not wield the same social or economic power. The same goes for players: some have more social capital, others have less. Everything being equal, the more clout a person has, the more likely he or she is to influence other people's choices and decisions. De Mesquita (2009:53–4) provides the following rationale for assigning numerical values to influence:

2.5 Introducing the Predictioneer's Model

Finally, figure out who you think has the most influence among your friends or family members if you assume that everyone thinks the choice is equally important. Give the person credited as being most persuasive a score of 100 and rate everybody else relative to that. If Harry is 100 and Jane is 60 and John is 40 in potential clout, and Jane and John want to see *The Sound of Music* and Harry wants to see *A Clockwork Orange*, then that means that John and Jane together just offset Harry's ability to persuade if they all care equally about choosing a movie. If Jane were 60 and John 70, then, all else being equal, they could persuade Harry to moderate his views and give more consideration to the movie Jane and John prefer. Of course, if someone else supported Harry's choice, that might create a strong enough coalition to defeat John and Jane. The dynamics get complicated, but the basic idea should be straightforward.

The scale for analyzing the influence of each of the 40 players in the language game played in colonial Africa is as follows:

Table 2.5. Influence Scale Matrix

No.	Influence Scale Matrix	Influence Matrix
1.	Europeans/White	100
2.	Expatriate (Asian and Middle Easterners)	90
3.	Euro-Africans	85
4.	Assimilated Africans	80
5.	African political elites	75
6.	African chiefs in British colonies	75
7.	African educated/employees	60
8.	African WW I and II veterans	50
9.	African chiefs in French/Portuguese colonies	50
10.	African chiefs in Belgian/German colonies	50
11.	African missionaries (black)	30
12.	Urban Africans	30
13.	Uneducated Africans/farmers	0

It is an uncontroversial fact that everywhere in colonial Africa, the European colonizer wielded an impressive amount of influence. This is so because the colonizers had a huge military, scientific, and economic edge over Africans. In African literature, whites were looked up to as having quasi-divine attributes. In fact, Keller (1995:158) notes that it was only after WW I and II that the image of the all-powerful, all-knowing, rich white person began to fade. Consequently, everywhere in the colonies, a white person, by virtue of the color of his/her skin, was automatically influential. Several notches under the white man and woman were all other non-black people in the colonies. Included in this category were Asians, Middle Easterners, and bi-racial individuals. Continuing in a descending order of influence were the assimilated Africans in French and Portuguese colonies, World War I and II veterans, paramount chiefs and emirs, educated civil servants, city dwellers, and indigenous missionaries. At the very bottom of the colonial society were uneducated African farmers who lived in rural areas. The numerical values assigned to the various players are based on a close reading of power asymmetry in colonial Sub-Saharan Africa.

2.5.5 The Pan-African language preference

At the heart of the Predictioneer's Model is the concept of **weighted mean**. It is a statistical formula that is widely used in mathematics, in medical statistics, in actuarial science, in polling analysis, and in many other areas where variable numerical values are calculated. De Mesquita uses the weighted mean formula in his assessment of security threats and risk analysis. As has been mentioned already, the CIA has rated the success of his predictions to be over 90%. The weighted mean formula is applied here to language planning because it can point us to a linguistic equilibrium, that is, a consensus outcome that the various players in the language game prefer. De Mesquita (2009:59) explains that the weighted mean is "Roughly speaking, an average of what people, with their influence and commitment to a given issue, want." In other words, the percentage that is derived from all the calculations points us towards the preferred language policy. When the various pieces of information collected from sections 2.5 through 2.5.3 are aggregated and calculated, we arrive at the weighted mean score of 67.32%, as shown in Table 2.6.

Table 2.6. Pan-African Weighted Mean

No.	Players	Influence Scale	Salience Scale	Position Scale	I × S × P	I × S
1.	French/Portuguese Catholic missionaries	100	75	100	750	7,5

(*Continued*)

Table 2.6. Pan-African Weighted Mean (*Cont.*)

No.	Players	Influence Scale	Salience Scale	Position Scale	I × S × P	I × S
2.	British Protestant missionaries	100	10	0	0	1
3.	Belgian missionaries	100	10	0	0	1
4.	German missionaries	100	10	0	0	1
5.	French and Portuguese teachers in lower elementary	100	95	100	950	9,5
6.	French and Portuguese teachers in upper elementary	100	95	100	950	9,5
7.	British teachers in lower elementary	100	10	0	0	1
8.	British teachers in upper elementary	100	95	25	237,5	9,5
9.	Belgian and German teachers in lower elementary	100	10	0	0	1
10.	Belgian and German teachers in upper elementary	100	10	0	0	1
11.	French/Portuguese colonial administrators	100	95	100	950	9,5
12.	British colonial administrators in Islamic areas	100	10	25	25	1

(*Continued*)

Table 2.6. Pan-African Weighted Mean (*Cont.*)

No.	Players	Influence Scale	Salience Scale	Position Scale	I × S × P	I × S
13.	British colonial administrators in other areas	100	50	25	25	1
14.	Belgian/German colonial administrators	100	10	0	0	1
15.	French and Portuguese business operators (white)	100	95	100	950	9,5
16.	British business operators	100	50	25	375	5
17.	Belgian and German business operators	100	50	25	125	5
18.	Euro-Africans in French/Portuguese colonies	75	95	100	712,5	7,125
19.	Euro-Africans in British colonies	75	95	25	178,125	7,125
20.	Expatriates in French/Portuguese colonies	90	95	100	855	8,55
21.	Expatriates in British colonies	90	95	75	641,25	8,55
22.	Assimilated Africans in French/Portuguese	80	95	100	760	7,6
23.	African political elite in French/Portuguese colonies	75	75	100	562,5	5,625

(*Continued*)

Table 2.6. Pan-African Weighted Mean (*Cont.*)

No.	Players	Influence Scale	Salience Scale	Position Scale	I × S × P	I × S
24.	African political elite in British colonies	75	75	25	140,625	5,625
25.	African political elite in Belgian colonies	75	75	0	0	5,625
26.	African educated/ employees in French/Portuguese colonies	60	75	100	450	4,5
27.	African educated/ employees in British colonies	60	50	25	75	3
28.	African missionaries in English colonies	30	10	0	0	300
29.	African missionaries in Belgian and German colonies	30	10	0	0	300
30.	African WWI and WWII vets in French and Portuguese colonies	50	75	100	375	3,75
31.	African WWI and WWII vets in British colonies	50	50	25	62,5	2,5
32.	African chiefs in French/Portuguese colonies	50	75	100	375	3,75
33.	African chiefs in British colonies	75	50	25	93,75	3,75

(*Continued*)

Table 2.6. Pan-African Weighted Mean (*Cont.*)

No.	Players	Influence Scale	Salience Scale	Position Scale	I × S × P	I × S
34.	African chiefs in Belgian and German colonies	50	10	0	0	500
35.	African Chiefs' sons in French/Portuguese colonies	50	75	100	375	3,75
36.	African Chiefs' sons in British colonies	75	75	25	140,625	5,625
37.	African manual workers in urban settings in French/Portuguese colonies	30	25	100	75	750
38.	African manual workers in urban settings in British	30	25	25	37,5	1,5
39.	African manual workers urban settings in Belgian and German colonies	30	25	0	0	750
40.	African uneducated/rural/farmers in French and Portuguese colonies	0	25	100	0	2,5
41.	African uneducated/rural/farmers in British colonies	0	0	25	0	0
42.	African uneducated/rural/	0	0	25	0	0

(*Continued*)

Table 2.6. Pan-African Weighted Mean (*Cont.*)

No.	Players	Influence Scale	Salience Scale	Position Scale	I × S × P	I × S
	farmers in Belgian and German colonies					
43.	Total				11,246,875	167,05
44.	Weighted mean				67.32%	

What does the score of 67.32% mean in relation to the five positions discussed in 2.5.2? AIM was rated at 100%, MM at 75%, DIM at 50%, TIM at 25%, and FIM at 0%. According to De Mesquita (2009:73) "Numerical values that are closer to the numerical value of the player's advocated position are liked better by the player than positions reflected by numerical values farther from the advocated position." Since 67.32% is closer to MM than to DIM, this means that if the various colonial powers had consulted with each other, they would have agreed on MM as a better language of education policy across Africa. All the players would have been in favor of using the European languages as media of instruction. However, they would also have liked African languages to be taught as academic subjects throughout elementary school. Instead, the French and the Portuguese went their way and imposed AIM. The Belgians and the Germans used FIM, while the British groped along until they eventually settled for TIM.

2.6 Summary

It is obvious from the presentation in this chapter that language planning qualifies as a game. As such, the Game theory is a serious theory that deserves a seat at the table where language planning is being debated. The theory has an impeccable pedigree in mathematics and economics. It has shown itself to be versatile and adaptable to various issues and situations. Its application to political science and economics make it particularly attractive to language planning. The fact that government agencies, corporations, military planners, and security firms trust it is an added bonus. The formula I x S x P is simple and yet powerful because it forces a stringent analysis of the players, the strategy, the payoff, and the outcome of every game. In so doing, according to Davis (1983:172), "[the Game theory] permits you to analyze many apparently different problems at the same time." Moreover, the theory is robust because it has both descriptive and predictive powers. Furthermore, De Mesquita's Predictioneer's Model is simple and intuitive because it mirrors the natural way in which human beings go about solving problems:

> It's important to note that most of us make these assessments of interests in any situation. We just do such calculations naturally with relative judgments of where people stand on a given issue. What I've sketched above is simply a formalization of that natural process – which becomes all the more needed the more complicated the problems in question become (De Mesquita 2009:54).

De Mesquita (2009:124) is not bashful about touting the success of his model. However, he warns that a careless application of his model will fail to predict the correct outcome if three important safeguards are not taken into account:

> Models fail for three main reasons: the logic fails to capture what actually goes on in people's heads when they make choices; the information going into the model is wrong – garbage in garbage out; or something outside the frame of reference of the model occurs to alter the situation, throwing it off course. The last of these is what happened to my health care analysis.

These warnings have been heeded in this book. Extreme care has been taken to make sure that players have been identified accurately and that the numerical values that are assigned to their positions, their salience, and their influence are based on reliable information that can be independently verified. Therefore, the weighted mean score of 67.32% represents a consensus-building model that the colonizers and the colonized could have used, had the Game theory existed back then. The same methodology will be used to provide guidance for African countries that are still in need of language planning.

Chapter 3
A Game-theoretic assessment of language of education policies in French and Portuguese colonies

Introduction

Generally, countries that were colonized by France and Portugal have fared more poorly in planning their indigenous languages than countries that were colonized by Belgium, Britain, and Germany. This state of affairs can be traced back to the fact that these colonial powers saw linguistic colonialism as a competitive zero-sum game. As a result, the language of education policy that they embraced led them to AIM. This chapter explains why and the impact that that policy has had on contemporary language planning efforts in francophone and lusophone countries of Africa. For the purposes of this chapter and the next, the colonial era is divided into three periods. The first period is known to historians as the "pacification" phase. It ran from the 1890s to the onset of World War I. This quarter of a century prepared the stage for what was to follow. It was the time of many battles between Africans and the invading European armies. The technological superiority of European weaponry did not only subdue Africans militarily, but it also paved the way for the ensuing cultural and linguistic subjugation. The second timeframe focuses on the period between the two world wars. It is the most sociolinguistically salient because it was during this time that the French and the Portuguese assimilation ideology was implemented to the fullest. The third colonial period runs from World War II to the eve of the independences. Most francophone countries gained their independence in 1960 while lusophone countries became independent around 1975. The present chapter focuses on these countries because their colonial masters were able to integrate the assimilation ideology into their colonial administrative style.

This chapter is divided into four sections. The first section serves two objectives. It addresses the relevance of Game theory to colonialism studies. It also serves as a review of the rationales for colonialism and the administrative model used by the French and the Portuguese. The second section applies the Game theory to French colonies. The analysis in the third section deals with lusophone countries. The discussions of the impact of French linguistic colonialism is far more detailed than that of the Portuguese because there is considerably less information in English and French on Portuguese colonialism. This lopsided analysis is due to the fact that I do not read Portuguese and have had to depend on secondary sources for my analyses. This caveat, as important as it may be, has only a residual effect on the overall findings because available sources in English and French are sufficient to shed light on the language game played by the Portuguese and their African subjects.

3.1 The Game theory and colonialism studies

A question that begs for an answer is the following: "How relevant is the Game theory to the study of colonialism?" De Mesquita (2009:ix-xiv) has already answered this question for us. The very first example used in his book to exemplify the relevance of the Game theory to colonialism comes from his analysis of King Leopold II's paradoxical behavior in Congo and in Belgium. He uses the Game theory to explain why Leopold II is remembered by the Belgians as an enlightened ruler while he is seen by Africans as a villain and a tyrant:

> King Leopold II, remembered today as Belgium's Builder King, reigned from 1865 to 1909. A constitutional monarch who, like many of his contemporaries, longed for the bygone days of absolute power, he was nonetheless an unusually influential and activist king who helped make Belgians free, prosperous, and secure. Belgium's good works during Leopold's reign are almost uncountable. He oversaw the expansion of political freedom with the adoption of universal adult male suffrage in competitive elections, putting his country on a firm footing to become a modern democracy. On the economic front, he encouraged free-market policies that guided Belgium to remarkable growth ... Though he never set foot in Africa, Leopold also ruled over Congo Free State for nearly a quarter of a century (1885–1908). He built his personal wealth in the Congo first by extracting high-priced ivory from the region and then by exploiting the even more lucrative rubber that developed there. Unlike in Belgium, there was no chef de cabinet (roughly prime minister), and no voters among Congo's approximately 30 million people to limit what he could do. Because it was his personal property, Leopold was free to exert the absolute rule he could not have at home. ... Perhaps as many as 10 million people were murdered at the hands of the Force Publique in their pursuit of wealth for Leopold and, of course, for themselves. ... How could King Leopold II have ruled two places at the same time in such dramatically different manners?

De Mesquita (2009) provides an answer to this important question by appealing to the Game theory. Since his analysis deals with political science, we will not bother with his findings. However, the methodology that he used to bolster his findings is applicable to linguistic colonialism.

Consequently, the I × S × P formula will be used to identify the key players of the colonial language game, their salience, their position on the language of education policy, and their influence.

3.2 The rationales for colonialism

Experts contend that European powers colonized Africa for three main reasons, all which begin with a "C": Commerce, Christianization, and Civilization. When these rationales are weighed one against the other, it is uncontroversial that Europe colonized Sub-Saharan Africa because of its immense reservoir of natural resources. Europeans came to tap into these vast riches to fuel their Industrial Revolution. Factories needed the abundant raw materials found in Africa to keep churning out manufactured goods for local consumption. However, since these countries produced more than they could consume, it was imperative that they find overseas markets also. So, Africa was a dream come true for capitalism: it supplied abundantly what was needed for European factories to run and it was also a place where European goods were moderately in demand. Christianization and Civilization were additional justifications for colonialism. However, they ranked second and third respectively. This ranking does not in any way trivialize or negate the importance of Christianization and Civilization in the overall colonial agenda. In fact, it will be shown in this chapter and in the next that the outcome of the language of education policy depended crucially on how seriously the colonists took the last two Cs. Taken together, the three "Cs" have left an indelible impact on the Africans economically, psychologically, culturally, and linguistically.

3.2.1 The indelible impact of colonialism

Two cataclysmic events of near apocalyptic proportion have befallen Africa since it came into contact with the Portuguese in the 16th century. The two events are slavery and colonialism. The first human slave cargo to reach the Americas was in 1525 and the last to arrive in the Americas was in 1867. For more than 342 years, the Dutch, the English, the French, the Germans, the Portuguese, and the Spaniards organized more than 35,000 slaving voyages from Africa toward destinations in the New World.[19] According to

---

19 Retrieved from http://www.slavevoyages.org/tast/index.faces on July 27, 2010.

Keim (1995:116), between 10 and 13 million Africans were brought alive into the New World. However, he notes that "millions more Africans died in the process of capture, in caravans taken captives to the coast, in quarantine while waiting for ships, in loading, and in the Atlantic crossing." Additionally Arabs took approximately 7 million slaves to North Africa and to the Middle East. Conservative estimates indicate that all in all between 15 and 20 million Africans were taken captive and sold into slavery. Slavery was one of the most lucrative businesses prior to the Industrial Revolution. It lasted for over three centuries because the average life expectancy of slaves was estimated to be less than ten years. For there to be enough supply, the trade had to go on and on. With the advent of the Industrial Revolution and the Enlightenment, and upon the objections of a new breed of religious leadership, the British parliament abolished slavery in Great Britain in 1807 and in all its colonies in 1833. The French followed suit and abolished slavery in France in 1830 and in all their territories in 1848. The Arabs, the Portuguese, and the Spaniards continued the slave trade well into the 1880s and 1890s (Keim 1995:124). The transatlantic slave trade ended only because of the British and French naval blockades and strict enforcement of anti-slavery laws. The city of Freetown in Sierra Leone was so named because it was a refugee town where freed slaves were sent after they had been rescued from slave ships on the Atlantic. As horrific and abominable as slavery was, it has had a very little effect on the daily lives of contemporary Sub-Saharan Africans. The cataclysmic event that contemporary Africans remember more vividly is colonialism.

The title of one of Ngugi wa Thiong'o's book, *Decolonizing the Mind*, attests to the fact that the 100 years or so of European colonialism has had a more ubiquitous effect on contemporary Sub-Saharan Africans than the three centuries of slavery. Every time Africans declare proudly or sheepishly that they are from this country or that country, or when they cheer loudly and boisterously for their country's soccer team, or when they are able to communicate with another African from a different ethnic group in English, French, Portuguese, or Spanish, they are consciously or subconsciously acknowledging the impact of colonialism on their lives. They are explicitly or implicitly acknowledging the historical realities that took place in Berlin between 1884–5. For a period of three months, Europeans met at a conference convened for the sole purpose of balkanizing Africa among them. It is not hyperbolic for Khapoya (1998:111) to state that it is impossible to understand contemporary Africa without first understanding the European colonization of the continent:

Colonization of Africa by European countries was a monumental milestone in the development of Africa. The Africans consider the impact of colonization on them perhaps the most important factor in understanding the present condition of the African continent and the African people. Therefore, a close scrutiny of the phenomenon of colonialism is necessary to appreciate the degree to which it influenced not only the economic and political development of Africa, but also of the African people's perception of themselves.

Assessing the impact of colonialism on Africans begins with understanding the objectives and the achievements of the Berlin Conference. One of the lasting legacies of the conference was the territorial carving up of Africa without any regard for linguistic or cultural homogeneity. The decisions made in Berlin and later on in Paris at the Treaty of Versailles have given us the present-day territorial configuration of Africa:

Table 3.1. Land Occupation

No.	European Powers	Before WWI	After WWI
1.	France	36%	37%
2.	Britain	30%	34%
3.	Belgium	8%	8%
4.	Germany	8%	0%[1]
5.	Italy	7%	7%
6.	Portugal	7%	7%
7.	Spain	1%	1%
8.	Uncolonized	3%	6%

Note:
1 The cases of Germany and Somalia will be discussed in Chapter 4.

European powers can be classified and cross-classified in various ways. Khapoya's classification reproduced in Table 3.1 uses territoriality as its main criterion. One could very easily use any one of the three "Cs," that is, Commerce, Christianization, or Civilization as a classificatory feature. Indeed, for the purpose of the outcome of the language game discussed in this chapter and the next, Christianization and Civilization will be used as the leading criteria. It will be argued in this chapter, for instance, that the similarities in language outcome between the French and Portuguese colonies are attributable to Civilization. Even so, a quick review of the three main rationales for the European colonization of Africa is in order before we proceed any further.

3.2.2 Commercial interests and the colonial enterprise

The European Industrial Revolution of the 18th century brought about an economic puzzle that begged for a solution. First, the factories in each country were producing more goods than the local consumer market could absorb. An increasing surplus of manufactured goods was becoming an economic nightmare. Secondly, European factories were in need of natural resources to keep churning out manufactured goods. The relative proximity of Africa and Europe made Africa the ideal place for Europeans to kill two birds with one stone. They could sell their surpluses in Africa and at the same time extract invaluable raw materials to produce more surpluses. A case in point is the invention of the bicycle and the automobile. Both of them need tires to run. Shellington (2005:334) explains how these two inventions created a huge need for rubber all over Europe. This need led to the development rubber plantations in Congo. Other agricultural products that European consumers needed were palm-nuts and groundnuts because they were used in manufacturing all kinds of consumer products such as soaps, cooking oil, and engine lubricants. Cotton was needed to fuel the growing fashion industry. Coffee and tea were for the educated palates of the new capitalist bourgeoisie. The Europeans' insatiable appetite for these products led to the development of cash crop agriculture all over Sub-Saharan Africa. The money that the farmers made was, in turn, used to purchase manufactured goods from Europe to which they became increasingly addicted.

Though trading in agricultural products was highly profitable, the most lucrative business of all was in the mining industry. Tin, aluminum, iron, ore, copper, and bauxite, to name a few, were in high demand. Shellington (2005:351) explains how extensive mining operations were:

> The sector of the colonial economy most profitable for capital investment was mining. Colonial authorities assumed all rights over minerals within their territories. These were leased for European-owned companies to exploit. The British thus took over the gold fields of Asante. ... The richest part of tropical Africa for European mineral exploitation in this period was the central African region of Katanga (Shaba) and the Northern Rhodesian 'Copperbelt.'

All in all, Europeans made huge amounts of money from their African colonies. Again, Shellington (2005:351) explains this economic bonanza for Europeans:

> Marketing at the coast was in the hands of a small number of large European merchant companies. They insured that prices paid to African

producers were maintained at the lowest possible level. If higher prices were obtained in Europe, the merchants kept the difference as extra profit for themselves. Those same merchants controlled the sale of manufactured goods imported from Europe; when prices rose in Europe, the increase was immediately passed on to the African buyer. In general then, during the 1920s and 1930s, African farmers were paid less for what they produced, but had to pay more for what they bought. This was particularly the case after the 'Great Depression' which struck Europe and the United States in 1929–30. With falling real incomes and constant pressure of colonial taxation, African peasants had to bring more and more land into cash-crop production. Food crops were neglected, soil became exhausted and in times of drought, famine struck. In 1931 famine killed nearly half of the populations in some areas of Niger."

The game-theoretic outcome of economic colonialism can be described as a 2-person, zero-sum game for European powers. They profited the most from colonialism. The long list of European agribusiness and mining companies doing business in colonial Africa attests to the fact that colonialism was a high revenue business. Normally it is hard for scholars to reach a unanimous consensus on economic matters, but when it comes to colonialism, one is hard pressed to find an expert to argue that colonialism was not economically profitable to Europe. However, there is no consensus as to whether or not Africans benefited economically from colonialism. To say that economic colonialism was a 2-person, zero-sum game for Africans does not in any way suggest that Africans were left without anything at all. The previous generations of colonialism scholars tended to make such claims. However, from a game-theoretical perspective, such a contention is not accurate. An example from the world of sports can be used to illustrate the 2-person, zero-sum outcome alluded to earlier. Take the championship game of the US Opens for tennis. The two finalists play. The winner gets the trophy but the loser does not go empty-handed. He/she receives some financial compensation for his/her efforts. Similarly, Africans did not win the trophy in the colonial economic game, but they did derive some benefits from it, albeit meager. Gilbert and Reynolds (2004:301) make this point very well:

> The new environments created by colonial rule also provided opportunities for new elites to be created. The expanding cash economy and rapid development of transportation infrastructures allowed some farmers and traders to amass considerable fortunes. Just because the imposition of colonialism was designed to benefit the colonial powers does not mean that some Africans were not able to exploit the new setting to their advantage.

In breaking away from the traditional assessment of economic colonialism, a new generation of scholars, including Khapoya (1998:143–6), Shellington (2005:338) and Gellar (1995:153) note rather accurately that, though Europeans benefited the most economically, some Africans, a tiny minority though it was, also took advantage of the system to improve their lot in life. The longer the economic colonialism game lasted, the more Africans became players in it. The impact of these entrepreneurs on the outcome of the colonial language game cannot and should not be underestimated.

3.2.3 Christianization and colonial enterprise

Scholars will debate for a long time to come the pros and cons of missionary involvement in the colonial enterprise. The overwhelmingly negative assessments which portrayed missionaries as accessories and accomplices of the political and economic exploitation of Sub-Saharan Africans is progressively giving way to a more balanced and nuanced appraisal such as the one proposed by Shellington (2005:291–2):

> Few Christian missionaries were directly active agents of European imperialism. But they were an essential ingredient of the increasing European presence which was a forerunner of imperial control. In a number of cases Christian missionaries played a significant role in promoting and shaping the advent of European colonialism. At times, especially in the final quarter of the century, European missionaries appealed to their home governments for various degrees of political or military 'protection'. This was usually in the face of local political conflict which threatened the safety of their missions. Nevertheless, when European governments responded positively to these requests, it was usually due more to their own wider strategic or commercial interests.

Moyo (2007:328–9) makes a useful distinction between three waves of missionary activities: the missionaries who came in the 15th century, those who arrived in the 18th century, and those who set foot on African soil in the 19th century. The Portuguese were first among the Europeans to come as missionaries. These were Jesuit and Dominican missionaries of the 15th century. However, Moyo deemed their work not to have been particularly successful. Shellington (2005:289) concurs with this assessment and adds that missionary work in the 18th century was also a failure:

> Looking back from the perspective of the late eighteenth century, it was clear that European Christianity, as a vehicle for religious and cultural

change, had made virtually no impact at all on the peoples of Sub-Saharan Africa. By contrast, the Christian revival of the early nineteenth century was a different matter. Though initially slow to take effect, eventually its impact proved to be both far-reaching and permanent. ... The evangelical missionaries saw their Christianity as part and parcel of their European cultural values – even to the extent of insisting African converts adopt European clothing. They preached a strict puritanical moral code. They opposed dancing, drinking, non-religious singing and any form of sexual freedom outside monogamous married. ... And since belief in the written word of the Bible was an essential ingredient of faith, the spread of Christianity also meant the spread of basic education for literacy.

More will be said in the next chapter about the relevance of missionary linguistics to the planning of indigenous African languages. For now, let me simply say that, according to Shellington (2005:289) "French Catholic missions followed later in the [19th] century." Furthermore, Laitin (1992:85) observes that "most Catholic Mission Society schools in Portuguese colonies were run by the French." Consequently, it can be stated categorically here without fear of contradiction that French and Portuguese missionaries had no beneficial impact on the planning and development of indigenous African languages. Missionary linguistic activities that count for indigenous language planning are Scripture translation and the development of literacy materials. On both counts, French and Portuguese missionaries were of no use at all. Combing through the history of Bible translation in African languages, I am yet to stumble on Scripture translation done in an African language under French or Portuguese rules in the 19th century. This confirms the observation made by Kaplan (1998:430–1) that Catholic missionaries ministered within the existing linguistic framework of the colonial powers, while Protestant missionaries did not. Recently Stroud (2008:79, 80) has made a similar observation, and so have the contributors to *Language* (2009:618–658).

In general, missionaries who originated from countries that were influenced by the Reformation tended to promote indigenous languages more vigorously than those whose countries were largely unaffected by the Reformation (see 9.4). As is well known, the Reformation was predicated upon two theological slogans, *Sola Scriptura* and *Ad Fuentes*. The former urged Christians to read the Bible for themselves in their own languages and not to rely on ecclesiastical interpretations. The second slogan insisted that Bible translation must be made on the basis of the original languages, Hebrew for Jewish Scriptures and Greek for Christian Scriptures. Missionaries who came from a Reformation tradition were so convinced that the people must read Scriptures in their "heart languages" that they went to great lengths to translate the Bible into various indigenous languages. However, since France and Portugal were Catholic countries, their missionaries did not give a lot of consideration to Bible translation. Jesuits and Dominicans built many schools in Sub-Saharan Africa, but the curriculums did not make room for the teaching of indigenous languages.

3.2.4 Civilization and the colonial enterprise

All the European powers had a civilizing mission statement. It is known under various euphemisms: the "White Man's Burden" for English speakers, "mission civilisatrice" for the French, and "lusotropicalism" for the Portuguese. These were ideological slogans designed to win the minds and hearts of European civil societies. France and Portugal camouflaged their colonial intentions behind the 'Civilization' ideology. Gilbert and Reynolds (2004:283) explain it as follows:

> Further, Colonial governments needed to legitimize their activities. Even if their ultimate goals were economic exploitation and a quest to prove racial superiority, colonial administrations were generally not willing to say, 'We are in it for the money and the power.' Rather, they sought to justify colonialism in terms of altruism. Indeed, the British notion of 'white man's burden,' and the French concept of the Mission Civilisatrice both represent the ways in which colonial powers sought to create an image of themselves as benevolent agents of civilization – selflessly toiling to bring the benefits of Western culture and technology to the "backward" races of the world.

The truest form of this ideology came to be known as "assimilation." France and Portugal believed in it so much that they made it the cornerstone of their administrative and educational policies. Gellar (1995:140–2) equates assimilation with a politically correct form of racism:

> Notwithstanding different patterns of European rule throughout the continent, colonialism was essentially a system of political, economic, and cultural domination forcibly imposed by a technologically advanced foreign minority on an indigenous majority. As a system, colonialism justified itself through ideologies which asserted the superiority of the colonizer and the inferiority of the colonized. Much of the rationale justifying the conquest and colonization of Africa had been based on evolutionary theories of history influenced by the ideas of Darwin, Spencer, Morgan, and Marx. Such

theories maintained that societies organized within the framework of the nation-state and industrial capitalism represented the most advanced human forms of civilization. Apologists for European colonialism and imperialism argued that it was right, indeed the duty, of the 'higher' civilizations to conquer the 'lower' civilizations in order to bring prosperity and 'progress' to all parts of the world. Such claims, often expressed in terms of the 'White Man's Burden,' or what the French referred to as their 'civilizing missions,' were reinforced by racial theories which asserted the biological superiority of the 'white race.' ... The racial character of the colonial system was not only reflected in the ideologies of the day but also in colonial social structures. Thus, in most colonies, European officials, businessmen, farmers, and missionaries constituted a privileged ruling caste open only to those of European birth.

For the French and the Portuguese, assimilation became the yardstick against which they measured the success or failure of their administrative and educational policies. As such, it can be used as a distinctive feature according to which colonial powers came to be classified. Thus, the seven European powers can be sub-categorized as follows:

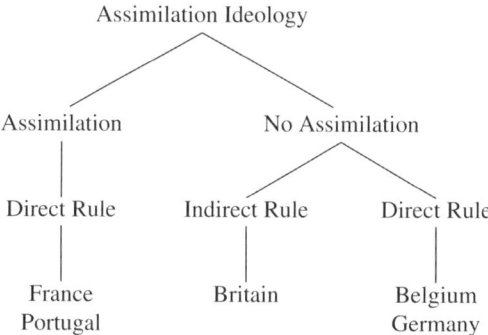

Figure 3.1. Colonial Ideology

France and Portugal practiced hard core assimilation while others avoided it. Africans and scholars of Africa have debated and will continue to debate the merits and demerits of assimilation. Some seem to prefer the French "Cartesianism" to the British "Empiricism" (Gellar 1995:144). Khapoya (1998:120–5) compares and contrasts French and British records on racial discrimination and votes in favor of assimilation:

> Obviously, the French were in Africa to 'civilize' and remake the African in their own image. The policy of assimilation required an educational system

that would transform Africans into French people. Since educational opportunities were extremely limited in French colonies, only a few Africans actually qualified for full rights as French citizens. Nevertheless, after World War II, following reforms that conferred French citizenship on Africans, the acculturated Africans, living in the cities of Senegal, Ivory Coast, Guinea, and elsewhere in the French empire do not recall having to use separate bathrooms, being sent to separate schools, having to sit on the opposite side of the aisle in the church, being forced to ride in separate train compartments, having to drink from separate fountains or even having to endure the humiliation of signs reading: 'Africans Only,' 'Europeans Only,' or 'Africans and Dogs Not Allowed.'

Another often mentioned advantage of assimilation is that it de-ethnicized French and Portuguese colonies, while its absence in other European colonies accentuated ethnolinguistic rivalries. As the saying goes, beauty is in the eyes of the beholder. Colonies under assimilation ideology may not have suffered from blatant racism of the type that Khapoya alludes to, but Whites in French and Portuguese colonies *did* discriminate against Blacks. Moreover, since the fate of African languages is the concern in this book, it can be stated unequivocally that assimilation was detrimental to local languages. This claim will be the subject for the rest of this chapter. Indeed, for the assimilation ideology to succeed, it first had to trash-talk and vilify African languages and cultures, as Wa Thiong'o (1986:16) has so eloquently stated it:

> The real aim of colonialism was to control the people's wealth. ... But its most important area of domination was the mental universe of the colonized, the control, through culture, of how people perceived themselves and their relationship to the world. To control a people's culture is to control their tools of self-definition in relationship to others. For colonialism this involved two aspects of the same process: the destruction or deliberate undervaluing of people's culture, their art, dances, religions, history, geography, education, orature and literature, and the conscious elevation of the language of the colonizer. The domination of a people's language by languages of the colonizing nations was crucial to the domination of the mental universe of the colonized.

The remainder of this chapter will focus on how the French and the Portuguese went about implementing the assimilation ideology in their colonies. The crux of the analysis will be based on the I × S × P formula. The players in the colonial language game will be identified first. Next, their interest (salience) in French and Portuguese will be rated. Then the language of education policy used by these two colonial powers will be discussed. Numerical values will be assigned to "I," "S," and "P" to measure the impact of colonialism on ancestral languages.

3.3 Overview of French colonialism

In addition to the three "Cs," Commerce, Christianization, and Civilization, geo-political and strategic considerations played some role in France's colonial ambitions in Africa. The prestige that France once held all over Europe was on the decline after France lost the Franco-Prussian war of 1871. This loss was accompanied by a territorial loss as well (Ager 1999:192). So, French politicians wanted to revive the nostalgia of "La Grande France" by stretching their empire from "Algeria to Congo." Their colonial strategy was to conquer all the territories west of the Libyo-Egyptian border and move southward to the Congo Basin. Their strategy of having a contiguous French-speaking empire in West Africa would have succeeded had it not been for the British colonies of Sierra Leone, Ghana, and the Gambia. The Portuguese also voided the French scheme by colonizing Guinea Bissau. In spite of this unwelcomed intrusion by the British and the Portuguese, France ended up with the lion's share of colonial territories in Africa. It controlled 36% of the continent from 1885 until 1918. After WWI, its territory was enlarged by 1% because the Treaty of Versailles gave it Togo and a large chunk of the Cameroons.

Another important feature of French colonialism is how it administered its Sub-Saharan territories. Its territorial administrative style has come to be known as the "Direct Rule." This policy was presumably designed by Louis Faidherbe, the French governor in Senegal (Gilbert and Reynolds 2004:287). It is called "Direct Rule" because the French presence was noticed all the way from Paris to its African subjects. In many colonies, it was customary to find a French administrator at all levels except at the village level. In some big villages, the French took it upon themselves to change the traditional political system by appointing chiefs. They were known as "Chefs de Canton" (Picoche and Marchello-Nizia 1994:89). So, in essence the French presence was felt via proxies from Paris all the way to the hinterlands of Africa. Direct Rule model required a fairly large number of French administrators. Where the number of colonists was not enough, adjustments were made, as was the case in Mauritania, Burkina Faso, Chad, and Niger (Gellar 1995:144). Except for these countries, Direct Rule generally applied. Picoche and Marcello-Nizia (1994:123) note, for example, that there were more than 5,000 French colonial administrators in Côte d'Ivoire before World War I.

France's Sub-Saharan empire consisted of two entities: French West Africa and French Equatorial Africa. The former was the largest and included eight countries: Benin, Burkina Faso, Côte d'Ivoire, Guinea, Mali, Mauritania, Niger, and Senegal. French Equatorial Africa comprised of four countries: Congo (The People's Republic), Chad, the Central African Republic, and Gabon. French West Africa had 13 million people in 1903 and 20 million in 1958. Between 1946 and 1955, the number of French administrators doubled in these countries. The population of French Equatorial Africa was 4 million in 1903 but it doubled to 8.5 million in 1958. Picoche and Marchello-Nizia (1994:102) note that the number of French administrators tripled in French Equatorial Africa colonies during this time frame.

3.3.1 Assessing players and their influence in French colonies

The first methodological step in all game-theoretic analyses, as explained in Chapter 2, is to identify and describe accurately the number of players that participate in a game. In all non-trivial games, there must be at least two players. The language game played in French colonies can be described as an n-person game because there were at least 14 groups of players. They fell into three groups: players who were citizens of France, expatriate players, and African players. Each group of players is further sub-divided, as will be shown shortly. The influence of each group and sub-group of players is rated on the influence scale.

3.3.1.1 French and Lebanese players

The French players fell into four sub-groups: teachers, missionaries, administrators, and business operators. They occupied the pinnacle of the colonial society. French missionaries and teachers exerted the greatest linguistic influence on Africans because they had more direct contact with the natives. Moreover, they interacted with more people than did colonial administrators and business operators. For this reason, their influence score is 100, while the score of administrators and business operators is set at 95. Missionaries were particularly influential because, in general, the first white person some Africans ever saw was the white "Father":

> Missionaries played a significant role in spreading European influence. They not only worked to convert Africans within the borders of the new colonies, but they often pushed the frontier of contact well beyond

administered zones, introduced Western education, and taught European values (Keim 1995:125).

An important segment of the expatriate community was made up of Lebanese. They were less influential in spreading French because many of them were not very fluent in it, and yet they passed on to their African collaborators the hybridized French that they had acquired. In this respect, I hypothesize that they helped spread an urbanized dialect of French. Gilbert and Reynolds (2004:278, 316) point out that in many parts of francophone Africa, Lebanese and other Middle Easterners were referred to as *"petits blancs,"* i.e. "little whites." They interacted with the French in French and they interacted with Africans in French. Because of their business acumen, they enjoyed a higher status than most Blacks. So, they too contributed in no small way to the spread of French. As a result, their influence score is rated at 90 while the influence of French citizens is rated at 100.

3.3.1.2 Hierarchy among African players

Africans under colonialism did not constitute a monolithic group of people. They were hierarchically divided into four main groups. Euro-Africans and "assimilated Africans" were in the upper echelons. Euro-Africans were people of mixed ancestry born to European and African parents. Gellar (1995:147) describes their status as ambiguous: "One interesting feature of the colonial system was the relatively privileged but ambiguous status of the Euro-Africans, who constituted a small Westernized elite midway between the European rulers and the African masses in the colonial racial hierarchy." Keim (1995:120) traces the origin of some of these Euro-Africans back to the days of slavery. Because of their privileged status, they are given a score of 80 for their influence in spreading French culture and language.

Next in influence came the assimilated Africans. These were educated men and women (more men than women) who later became the professional and political elite. According to Gilbert and Reynolds (2004:288), by 1922, after nearly 100 years under colonial rule, the French had granted assimilated status to only 100 Africans. Out of more than 17 million Africans in the federated French colonial empire, less than 500 Africans were fully assimilated by the time World War II began. Shellington (2005:355) contends that the French were manipulative and unwilling to dole out citizenship even if the people met the draconian cultural and linguistic requirements. They dangled the assimilation carrot in front of Africans but did not allow many to reach it. He argues that "the French continued to hold up potential assimilation as an ideal which all Africans should strive for. But French authorities made the educational qualifications for African assimilation extremely difficult to achieve." The influence of the few that reached the assimilated status is rated at 80.

Below the Euro-Africans and the assimilated Africans is another group of Africans who was granted an "elevated status." One of the main advantages attached to this status was that these persons were exempt from the *corvée* (forced labor). Picoche and Marchello-Nizia (1994:89) estimate that 10% of Africans were promoted to this rank. This group included county chiefs appointed by the French, African employees of the colonial administration, elementary school graduates, and the veterans of WWI and II. Their influence is rated at 50. The veterans of WWI and WWII need to be singled out for special mention. During their deployment elsewhere in Africa or in France, they were taught enough French to facilitate communication with other African soldiers or with French soldiers. Some did actually excel in French, as is the case of Sembène Ousmane who went on to become a well-known writer and movie maker. The number of veterans who participated in WWI and WWII[20] was impressive, and so was their political influence. Picoche and Marchello-Nizia (1994:89, 100) state that 256,000 Sub-Saharan African soldiers, derogatorily called "tireailleurs sénégalais," were conscripted in WWI and WWII. A total of 49,000 of them died in combat for the Allies. According to *Jeune Afrique L'Intelligent*,[21] 72,000 were wounded. The veterans who returned were a nightmare for French colonial administrators. Upon demobilization, many of them took advantage of their proficiency in French to acquire paid positions as police officers, bodyguards, chauffeurs, cooks, etc. Others lent their services to the political elite who were agitating for more civil rights and reforms. Moreover, upon their return home, the demobilized veterans helped to undermine the myth that all Europeans were wealthy, healthy, and civilized. Keller (1995:158) describes their eye-opening experiences as follows:

> Many Africans were also drafted into the armies of the colonizing powers, where they served in various capacities, such as combatants, porters, servants, cooks, and drivers. In many cases, the war experience enabled African soldiers to see another side of their European masters. Rather than being invincible, self-assured, emotionless gods, European soldiers proved

---

20 More than 193,000 participated in WWI and 63,000 in WWII.
21 *Jeune Afrique l'Intelligent*, No. 2142, January 29-February, 2002, p. 24.

to be as human as any African. There were rich and poor Europeans. In the heat of battle they displayed the emotions of fear and apprehension just as all people do.

Gilbert and Reynolds (2004:304) remark that WWI and WWII veterans had both political and social clout. Consequently, their sociolinguistic influence cannot be underestimated. Just as Alexander the Great's soldiers contributed to the spread of Koine Greek 2000 years earlier, it is quite likely that the hundreds of thousands of demobilized soldiers who returned from the battlefields of France played a role in spreading the influence of the French language and culture as much as they were able to. There are plenty of anecdotal stories of veterans who, upon returning to their villages, claimed to have forgotten their native language(s)! There were even some who wailed in French at funerals!

The last two rungs of the colonial social ladder were occupied by more than 85% of the population. The French classified them as indigènes, i.e., unassimilated natives. They fell into two groups: urban indigènes vs. rural indigènes. The common characteristic that these two groups shared is they were all illiterate. Many of them moved to the burgeoning colonial cities to work as day laborers, cooks, housecleaners, night watchmen, gardeners, garbage collectors, etc. Because they lived in towns and cities, they were not under the direct jurisdiction of village chiefs, so they were not required to do forced labor. Rural dwellers, on the other hand, were regularly forced to work for free on colonial projects: building schools, hospitals, roads, bridges, railroads, etc. They were beaten, humiliated, and ill-treated at least once a year for two weeks to a month. Many Africans under French colonial rule fled to neighboring English-speaking countries to avoid the corvée altogether. In fact, my grandparents were among the fugitives from Côte d'Ivoire who fled to Ghana. Both of my parents were born in Ghana and did not return to Côte d'Ivoire until they were in their twenties, after Houphouet-Boigny introduced legislation into the French Assembly banning the corvée. The legislation passed on April 11, 1946, and the corvée was banned in all French colonies in 1946.[22]

All in all, there were 14 types of players in the language game played in French Sub-Saharan colonies. All the players except the rural indigènes played some role in spreading the French language with varying degrees of

---

22 Retrieved from http://www.contreculture.org/AL%20Abolition%20du%20travail%20forc%E9.html on June 17, 2011.

importance. The Table 3.2 in 3.4 lists all the players and rates their influence, their position, and their salience.

3.3.1.3 Language of education policy in former French colonies

In the colonial language game under consideration, "Position" refers to the language of education policy implemented by colonial authorities. There were five models discussed in 2.5.

Given the assimilation ideology that undergirded French colonial policies, it would not come as a surprise to know that they implemented AIM from first grade upward. Picoche and Marchello-Nizia (1994:127) note that in colonial times, and even today, a person is considered "francophone" if he/she has completed six years of formal education in French. To understand the rationale behind the French's decision to use their language as the sole medium of instruction, we must first provide some background about how the French felt (and still feel) about their language. In his book, *Identity, Insecurity, and Image: France and Language*, Ager (1999) provides valuable insights that can help us understand the unparalleled symbiosis between the French people and their language. Some landmark dates need to be highlighted for us to better understand why the French felt the way they did regarding the use of their language in colonial Africa. In 1539, a law was passed that made French the official language of France. In 1635, the French Academy was created to regulate the use of standard French. In 1660, that is, 25 years after the creation of the French Academy, a seminal book on French Grammar, *Grammaire Générale et Raisonnée* was written by Antoine Arnauld and Claude Lancelot. Here is how Ager describes the formative role of this book in shaping French linguistic identity:

> The *Grammaire Générale et Raisonnée* of 1660, and particularly later commentators like Voltaire and Rivarol, ascribed qualities to written French which made it almost a measure of perfection, and the ideology of language which was generated then has remained with many commentators today. At this time was born the belief in the universality of standard French, in its innate clarity, precision, logic and elegance, and its superiority over any other language.

A century or so prior to colonialism, French was the diplomatic language of Europe and also the language of cultural sophistication. Picoche and Marchello-Nizia (1994:149–156) note that European countries copied French culture, architecture, and fashion. The spread of French in Europe flattered the ego of Frenchmen and women and made them believe in the myth about the universality and the superiority of their language to any other language. Consequently, by the time the French conquered their colonies in Sub-Saharan Africa, they were so enamored with their own language that they could not fathom not using it as the sole medium of instruction for "civilizing" Africans. Ager (1999:192) accounts for the exclusive use of French in African schools as follows:

> The discourse of support for the teaching of the language abroad, and for the dissemination of French culture, has for long used the argument of duty a civilized country has to bring enlightenment to others. Indeed, France had a mission to civilize others by insisting that they benefit *from her language*, her enlightened understanding of the world and her culture, *which naturally required the extinction of their own in the pursuit of universality*. [Emphasis added]

Linguistic narcissism aside, no African language was used in colonial schools because, according to Ager (1999:24), Articles 6 and 7 of the 1793 Education Reform Act explicitly forbade the use of any other language in schools except French:

> Article 6. *Public education is to be carried out everywhere so that one of its benefits should be that French quickly becomes the familiar language in all parts of the Republic.*
>
> Article 7. *Throughout the Republic instruction will take place solely in French.*

This Education Reform Act applied equally to schools inside and outside of the metropole. Another important characteristic of this law is that it explicitly prohibited private schools from teaching any other language but French. As a result, though half of the schools in the colonies had religious affiliations, they were required by law to use French and French only as the medium of instruction (Picoche and Marchello-Nizia 1994:94). The law was initially passed to prohibit regional dialects and languages from school grounds. Linguistic bullying and intimidation measures were used to enforce the use of standard French at school. Ager (1999:29) describes these tyrannical methods as follows:

> At this point the duty of the Ministers of Education and all the teachers, particularly in the primary schools throughout the land, was not merely to

teach French but to ensure that regional languages and local dialects were systematically excluded from school, even from school grounds. Methods used to ensure this included ridicule of children speaking local languages by forcing them to wear a dunce's cap or a placard around their necks, and systematically ensuring that local cultures and customs were regarded as backward

These same methods were transplanted in schoolyards all over French-speaking Africa. Teachers enforced this law scrupulously. Wa Thiong'o (1986:11) describes with an unsurpassable eloquence his experience of the token as a middle-school student in Kenya. His description is cited here in full because all the necessary background information is needed to help us understand the torment and humiliation that students in colonial Africa felt:

> Language was not a string of words. It had a suggestive power well beyond the immediate and lexical meaning. Our appreciation of the suggestive magical power of language was reinforced by the games we played with words through riddles, proverbs, transpositions of syllables, or through nonsensical but musically arranged words. ... And then I went to school, a colonial school, and this harmony was broken. The language of my education was no longer the language of my culture. ... English became the language of my formal education. In Kenya, English became more than a language: it was *the* language, and all the others had to bow before it in deference. Thus, one of the most humiliating experiences was to be caught speaking Gikuyu in the vicinity of the school. The culprit was given corporal punishment – three to five strokes of the cane on bare buttocks – or was made to carry a metal plate around the neck with inscriptions such as I AM STUPID or I AM A DONKEY. Sometimes the culprits were fined money they could hardly afford. And how did the teachers catch the culprits? A button was initially given to one pupil who was supposed to hand it over to whoever was caught speaking his mother tongue. Whoever had the button at the end of the day would sing who had given it to him and the ensuing process would bring out all the culprits of the day. Thus children were turned into witch-hunters and in the process were being taught the lucrative value of being a traitor to one's immediate community.

Chaudenson (2008:183) recounts a similar story. The British borrowed this practice from the French who had been using it to enforce the superiority of standard French for at least a century. On the basis of the information presented so far, the salience of French among the various players of the colonial language game can be rated as follows. Colonial administrators and teachers have the highest score on salience because they were required by law to teach French alone. Colonial business operators were also interested in hiring Africans who knew French well enough to be book-keepers and junior managers. So, their salience is rated at 95. Catholic missionaries receive a score of 75 because some of them would have preferred to minister in indigenous languages if they had been allowed to do so. In fact, some went to great lengths to study and describe indigenous languages even though they knew full well that these languages were never going to be used as media of instruction in colonial schools. African players are given a salience score that ranges from 75 to 25 because, from WWI onward, they realized that learning French was the new linguistic order. The French won the pacification battles very decisively. From then on, African rulers put into practice the saying "if you cannot beat them, join them." They and their subjects began to embrace French education wholeheartedly.

At first school attendance was very low. Robertson (1995:314) contends that "some rulers, when urged by missionaries to send their children to school, sent the children of their slaves instead, considering that education was unimportant and that they could more easily control low-status educated persons" However, after WWI, the demand for schooling skyrocketed, because "it soon became evident to Africans that high status under colonialism involved choosing to accept the domination of European culture in everything from dress to religion and schooling" (Robertson 1995:314). Boarding schools were built to house students who traveled over long distances from home. The demand for education continued to grow at an astronomical pace, but the French government could not keep up with the demand. Between 1926 and 1927, 26,000 pupils were enrolled in schools throughout French West Africa. Twelve years later, that is, in 1938, there were 71,000 students in primary schools across West Africa (Picoche and Marchello-Nizia 1994:94). Of these, only a few hundred, the best and the brightest, were allowed to move on to regional high schools in Brazzaville, Libreville, Bangui, Fort-Lamy, Bingerville, and Dakar. Of these hundreds, only an infinitesimal number of the graduates would make it to France where they would enroll in universities. Among these were the political elite who wrestled political independence away from France. It is worth noting that nearly all these political leaders were French citizens through assimilation. Even though they fought valiantly for political independence, they did not challenge the colonial language of education policy. In fact, upon independence, the constitutions of their countries endorsed French as the only official language, thus perpetuating the linguistic dominance of French as the sole language of education from elementary school onward.

3.4 A Game-theoretic analysis of players' preference

The previous information can help us calculate the weighted mean score, i.e., the level of preference for French among all the players in colonial Africa. De Mesquita (2009:59) says that the weighted mean score represents, roughly speaking what the people want. The aggregate of all the numerical values gives a score of 97.02%.

Table 3.2. Weighted Mean in French Colonies

No.	Players	Influence Scale	Salience Scale	Position Scale	I × S × P	I × S
1.	French Catholic missionaries	100	75	100	750	7,5
2.	French elementary school teachers	100	95	100	950	9,5
3.	French colonial administrators	100	95	100	950	9,5
4.	French business operators	100	95	100	950	9,5
5.	Euro-Africans in French colonies	75	95	100	712,5	7,125
6.	Expatriates in French colonies	90	95	100	855	8,55
7.	Assimilated Africans	80	95	100	760	7,6
8.	African political elite in French colonies	75	75	100	562,5	5,625
9.	African educated/ employees in French colonies	60	75	100	450	4,5
10.	African WWI and WWII vets in French colonies	50	75	100	375	3,75
11.	African chiefs in French colonies	50	75	100	375	3,75

(*Continued*)

Table 3.2. Weighted Mean in French Colonies (*Cont.*)

No.	Players	Influence Scale	Salience Scale	Position Scale	I × S × P	I × S
12.	African chiefs' sons in French colonies	50	75	100	375	3,75
13.	African manual workers in urban settings in French colonies	30	25	100	75	750
14.	African uneducated/rural/farmers in French colonies	0	25	100	0	2,5
15.	Total				8,140,000	83,9
16.	Weighted mean				97.02%	

We saw in 2.5.2 that there were five language of education models in colonial Africa. The weighted mean score of 97.02% corresponds to AIM. We conclude therefore that the consensus among an overwhelming majority of players was that they wanted French to be used exclusively as the medium of education in primary schools. There was a consensus on French among all the players in the language game. For Francophones, French was perceived as the magical language that could make their dreams of upward socioeconomic mobility come true. This finding is supported by available historical evidence. To the best of my knowledge, apart from Protestant missionaries who lamented the growing influence of French, there were hardly any calls from Africans and French authorities for the use of African languages in colonial schools. Everybody accepted the use of French as the sole medium of instruction to be a foregone conclusion.

3.5 Overview of Portuguese colonialism

The Portuguese were the first Europeans to establish settlements in Africa, but they were the last to leave the continent. Keim (1995:115) traces the very first contact between Africans and the Portuguese to Henry the Navigator. He allegedly came to Africa to fulfill a personal dream of "bypassing the Arabs who controlled North Africa and establishing direct trade, especially in gold, with the great civilizations of West Africa." This trip took place on the eve of the 15th century. He used Cape Verde as his refueling station. Soon many other Portuguese explorers followed in his footsteps. Vasco de Gama reached the Indian Ocean in 1497, some 10 years after his compatriot, Bartholomew Diaz, arrived at the Cape of Good Hope. En route to the Indian Ocean, many explorers established trading posts along the seashore of the Gulf of Guinea. City names such as Elmina, San Pedro, and Sassandra attest to the early Portuguese presence in these parts of West Africa. These early settlements gave the Portuguese a formidable advantage in the slave trade that followed shortly afterward.

In the 19th century when the European powers were scrambling to colonize the continent, the Portuguese were there. Portugal's territorial game plan, according to Cole and De Blij (2007:696) was "to link its territorial claims in Mozambique with those of Angola in a cross-African axis." However, this plan was foiled by the Belgians, the British, and the Germans. In the end, the Portuguese were left with only five colonies in Africa: Angola, Cape Verde, Guinea Bissau, Mozambique, and Sao Tome y Principe. Their administrative management style was the "Direct Rule," like the French. However, unlike the French, the Portuguese considered their African territories, especially those of Angola and Mozambique to be "provinces" of Greater Portugal (Cole and De Blij 2007:88, 682).

It seems that the Portuguese pursued a more aggressive assimilation policy than did the French. Not only did their presence in Africa last longer, approximately 500 years, but there were also more Portuguese nationals in their African colonies than there were of French. Cole and De Blij (2007:88, 682) estimate that the number of Portuguese immigrants was 400,000 for Anglola and 150,000 for Mozambique. Two reasons are given for the large influx of Portuguese into Africa. Gilbert and Reynolds (2004:296) attribute it to a new restriction that the United States placed on immigration around 1917. Illiterate immigrants were barred from entering America. So, they contend that "this new policy largely shut out the great bulk of Portuguese from the United States, and would-be migrants chose the path of least resistance by simply moving to areas under Portuguese colonial rule." The second reason, according to Cole and De Blij (2007:696, 697), is that Portugal was poor and its citizens fled to Africa to improve their socio-economic conditions:

> Throughout its tenure in Africa, Portugal was a poor country: its per capita income and literacy rates were the lowest in western Europe; a considerable proportion of its people lived at subsistence level; infant mortality rates were among the highest in Europe, while birthrates were among the

highest in the world; the majority of Portugal's inhabitants made their living from agriculture, while manufacturing contributed little to the national economy; freedom of thought and action were not tolerated by dictatorships; and the Portuguese remained largely uninformed about changing world conditions and were very conservative in their attitudes. Little wonder that 'development' was so painfully slow in Angola (and Mozambique). Portugal looked upon its colonies (officially referred to as 'provinces' after 1951) as reservoirs of human labor and natural resources to be exploited for the benefit of the metropole first, Portuguese settlers second, and the Africans last.

3.5.1 Assessing players' influence in Portuguese colonies

The Portuguese's colonial ideology was a carbon copy of the one that the French used in their colonies. Therefore, there is roughly the same number of players in both colonial language games. The influence scores are also identical. The only noteworthy exception is that there was a large contingent of Lebanese business entrepreneurs in francophone Africa, but in Portuguese colonies Portuguese citizens occupied all such positions:

> Colonial Angola had the second largest European population in Subsaharan Africa (after South Africa) but its colonists never had high educational standards. 1950, for example, half of the colonists had no formal education at all; only 17% had attended school for 5 years or more. Fewer than 2% of the immigrants arriving between 1953 and 1964 had more than 4 years of education. In Angola, colonists were the elite, but in Portugal, ironically they represented the poor majority. Although Portugal gave emphasis to its settlement projects, the overwhelming majority of the Portuguese were employed in commerce, not farming. Portuguese monopolized positions as waiters, bus drivers, bank clerks, and taxi drivers, jobs commonly held by Africans elsewhere in colonial Africa (Cole and De Blij 2007:697).

As for the social hierarchy, Portuguese nationals were the most privileged class. The next influential group was the "mestizos," that is, biracial individuals of Portuguese and African descent. Their number was extremely high because one aspect of the Portuguese lusotropicalism theory, i.e., assimilation strategy, was racial mixing (Cole and De Blij 2007:675, 697). In Angolan society alone, there were more than 150,000 mestizos. The "*assimilados*" (assimilated) ranked lower than the mestizos in influence. Here too, the Portuguese were far more generous than the French in granting citizenship to their African subjects. There were four requirements for assimilation and whoever met them could qualify for Portuguese citizenship: "The mastery of the Portuguese language, a commitment to monogamy, evidence of employment and true Catholic faith" (Stroud 2008:79). It is estimated that by 1961, the year of the abolition of this system, there were 40,000 assimilados in Angola. Spencer (1974:169) reports lower numbers of assimilados for Mozambique and Portuguese Guinea. According to the 1950 census, only 4,353 attained the assimilado status in Mozambique. Spencer also notes that there were only 1,478 assimilados in Guinea Bissau even though the population of the colony was more than 500,000 people. It has been suggested that between 1950 and 1961, several thousand more people became assimilated. However, the vast majority of Africans were classified as *"Indignato,"* that is, indigènes. These people needed special papers to travel outside of the territorial circumscription (Cole and De Blij 2007:697; Gilbert and Reynolds 2004:289).

3.5.2 Language of education policy in Portuguese colonies

The situation in Portuguese colonies is identical to that of French colonies in that Portuguese was the only language of instruction at all levels of education. Laitin (1992:134–5) indicates that the dominance of Portuguese was never questioned:

> The particular nature of Portuguese colonialism, in which a besieged administration and foreign missionary contingent both supported Portuguese language use led to a situation where Portuguese was well understood among elites throughout much of the colonial territories. Nationalist elites (perhaps because so many of them came from mixed African and Portuguese parents) never seriously questioned Portuguese's dominant role. In 1981, in Mozambique, the Peoples' Assembly approved a document with an objective 'to spread, by the means of education, the Portuguese language, [in order] to contribute to the consolidation of national unity. Accordingly the legislators recognized that Portuguese would 'continue to be the only language of instruction at all levels of education'.

Since Portuguese was seen as the language of upward social mobility, Africans from all walks of life were keenly interested in acquiring it. Unfortunately for most, the Portuguese could not build schools fast enough to satisfy the demand. Stroud (2008:78) notes that in 1890 there was only one school in the whole country of Mozambique. Twenty-five years later, that

3.5 Overview of Portuguese colonialism 101

is, in 1915, the number of schools had increased to 68. Yet the supply was much lower than the demand. For those Africans who were lucky enough to attend school, Portuguese authorities ensured that their language remained the only medium of instruction in their colonies by keeping a very close watch on the curriculum:

> At the same time, Portuguese was spread throughout the territory in the wake of the expansion of institutions such as schools, clinics and maternity wards, an infrastructure that, like the new administrative structures, was associated with use of Portuguese. Education, for example, was conducted solely in Portuguese and school personnel were transferred to parts of the country whose local language they did not know, to ensure that only Portuguese would be used in the classroom. Portuguese usage was strictly regimented in teacher method handbooks, especially in extensive model exercises, classroom dialogues, and drill patterns. Furthermore, language use in exams was monitored by all institutions in the hierarchy, including the local education offices, the provincial education directorates, and the Ministry of Education (Stroud 2008:81).

When colonial authorities realized that English and French could undermine the spread of Portuguese, policymakers in Lisbon did not hesitate to take vigorous actions to protect their language. They preemptively banned English and French from schools in 1903. Seventeen years later, Decree no. 77 was published banning the use of indigenous vernaculars in schools. The decree went so far as to prohibit "the publication of anything in the vernacular, except as a parallel text to Portuguese" (Laitin 1992:85). French missionaries were allowed into Portuguese colonies only if they agreed to abide by the rule that Portuguese was the only medium of instruction in elementary school. This and other protective measures ensured the spread of Portuguese at all levels. Therefore, colonial officials and all Portuguese nationals, rich or poor, educated or uneducated, are given a salience rating of 95. Catholic missionaries are rated at 75. The rating score of non-assimilated Africans ranges from 75 to 25.

3.5.3 A Game-theoretic analysis of players' preference

When the various numerical values are assigned to the players in the Portuguese language game in accordance with the I × S × P formula, we arrive at the weighted mean score of 96.68%, as displayed in Table 3.3:

Table 3.3. Weighted Mean in Portuguese Colonies

No.	Players	Influence Scale	Salience Scale	Position Scale	I × S × P	I × S
1.	Portuguese Catholic missionaries	100	75	100	750	7,5
2.	Portuguese teachers in elementary school	100	95	100	950	9,5
3.	French/Portuguese colonial administrators	100	95	100	950	9,5
4.	Euro-Africans in Portuguese colonies	75	95	100	712,5	7,125
5.	Other Portuguese citizens	100	95	100	950	9,5
6.	Assimilated Africans in Portuguese colonies	80	95	100	760	7,6
7.	African political elite in Portuguese colonies	75	75	100	562,5	5,625
8.	African educated/ employees in French/Portuguese colonies	60	75	100	450	4,5
9.	African WWI and WWII vets in Portuguese colonies	50	75	100	375	3,75
10.	African chiefs in Portuguese colonies	50	75	100	375	3,75
11.	African Chiefs' sons in Portuguese colonies	50	75	100	375	3,75
12.	African manual workers in urban	30	25	100	75	750

(*Continued*)

Table 3.3. Weighted Mean in Portuguese Colonies (*Cont.*)

No.	Players	Influence Scale	Salience Scale	Position Scale	I × S × P	I × S
	settings in Portuguese colonies					
13.	African uneducated/ rural/farmers in Portuguese colonies	0	25	100	0	2,5
14.	Total				7,285,000	75,35
15.	Weighted mean				96.68%	

The weighted score of 96.68 corresponds to the language of education policy described in 2.5.2 as AIM. This means that all the players in the language game agreed that using Portuguese as the medium of instruction in all colonial schools for all grades was what they wanted. Portuguese nationals wanted it. Assimilated Africans, Euro-Africans, and all the colonized people wanted it because they saw that acquiring Portuguese was their ticket for upward socio-economic mobility. The protective measures taken by the authorities in Lisbon to banish local and competitive European languages such as English and French paved the way for its spread. So, in the competitive language game played in colonial Africa, Portuguese won hands down.

3.5.4 The outcome of the language game

In the final analysis, French and Portuguese beat African languages even though the latter had home court advantage. The visiting languages won because they had the support of the colonial authorities, the missionaries, the business community, and the biracial community. The visiting teams were also able to co-opt some players from the home teams by offering them citizenship and employment incentives. The payoffs were simply too good to ignore. As a result, little by little, as was discussed in 2.4.1 in the case of the Tragedy of the Linguistic Commons, the speakers of the indigenous languages began acquiring the languages of the foreign powers. Since then, some speakers have been switching their language preference from their native tongues to French or Portuguese. The process of language shift is proceeding at an uneven pace from country to country. However, Picoche and Marchello-Nizia (1994:94) provide us with the data below which can help us anticipate what the final outcome will be if nothing is done to change course:

Table 3.4. Postcolonial Spread of French

No.	Countries	Percentage of Francophones
1.	Benin	65%
2.	Burkina Faso	13%
3.	Chad	25%
4.	Congo	100%
5.	Cameroun	85%
6.	Côte d'Ivoire	80%
7.	Central African Republic	65%
8.	Gabon	100%
9.	Guinea	33%
10.	Madagascar	50%
11.	Mali	35%
12.	Niger	20%
13.	Senegal	40%
14.	Togo	65%

A "francophone" is defined as a person who has completed six full years of elementary school in French. The data indicates unambiguously that French is still winning the language game because the language of education that was set in motion some 150 years ago is continuing unabated. Information gleaned from Stroud (2008) suggests that the situation in Lusophone Africa is remarkably similar to the one in French-speaking Africa. Former Portuguese and French colonies continue to implement AIM as their preferred language of education policy.

3.6 Implications for language planning in French and Portuguese colonies

The sociolinguistic situation that Francophone and Lusophone countries inherited from their former colonial powers is one of diglossia à la Fishman. Ferguson originally coined the word 'diglossia' to describe situations such

3.6 Implications for language planning in French and Portuguese colonies 105

as in Germany, Switzerland, the Arabic-speaking world, Haiti, etc., where the same language has two sociolinguistically marked divisions of labor. One variety, the most prestigious one, is used for all official and formal functions, whereas the low variety is used to fulfill informal and familial functions. Education and all things related to literacy call for the use of the high variety. Fishman took this original definition and extended it to colonial settings such as those discussed in this chapter, where a colonial language wins over indigenous languages. The main distinction between diglossia à la Ferguson and diglossia à la Fishman is bilingualism. In the former, widespread bilingualism is expected, especially if literacy is widespread. However, in the latter, bilingualism need not exist. For instance, most colonists lived in the diglossic environment of colonial Africa without knowing a single African language. As for the Africans themselves, many including, the assimilated, the "political elite," the educated classes, and the urbanites will be reasonably bilingual, while the dwellers in rural areas will remain essentially monolingual unless they have access to public education. Another important characteristic of diglossia à la Fishman, arguably the most important characteristic, is that all educated individuals in former French and Portuguese colonies will be literate in one and only one language. That language will be either French or Portuguese. The colonial language ideology was such that indigenous African languages were given very low prestige, and as such did not deserve to have any role in education.

Laitin (1992:134) describes situations of this type as a case of 2-language outcome. He notes that Mozambican authorities "are working toward a program to develop 'a positive form of bilingualism.'" Since independence, all former French and Portuguese colonies have had linguistic reforms on their agendas. However, it seems that the more they talk about it, the more complacent they become. The following example cited in Stroud (2008:87) describes a situation that is all too common in French and Portuguese-speaking Africa:

> A recent example of this is when President Guebuza [of Mozambique] delivered an Easter speech in Portuguese to an audience of Changana/Tsonga-speaking women, despite the fact that he is a fluent and native speaker of this language himself. The occasion was in honor of a feminist organization, and the speech was translated, as well as subsequent interactions, on the spot by a Portuguese-Changana/Tsonga translator. The performance of this event enacted and underscored the link between modernity and feminism (in Portuguese), on the one hand, with tradition and womanhood (in Changana), on the other.

Sociolinguistic performances such as this one underscore the pervasive impact that linguistic assimilation has had on francophone and lusophone countries in Africa. So long as African languages continue to be excluded from the formal education setting, indigenous languages will keep losing ground. One should not be surprised if in a century or two, the Tragedy of the Linguistic Commons runs its course in these countries.

3.7 Summary

The charts in this chapter and the next are interpreted as follows. A high weighted mean score shows that all the players in the language game agreed that the European languages should be used as the media of instruction at school. A low weighted score indicates the players' preference for the use of African languages as the media of instruction. The weighted mean score is then aligned with the information in 2.5.2, Table 2.3, to determine the model of education used in colonial times. As noted previously, DIM and MM were never implemented in colonial Africa. If they had been implemented, and if the European powers had known about the Game theory, they would have used MM as their preferred model of education because the pan-African weighted mean score was 67.32% (see the analysis in 2.5.4).

The weighted mean scores are 97.02% and 96.68% respectively, as shown by the comparative bar graphs below:

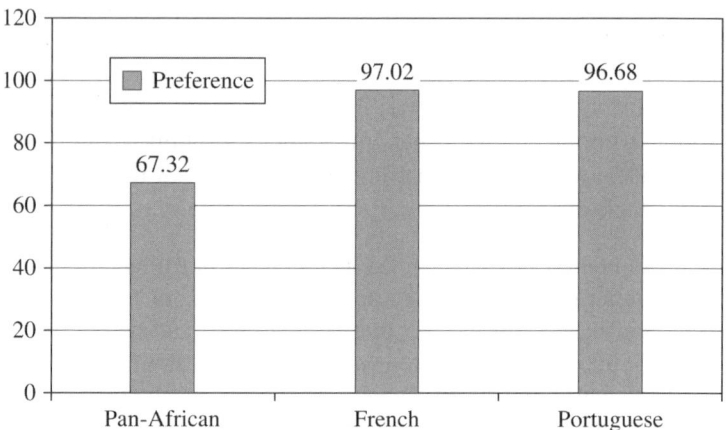

Figure 3.2. Comparative Weighted Mean of Position

These scores indicate that the players in the language game French and Portuguese colonies used AIM as their preferred language of education model. The assimilation ideology pursued by these two colonial powers succeeded in creating an environment where the outcome of the language game favored of their respective languages and downgraded African languages. The language of education policies that the colonists set in place 100 years are still the ones being implemented in schools today. Laitin (1992) states that policymakers in lusophone Africa have been making plans for "positive bilingualism," that is, a language of education policy whereby African languages would be introduced into the school curriculum. Similar plans have been made in francophone Africa. But so far these proposals have not been implemented, or should I say, cannot be implemented because they fail to bring about linguistic equilibrium. Moreover, the proposals do not address the pertinent issues of ethnolinguistic loyalty, the low marketability value of African languages, parental opposition, and the other impediments discussed in Chapter 1 that stand in the way of mother-tongue education in Africa.

Chapter 4
A Game-theoretic assessment of language of education policies in Belgian, British, and German colonies

Introduction

In this chapter, our attention is focused on the linguistic legacy that the British, the Belgians, and the Germans had left behind by the time colonialism was officially over. These three countries are grouped together because they pursued a non-assimilation ideology in their colonies. Unlike the French and the Portuguese, they did not seek to turn their Sub-Saharan African subjects into carbon copies of their respective metropoles culturally and linguistically. As a result, the language game played in these colonies can be described as having a cooperative non-zero sum outcome. The game theoretic analysis will again be used in this chapter to measure the level of interest of all participants in the colonizer's language.

4.1 The legacy of the pluralistic language ideology

Many African linguists, including me, have mistakenly thought that the administrative style of the colonies had a more direct impact on the status of African languages than the language ideology of the colonists. As it turns out, Direct Rule or Indirect Rule had an inconsequential impact on indigenous African languages. What mattered the most was the ideological orientation of the colonizing power. As indicated in Figure 3.1 in Chapter 3, all the European powers except England administered their colonies using Direct Rule. Yet, the linguistic outcomes in Belgian and German colonies are more in line with English colonies than with French and Portuguese colonies. Upon a closer examination, it becomes obvious that the single most important predictor of how African languages fared was the language ideology espoused by European powers. By and large, African languages fared worse (and are still faring worse) under colonial powers that espoused the assimilation ideology than those that did not. This can be explained by the fact that the British, the Belgians, and the Germans did not treat African languages with the same level of disdain as did the French and the Portuguese.

Khapoya (1998:114) laments the fact that African languages were banned in mission schools run by French and Portuguese and that the African heritage was ridiculed and suppressed. This was diametrically opposed to the clement attitude that the British adopted towards African languages. In fact, according to Gilbert and Reynolds (2004:291), British colonial officers were made to promise not to "threaten local cultural norms" and "were required to learn to speak local languages." McLaughlin (2008:70–1) informs us that "British officials of the Sudan Political Service were required to become proficient in Arabic if they were posted in the north, but also rewarded for studying a select number of southern languages if they were based there." Moreover, since cultural assimilation was not their goal, the British, the Belgians, and the Germans did not go out of their way to try to impose their native languages on their African subjects. In fact, we will see in 4.3 and 4.4 that the Belgians and the Germans were reticent to use their native languages in colonial schools. As for the British, they designed a flexible language policy that they applied differently to different colonies or regions within the same colony, as local circumstances allowed.

4.2 Overview of British colonialism

Britain is second only to France in the number of countries and territories that it colonized. Historians of the colonial era note that the British were the only European power to have used Indirect Rule approach in the administration of their colonies. The person whose name is often associated with the British Indirect Rule system was F. D. Lugar. He served two tours of duties in Africa, first in Uganda and later in Northern Nigeria. Gilbert and Reynolds (2004:287, 290–1) compare and contrast Lugar's approach to that of Faidherbe:

> The original architect of this policy for the French was Louis Faidherbe, the military officer largely responsible for French expansion in the Senegambia in the mid-1800s. Faidherbe's concept of assimilation really worked on two levels. First was the ideal that new colonial territories would be "assimilated" into existing French administrative systems and would be part and parcel of a "Greater France" – a concept already somewhat established in Algeria. Second, however, was the idea that subject peoples would ultimately become French citizens who were culturally indistinct from their counterparts at home. ... Quite in contrast to their colonial powers, the British in Africa developed a system known as indirect rule. As the name implies, the British sought not to displace African systems of authority and

administration, but rather to rule through them whenever possible. The system of indirect rule built on British colonial experience elsewhere in the world, particularly India. Credit for the codification of indirect rule itself goes to F. D. Lugard, who served as a colonial officer in Uganda and later in Nigeria. Indeed, it was his experience in Northern Nigeria that led him to formulate his perspective on indirect rule. In 1922 he published a book, *Dual Mandate in Tropical Africa*, which outlined his ideas for colonial administration in considerable detail. The text quickly became a statement of policy for British colonial rule in Africa (Gilbert and Reynolds 2004:287, 290–1).

Indirect Rule meant that the British did not meddle directly in the affairs of Africans, as the French and the Portuguese did. The British usually appointed a colonial officer to be the governor of a specific colony. He, in turn, ruled through local chiefs. Some commentators contend that the British opted for this administrative style because they were involved in a vast colonial empire stretching from Asia to Africa. Consequently, they lacked the human resources they needed to manage all their territories. Being quintessentially pragmatists, the British allegedly opted for an administrative model that did not require a large number of British citizens. Gellar (1995:145) notes for instance that for the vast area of Northern Nigeria, "there was only one British administrator for every 100,000 persons." Moreover, he explains that

> The system of Indirect Rule permitted rulers and chiefs to govern certain areas under the careful supervision of the Europeans. The survival of traditional authority did not alter the fact that rulers and chiefs were clearly subordinate to the colonial power structure and could be deposed if they did not follow the dictates of the colonial administration. The ideal chief under the colonial system was loyal, accepted the hegemony of the colonizer, maintained order, collected taxes for the colonial regime, encouraged his people to produce cash crops for export economy, and provided forced labor for public works projects and cheap labor for European enterprises.[23]

Scholars have argued back and forth about the merits and demerits of Indirect Rule. Clearly, for the British, it was a win-win situation from an economic standpoint. They got as much as possible out of their colonies with the least amount of investment in human resources. However, the merits and demerits of Indirect Rules for Africans are still being vigorously

---

23 Also, see Khapoya (1998: 138–140) for a description of the complicity of African chiefs in colonial exploitation.

debated. Many see the preservation and even strengthening of local ethnicity under Indirect Rule as a beneficial development (Gilbert and Reynolds 2004:294). However, others have charged that the strengthening of local ethnicity caused a sense of "national identity crisis" or a lack of nationalistic commitment among former British colonies (Gilbert and Reynolds 2004:294). Simpson and Ayetade (2008:178) give an example from Nigeria that illustrates the pro and cons of Indirect Rule:

> The rationale for indirect rule was that it would minimize the administrative costs of governing the huge territory, and reduce the general visibility of the British colonial presence and its intrusion in the country. Indirect rule was heralded as a great success in the north, where the British allowed Fulani rulers to continue in their role as emirs and leaders of the northern population, promising minimal interference in the daily life of those in the north and a guaranteed respect for the continued practice of Islam. Christian missionary activity which was permitted in the north was consequently only permitted in those areas which were not Islamic. Elsewhere, in the south, however, the policy of indirect rule resulted in much resentment as it often created local rulers with powers far greater than those traditionally permitted in indigenous societies such as those of the Yoruba and the Igbo.

The political and economic merits or demerits of Indirect Rule will, no doubt, continue to be vigorously debated. However, we will confine our observations only to the linguistic legacy of British colonialism in so far as it impinges on planning indigenous languages. To do so, let us examine how Indirect Rule played out in the different areas of Sub-Saharan Africa that were under British rule.

4.2.1 The implementation of indirect rule in Northern Nigeria and Sudan

It is true that the British invented Indirect Rule. It is also true that they ruled most of their colonies according to the principles of Indirect Rule. However, it is not true to say that they applied Indirect Rule uniformly to all their colonies. The British modified their administrative style to fit the local realities in Nigeria and Sudan. The British had three colonies in Nigeria: the Lagos Colony, the Southern Protectorate and the Northern Protectorate. In 1906, the Crown Colony of Lagos was officially incorporated into the Southern Protectorate. From 1906 onward, Nigeria consisted of only two colonies: the North and the South. This geographical and political division remained

4.2 Overview of British colonialism 113

in place until Nigeria became a federal republic in 1954.[24] The British administered the two colonies in Nigeria differently. The Northern Colony was for all practical purposes an autonomous colony in the hands of predominantly Hausa-speaking Fulani emirates. British authorities enforced their policy of Indirect Rule so strictly in the Northern Colony that they prevented missionary activities there. Laitin (1992:84) offers the following explanation for this decision:

> In the Muslim north, Lugar feared a potential rebellion, similar to what plagued the British in the Sudan. He therefore proscribed Christian missionaries from operating in northern Nigeria, thereby holding back formal education in northern Nigeria. Eventually a Church Missionary Society (CMS) project to set up a boarding school for the sons of Muslim chiefs was accepted, but the CMS was not permitted to implement it.

Virtually all formal education in British colonies was in the hands of missionaries. This meant that for nearly 100 years, the inhabitants of northern Nigeria did not have access to English. The British decided early on to let Hausa be the administrative language of their Northern Colony. They interfered only minimally with Hausa by replacing the traditional Ajami script with a Romanized script. Literacy in English came much later. Cole and De Blij (2007:326) note that "as late as 1931, less than 3% of the population in the northern part of the country could read [English]." In the Southern Colony, literacy in English was much higher. As a result of these historical factors, the control of English is, up to the present, unevenly distributed. Simpson and Oyetade (2008:190) report that Hausa speakers have a very high level of loyalty to their language and a significantly lower proficiency in English.

The situation of English in Sudan is almost a carbon copy of the one found in Nigeria. In Sudan also, there is a great divide of proficiency in English between the north and the south. In 1898, the Egyptians allied with the British and conquered Sudan. Shortly thereafter, Egypt itself became a protectorate of Britain. Administratively, northern Sudan was a quasi autonomous state where Indirect Rule was vigorously enforced. Moreover, Arabic was used as the administrative language of northern Sudan. The British dissuaded missionaries from evangelizing in the north. James (2008:70) lauds the flexibility of the British colonial rule in Sudan. He observes that

---

24 By 1960, the time of independence, the Federal Republic of Nigeria consisted of three regions: the Western Region, the Eastern Region, and Northern Region. As of 1996, there were 36 states, plus the Federal District.

"administrative structures, though based in 'Indirect Rule' all over the country, were more direct in the case of the three southern provinces." Since these southern provinces were ruled 'directly' by the British, missionary activities were encouraged. Schools were built and the English language spread:

> The tremendous linguistic richness of the south has been much studied (by comparison) and has been woven into the history of the arguments over cultural and educational policy of the modern era. Education in the south was initially entrusted to missionary organizations, and eventually English became the lingua franca of the educated. ... The English language was promoted not only in education but also administration, while the missions were encouraged also to pursue the use of vernacular languages both in church and in school (James 2008:64, 70).

4.2.2 A Game-theoretic assessment in Islamic areas

The survey in the previous sections allows us to identify two groups of players in the language game in these areas of Sub-Saharan Africa. The first group consisted of a negligible contingent of missionaries, a small group of colonial teachers, administrators, and business operators. The second group was made up of local Muslim chiefs, their sons, and the uneducated rural inhabitants. The position held by the British colonial authorities is that the LWC in each Islamic area should be used in the administration of that particular area. The system of Indirect Rule empowered the emirates and other local chiefs. Those who supported the British became very influential. To please the emirs, the British deliberately restricted the presence of Christian missionaries in these areas. They went to great lengths to find and hire secular teachers for these areas (Laitin 1992:84–5). However, English was not banned altogether from these areas because we know that "the sons of Muslim chiefs" were sent to British school and some of their education was in English. The chiefs wanted their sons to know English for the employment opportunities that it afforded them. Simpson and Oyetade (2008:182–3) suggest that the chiefs foresaw knowing English as a way of positioning their sons for political roles in post-colonial Nigeria. Business operators who were involved in the import and export of goods had an interest that some of the people living in these Islamic areas learn English because they needed book-keepers, petty accountants, and other junior associates to help them. Piecing together the players' influence, their salience, and their position, we arrive at the information displayed in Table 4.1:

Table 4.1. Weighted Mean in Islamic Areas

No.	Players	Influence Scale	Salience Scale	Position Scale	I × S × P	I × S
1.	British Protestant missionaries	100	10	0	0	1
2.	British teachers in secondary	100	50	0	0	5
3.	British colonial administrators in Islamic areas	100	10	0	0	1
4.	British business operators	100	50	25	125	5
5.	Muslim chiefs	75	50	25	93,75	3,75
6.	Muslim Chiefs' sons	75	75	50	281,25	5,65
7.	African uneducated/ rural/farmers in British colonies	0	0	0	0	0
8.	Total				500	21,4
9.	Weighted mean			23.36%		

The weighted mean score 23.36% shows that all the players were pleased to use Hausa as the medium of instruction in elementary school. However, the fact that the score is fairly high shows that they were not entirely satisfied with this choice. They would have been satisfied with TIM which would have taught Hausa in lower elementary and English in higher elementary. Though it was not implemented, British colonial authorities saw the need for it and responded to it by teaching English in secondary school. A teacher by the name of Hanns Vischer was hired according to Laitin (1992:84–5) to implement this curriculum at the request of Muslim chiefs for their sons.

4.2.3 English and African languages in West Africa

Britain colonized the following countries in West Africa: the Cameroons,[25] Ghana, the Gambia, Nigeria, and Sierra Leone. The players in the West

---

25 See sections 4.4 and 4.4.1 for additional information about the Cameroons.

African language game are essentially the same as those in Islamic Africa with the exception of missionaries. They were numerous in West Africa and had a very profound impact on the language situation in the regions where they ministered. An important caveat is necessary here because most people associate the term "missionary" only with Europeans. This is not entirely true in West Africa. Christianization of West Africa was underway well before British missionaries arrived. The pioneer missionaries in this area were freed slaves that the British anti-slavery naval forces intercepted on the Atlantic Ocean. The freed slaves were relocated to Freetown in Sierra Leone. By 1827 the number of freed slaves had grown considerably. British abolitionists created the Fourah Bay College to educate them. They were trained in theology, biblical languages, agriculture, and medicine. A large number of the graduates fanned out across West Africa. Some became itinerant evangelists who propagated the Gospel from the coastal areas into the hinterland. Some translated the Scriptures into African languages. Others were engaged in medical missionary ministry. A group of them led an agricultural ministry as far as Niger. Some graduates set up makeshift schools where local populations were taught literacy skills in their own languages. Some of the pioneer missionaries made literacy in one's native language a prerequisite for baptism and confirmation.[26] Schaaf (1994:62) reports that in 1841, 500 Yoruba-speaking Sierra Leoneans returned to live permanently in Nigeria and helped spread the Christian message among their own people. In 1843 Samuel Crowther, one of the most prominent graduates of Fourah Bay College, was invited to England to be ordained a minister in the Church of England (see 9.5 through 9.5.3 for an expanded description of his achievements). Two years earlier, his travel account of the ill-fated first British missionary journey into West Africa was published and widely distributed in England. In it, Crowther explained how the first 145 European missionaries to West Africa lost their lives. While he was in England, Crowther encouraged European churches to send missionaries to Africa. His appeals were heeded and soon native African missionaries were joined by English, Scottish, and German missionaries. By 1850, African missionaries and European missionaries were ministering together in West Africa. Fage (1988:348)[27] explains this collaboration as follows:

---

26 Most of the historical information in this section is taken from Schaaf (1994).
27 Fage (1988: 223, 234–5, 328) provides useful information on profitability of trade with Africa. The number of slaves transported to the New World is discussed on p. 254–5. He discusses the geopolitical prestige in owing African colonies on p. 327.

Up to the 1870s, the work of spreading a Christian European influence in West Africa was essentially a partnership between Europeans and Africans, and it would not have advanced as rapidly as it did without the latter. Men like the Saro, Samuel Ajayi Crowther, who in 1864 became the first Bishop of the CMS (Christian Missionary Society) Niger Mission; the West-Indian-born Dr. E. W. Blyden, whose active career in Liberia, Sierra Leone and Lagos spanned the years 1851–1911, and embraced exploration as well as pioneer work in education and in attempting a rational synthesis of African, Christian and Muslim ways of thoughts and life; or the Fante surveyor, G.E. Ferguson, who led British expeditions to the Gold Coast hinterlands in the 1890s – these and men like them were just as much strangers to the interior African societies as any European.

More will be said in Chapter 9 about the exploits of some of these men and the strategies in indigenous language planning in 19th century Africa.

4.2.4 Mission schools in West Africa

European missionaries brought money and technology that pioneer African missionaries did not have. Together, they expanded and modernized the network of mission schools in several other places in West Africa. Between 1843 and 1884, mission schools had a single purpose, namely to train Africans for church work in their own native languages or in the lingua franca of the area. However, from 1884 onward, after the pacification battles had been fought and won, British colonial officers began subsidizing mission schools because they needed petty officers, bureaucrats, and a somewhat educated personnel to help them run their colonies. The subsidies that they offered helped to increase the number of West Africans who enrolled in mission schools. Mission schools that accepted the largess of colonial authorities were required to expand their curriculum to include English as a medium of instruction in the upper elementary levels. Until that time mission schools had provided education exclusively in indigenous languages. Some mission agencies gladly accepted the subsidies because money was always tight. Except for the stipulation that mission schools offer English in upper elementary grades, the British did not interfere with the school curriculum. Khapoya (1998:153–4) describes this collaborative effort between mission schools and British colonial officers as follows:

> Mission education had three modest goals: First, to provide the basic literacy that would enable Africans to absorb religious education and training and help in the spread of the Gospel; second, to impart the values of Western

society, without which missionaries believed the Africans could not progress; and third, to raise the level of productivity of the African workers (both semiskilled and clerical) without necessarily empowering them sufficiently to challenge colonial rule. Mission education was, generally speaking, inadequate, especially in its emphasis on a religious education that Western society was already finding anachronistic. But, limited or flawed as it might have been, it was enough to whet the appetite of African people for more education and to pique their political consciousness.

So, from 1884 onward, many missionaries introduced TIM to Africa. The prevailing approach was the exclusive use of dominant indigenous languages from grades 1 to 3, while grade 4 served in most cases as a transition year. From grade 5 onward English became the language of education for nearly all the subjects. In many instances, religious studies and creative writing were done in both English and the indigenous languages. In 1922 the Phelps-Stokes Commission recommended "that the local languages be used as mediums of instruction in the lower primary classes, and English at the upper levels, and that indigenous languages be used alongside English" (Spencer 1974:164–5). For many missionary schools, this recommendation was nothing new because it had been in use for nearly a century. However, Anyidoho and Dakubu (2008:147–8) report that German missionaries working in Ghana under the auspices of the Bremen Mission and the Basel Mission ignored this policy and continued instructing their students in Ewe and Ga. The choice of the language of education set off a debate among mission schools on the one hand, and between mission schools and parents on the other. Some diehard mission schools that had refused British subsidies were confronted by parents who desired for their children to learn English. As noted before, Yoruba and Igbo parents voiced their concerns to Protestant missionaries that they were putting too much emphasis on the pupils'"heart language," i.e., native language at the expense of "head language," i.e., English. Parents saw knowing English as a tool of economic advancement in colonial Africa. Many parents opposed the Protestant missionaries' decision to postpone the use of English until secondary school. Laitin (1992:121–2) describes the conflict between missionaries and parents over the language of education policy as follows:

> Nigeria's Northern Region was administered largely in Hausa, while in the East and West, English became the language of administration. ... Already families in the East and West were in a race to see how many qualified civil servants they could produce to run the country when the British handed over power. They sought English education for their children. In the East, people

demanded that missionary schools stop seeking to reach their souls through the Igbo medium and start helping their pocketbooks through English.

Laitin (1992:122) explained the rapid expansion of the Catholic Church in Yoruba and Igbo areas by the fact that disgruntled parents refused to enroll their children in Protestant mission schools because of their language policy. Enrollment in Catholic schools soared rapidly because, unlike Protestants, they used only English as the medium of instruction at all grades. The refusal of a sizable number of Igbo and Yoruba parents to send their children to schools where Igbo or Yoruba would be the sole medium of instruction was a forerunner to the contemporary debate about the role of the mother tongue in the education of African pupils. Chaudenson (2008:183) comments that "it is common knowledge that in Africa those who are the most opposed to usage of the local vernaculars in schools are the students' parents themselves."

4.2.5 A Game-theoretic assessment of English West Africa

The weighted mean score for West Africa is displayed in Table 4.2. It sums up the preference of all the players for the language of education policy in colonial schools.

Table 4.2. Weighted Mean in West Africa

No.	Players	Influence Scale	Salience Scale	Position Scale	I × S × P	I × S
1.	British Protestant missionaries	100	10	0	0	1
2.	British teachers in lower elementary	100	10	0	0	1
3.	British teachers in upper elementary	100	95	25	237,5	9,5
4.	British colonial administrators	100	50	25	125	5
5.	British business operators	100	50	25	125	5
6.	African political elite in British colonies	75	75	25	140,625	5,625

(Continued)

Table 4.2. Weighted Mean in West Africa (*Cont.*)

No.	Players	Influence Scale	Salience Scale	Position Scale	I × S × P	I × S
7.	African educated/ employees in British colonies	60	50	25	75	3
8.	African missionaries in English colonies	30	10	0	0	300
9.	African WWI and WWII vets in British colonies	50	50	25	62,5	2,5
10.	African chiefs in British colonies	75	50	25	93,75	3,75
11.	African chiefs' sons in British colonies	75	75	25	140,625	5,625
12.	African manual workers in urban settings in British colonies	30	25	25	37,5	1,5
13.	African uneducated/ rural/farmers in British colonies	0	0	25	0	0
14.	Total				1,037,500	43,8
15.	Weighted mean				23.68%	

The weighted mean score of 23.68% shows that TIM met the language of education needs of all the players in West Africa who were under colonial rule. They were perfectly content in the colonial period to use indigenous African languages as the medium of instruction in the lower elementary grades and English in the upper elementary grades. Apparently, the level of satisfaction has not changed, at least for Nigerians. Adegbija (2000:94) reports that in a survey of 600 Nigerians, he found that 76.6% of them still like this language policy and do not want to see English be replaced by indigenous Nigerian languages in elementary school. We noted in 1.5 that there was an attempt made in Ghana to move from TIM to an AIM. However, there was such an outcry that the Ministry of Education reversed its own decision (Essegbey 2009:129). Fage (1988:412) seems to suggest that this language policy worked well for West Africans. It helped the British train the cadres they needed. Since there were not enough British colonists to do the job, they recruited heavily among West Africans to get the job done. They appointed educated Africans as district commissioners, judges, and medical officers. It is said that "in the 1880s, one quarter of the small senior British establishment in the Gold Coast was black." This was a strong incentive for West Africans to learn English without sacrificing their indigenous languages.

4.2.6 English and African languages in South Central Africa

The British colonies in South Central Africa included Uganda, Zambia, Malawi, and Botswana. Most of what was said in the previous paragraph about West Africa also applies to this region. The only notable exception is that in this region, pioneer missionaries were overwhelmingly white. Moreover, historians are in a better position to reconstruct various facets of the European colonization of this region because missionaries wrote journals, travelogues, and letters to their supporters back home. From this data, we know that pioneer missionaries vigorously promoted indigenous languages as part of their overall evangelization strategy. Krapf (1810–1881), the tireless German missionary-linguist, for instance, dreamed of twelve missionary stations stretching from East Africa all the way to West Africa. He and others translated the Bible into indigenous languages of South Central Africa and came up with a very imaginative approach to spread literacy in indigenous languages. While many missionaries in West Africa relied on rote memorization and oral recitation of catechism materials as a precondition for baptism, missionaries in this region required that candidates for the Christian sacraments be able to read in their native language(s) before receiving baptism or confirmation. In Uganda where the Scottish missionary Alexander Murdoch Mackay (1849–1890) pioneered this approach, literacy increased rapidly. According to Schaaf (1994:78, 121), 6,905 people were baptized and 50,000 others were waiting to be baptized in a ten year period. In other words, as far back as 1896, the year of the publication of the entire Bible, there were at least 50,000 people who could read Luganda! Schaaf (1994:135) tells us that many missionaries, including Robert Moffat (1795–1883), used the same strategy for his ministry in Botswana. He and his wife spent 46 years among the Setswana and learned their language. It is reported that by 1825 he was already preaching in Setswana. He began his translation work in 1830 and started a school where he taught the language. By 1840, he had completed the New Testament and in 1843 printed 2,000 copies of it. He completed the whole Bible in 1857 and literacy in Setswana took off from there.

From 1885 onward, British colonies in this area of Africa were forced to adapt their curriculum and make room for English. Here, as in West Africa, indigenous languages were used as the medium of instruction in lower elementary school, while English became the language of instruction for upper elementary and beyond. The players in the language game were similar to those in West Africa. Parents encouraged their children to learn English. In Zambia, for instance, interest in English was so high that in 1965 it became the only medium of instruction in all schools. However, eleven years later, they went back to the century-old tradition of using indigenous languages in lower elementary grades.[28] The linguistic situation of the rest of the countries in this region is similar. In each country, there are three to four indigenous lingua francas which were promoted by European missionaries. The Holy Scriptures were translated into these languages. Since independence, the linguistic priorities set by missionaries are still in force. The weighted mean score regarding the language of education policy pursued in this area is as follows:

Table 4.3. Weighted Mean in South-Central Africa

No.	Players	Influence Scale	Salience Scale	Position Scale	I × S × P	I × S
1.	British Protestant missionaries	100	10	0	0	1
2.	British teachers in lower elementary	100	10	0	0	1
3.	British teachers in upper elementary	100	95	25	237,5	9,5
4.	British colonial administrators in other areas	100	50	25	25	5

(*Continued*)

---

28 Marten and Kula (2008:297) report that the 1991 constitution of Zambia makes proficiency in English a prerequisite for running for parliament. To the best of my knowledge, the only other African country that has such a requirement is Djibouti (Appleyard and Orwin 2008:282–3).

Table 4.3. Weighted Mean in South-Central Africa (*Cont.*)

No.	Players	Influence Scale	Salience Scale	Position Scale	I × S × P	I × S
5.	British business operators	100	50	25	375	5
6.	Euro-Africans in British colonies	75	95	25	178,125	7,125
7.	Expatriates (Indians)	90	95	75	641,25	8,55
8.	African political elite in British colonies	75	75	25	140,625	5,625
9.	African educated/ employees in British colonies	60	50	25	75	3
10.	African missionaries in English colonies	30	10	0	0	300
11.	African WWI and WWII vets in British colonies	50	50	25	62,5	2,5
12.	African chiefs in British colonies	75	50	25	93,75	3,75
13.	African Chiefs' sons in British colonies	75	75	25	140,625	5,625
14.	African manual workers in urban settings in British	30	25	25	37,5	1,5
15.	African uneducated/rural/ farmers in British colonies	0	0	25	0	0
16.	Total				2,006,875	59,475
17.	Weighted mean				33.74%	

The weighted score of 33.74% can be interpreted to mean that the players expected English to play a greater role in the curriculum than it did. The dissatisfaction may have come primarily from the expatriate Indian community. They were petty officers, lower range managers, bookkeepers, office clerks, railroad workers, and shopkeepers that the British had brought to eastern Africa during the colonial era. By and large, they considered themselves superior to Africans. In the colonial social pegging order, they found themselves lower than whites but higher than blacks. Many frowned on the idea of having their children schooled in African languages first. As a result, they preferred sending their children to schools where the medium of instruction was entirely in English. In some instances, they created a parallel school system where their children were taught English and Hindi. If the Indian community is removed from the analysis, the weighted mean score is 26.81%, which means that the remaining players in the language game were completely satisfied with TIM which consisted in using the local languages as media of instruction in lower elementary school and gradually switching over to English in upper elementary.

4.2.7 English and African languages in settlement colonies

Three British colonies, Kenya, Zimbabwe, and South Africa, have been described by experts as "settlement colonies." The main difference between settlement colonies and other British colonies in Africa has to do with the sheer number of colonists who lived in these areas and their reasons for living there. Fage (1988:426–7) notes that three million Europeans had settled in South Africa by the close of the 19th century, 295,000 in Zimbabwe, and 60,000 in Kenya. Unlike other colonizers, these Europeans saw the colonies as their new home. They had come to settle there permanently. This was the new home for them, their children, and their children's children. In order to understand how they affected the language of education policies in these areas, let's see how Fage (1988:428) compares them with their African neighbors:

> The European settlers were also significant in that they had for the most part gone to Africa, and had committed themselves, their families, and their fortunes to it, during the high tide of imperialism. When they had arrived, they had had a real superiority over most Africans in military strength, in wealth, in education, technology and organization, and they naturally wanted to maintain the privileged positions they had built up with this superiority.

How these settlers viewed themselves in relation to the Africans in the midst of whom they were living was sociolinguistically significant. Their influence on their African neighbors is rated at 100. The settlers' interest in using English[29] as the language of instruction for their children, and indeed for other inhabitants of the colony, is rated at 95, and their position on whether to use English as the medium of instruction is rated at 100. By and large, the settlers made important investments to have similar standards of living as the people back home. Settlement colonies therefore benefitted from a substantial investment in road, school, hospital, and agriculture infrastructures.

Table 4.4. Weighted Mean in Settlement Colonies

No.	Players	Influence Scale	Salience Scale	Position Scale	I × S × P	I × S
1.	British Protestant missionaries	100	10	0	0	1
2.	British teachers in lower elementary for African children	100	10	0	0	1
3.	British teachers in lower elementary schools for settler children	100	95	100	950	9,5
4.	British teachers in upper elementary for African children	100	95	25	237,5	9,5
5.	British teachers in upper elementary schools for settler children	100	95	100	950	9,5

(*Continued*)

---

29 Settler communities were linguistically diverse. In the case of South Africa, for instance, they formed homogeneous societies on the basis of their language of origin. However, since our focus is on English, we will not pay attention to other groups except British settlers.

Table 4.4. Weighted Mean in Settlement Colonies (*Cont.*)

No.	Players	Influence Scale	Salience Scale	Position Scale	I × S × P	I × S
6.	British settlers (policy towards Africans)	100	50	25	25	5
7.	British settlers (policy towards other settlers)	100	95	100	950	9,5
8.	British business operators (policy towards Africans)	100	50	25	375	5
9.	British business operators (policy towards other settlers)	100	95	100	950	9,5
10.	Euro-Africans in British colonies	75	95	25	178,125	7,125
11.	Expatriates (non-whites)	90	95	100	950	9,5
12.	African political elite in British colonies	75	75	25	140,625	5,625
13.	African educated/ employees in British colonies	60	50	25	75	3
14.	African missionaries in British colonies	30	10	0	0	300
15.	African WWI and WWII vets in British colonies	50	50	25	62,5	2,5
16.	African chiefs in British colonies	75	50	25	93,75	3,75
17.	African Chiefs' sons in British colonies	75	75	25	140,625	5,625

(*Continued*)

Table 4.4. Weighted Mean in Settlement Colonies (*Cont.*)

No.	Players	Influence Scale	Salience Scale	Position Scale	I × S × P	I × S
18.	African manual workers in urban settings in British colonies	30	25	25	37,5	1,5
19.	African uneducated/rural/ farmers in British colonies	0	0	25	0	0
20.	Total				6,115,625	98,425
21.	Weighted mean				62.13%	

The weighted mean score of 62.13% helps us understand the difficulties that the players of the language game in settlement colonies faced. According to de Mesquita (2009:73), players prefer numerical values closer to their advocated position than scores that are further away. But the score of 62.13% is almost at equal distance between 50 and 75. According to the discussions in 2.5.2, a score of 50 suggests that the preferred language of education policy is DIM whereas a score of 75 indicates a preference for MM. Neither of these two models was implemented in colonial Africa. This means that the players could not agree on a single language as the ideal medium of instruction. Since there was no consensus schools were segregated along racial or ethnic lines. In Black schools, colonists implemented TIM. The weighted mean score is 26.81% if British and other settlers are removed from consideration. This percentage is consistent with the British language of education in their other colonies. Proficiency in English was required for Africans in settlement colonies who wanted to advance socio-economically. However, for their own children and for all the non-Blacks who cared to send their children to schools run by the colonists, the British used English as the sole medium of instruction in elementary school. We all know that this led to Apartheid in South Africa. Khapoya (1998:1205) explains that school segregation happened in Kenya. That the Predictioneer's Model could have predicted school segregation in settlement colonies is an unexpected finding!

128 *A Game-theoretic assessment of language of education policies*

4.2.8 Weighted mean scores of English in Africa

It is time to summarize the scores from the different British colonies and draw some conclusions about the overall use of English in colonial schools and even now. When the various weighted mean scores in former British colonies are compared and contrasted with the weighted mean scores in French (97.02%) and Portuguese (96.68%) colonies, we see readily that the British made a concerted effort to include African languages in the educating Africans in their colonies. The weighted mean scores summarized below are supported by historical data. Spencer (1974:167) reports that "by 1950 there were ten vernacular literature bureaus or committees established in British Africa for the production of teaching and reading materials and for studying the technical, linguistic, and practical problems involved. At that time altogether 91 languages were in use in schools in British Africa (UNESCO 1953b)."

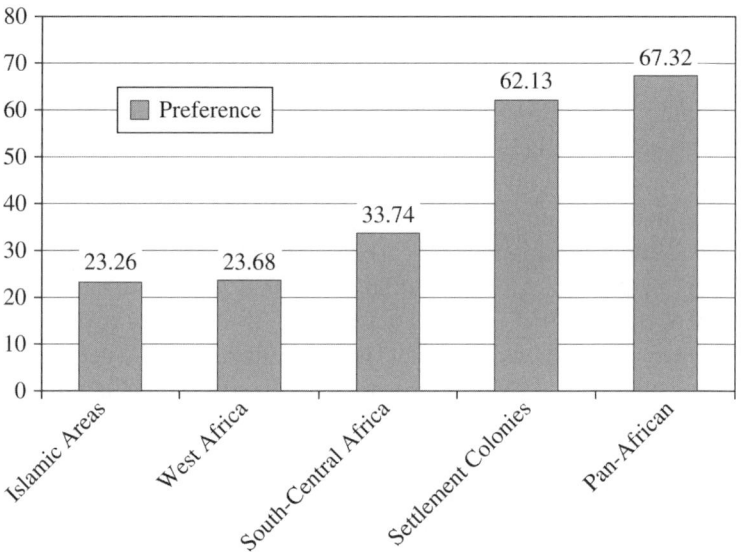

Figure 4.1. Weighted Means of English in Africa

When Indian expatriates and white settlers are excluded from the calculation, the combined weighted mean score in South-Central Africa and in Settlement Colonies is 25.14%. This is a strong indication that TIM that the British implemented from 1922 onward worked very well for the overwhelmingly indigenous African populations. The longer colonialism lasted, the higher the interest in English grew. The salience score of 44.96 shows that interest in English was on the rise in all the colonies. This salience score is calculated by adding together all the individual salience scores and dividing the sum by the number of players in the game. Adegbija (2000:83) explains the ever increasing interest (salience) in English in socio-economic terms:

> Knowledge of them [i.e. colonial languages] is synonymous with being educated, with making it, with being up there, with power, with prestige, with achievement. Partially, this is because they had almost exclusive monopolistic function in the domain of higher education and in official circles. The status quo has remained the same today, and so has the power of these languages in West Africa and, consequently, their being continually positively associated with power, prestige, and achievement.

To be sure, Adegbija's analysis is restricted to West Africa. But the studies coming from other parts of Africa underscore the fact that the appetite that Africans have for English has not lessened, quite the contrary. Globalization and the worldwide appeal of English have made it a "must know" language. Even in Kenya, South Africa, and Tanzania, where African languages have been seriously and deliberately promoted, interest in English continues to rise. Batibo (2008:64) notes with a tinge of sadness how English is spreading in cities across Botswana. Mazrui (2008:196–8) shows that even though localization of search engines is available in both Kiswahili and English, native speakers of Kiswahili in Mobassa prefer to browse the internet via English instead of Kiswahili. Kamwangamalu (1997:245) uses the language marketability rationale to explain why black South African parents in post-Apartheid era are eager for their children to learn English and learn it well:

> The term language marketability refers to the potential of a language to serve as a tool by means of which its users can meet their material needs. It implies empowering the users so that they can achieve upward social mobility and improve their standards of living. Compared to English and Afrikaans, the status of African languages is relatively low. It does not take long for the language consumer to realize that education in an African language does not ensure one social mobility and better socio-economic life; that those who can afford it, and among them policymakers themselves, send their children to English-medium schools, and when all is told, only education in English opens up doors to the outside world as well as high paying jobs. ... people would not want to be educated in their indigenous language if that language has no cachet in the broader social, political, and economic context.

Mesthrie (2008:332–3) concurs with Kamwangamalu. He cites examples from South African parents who prefer English over their own native language because "[they] appear to be distrustful of using African languages as mediums of instruction as they associate this with the disadvantage fostered by the apartheid education." Mesthrie puts the blame on apartheid to explain why parents are suspicious about using local languages as media of instruction at school. However, this may not be the most compelling explanation. The same behavior is seen all across Africa, even in places where apartheid has never existed. Elsewhere in Africa, Djité (2008:59), Anyidoho and Dakubu (2008:150–1) lament what is called a "backward move" in Ghana because in 2001 the government decided to do away with indigenous languages in lower elementary school in favor of an English-only policy. Djité (2008:64) again complains about the increasing role of English in Tanzania.

Another reason why English is popular in former British colonies is its perceived neutrality in the hotly contested ethnolinguistic landscape of Africa. Since English has no primordial ties to any one ethnic group, it is seen as ethnolinguistically non-threatening. English has played its role of "non-partisan" and honest broker in many linguistic disputes across the continent. Laitin (1992:134) notes, for example, that in post-independent Zimbabwe, the feuding Shona (70.8% of the population) and Ndebele (14.6%) were opposed to selecting each other's language as the national language of Zimbabwe; "meanwhile, English is the lingual franca that unites the elites of these two groups: neither Shona nor Ndebele has played a role as an important lingua franca." Virtually all the contributors to *Language and National Identity in Africa* agree that keeping the ex-colonial languages as official languages of African countries has kept the ethnolinguistic peace. The view that English is an "equal opportunity" language has allowed it to continue to spread and continues to make it a very desirable language to know.

4.3 Overview of Belgian colonies: Congo, Burundi, Rwanda

The Belgian's colonial administrative style can be described as a Direct Rule. However, their colonial ideology was one of radical non-assimilation. Much has been written about how the Belgians ruled ruthlessly in Congo from 1884 to 1960. For those who are not well versed in African history, it is worth noting that Congo has undergone several name changes. First it was the Congo Free State; later it became known as Zaire. Now, the official name is the Democratic Republic of Congo, or the DRC for short. Unlike other European colonies that were the property of the state, the DRC was first the

4.3 Overview of Belgian colonies: Congo, Burundi, Rwanda 131

private property of King Leopold II. However, from 1908 until its independence on June 30th 1960, it became the property of the Belgian government. The king was dispossessed of his prime real estate in central Africa because of the inhumane way in which he ran his colony. Though persistent rumors had been circulating about the atrocities being committed in Congo, nothing was done until the following excerpt from Reverend J. B. Murphy's letter was printed in *The Times of London* on November 18, 1895:

> It [Belgian rule] has reduced people to a state of utter despair. Each town in the district is forced to bring a certain quantity [of rubber] to the headquarters of the commissaire every Sunday. It is collected by force. The soldiers drive the people in the bush. If they will not go they are shot down, and their left hands cut off and taken as trophies to the commissaire. The soldiers do not care who they shoot down, and they more often shoot poor helpless women and children. These hands, the hands of men, women, and children, are placed in rows before the commissaire, who counts them to see that the soldiers have not wasted cartridges. ... In November last [1894] there was heavy fighting upon Bosira, because the people refused to give rubber, and I was told upon the authority of State officer that no fewer than 1,890 people were killed (Shillington 2005:333).

King Leopold II was interested in Congo particularly because of its enormous economic and mining potentials. From the 1890s on, wild rubber from Congo contributed to the manufacturing of tires for bicycles and motorcycles in Europe. It was also a very lucrative business for the nascent automobile industry. Gilbert and Reynolds (2004:251–3) give us some important insights into why King Leopold II demanded an ever increasing collection of rubber. From 1890 to 1895, he had borrowed a total of 32 million francs to develop the Congo Free State. Not only did he need to pay back the loan, but according to De Mesquita (2009:ix), he also needed to make a handsome profit to continue his grandiose and lavish building and other infrastructure projects.

4.3.1 The linguistic impact of Belgian colonialism

As noted earlier, the Belgians practiced the most radical form of linguistic non-assimilation in the Congo Free State. Because of the linguistic feud between Flemish-speaking and French-speaking Belgians, it has been argued that Belgian authorities were in a linguistic dilemma as to which of their two official languages to use in Congo. As a result of this internal linguistic squabble, colonial authorities tried to remain neutral. Schaaf (1994:189) notes, for instance, that early in the 1960s, the Belgian equivalent of the Yellow Pages appeared both in French and Flemish. Belgian authorities did not want to promote French at the expense of Flemish, nor did they want to promote Flemish at the expense of French. The compromise that was found was to select some indigenous Congolese languages which had regional appeal to be the administrative languages of specific areas. Bokamba (2008b:101) lists six such regional lingua francas: Kikongo, Kiswahili, Lingala, Lomongo, Tshiluba, and Zande. These six languages were chosen out of some 217, Ethnologue (2009:34). Of the six lingua francas, Kikongo, Kiswahili, Lingala, and Tshiluba have been elevated to the status of "national languages" since independence. Missionaries and colonial officials effectively promoted Lingala and elevated it to the status of a national lingua franca even before independence. Though pockets of the country used Flemish, French was the de facto language of the colonial administration simply because of the large number of French-speaking missionaries and administrators. Schaaf (2004:236) notes, for instance, that there were 7,500 French-speaking Catholic missionaries in Congo but only 2,000 missionaries from the Flemish-speaking areas of Belgium, Germany, Holland, Italy, Portugal, and the USA combined.[30] In Congo, Picoche and Marchello-Nizia (1994:95) also observe that most of the 2,200 colonial administrators spoke French.

We learn from Gilbert and Reynolds (2004:289) that the Belgians relied almost entirely on missionaries to provide an education to the Congolese. We also learn from O'Toole (2007:50) that "The Belgians, unlike the French, deliberately limited African education to the primary levels and geared it entirely to semiskilled occupational training." Spencer (1974:167) makes a similar observation and contrasts the Belgian educational practice with that of the British: "Belgian practice in the Congo ran to some extent parallel to that of the British in the East and Central Africa. They resisted, however, until the very last years of colonial rule, all pressure for the establishment of facilities for higher education, and before 1954 placed very severe restrictions upon Africans who might wish to study in Belgium." According to Picoche and Marchello-Nizia (1994:95), in 1920 there were 100,000 Congolese children enrolled in Catholic mission schools, and 85,000 in Protestant mission schools. In the vast majority of these schools, the languages of instruction were indigenous Congolese languages. Statistical

---

30 Belgian Congo had the highest number of missionaries in all of Africa. Welmers (1974:192) estimates that "by 1957, there were probably between 8,000 and 10,000 missionaries, Catholic and Protestant, in Sub-Saharan Africa.".

4.3 Overview of Belgian colonies: Congo, Burundi, Rwanda 133

evidence provided by Fage (1988:424) shows that 8.3% of the Congolese attended school by 1953. Such a relatively high rate of literacy (it was high for pre-independent Africa) was not found elsewhere in Sub-Saharan Africa except in Northern Rhodesia (present day Zimbabwe). Unfortunately, this high level of literacy did not extend beyond elementary school. When it came to secondary schools, Congo had the worst ratio of all of Sub-Saharan Africa. There was only one secondary school for 870 primary schools! It is therefore not surprising that at independence, in the entire Congo Free State, there was only one Congolese with a college degree (Khapoya 1998:132). Cole and De Blij (2007:413) also offer a bleak assessment of the Belgian educational legacy in Congo:

> Few Congolese had any formal education at all, and in such critical institutions as the Force Publique and Gendarmerie, only a small minority were even literate. In fact, Belgian paternalism meant that few Congolese had been educated beyond the primary level; the positions that required education were occupied by Europeans. The Belgian Congo's Force Publique, the national army, was made up of 23,000 soldiers, almost all of whom were illiterate, and 1,000 Belgian officers. At independence in 1960 there were no Congolese physicians, engineers, or even veterinarians.[31]

Missionary education was geared exclusively towards spiritual formation. It is believed that this policy of linguistic indigenization helped the church in Congo grow by leaps and bounds. One should be careful not to attribute the phenomenal growth of the church to white missionaries only. Once the Congolese became schooled in their indigenous languages, they fanned out across their huge country on evangelization missions. Most native missionaries were bilingual: they were schooled in their regional lingua franca. They had also acquired reading proficiency in Lingala. One of the most well-known native evangelists of the colonial era was a prophet and miracle worker by the name of Simon Kimbangu. The church grew tremendously under his leadership because he gave it an "authentic African" flavor. Though Belgian authorities arrested him and kept him in jail for 30 years until his death, his followers spread his message to the four corners of Congo and even into Angola. Lingala was the liturgical language that the

---

31 The situation did not improve significantly in the first decade after independence, as explained by Makouta-Mboukou (1973:48). He writes that 13 years after independence, there were only 6 licensed teachers in the whole country: four licensed teachers of French, one of mathematics, and one of history.

Kimbanguistes used to preach and teach (Schaaf 1994:232). Its widespread use by Kimbanguistes in the colonial times paved the way for the Catholic Church of Congo to choose it as the Church's official language in June 1966 and to require it in the training of its clergy (Bokamba 2008b:224).

The linguistic landscape of Congo, i.e., the existence of some 217 indigenous languages, the presence of 6 regional lingua francas, and the widespread use of Lingala as an indigenous national lingua franca, makes for an interesting game theoretic analysis of the language game played there. The influence of white missionaries, school teachers, and colonial administrators is rated at 100. However, their level of interest in using French as a colonial language varies. Missionaries, elementary school teachers, and colonial administrators were not much interested in doing so. Therefore, their salience is rated at 10. The only group of players who seemed genuinely interested in French was the expatriate business community. As news spread about the immense and untapped natural and mining resources found in Congo, many business opportunists began flocking there. Fage (1988:426) estimates that there were more than 75,000 Westerners living in south eastern Congo by the time of independence. The increase in business opportunities and of the expatriate population created an appetite for French. However, French was needed only if international clients were involved. Domestically, Lingala was sufficient for most business transactions. Consequently, there was not an urgent need for a large number of Congolese who were educated in French. This is the reason why the salience of business operators is rated at 50 and their position at 25. Picoche and Marchello-Nizia (1994:94–5) note that in 1920 there were 1,861 children out of some 180,000 enrolled in schools where the medium of instruction was French. This represents a French penetration rate of about 1%. Table 4.5 provides us with the relevant numerical values for all the players:

Table 4.5. Weighted Mean in Congo

No.	Players	Influence Scale	Salience Scale	Position Scale	I × S × P	I × S
1.	Belgian missionaries	100	10	0	0	1
2.	Belgian teachers in lower elementary	100	10	0	0	1
3.	Belgian teachers in upper elementary	100	10	0	0	1

(*Continued*)

4.3 Overview of Belgian colonies: Congo, Burundi, Rwanda

Table 4.5. Weighted Mean in Congo (*Cont.*)

No.	Players	Influence Scale	Salience Scale	Position Scale	I × S × P	I × S
4.	Belgian colonial administrators	100	10	0	0	1
5.	Belgian business operators	100	50	25	125	5
6.	African political elite in Belgian colonies	75	75	0	0	5,625
7.	Africans-missionaries (Kimbanguistes)	85	10	0	0	850
8.	African WWI and WWII vets in Belgian colonies	50	50	25	62,5	2,5
9.	African chiefs in Belgian colonies	50	10	0	0	500
10.	African manual workers in urban settings in Belgian colonies	30	25	0	0	750
11.	African uneducated/ rural/farmers in Belgian colonies	0	0	25	0	0
12.	Total	790	260	75	187,5	19,225
13.	Weighted mean				9.75%	

The weighted mean score of 9.75% confirms that the language of education policy was firmly anchored in FIM. Congolese languages were used as media of instruction for all the years of elementary school. This also confirms the radical non-assimilation linguistic policy pursued by Belgian colonial authorities. So long as they could exploit the natural resources of Congo without building educational facilities or investing in secondary level education, they did not see any need to promote French. In fact, French was not used in most Congolese primary schools until around 1948 when an educational reform act was enacted. The new policy adopted TIM. Congolese languages were to be used as media of instruction during the first three years of elementary school. The fourth year was to be a transition year where French would be introduced as an academic subject. From the fifth grade onward, French was to become the medium of instruction. Colonial authorities became impatient with the results of the new policy because it did not bear fruits fast enough. The pace of "francophonization" was deemed to be too slow. In 1958, another reform was introduced which made French the only medium of instruction in all schools. Bokamba (2008b:104) notes that the latter mandate was followed by an across-the-board failure because there were not enough qualified teachers to teach French. In fact, Picoche and Marchello-Nizia (1994:94–5) found that 14 years after independence, only 10% of children in school learned French. Bokamba (2008b:103) seems to concur with this assessment because he reports that only 12 to 15% of the Congolese population speak French as a second language. These percentages agree remarkably well with the game-theoretic findings in Table 4.5.

The Belgians' use of indigenous Congolese languages as the only media of instruction came under heavy criticism by French-educated Africans from other Francophone countries. According to Picoche and Marchello-Nizia (1994:92–3), these black colonial elites interpreted the Belgian language policy as a deliberate ruse for keeping Congolese in the dark by not teaching them French. Shellington (2005:361) seems to concur with this assessment, noting that "In the decades preceding and following the Second World War, Africans who were determined to seek further education had to go abroad. French-speakers went to France, while English-speakers went mostly to African-American institutions in North America." However, the Belgians did not send Congolese anywhere. Bokamba (2008a and 2008b) has put a positive spin on the Belgian colonial language policy. He sees it as a language planning blessing in disguise. He contends that the lack of a widespread penetration of French helped forge a national linguistic identity built around Lingala. This is certainly true. Congo is one of the most successful French-speaking countries in Africa that has valorized its vast linguistic resources. Picoche and Marchello-Nizia (1994:128) report that 90% of popular songs in Congo are in Lingala, that 94% of TV commercials are in Lingala, and that 60% of radio and television broadcasts are also in Lingala. Bokamba (2008a:231) sees an additional benefit to the Belgian language policy in Congo because the Congolese do not have the linguistic inferiority complex that plagues other French-speaking Africans. He claims that "there is very little evidence, generally speaking, that the Congolese in the post-independence era who do not speak French or any other LWC feel linguistically inferior or ashamed." This claim should be understood as a hyperbolic statement and taken with a grain of salt because we read in Picoche and Marchello-Nizia (1994:95) that "The language of upward mobility was French and to some extent Flemish; those who were only educated in indigenous languages were frustrated because they suffered from racial segregation akin to that in South Africa."

4.4 Overview of German colonies

Germany colonized Burundi, Cameroon, Namibia, Rwanda, Tanzania, and Togo, that is, a total of 8% of the African continent. However, German rule in these colonies was short-lived. It was dispossessed of all its African colonies by Article 22 of the Treaty of Versailles that it signed on June 28, 1919. World War I was fought on many fronts: in Europe but also in Africa. Gilbert and Reynolds (2004:300) describe some aspects of these battles where thousands of Africans lost their lives. Because Germany lost the war, its African territories became the spoil of war and were divided among the Allies. Burundi and Rwanda were ceded to Belgium. Cameroon was divided between the French and the British; the French received the lion's share. Namibia was entrusted to the care of South Africa. Tanzania was handed over to the British, and Togo was made a French colony. According to the spirit of the Treaty of Versailles, Belgium, Britain, France, and South Africa were caretakers of former German colonies, but as Shillington (2005:347) writes, "In practice, the European victors treated their new acquisitions much like any other colony." Even before World War I, the Germans did not have an easy time with their Namibian and Tanzanian colonies. For example, the Hereros of Namibia rebelled against German settlers who were pushing them further and further into dry and desolate lands. The Germans responded harshly against the Hereros and nearly annihilated them. Of the original 80,000 Hereros, a mere 16,000 were left by the time the rebellion was over in 1905. In Tanzania, during the Maji Maji rebellion, German soldiers massacred at least 26,000 Tanzanians. They also adopted a scorched earth policy as a war strategy. This caused a huge famine in which an estimated 50,000 Tanzanians lost their lives (Shillington 2005:340–1, Gilbert and Reynolds 2004:290–1).[32]

---

32 Shillington (2005:336) indicates that 16,000 people from French Congo died in railroad projects alone! He also describes the French genocide of the Baya as follows: "An important and little-known exception was a rebellion by 350,000 Baya in French Equatorial Africa in the late 1920s. The slaughter that accompanied the violent suppression of this revolt in 1928–31 was one of the great atrocities of colonial rule in tropical Africa" (p. 361).

When these atrocities were finally reported, the news did not settle well with German public opinion. The news of the massacres perpetrated by the Germans coincided with the reports of Belgian atrocities in Congo. The Germans decided to change course and introduced a new colonial policy known as "Scientific Colonialism" (Khapoya 1998:130). Fage (1988:409) explains what the Germans meant by this phrase:

> From 1907 onwards, there was considerable rethinking about the policy and administration needed in the German colonies. German colonial secretaries were virtually unique at this time in touring the colonies – foreign as well as German ones – to see what was going on and what needed to be done. As a result, the old, automatic Prussian style of authoritarian administration began to be relaxed. Money was made available not only for such aids to development as railway building on a considerable scale, but also for sound research into problems of development in the tropics; for example, how best to combat animal and human diseases, or how to improve crops and their yields. By 1914, it would not be unreasonable to say that German colonial administration was earning the respect and admiration, if not the love, of the African people subjected to it. But there was not time to see how the new German colonial policies might have worked out, because, as a result of the 1914–18 war, the German colonies were repartitioned between France, Belgium, Britain, and the new self-governing British dominion of South Africa.

Though the German political rule of Africa was short lived, we will see in the following section that their linguistic legacy continues to live on and will continue to do so for centuries to come.

4.4.1 The linguistic impact of German colonialism before 1905

The Germans had the best missionary-linguists among all the colonists. The linguistic description of African languages that they did was unmatched both in quality and in quantity. Johann Ludwig Krapf and many other Germans who worked under the auspices of the Christian Missionary Society (CMS) crisscrossed the continent studying, analyzing, and translating the Bible into many eastern and southern African languages. Krapf was personally involved in the translation of significant portions of the Bible into Oromo, Swahili, and Nyika, (Schaaf 1994:83–88). He also trained a large contingent of German missionaries to do linguistic fieldwork across Africa. For all his efforts in favor of African languages, he received an honorary doctorate from the University of Tubingen in 1842. Meanwhile, his fellow missionary-linguist and compatriot Sigismund Koelle (1820–1902) was doing pioneering linguistic work on Bantu languages. Around the same time, another German scholar, Wilhelm H. Immanuel Bleek (1827–1875) was describing southern African languages.

In West Africa, Diedrich Westermann (1875–1956), another missionary-linguist, and his teammates from the Bremen Mission embarked on the analysis of a number of languages. His groundbreaking analysis of Niger-Congo languages is a classic in the annals of African linguistics. The Basel Mission Society did remarkable Bible work into Akuapem, Ewe, and Ga from 1840 to 1866. Their evangelism strategy is summarized by Anyidoho and Dakubu (2008:147–8) as follows:

> Unlike the Wesleyans, the Basel Mission believed from the start that spreading the gospel would be accomplished best if the converts could read the Bible in their own language. Thus, the teaching of literacy and content subjects were developed in the local language. The Bremen Mission began work among the Ewe in 1847, using Ewe language in their schools.

German missionaries used the same philosophy in their missionary work in Tanzania. In his survey of the history of the development of Swahili, Topan (2008:252–7) finds three important phases: the pre-colonial spread, the colonial period, and the post-colonial period. He credits the missionary activities of Krapf and his assistant Rebmann with the astounding spread of Swahili in colonial times. According to Topan, the colonial phase of the spread of Swahili may appropriately be called the "German" phase because German missionaries devoted themselves to studying the language linguistically and became true "scholars of Swahili." Even their squabbles over which dialect of Swahili to standardize reflects the depth of knowledge that they possessed about variationist sociolinguistics as far back as the 19th century. Krapf and his disciple Rebmann opted for the Mombassa dialect, while and Roehl and others opted for the dialect spoken in Zanzibar, i.e., the KiUnguja. Bibles were translated in both dialects from 1878 onward. Even though British missionaries are credited with having brought about the "Union Bible," much of the preliminary analysis that made it possible should be credited to German missionaries (Schaaf 2004:126–7). As early as 1888, the Germans began publishing a newspaper in Swahili. In 1894, they introduced a monthly magazine. When Tanzania was given to Britain in 1919, the British just continued on with the linguistic infrastructure that the Germans had built. "The British, in the main," Topan (2008:256) writes, "built upon the system introduced by the Germans and consolidated the development of Swahili in many respects."

Namibia, formerly known as South-West Africa, was the only settlement colony that the Germans had in Africa. German farmers confiscated the traditional lands of the Nama and the Herero. Cole and De Blij (2007:644) write that five years after the German occupation, they controlled 72% of the best lands in the colony. Dispossessed African landowners were being continually pushed towards the barren and unproductive desert lands. This led to the genocide alluded to in 4.4. It is believed that after the introduction of the so-called Scientific Colonialism, German colonists took a keen interest in developing their settlement colony of South West Africa. It was estimated that there were some 15,000 in Namibia before 1914. Over time the number of Germans grew, especially when South Africa was made the caretaker after WWI. It is unclear at the moment what the Germans' linguistic policy in Namibia was like before they were dispossessed of their colony. We know that they initiated the translation of the New Testament in Nama which began on 1830 but was not completed until 1966, that is, some 136 years later. The translation of the Bible into Tswana lasted even longer, 153 years from start to finish, that is, from 1840 to 1993. There is also very little known about the linguistic works of the Germans during their tenure in Burundi, the Cameroons, and Rwanda. They did not seem to have succeeded in fashioning a language of education policy in the Cameroons. Biloa and Echu (2008:204) attribute this to the competition between missionaries from different nationalities. They contend that the competition did not favor the development of a single language. Instead, four regional LWCs emerged: Duala, Mungaka, Bulu, and Ewondo. German Missionaries with the Basel Mission agency worked predominantly among the Duala and the Mungaka. However, it is not known what the language of education policy was for those schools or if the Germans even had time to establish schools. Fage (1988:395) explains the lack of information by the fact that "German campaigning in nearby Cameroun was hardly complete before the Germans were themselves ousted by the British and the French forces (again, largely consisting of African soldiers) in 1914–16." It is unclear if the linguistic analyses that served as the basis of the orthographies of Kinyarwanda and Kirundi were initially done by Germans. For this reason, we turn to Togo to get a clearer picture of the language of education policy pursued by the Germans in their model colony of Togo.

4.4.2 The language game in German Togo before 1905

Togo was the poster child of German colonialism in Africa. It was deemed a "model colony" because it was the only German colony in Africa that was economically self-supporting (Fage 1988:406). Cole and De Blij (2007:367) speak of important investments that the German colonial administration made for public works projects and road and railroad infrastructures from Lomé, the capital, towards the interior of the country. On the linguistic front, Westermann and his fellow missionaries from the Bremen Missionary Society immersed themselves completely in the study of Ewe. According to Afeli (2003:159), many German missionaries spoke Ewe fluently. On pages 141–93, he provides us with an impressive record of German linguistic study of Ewe. In the area of phonetics, phonology, and pronunciation, two important works were published in 1890 and 1896. Many more followed. The Germans wrote eight important grammar books of Ewe between 1857 and 1914. The first Language Arts book on Ewe was published in 1897. Between 1897 and 1914 ten more Language Arts books appeared. The first trilingual dictionary, Ewe-English-German, became available in 1891. A German-Ewe dictionary appeared in 1897. By 1910, there were eight different bilingual dictionaries involving Ewe and German, or Ewe and English. A book to teach arithmetic to school children was available in 1881. By 1858, the New Testament was already available in Ewe. This quick review speaks to the breadth and depth of German linguistic work in Ewe.

The Germans' language of education policy was unmistakably FIM, which means that they used a local language as the medium of instruction all through elementary school. Ewe fulfilled that role for Togo. It was used and promoted as the administrative language of the colony. In 1912, 97% of the 14,246 students in 352 schools in German Togo attended schools run by missionaries (Afeli 2003:177). These students received instruction only in Ewe. German colonial schools consisted of three cycles, namely the primary cycle of four years, the middle cycle of two to three years, and the seminary cycle of five to six years. Ewe was the sole language of instruction in the primary cycle for all the subjects. In the secondary and the seminary cycles, English and German were used alongside Ewe. Additionally, a small percentage of gifted and talented students attended a special school called "Fortbildungschule" located in Lomé (Afeli, p. 186). This was the language policy that prevailed throughout Togo until the advent of "Scientific Colonialism" in 1906.

On the basis of the preceding information, it is now possible to calculate the weighted mean score for Togo:

Table 4.6. Weighted Mean of German in Togo before 1905

No.	Players	Influence Scale	Salience Scale	Position Scale	I × S × P	I × S
1.	German missionaries	100	10	0	0	1
2.	German teachers in lower elementary	100	10	0	0	1
3.	German teachers in upper elementary	100	10	0	0	1
4.	German colonial administrators	100	10	0	0	1
5.	German business operators	100	50	25	125	5
6.	African missionaries in German colonies	30	10	0	0	300
7.	African chiefs in German colonies	50	10	0	0	500
8.	African manual workers urban settings in German colonies	30	25	0	0	750
9.	African uneducated/ rural/farmers in German colonies	0	0	25	0	0
10.	Total	610	135	50	125	10,55
11.	Weighted mean				11.84%	

The score of 11.84% confirms FIM as the one that all the players of the language game preferred. This was the situation that prevailed before 1905.

4.4.3 The linguistic impact of German colonialism between 1905 and 1914

The success of Germany in hosting the Berlin Conference, which led to the partitioning of Africa, confirmed the growing importance of Germany on the world scene. Confidence led to pride and pride gave way to unbridled nationalism. On the eve of WWI, nationalistic feelings were running very high in Germany. Policymakers back in Germany began a subtle but clever way of injecting German nationalism into colonial schools by offering to subsidize mission schools financially if they agreed to increase the hours devoted to the teaching of German. The first six hours per week in primary schools, eight hours in middle/secondary schools, and ten hours per week in seminary. Afeli (2003:179–93) states that Bonn lured and enticed missionary schools by increasing its subsidies from 8000 marks in 1905 to 15,000 in 1910, and to 30,000 in 1914. This created some tensions between German missionaries who were pro-subsidies and those who were against them. In the end, the pro-subsidy forces prevailed. This led to a substantial revision of the Germans' language of education policy in Togo. In a rapid turn of events, German authorities replaced FIM with TIM in elementary school and in middle school. During the seminary cycle, which lasts five to six years, English was eliminated and German was given more prominence than Ewe. The most noteworthy development regarding language of education policy in Togo happened when the "gifted and talented," the best and brightest in Togo, were offered scholarships to pursue advanced degrees in Germany. The hours devoted to teaching Ewe remained fairly constant. Interest in German increased as well. In about ten years, there was a drastic change in the weighted mean score. It grew from 11.84% to 88.91%, as seen below:

Table 4.7. Weighted Mean of German in Togo between 1905–1914

No.	Players	Influence Scale	Salience Scale	Position Scale	I × S × P	I × S
1.	German missionaries after 1905	100	95	100	950	9,5
2.	German teachers in lower elementary after 1905	100	50	50	250	5
3.	German teachers in upper elementary after 1905	100	95	90	855	9,5
4.	Level 2 school graduates	50	90	90	405	4,5
5.	Level 2 Gifted and Talented graduates	75	95	100	712,5	7,125

(*Continued*)

Table 4.7. Weighted Mean of German in Togo between 1905–1914 (*Cont.*)

No.	Players	Influence Scale	Salience Scale	Position Scale	I × S × P	I × S
6.	German colonial administrators after 1905	100	95	100	950	9,5
7.	German business operators after 1905	100	25	100	250	2,5
8.	African missionaries in German colonies	30	10	0	0	300
9.	African chiefs in German colonies	50	10	0	0	500
10.	African manual workers urban settings in German colonies	30	25	0	0	750
11.	African uneducated/rural/ farmers in German colonies	0	0	25	0	0
12.	Total	735	590	655	4,372,500	49,175
13.	Weighted mean				88.91%	

The Germans' language of education policy changed drastically. It went from favoring FIM to a model that closely resembles AIM, the assimilationist model used by the French and the Portuguese. However, this new language policy had very little impact on the Togolese because the trend to promote German above Ewe was short lived. It lasted for only nine years before World War I started.

4.4.4 The linguistic impact of German colonialism after 1918

Schaaf (2004:137) writes the following eulogy that encapsulates the linguistic legacy of German colonialism in Africa:

Because it lost its colonies in World War I, and also because of internal economic difficulties and of the rise of the Nazi movement, German involvement in missions and in Bible Societies diminished considerably. During the Third Reich (1933–1945), German churches stood on the sidelines of worldwide Christendom and were no longer able to be involved internationally.

Today, very little is left of German colonial presence in Africa. None of its former colonies uses German as its official language. Except in South Africa and Namibia where a remnant of German speakers is found, nowadays one would be hard pressed to find speakers of German in Burundi, Cameroon, Rwanda, Tanzania, or Togo. Kadt (2000:69–93) estimates that there are some 40,000 South African Germans who live in Wartburg. According to Ethnologue (2009:161) 22,000 Namibians speak "Standard" German. The adjective "standard" is apparently used to contrast this form of German with the one spoken by an estimated 15,000 bi-racial Namibians of mixed African and German ancestry who speak a non-standard dialect of German.[33] The reason why German is not spoken in Burundi, Cameroon, Rwanda, Tanzania, or Togo is that, as soon as the Allies took over, every effort was made to stamp out the German presence. Togo was partitioned between the British and the French. Two-thirds of the original German Togoland was added to the British colony of Ghana, and 1/3 was put under the care of the French. We read in Afeli (2003:111) that the first moves the French made were to expel all German missionaries from Togo, to close all schools, and to reopen them a year later completely transformed in the image of the French colonial school system. Shortly after the French takeover, Ewe was booted out of the classroom. The French then imposed AIM on Togo and the area of the Cameroons under their control. In neither country is German spoken today. In Togo, French is the only official language. Cameroon is officially a bilingual country, but Biloa and Echu (2008:198 and 205) note that since the French controlled five out of seven provinces (approximately 2/3 of the country). They also managed through legal tricks and maneuvering to impose their language on 80% of the population. The Belgians used French as their colonial language in Rwanda and Burundi but did not seek to banish Kinyarwanda and Kirundi from elementary school. In Namibia, German speakers represent about 20% of the population, yet the Namibian constitution of 1992 bypassed it and chose English as the official language of the country.

---

33 Information obtained from Robert Pearce, Chief librarian at Nelson Mandela Metropolitan University during a conversation on the use of colonial languages in South Africa and Namibia, November 8, 2010.

4.5 Summary

The language of education policies of the former colonial powers can be summarized by the chart below:

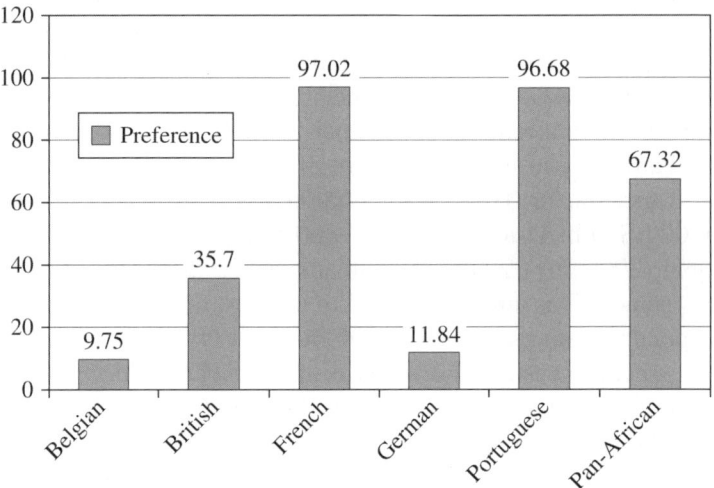

Figure 4.2. Summary of Weighted Means

The weighted mean scores of 9.75% and 11.84% show that the Belgians and the Germans implemented FIM, that is, they used dominant African languages as the media of instruction in elementary school. The overall score of 35.70% reflects the British preference for TIM which consisted in using African languages as media of instruction in lower elementary grades and English in upper elementary. The scores of 97.02% and 96.68% show that the French and Portuguese preferred AIM. Their language of education policy is part and parcel of the assimilation ideology that undergirded their views and actions in their colonies. It is important to note that none of the language of education policies matched the pan-African preference of 67.32%. I will contend in the rest of the book that the secret to successful mother-tongue education is to come up with a language of education policy that closely matches what the contemporary players of the language game in each African country want. Côte d'Ivoire will be used as a case study to show how the Predictioneer's Model can help meet this objective.

Chapter 5
Case study: Rethinking mother-tongue education in Côte d'Ivoire

Introduction

Côte d'Ivoire has a sociolinguistically complex landscape. To begin with, the 21,395,198 people reported by the Institut National de la Statistique (National Institute of Statistics) to be living in the country in 2009 speak more than 60 different languages. From about 1884 until now, French has been used as the only language of instruction in the country from primary, secondary, and tertiary schools. Furthermore, sociolinguistic studies report that French is more pervasive in Côte d'Ivoire than any other country formerly colonized by France. The position of French as the only language of instruction has gone largely unchallenged. However, an experiment in mother-tongue education was initiated in 1996 and a new Constitution was approved in 2000, which together have left opened the possibility of Ivorian languages playing some future role in educating the next generations of Ivorians. But for now the country is in search of a language planning model that can maintain the socio-economic advantages linked to knowing French, while promoting its indigenous languages. The population has, for the most part, been unimpressed by TIM that *Savane et Développement*, a non-governmental organization, has been experimenting with in lower primary school in ten indigenous languages. The goal of this chapter is to look for a model of mother-tongue education that can meet the sociolinguistic aspirations of all the players in the Ivorian language game. The Predictioneer's Model that we have encountered in the previous chapters will be used again here to help discover the language of education policy that most can agree on.

5.1 Sociolinguistic survey of Côte d'Ivoire

There are, according to Ethnologue (2009:34, 692), 71 indigenous languages spoken in Côte d'Ivoire. This figure must be taken with caution because *Ethnologue* counts Anyi Sanvi and Anyi Morofou as two separate languages even though they are mutually intelligible dialects. Furthermore, even though the Bété constitute a single ethnic group, those in Daloa and

148 *Case study: Rethinking mother-tongue education in Côte d'Ivoire*

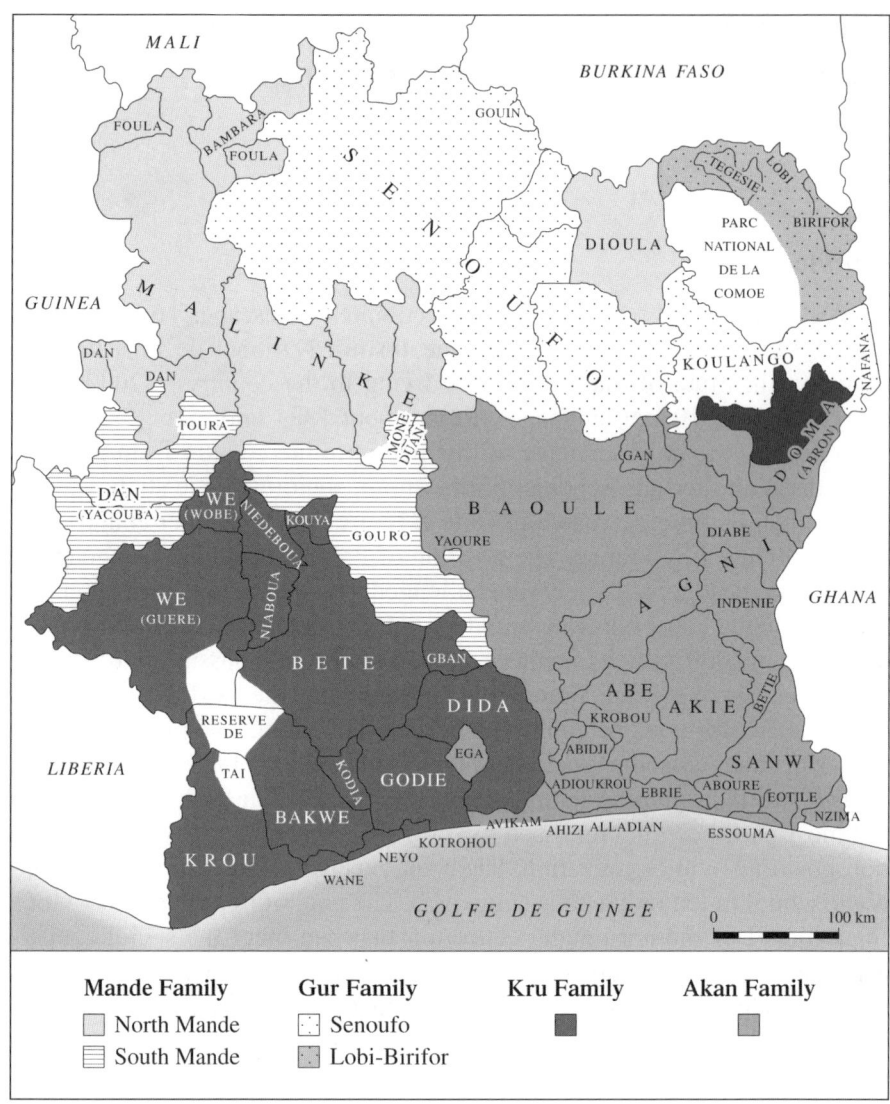

Figure 5.1. Language Family Map of Côte d'Ivoire[34]

---

34 Adapted from Kipré (1992).

those in Gagnoa do not understand each other well. Yet, the Bété of Gagnoa understand the Dida dialect spoken in Lakota but have a hard time communicating with the Dida in Yocoboué. Some Anyi dialects are mutually intelligible with some Baule dialects but not with all of them. The dialectological picture is so muddled and so complex that many Ivorian linguists are more circumspect in counting the number of languages spoken in the country. They content themselves with a vague statement such as "there are more than 60 languages" spoken in Côte d'Ivoire. All these languages belong to the Niger-Congo phylum. It is an extremely large phylum that covers nearly all of Sub-Saharan Africa except for a small area in southern Africa where the Khoisan phylum is found (Williamson and Blench 2000:12). The Niger-Congo phylum is, in turn, sub-divided into 8 Proto families, namely, Proto-Mande, Proto-Atlantic, Proto-Ijoid, Proto-Dogon, Proto-Kru, Proto-Gur, Proto-Kwa, and Proto-Benue-Congo. Ivorian languages belong to four of the eight proto-families, as shown on the map on the preceding page.

The Ivorian National Institute of Statistics' figures show the population of Côte d'Ivoire was 21,395,198 in 2009. However, the demographic figures used for this analysis are based on the 1998 census because it is the only official document that provides reliable ethnolinguistic data. Botau (2004:4) reports that the annual population growth rate is 3.3%. With this piece of information, it is easy to estimate the current size of each linguistic community in the country.

The 1998 census reported that there were 15,043,950 people living in the country. Of these, 11,043,903 were citizens and 4,000,047 were non-citizens. The percentage of citizens was 73.41% and that of non-citizens was 26.59%. The latter figure, I'm told, is the highest in the world.[35] The findings of the 1998 census most likely contributed to the emergence of the "Ivoirité" (Ivorianness) ideology which rescinded the voting rights of non-citizens. In the late 1980s, the first president of Côte d'Ivoire, Félix Houphouët-Boigny, whom American political theorists and journalists have described as a "benevolent dictator," feared that he might lose the election to Laurent Gbagbo, his political foe. Consequently, he gave voting rights to non-citizens. Shortly after his death in 1993, his successor Henri Konan Bédié rescinded

---

35 By way of comparison, according to the census figures released in December 2010, the US population stands at 308,745,538 people. The US Community Census results indicated in 2007 that there were 12.6 million people living in the US who are classified as non-citizens. They represent 4.08% of the US population. Non-citizens do not have the right to vote in US elections. Retrieved from http://www.census.gov/prod/2010pubs/acs-12.pdf on December 21, 2010.

the rights of non-citizens to vote. The passage of this restrictive new legislation lies at the core of the socio-political crisis that the country has been experiencing since 1999. Each of the four language families is described succinctly below in order to provide background information for the language of education proposal that will be made later on in the chapter.

5.1.1 Focus on the Gur family

The Gur family of languages occupies the northeastern portion of Côte d'Ivoire. Two groups of Gur language people migrated to Côte d'Ivoire over two millennia (Mabille et al. 1987:71). The first to occupy the land were the Senoufos. Historians are not completely sure about their ancestral homeland but it is generally accepted that they may have migrated from somewhere between eastern Mali and Western Burkina Faso. Mabille et al. (1987:74) note that the various Senoufo dialects enjoy a high degree of mutual intelligibility and occupy a large section of the country stretching from the northeast all the way to Katiola in the center. The second group of Gur immigrants is the Lobi. They settled in the far northeastern corner of the country, in the area of Bouna. The languages that belong to this family are listed alphabetically as follows: Birifor (Southern), Ceebaara Senoufo, Cerma, Khisa, Koulango (Bondoukou), Koulango (Bouna), Ligbi, Lobi, Senoufo (Djimini), Senoufou (Palaka), Senoufo (Nyarafolo), Senoufo (Shempire), Senoufo (Tagwana), Teen. The speakers of the Gur language family represent 18.07% of the Ivorian population. The Senoufos are the largest ethnic group inside of the Gur family. They alone make up 59.40% of the whole group.

5.1.2 Focus on the Mande family

Ethnologue (2009:692) includes the following languages under the Mande family: Bambara, Beng, Dan, Gagou, Gouro, Jula, Koro, Koyaga, Mahou, Mbre, Mwan, Toura, Wan, Wojenaka, Worodougou, and Yaouré. The Mande family is divided into two main sub-groups: the Southern and Northern (Kipré 1992:23–37 and Mabille et al. 1987:69–70). The former inhabit the forested and mountainous areas of Western Côte d'Ivoire. Historians postulate that they were among the first groups to migrate south from the former kingdoms of Ghana and Mali around the 9th century. They constitute three main groups: the Yacouba (also known as the Dan), the Gagou (Gban), and the Gouro (Kwéni). Initially, they occupied the northwestern regions of the country. However, when a new wave of Mande immigrants came to the

5.1 Sociolinguistic survey of Côte d'Ivoire 151

region between the 14th and 15th centuries, they pushed their predecessors further south and took possession of their lands. The newcomers are called Northern Mandes even though Ivorians lump northerners and Muslims together as Diula (Knutsen 2008:162). Technically, though, the Diula and the Malinke are two different ethnolinguistic groups. The Malinké are more numerous. They alone are 53.31% of the Nothern Mande whereas the Diula represent only 27% of the same family. Kouadio (2009) is of the opinion that the two groups should be considered as one because of the high degree of mutual intelligibility between them. The Southern and Northern Mandes are two separate linguistic groups because there is no mutual intelligibility between them. Overall, the Mande family makes up 27.30% of the Ivorian population. Within their language family, the Diula-Malinke are 80.31% of the Northern Mande subgroup, while the Yacouba represent 55.10% of the Southern Mande subfamily. The languages within the two sub-groups are not mutually intelligible.

5.1.3 Focus on the Kru family

The languages of the Kru family are listed as follows: Bakwe, Bété (Daloa), Bété (Guiberoua), Bété (Gagnoa), Daho-Doo, Dida (Lakota), Dida (Yocoboue), Glio-Oubi, Godie, Kodia, Kouya, Krahn (Western), Krumen (Pye), Krumen (Tepo), Krumen (Plapo), Neyo, Nyabwa, Wane, Wè (Northern), Wè (Southern), and Wè (Western). The speakers of the languages that are part of the Kru family represent 11.34% of the Ivorian population. Mabille et al. (1987:77) express scholars' bewilderment as follows:

> The origin of the Kru has given way to various hypotheses. Some [scholars] hypothesize that they originated from the West, that is, from Guinea or from present-day Liberia. Others claim that they came from the North, yet others postulate that they are indigenous to Côte d'Ivoire.

The peoples of the Kru language family occupy a large territory that stretches from the Liberian border on the West to the banks of the Badaman River. Scholars have attempted to reconstruct the migration patterns of the peoples of this language family without much success. There is no clear picture of the settlement patterns because the group splintered into many factions. The following description provided by Marchese (1989:123) explains why it is hard to have a good grip on the Kru language family of Côte d'Ivoire:

> Of the two groups [Eastern Kru vs. Western Kru], Eastern Kru is by far the more homogeneous. Spoken exclusively in Ivory Coast, this group contains two major sub-groups: the Bété complex and the Dida complex. Though the

Bété can be viewed as a sociological unit, it is divided into two main speech vairieties (languages?): one spoken in the region of Gagnoa where the principal dialect of Gbadi (Eastern Bété) and one spoken in a wider area, including Soubre, Guibéroua, Issia, and Daloa (Western Bété). This latter group is further subdivided into two mutually intelligible dialects: one spoken in Soubre-Issia-Daloa. Dida is also divided into at least two groups: Western Dida and Eastern Dida. Eastern Dida is divided into six dialects. Western Dida is made up of a number of dialects that may be subdivided into two groups.

As if this picture were not muddled enough, Kouadio (2009) notes that mutual intelligibility between some Bété groups is not high. Zogbo, a Kru expert, has informed me in a personal correspondence that the New Testament has been translated into three Bété dialects/languages because of the less than perfect mutual intelligibility between them. The dialect of the Bété continuum spoken in Daloa has the largest number of speakers, about 39.30% of the Kru language family. However, I have been told by many Bété speakers that the dialect used on radio and television is the one spoken in the area of Soubré.

5.1.4 Focus on the Akan family

Collectively, the Akan group has the largest number of speakers. They make up 43.29% of the Ivorian population. The languages that belong to this family are Abe, Abidji, Abron, Abure, Adioukrou, Alladian, Anyi (Morofou), Anyi (Sanvi), Apromou Aizi, Attie, Avikam, Baule, Beti, Ebrie, Krobou, Mbatto, and Nzema. In Côte d'Ivoire, they are divided into three main groups according to their settlement patterns. The Baule are also called the mid-country Akans because they are found in the middle of the country. The Anyi and Abron are nicknamed borderland Akans because of their proximity to Ghana. The third group is known as lagoon Akans (Ebrié, Abouré, Adioukrou, Nzema/Apolloniens) because they inhabit the lagoon coastlands. Historians (Mabille et al. 1987:90–108) are fairly confident about the origins and migration patterns of this group because many of them settled in the eastern corner of Côte d'Ivoire relatively late, that is, around the 18th century. By and large the Akan left Ghana because of wars and rifts between the various antagonistic factions within the Ashanti Kingdom. Kouadio (2009) contends that the Akan languages have been better studied than any other language family in the country. The Anyi-Baule continuum is the largest group among the Akans. Because of its central geographical location, the Anyi Morofou dialect spoken around Bongouanou enjoys a high degree of mutual intelligibility with all Anyi dialects and with most Baule dialects.[36] The Morofou dialect can serve as the basis for a harmonized and standardized written dialect.

In summary, the National Institute of Statistics indicates that 17 of the languages listed above are spoken by 100,000 people or more. The languages in question are the following: Baule (23.81%)[37], Senoufo (10.73%), Malinke (9.04%), Anyi (6.84%), Yacouba (5.7%), Attie (4.29%), Diula (4.58%), Bété (4.46%), Guéré (2.66%), Koulango (2.62%), Mahou (1.95%), Lobi (1.86%), Abbey (1.77%), Dida (1.63%), Abron (1.47%), Wobé (1.39%), and Adjoukourou (1.08%). The country is divided administratively into 19 prefectures which are equivalent to counties in the United States. The county lines match up perfectly with the ethnolinguistic settlement patterns of the country. The counties are listed alphabetically as follows: the Agnébi, the Bafing, the Bas-Sassandra, the Denguélé, the Fromagers, the Haut-Sassandra, the Lacs, the Lagunes, the Marahoué, the Montagnes, the Moyen-Cavally, the Moyen-Comoé, the Nzi-Comoé, the Savanes, the Sud-Bandama, the Sud-Comoé, the Vallée du Bandama, the Zanzan, and the Worodougou. Baule, the largest ethnic group in the country, is the regional LWC of two counties: The Lacs region and the Vallée du Bandama region. The correlation between administrative mapping and linguistic zoning is a good foundation for MM of the language of education policy that will be discussed in 5.4.2 through 5.4.10. But first, let us examine how the indigenous Ivorian languages have cohabitated with French for nearly 130 years.

5.2 The co-habitation of French and indigenous Ivorian languages

The Berlin Conference of 1884–5 permanently fixed the boundaries of Côte d'Ivoire. Since then, the indigenous Ivoirian languages listed above have cohabitated with French. The territorial organization of the country which

---

36 Kipré (1992:35) notes that the Kodè dialect spoken around Béoumi and Botro is hard for other speakers of Anyi-Baule to understand. However, they have no difficulty understanding the Anyi Morofou dialect.

37 The percentages listed here are only for the citizens of Côte d'Ivoire. The percentages reported by Leclerc (2010) and others are based on the general population which includes citizens and non-citizens alike. However, since the model of language planning advocated here deals only with indigenous Ivorian languages, I have not seen fit to include non-citizens.

was alluded to in the previous paragraph follows a linguistic logic to the point that county lines correlate fairly well with linguistic zoning. Consequently, the country can be seen as consisting of 17 contiguous and fairly homogeneous linguistic enclaves. Most regions have one major regional LWC and several minority languages that belong to the same language family as the regional LWC. This has brought about a situation of widespread bilingualism between the regional LWC and the smaller languages spoken within the same region. However, in all regions of the country French reigns supreme as the "superlanguage." The absolute dominance of French can be attributed to two factors. First, no indigenous language is spoken by 25% or more of the population. Consequently, French faces no real competition. Secondly, the first president of Côte d'Ivoire, Félix Houphouet-Boigny, was absolutely convinced that multilingualism was a liability for nation-building. Botau (2004:8) explains this sentiment as follows:

> It should be pointed out that, in order to strengthen national unity, the authorities that have governed the country since independence have opted for a sort of "linguistic dualism". Given the linguistic patchwork in Côte d'Ivoire, and fearing that the adoption of one language rather than another might cause animosity between the different ethnic groups, the authorities made French the official language, to be used exclusively by government bodies and at all levels of education, while national languages were reserved for private use.

The excessive fear that multilingualism is detrimental to national cohesiveness led Ivorian policymakers to promote French vigorously at the expense of indigenous languages. The country wasted no time in 1960 in stating in Article 1 of the Constitution that "French shall be the official language of the Republic of Côte d'Ivoire." Three years later, that is, on January 1, 1963, Legislation No. 63 amended Article 1 by changing the future tense *"shall be"* to the present tense *"is."* The revised Article 1 reads, "French is the official language of the Republic of Côte d'Ivoire." Political and opinion leaders, including Philip Yacé, the former president of the National Assembly of Côte d'Ivoire, defended the choice of French as the sole official language of Côte d'Ivoire in the United Nations General Assembly saying:

> In all truthfulness, I must confess that as far as my country is concerned, the adoption of French as the first article of our Constitution, has without any doubt, been a facilitating factor that has contributed quickly and positively to the nation-building efforts of His Excellency, President Félix Houphouët-Boigny. This was the top priority of his political action. We adopted French

5.2 The co-habitation of French and indigenous Ivorian languages

freely and willingly, and this has been a cohesive factor in Côte d'Ivoire and has made it possible to bring together some one hundred ethnic groups in our country (Leclerc 2010).[38]

The decade of the 1970s was marked by the African Renaissance. It was ideology epitomized in French-speaking Africa by the late presidents of Congo DRC and Togo. They climbed to power through military coups, they embraced this ideology as a way of consolidating their grip on power. The two strongmen exchanged their French first names for "authentic" African first names. Thus, Josepeh-Désiré Mobutu of Congo became Sese Seko Mobutu. Similarly, Etienne Eyadéma of Togo became known as Gnassingbé Eyadéma. They also forced their countrymen and women to adopt African first names. The undercurrent of the African Renaissance ideology was particularly strong among the intellectuals. Ivorian leaders responded to this ideology by enacting the Education Reform Act of 1977. Articles 67 and 68 read as follows:

> Article 67: *The introduction of national languages into the official education system must be conceived as a factor of national unity and a way of revalorizing the Ivorian cultural heritage.*

> Article 68: *The Institute of Applied Linguistics is charged with paving the way for the introduction of national languages in the school curriculum by describing, codifying, identifying, cataloguing their grammars and their lexicons; by producing textbooks and developing literary productions so as to guarantee their cultural distinctiveness.*

A commission was set up to examine the feasibility of implementing the educational reform. Knutsen (2008:166) reports their conclusion as follows:

> This commission brought together people from the public and civil society, including teachers, parents, and members of village associations. Although those consulted agreed on the importance of integrating national languages in the school system, they did not agree on which languages should be promoted. Some of the members of the commission advocated the promotion of one major language from each of the four main linguistic and ethnic

---

38 This quote and all other statements, including the articles of the constitution and legislations passed in Côte d'Ivoire have been translated from French into English by me.

groups of the country in order to progressively assure communication between various groups. Others objected that because of important interregional migration, schools could not be considered as regional but national entities and that consequently the promotion of different regional languages would constitute a political problem.

In the end, after numerous discussions, nothing happened. In my opinion, Houphouët-Boigny allowed this legislation to pass just to placate the boisterous academics at the University of Abidjan who were clamoring for African cultural renaissance. No sooner was the legislation passed than it was ignored. So, French continued to be used as the only medium of instruction in Ivorian schools. In 1995, Legislation No. 95–696 was passed in September which called for the teaching of Ivorian languages in schools. The text of the law reads in part:

> *The teaching of national languages, the teaching of arts and crafts, the teaching of technology and menial work, physical education and sports, contribute to the training of citizens.*

This second legislation also fell on deaf ears. On July 23, 2000, a new constitution was adopted which explicitly mentioned indigenous languages. Language policy matters are discussed in Article 29, sections 5 and 6. Section 5 is a verbatim repetition of the disposition that made French the official language of Côte d'Ivoire. Therefore, it is not worth repeating it. Section 6, on the other hand, contains the following new language:

> Section 6: *The law determines the conditions under which national languages are to be promoted and developed.*

No action has been taken to modify the terms of the linguistic co-habitation between French and indigenous Ivorian languages since the passage of the new constitution. In a nutshell, the AIM introduced by French colonial authorities in 1884 has been implemented continuously for nearly 130 years. The linguistic dispositions of the new constitution have not taken effect because the country has been embroiled in chronic political crisis since 2002. This sociolinguistic background is necessary for understanding the ramifications of Laitin's (1992:144) forecast about language outcome in Côte d'Ivoire:

> The country is now on a linguistic track not dissimilar to France in 1539 when François 1er issued the Edict of Villiers-Cotterêts, establishing Francien the dialect of Ile-de-France, as the only official language of state. ...

5.2 The co-habitation of French and indigenous Ivorian languages 157

> An increasing number of Ivorian youth are reporting that French is their mother tongue.

The youth that Laitin referred to in 1992 are all adults now. People of their generation and those younger are predominantly monolingual in French if they live in semi-rural and urban areas. It must be acknowledged that younger Ivorians are not the only ones who take pride in having French as their native language. Leclerc (2010) quotes the Ivorian representative to the International Organization of Francophone countries as having made the statement below:

> French is one of our mother tongues. It is history that creates linguistic communities. One is born in it. One must accept it as it is! I speak French, I speak Bété. I'm a Francophone. I'm a Bétéphone. Let's rid ourselves of inferiority complexes and claim French as an Ivorian language.

AIM that has been implemented since colonial times has contributed significantly to the diffusion of French in Côte d'Ivoire. Picoche and Marchello-Nizia (1994:135) note that after six years of schooling, Ivorian school children can express themselves clearly and effortlessly in French:

> In Côte d'Ivoire, where it [French] is obligatory at school, even during recess, pupils learn it amazingly quickly and effortlessly. After two months of schooling, they can understand the basic instructions given by the teacher. By the time they reach sixth grade, they know French well enough to express themselves spontaneously, without any more difficulty than French or Quebecois kids of their age, but of course, in the 'popular variety'.

They report that French has emerged as the only truly national language because it is the only language used by 60% of the population. Furthermore, they note that 73% of Ivorians prefer French to any other language as the national language of Côte d'Ivoire. The socially stratified dialects of French are known collectively as "Français Popular Ivorien" (Ivorian Vernacular French). Picoche and Marchello-Nizia (1994:129) describe these varieties as follows:

> There are varying levels of proficiency in French [in Africa]. In Côte d'Ivoire, the ruling elite (5%) who are university graduates, some of whom had lived in France for a long time, are scrupulously attentive to the rules of grammar. The educated upper middle class, high school graduates (5%), speak a regional variety. Traders, often Lebanese and Moroccans, often

disregard grammar rules. The rest of the population, illiterate or barely literate, that is, elementary school graduates (Malians and Burkinabes), resorts to a pidginized variety called Ivorian Popular French when the social encounters call for it. Some believe that this variety is undergoing creolization. This variety is spreading quickly in towns all over the country. Because it is widely used, its phonology, syntax, and lexicon are undergoing stabilization. This variety is accessible to everybody. It allows a person who did not go to school to communicate with one who attended school if they speak different indigenous languages. Until schooling is widespread, this variety has set in motion linguistic unification. It is now even spoken in rural areas.

This quote and the survey figures reported by Picoche and Marchello-Nizia (1994) underscore the fact that French is far more pervasive in Côte d'Ivoire than linguists have been willing to acknowledge. They note, for instance, that in urban settings, an Ivorian will not greet another African in any other language except in French. This contrasts with the widely quoted claim posted on the website of the National Institute of Statistics that 88% of conversations in the markets in Abidjan are done in indigenous Ivorian languages. This figure is valid if and only if the interlocutors have had a previous encounter in which it has been established that they spoke the same language. Otherwise, it is unheard of in Côte d'Ivoire to walk to a stranger in an urban setting and speak to him/her in any other language than French. This contrasts with my experiences in Cotonou (in Benin), Lomé (in Togo), Accra (Ghana), Ouagadougou (Burkina Faso), Dakar (Senegal) and Nairobi (Kenya), where people addressed me respectively in Fon, Mina, Akan, Moore, Wolof, and Swahili as soon as I showed up in the market. The widespread use of French in Côte d'Ivoire seems to be markedly different from the situation in Congo, DRC as described by Bokamba (2008a:109), "For example, asking to buy, or offering a Congolese, some goods in French at a marketplace in Kinshasa is perceived as educational arrogance. Such a behavior can cost a buyer a higher price, more typical of an expatriate, or can lead the potential buyer to decline the transaction." Again, on page 113, he states, "Initiating a conversation in French a Congolese in Mbandaka, unless one knows the interlocutor personally, is generally viewed not only as arrogant, pedantic, but also in very bad taste. Our survey of six families in Mbandaka reveals that there is, generally speaking, little evidence and incentive to shift to French." The sociolinguistic situation in Côte d'Ivoire is clearly the opposite of what Bokamba describes for Congo DRC. It is a serious sociolinguistic faux-pas to address an Ivorian whom one does not know in any other language except French, whereas in Congo the linguistically correct behavior is to avoid using French.

5.2.1 The psycholinguistic side-effects of the widespread use of French

Jules Hié Nea, a former minister of culture, offers the following explanation for why French has spread far and wide in Côte d'Ivoire:

> One must not forget that Côte d'Ivoire has chosen a development path that embraces the outside world. Given this choice, we have imposed on ourselves the necessity to use an international language. French is not only the language of the economy, of the administration, but also the language used by most of our writers.

The diffusion of French has been achieved not without a hefty psycholinguistic price tag. The sociolinguistic situation described previously has given way to a condition bordering on "linguistic schizophrenia." Many Ivorian parents feel powerless in the face of the gradual but steady encroachment of French on ancestral languages. Parents of school age children are puzzled by the language shift that is taking place under their very own eyes. Furthermore, a growing number of them feel like ethnolinguistic traitors for having sacrificed their mother tongues on the altar of socio-economic mobility and modernity. Mufwene (2010:927) describes a similar situation as "an awful feeling." Increasingly, the citizenry is looking for a workable solution to this sociolinguistic paradox. In their heart of hearts, Ivorians do not want to give up their ancestral languages, yet they do not want to downplay the importance of French as a language of modernity, social mobility, between-group communication, and global citizenship. They are hungry and thirsty for a workable mother-tongue education model that can help them balance the gains made in education through French with the need to promote their ancestral languages in the educational system. They seem to concur with Grenoble and Whaley (2006:51) that mother-tongue education is the first line of defense against language shift.

5.3 Experimentation with TIM

The Education Reform Act of 1977 which recommended that Ivorian languages be used in education went unheeded. Tchagbalé writes in *Fraternité Matin* of April 10th 2003 that an experiment was performed jointly by the Institut de Linguistique Appliquée and the Institut de Recherches

Mathématiques of University of Abidjan from 1980 to 1986. Lower primary school children were taught in five local languages: Adioukrou, Baule, Malinké, Senoufo, and Yacouba. He claims that the experiment was successful. However, he does not explain why it was discontinued. Ten years after this experiment, a non-governmental organization known as *Savane et Développement* began a similar experiment in Bondiali, in the northwestern corner of the country. The experiment was carried out in Malinké and Senoufo. From first grade to third grade Senoufo and Malinké were used as the sole media of instruction. French was introduced as the language of instruction in upper primary school, that is, from fourth grade to sixth grade. Since then, according to Dally (2000), ten more villages in ten different languages (Abidji, Anyi, Attié, Baule, Bété, Guéré, Dan, Koulango, Mahou, Malinké, and the Senoufo dialect spoken in Korogho) have been asked to experiment with this model of mother-tongue education.

Though TIM is new to Côte d'Ivoire, we learned in Chapter 4 that it has been in use in many former British Sub-Saharan African colonies since 1922. It is the preferred language of education policy of language planners presumably because it produces better academic results. The literature is replete with claims about its merits. Even scholars who are otherwise very circumspect in their statements have repeated the same claims without providing the slightest shred of evidence to back them up. The latest linguist to do the same is Mufwene (2010:923). He states that "many studies have argued convincingly that children do better at school when their mother tongue serves as a medium of instruction." Yet he does not cite a single source to substantiate this claim. Regardless of what linguists may think, Ivorian parents have remained unconvinced by the alleged merits of TIM. Now Grenoble and Whaley (2006:55) seem to indicate that the model is falling in disfavor among some language planners:

> Partial-immersion programs are bilingual programs, with some classes conducted in the local language, and some in the language of wider communication. The basic difficulty with partial immersion programs is that they often develop into, or simply are, transitional bilingual programs. In general, the classes conducted in the local language are language-learning classes, or parts of classes, and the other subjects are taught in a language of wider communication. Thus, the local language is taught as a foreign language or second language. This is not a model which we advocate, nor does it hold wide support. Yet it is arguably the most frequently encountered model, in particular in certain parts of the world such as the Americas, the former Soviet Union, and elsewhere, and so merits discussion. Note that language activists advocate against partial-immersion programs.

5.3.1 A critical appraisal of TIM

The advocates of TIM in Côte d'Ivoire and elsewhere have used the alleged high rate of failure in primary school as iron-clad evidence against the use of ex-colonial languages in lower primary education. They have gone on to conclude that if the indigenous language spoken by the child is used as the medium of instruction, there will be less failure. It can be stated categorically and emphatically that at least for Côte d'Ivoire, 30 years of student achievement data do not support this allegation. In fact, the Ivorian data runs contrary to conventional wisdom. However, before disproving this claim, we must first provide a short explanation of the education system of Côte d'Ivoire. The school system is divided into three cycles: a primary cycle of six years, a lower secondary cycle of four years, and an upper secondary cycle of three years. Students pass a national standardized exam to move from one cycle into another. Let's examine the pass/fail rates of the exams in each cycle. These figures were released by incumbent President Laurent Gbagbo during the 2010 presidential debate and were reported by the newspaper, *Le Patriote* of November 26, 2010.

Table 5.1. Success Rate at National Exams

No.	Grade Level	1991	1994	2002	2004
1.	Seventh Grade Entrance Exam	21%	37.34%	64%	68.94%
2.	O Level Exam	32%	7.85%	36.47%	31.43%
3.	A Level Exam	27.25%	13.52%	27.25%	23.71%

A cursory glance at the table reveals that for a period of 13 years, the average passing rate for elementary students is 47.82%. The average passing rate for lower secondary students is 26.93% while that of upper secondary students is 22.93%. In other words, the failure rates are respectively 52.18% for elementary students, 73.07% for middle school students, and 77.07% for high school students. Given the fact that the rate of success is higher in elementary school than in secondary school, it is hard to blame the failure on language. If language were the issue, we would expect more failure in elementary school than in secondary school. However, this is not the case. To show that language is not the culprit for school failure, let's consider the following set of data from Loucou et al. (1987:284). The researchers tracked a group of students from 7th grade until the end of 13th grade and provide us with the information in Table 5.2:

Table 5.2. Success Rate in Secondary School

No.	Grade Levels	1969
1.	7th Graders	15,925
2.	8th Graders	12,531
3.	9th Graders	9,018
4.	10th Graders (O Level Exam)	5,362
5.	11th Graders	1,786
6.	12th Graders	820
7.	Passed BAC (13th A Level Exam)	570

Of the 15,925 students who passed the Seventh Grade Entrance Exam in 1969, only 5,362 students passed the O Level Exam. This represents a success rate of 33.67%. Or to put it negatively, 66.33% failed. In those days, there were two separate exams: the O Level Exam and the 11th Grade Entrance Exam. Of the 5,362 students who passed the O Level Exam, only 10.63% were allowed to move on to Eleventh Grade. In other words, 89.37% of those who passed their O Level Exam failed their 11th Grade Entrance Exam. Now, of those who entered 11th grade, only 31.91% graduated with their A Level diploma. If we track down the progress of the seventh grade entering class all the way to thirteenth grade, we see that only 3.57% of the 15,925 students passed their A Level exam. This represents a failure rate of 96.5%! Loucou et al. (1987:291) report a higher rate of failure in a longitudinal study involving 500,865 students who enrolled in elementary school in 1970–71. Of these, only 3,092 graduated from college with a BA degree. This represents a success rate of 0.61%, or a failure rate of 99.38%. If language were indeed the culprit, we would expect less failure as students moved up in grades. As is well known in Africa, proficiency in the colonial languages correlates very highly with levels of education. In other words, the higher the educational attainment, the higher the proficiency in European languages. However, we see that in this case, the correlation does not hold. Higher proficiency levels in French translate into higher rates of failure. This shows then that the use of French as the medium of instruction is not responsible for academic underperformance.

It has also been postulated that failure to use the child's mother tongue as the medium of instruction accounts for high drop-out rates in elementary school. This argument also is not validated in the case of Côte d'Ivoire, and there is data to prove it. The National Institute of Statistics provides us with the following data on elementary school enrollment, retention and dropout rates:

Table 5.3. Enrollment, Retention and Dropout Rates

No.	Primary School Data	1993	1996	1998	2000	2002
1.	Enrollment Rate	48.8%	51.1%	52.8%	56.9%	56.5
2.	Completion Rate	47.9%	46.4%	45.2%	49.1%	NA
3.	Failure Rate	0.9%	4.7%	7.6%	7.8%	NA

A quick glance at the data shows that for a period of seven years, the average dropout rate was 5.25% compared with the average retention rate of 47.15%. It is not possible to compare this data with data in the United States where education is compulsory until the age of 16. However, high school dropout rates in America can help dispel the allegation that the language of instruction is the main culprit when students drop out. From 2002–2003, nationwide, 26.60% of American high school students dropped out. In Minnesota, a state nationally recognized for its excellence in education, 15.2% of the students dropped out. Among white students, the dropout rate is 7.2%.[39] If language were the main culprit, all white Minnesotan students would have graduated from high school because they are almost all native speakers of English. The Federal Dropout Prevention Center has highlighted seven important dropout indicators: attendance data, failing grades, number of suspensions, low credit accumulation, disciplinary referrals, health crisis (including unexpected pregnancies), and family poverty. Dropout occurs whether the child's native language is used as the medium of instruction or not. Take the state of Mississippi for example. It has the highest dropout rate in the nation, 26.60%. Since dropping out of school is a common phenomenon, it is premature to blame the relatively small dropout rate in elementary school in Côte d'Ivoire on the fact that French is the only medium of instruction.

The high rate of failure at entrance exams in Côte d'Ivoire has less to do with French as the medium of instruction in elementary school and more to do with the fact that the whole education system is geared toward

---

[39] Retrieved from http://education.state.mn.us/MDE/Academic_Excellence/Implement_ Effect_Practic/Dropout_Prevent_Reten_Grad_Init/Resources_Tools/index.html on June 23, 2011.

meritocracy and the pursuit of academic elitism. Roadblocks in the form of entrance exams are deliberately built into the curriculum to weed out students. A host of other indicators may legitimately account for the high rates of failure at entrance exams. Loucou et al. (1987:288) mention class sizes as a possible culprit. In 1971, there were 35 students per classroom in primary school. By 1976, the number of students per classroom had climbed to 44. At the beginning of 1980, there were 55 students. The construction of new schools has not kept pace with the demographic explosion in the country. Other contributing factors may include undiagnosed disabilities ranging from poor vision, poor hearing, and learning disabilities to various forms of attention deficit disorders. By and large, the Ivorian general public has grown skeptical and tired of scapegoating French as the essential cause for academic failure. People are no longer persuaded by the same age-old explanation that academic failure is due to the nonuse of indigenous Ivorian languages as media of instruction. Moreover, the fact that elementary school children have consistently outperformed their seniors in national exams has rendered the language of instruction argument innocuous. In 2009, according to the leading newspaper, *Fraternité Matin* of July 7, 2010, 73.94% of them passed their Seventh Grade Entrance Exam. In light of these relatively good results in primary school, parents of school age children are unconvinced that French is an obstacle to success. There is a disconnect between the arguments put forth by the proponents of mother-tongue education and the educational realities as witnessed by parents of school age children. Mufwene (2010:928) alludes to this divide as follows:

> Languages represent invaluable world views and typological specimens that must be maintained at any cost, almost romantically, or, should I say with some embarrassment, in the interest of linguistics as a discipline. Unfortunately, no concrete suggestions have been articulated for the best ecological conditions under which both the linguists' interests and the speakers' interests can be satisfied.

This observation is in reality an indictment of applied linguistics. As was noted in 1.5, its record on mother-tongue education has been described as "a catastrophic success" precisely because it has not responded to parents' felt needs. Instead, applied linguists have sought to impose on them models of language of education that suite their ideological and academic interests. Instead of acknowledging this reality, emotive arguments are used to shame Ivorian parents for their willingness to sacrifice their ancestral languages on behalf of French. In an interview reported in the *Notre Voie* of November 2002, Professor Sery Bailly, the then minister of Higher Education and Scientific Research, alleged that mother-tongue education has stalled in Côte d'Ivoire since the passage of the Education Reform Law of 1977 because of "fear, prejudice, and alienation." However, Mufwene (2004:924) may have a better explanation for the Ivorian situation:

> People prefer education in the European language because common sense dictates it for them, since they hope that their children will be more competitive than themselves on the current job market. Using the languages of marginalized populations will not necessarily empower the latter economically if the political system continues to exploit them economically.

Name-calling and shaming have not succeeded in persuading Ivorian parents to embrace mother-tongue education. Even though parents love their ancestral languages, the payoff they offer is too insignificant compared to the benefits that are attached to being educated in French. In the remaining sections, the Predictioneer's Model will be used to formulate a win-win language of education policy. Parents will be able to have the best of both worlds: their children will continue to be educated in French and also acquire literacy in local Ivorian languages at school.

5.3.2 Toward an optimal solution

It is my contention that the Predictioneer's Model can help us find an optimal solution for the language of education conundrum in Côte d'Ivoire. For this language game, a total of 56 players have been identified. These players represent groups of people who have a vested interest in both French and Ivorian languages. Some hold advanced degrees but others are preliterate. Within each category of players, the labels "Committed," "Undecided," or "Lip service" are used to gauge the level of interest (salience) in mother-tongue education. The level of interest of Committed players is rated at 95, while that of the "Undecided" is rated at 50. The category "Lip service" includes people who say publicly that they support mother-tongue education but do not believe in it and would not send their children to schools that teach Ivorian languages. They say with their mouths that they are for it but their actions prove otherwise. Their salience is rated at 10 only. Table 5.4 below contains all the information needed for the calculation of the weighted mean score.

166 *Case study: Rethinking mother-tongue education in Côte d'Ivoire*

Table 5.4. Preference Level of French in Côte d'Ivoire

No.	Players	Influence Scale	Salience Scale	Position Scale	I × S × P	I × S
1.	Ph.D. and Advanced Degree Holders – Committed	100	95	100	950	9,5
2.	Ph.D. and Advanced Degree Holders – Undecided	100	50	50	250	5
3.	Ph.D. and Advanced Degree Holders – Lip service	100	10	0	0	1
4.	Politicians – Committed	100	95	100	950	9,5
5.	Politicians – Undecided	100	50	50	250	5
6.	Politicians – Lip service	100	10	0	0	1
7.	Linguists-ILA – Committed	100	95	100	950	9,5
8.	Linguists – Undecided	100	50	50	250	5
9.	Linguists – Lip service	100	10	0	0	1
10.	Linguists-SIL – Committed	100	95	0	0	9,5
11.	MA. and College Graduated – Committed	100	95	100	950	9,5
12.	MA. and College Graduated – Undecided	100	50	50	250	5

(*Continued*)

Table 5.4. Preference Level of French in Côte d'Ivoire (*Cont.*)

No.	Players	Influence Scale	Salience Scale	Position Scale	I × S × P	I × S
13.	MA. and College Graduated – Lip service	100	10	0	0	1
14.	Armed & Security Forces	100	95	100	950	9,5
15.	Educated Parents of School Age Children – Committed	100	95	100	950	9,5
16.	Educated Parents of School Age Children – Undecided	100	50	50	250	5
17.	Educated Parents of School Age Children – Lip service	100	10	0	0	1
18.	French Expatriate Community	100	95	50	475	9,5
19.	Civil Servants – Committed	90	95	100	855	8,55
20.	Civil Servants – Undecided	90	95	50	427,5	8,55
21.	Civil Servants – Lip service	90	95	0	0	8,55
22.	Teachers' Unions – Committed	80	95	100	760	7,6
23.	Teachers' Unions – Undecided	80	50	50	200	4
24.	Teachers' Unions – Lip service	80	10	0	0	800

(*Continued*)

Table 5.4. Preference Level of French in Côte d'Ivoire (*Cont.*)

No.	Players	Influence Scale	Salience Scale	Position Scale	I × S × P	I × S
25.	Students' Unions – Committed	60	95	100	570	5,7
26.	Students' Unions – Undecided	60	50	50	150	3
27.	Student's Union – Lip service	60	10	0	0	600
28.	Abidjan city dwellers – Committed	60	95	100	570	5,7
29.	Abidjan city dwellers – Undecided	60	50	50	150	3
30.	Abidjan city dwellers – Lip service	60	10	0	0	600
31.	Catholic Clergy – Committed	50	95	100	475	4,75
32.	Catholic Clergy – Undecided	50	50	50	125	2,5
33.	Catholic Clergy – Lip service	50	10	0	0	500
34.	Protestant Clergy – Committed	50	95	100	475	4,75
35.	Protestant Clergy – Undecided	50	50	50	125	2,5
36.	Protestant Clergy – Lip service	50	10	0	0	500
37.	Islamic Clergy – Committed	50	95	100	475	4,75
38.	Islamic Clergy – Undecided	50	50	50	125	2,5
39.	Islamic Clergy – Lip service	50	10	0	0	500

(*Continued*)

Table 5.4. Preference Level of French in Côte d'Ivoire (*Cont.*)

No.	Players	Influence Scale	Salience Scale	Position Scale	I × S × P	I × S
40.	Lebanese Expatriate Community	40	95	50	190	3,8
41.	Western Expatriate Community – (Germans, Spaniards, Americans)	40	95	50	190	3,8
42.	International Business Community	40	95	50	190	3,8
43.	Residents of secondary cities – Committed	30	95	100	285	2,85
44.	Residents of secondary cities – Undecided	30	50	50	75	1,5
45.	Residents of secondary cities – Lip service	30	10	0	0	300
46.	Urban unskilled workers– Committed	20	95	100	190	1,9
47.	Urban unskilled workers– Undecided	20	50	50	50	1
48.	Urban unskilled workers–Lip service	20	10	0	0	200
49.	Urban unemployed or underemployed – Committed	20	95	100	190	1,9

(*Continued*)

Table 5.4. Preference Level of French in Côte d'Ivoire (*Cont.*)

No.	Players	Influence Scale	Salience Scale	Position Scale	I × S × P	I × S
50.	Urban unemployed or underemployed – Undecided	20	50	50	50	1
51.	Urban unemployed or underemployed – Lip service	20	10	0	0	200
52.	West African Expatriate Community	10	95	50	47,5	950
53.	Informal business community	10	10	50	5	100
54.	Rural/Farmers – Committed	10	95	100	95	950
55.	Rural/Farmers – Undecided	10	50	50	25	500
56.	Rural/Farmers – Lip service	10	10	0	0	100
57.	Total	3,5	3,285	2,75	14,490,000	210,75
58.	Weighted Mean				68.75%	

The weighted mean score is 68.75%. The Position Scale Matrix discussed in 2.5.2 indicates that a score of 75 corresponds to Maintenance Model. Even though 68.75% is 6.25% away, according to De Mesquita (2009:73), "Numerical values that are closer to the numerical value of the player's advocated position are liked better by the player than positions reflected by numerical values further from the advocated position." On this basis, we conclude that the language of instruction policy that is most likely to work in Côte d'Ivoire is MM. Picoche and Marchello-Nizia (1994:128) report that a study done a decade or so earlier had found that 73% preferred French as the medium of instruction. Our analysis is 4.5% lower, but both studies are in agreement.

5.4 Workable models of language of education

The score of 68.75% can be interpreted as a clear indication that Ivorians reject FIM and TIM. The same score shows clearly that they do not want AIM that has been in place since colonial times. They are therefore in search of a new language of education model. Three of the five models listed in 2.5.2 have been implemented since colonial times. The only two that were never experimented with are DIM and MM. Let's review them to see what they might contribute to the players in the Ivorian language game.

5.4.1 The core principles of DIM

DIM is becoming widely popular in the United States. It started in 1963 but has been growing by leaps and bounds since. The Center for Applied Linguistics (2010) reports that, on average, 40 new Dual Immersion schools are started every year. DePalma (2010:6) reports that there were 346 DIM programs in 2009. The common features shared by the vast majority of DIMs are listed by Lessow-Hurley (2000:17) as follows:

1. The ratio of speakers of each language is balanced
2. The languages are carefully separated
3. The minority language is emphasized in early grades
4. Instruction is excellent and emphasizes core academics
5. Parents have a strong and positive relationship with the school

Proponents of DIM sell their program by emphasizing that it promotes both bilingual and biliteracy skills. Presumably, a graduate from such a program has "the full range of understanding and skills appropriate for an educated speaker of two languages" (Lessow-Hurley 2000:87). For this reason, the Dual Immersion curriculum and syllabus insist that core academic subjects such as mathematics, science, language arts, and social studies be taught in both languages. The main stumbling block that makes it impossible to implement this model in Côte d'Ivoire is its insistence on having two teachers per grade level: one teacher for the LWC and another one for the minority language. Carrera-Carillo and Rickert Smith (2006:5) justify this stringent requirement as follows:

> The two languages are kept distant and never mixed during instruction. For example, in an English-Spanish dual language program, two teachers are responsible for instructing a group of students. Both teachers are considered pure language models. The English-speaking teacher instructs only in English and the Spanish-speaking teacher instructs only in Spanish.

Loucou et al. (1987c:284) inform us that there were 10,000 elementary school teachers in 1970. My estimate of the current number of teachers in Côte d'Ivoire is 39,798 elementary school teachers. This means that if this model were implemented in 2010, the government would have to double the number of teachers currently available. Since an elementary school teacher makes on average $463 a month, this would mean that the government would have to budget $442,235,376 annually for teachers' salary alone (see 8.3.5 for additional details). DIM is financially impossible for cash-strapped Côte d'Ivoire. It cannot afford two elementary school teachers per classroom. Grenoble and Whaley (2006:45) note rather correctly that language planning programs regularly fail for lack of adequate funding: "A lack of financial resources can limit the kinds of programs a community can realistically implement, and so an early-on evaluation of potential resources – both internal and external – is critical." The exorbitant price tag of DIM makes it impossible to implement.

5.4.2 Introducing MM

The remaining model to be discussed is MM. It has four core characteristics:

1. It maintains language vitality by fostering bilingualism and biliteracy in indigenous languages.
2. It is economically sustainable for medium and long term by promoting a profitable indigenous language industry.
3. It uses the Repertoire Model to select which languages should be used as media of instruction.
4. It meets parental expectations and receives parental cooperation because it does not jeopardize the position of French as the language of upward socio-economic mobility while at the same time promoting ancestral languages.

Grenoble and Whaley (2006:13) make it clear that this model is not ideal for language revitalization. It does not work for moribund languages that have undergone a prolonged period of decay. However, it can help maintain current levels of proficiency in languages that are under stress but are still vital. Unlike other Francophone countries where amcestral languages are holding their own in their competition with French, in Côte d'Ivoire French is becoming a real menace for the welfare of indigenous languages, as was noted in 5.2. Consequently, there is an urgent need for Ivoirian languages to be maintained by teaching them at school. The ideal grade level for this to be done is in secondary school. Let's see how MM may be implemented.

5.4.3 Overview of the secondary school curriculum

A quick survey of the school system was provided in 5.3.1. The information in this section deals exclusively with the secondary school curriculum. Passing the Seventh Grade Entrance Exam automatically gives primary school students the opportunity to enroll in secondary school. Secondary school lasts seven years and consists of two cycles. The lower secondary (equivalent to middle school in the United States) lasts four years and goes from 7th grade to 10th grade. The high school lasts three years, from 11th to 13th grades. At the end of the 13th grade, all students must take the dreaded high school graduation exam called "Baccalaureat", for BAC for short. It is equivalent to the A Level Exam in the Commonwealth countries. All core academic subjects: Language Arts, History, Geography, Mathematics, Physics, Chemistry, and Foreign Languages are taught in secondary school. As far as foreign languages are concerned, English is introduced as the first foreign language in 7th grade. German and Spanish come later in 9th grade. Students have the choice of studying either German or Spanish, but not both concurrently. English, German, and Spanish are compulsory foreign languages. They are examinable subjects for the A Level graduation exam. Students have to demonstrate written and spoken proficiency in their language pairs: English and German, or English and Spanish. I propose that the studying of German and Spanish be delayed until college for those who want to study these languages. I also propose that regional LWCs be taught in their stead.

The proposal being made here is neither germanophobic nor is it hispanophobic.[40] It is simply motivated by the fact that there is no convincing rationale for teaching these two languages in high school and that the space they currently occupy in the curriculum can be put to good use by teaching indigenous Ivorian languages. The need to study English in secondary school can be justified by the need of regional cooperation and integration. Côte d'Ivoire has two English-speaking neighbors: Liberia on the west and Ghana on the east. Additionally, Côte d'Ivoire belongs to the Economic Organization of West African States which has four Anglophone countries: Ghana, Gambia, Liberia, and Nigeria. Moreover, English is now truly a global language worth knowing. However, as for the presence of German and Spanish in the curriculum of Ivorian secondary schools, there is no convincing explanation for it

---

40 As a graduate of the Ivorian school system, I too, took Spanish in secondary school to fulfill the foreign language requirements. I enjoyed warm German hospitality in German homes when I toured the country for a month some years back.

except to claim that it is a colonial education legacy. As noted in Chapter 3, the educational system in colonial Francophone Africa was a facsimile of the one in the metropole. It made sense for the French to teach German and Spanish in the schools of the metropole because they had the speakers of these two languages as their neighbors. However, it does not make much sense now for Côte d'Ivoire to keep teaching German and Spanish.

In real economic terms, keeping German and Spanish in secondary school is an economic liability because there is no return on this educational investment. Teachers' salary alone amounted to $93,243,672 in 2010 (see 8.4.3). The overwhelming majority of high school graduates who study these two languages never use them in real life. They do not travel to Germany or Spain, nor do they do business in these languages. Worse, no sooner do they graduate from secondary school than they forget them. Yet the government of Côte d'Ivoire continues to sink millions of its hard earned money into an unprofitable academic venture. Year after year, as it has done for the past 50 years, the country continues to pay the salary and fringe benefits for German and Spanish language teachers. Why waste students' time and effort on the study of languages that will never be put to good use by the vast majority of them? Why spend so much money on an investment which yields no benefit for the nation? Why spend so much time, energy, resources, and brain power on teacher training and preparation for skills that students do not need nor use once they graduate from high school? Why not invest the same amount of money, time, energy, and talents on promoting and developing indigenous Ivorian languages? In fact, it will be argued in Chapter 8 that replacing German and Spanish with Ivorian regional LWCs will contribute positively to the economic development of the country.

5.5 MM and the 3±1 language outcome

How can one go about implementing MM in a multilingual country such as Côte d'Ivoire? The answer to this important question can be found in Laitin's (1992) Repertoire Model discussed in 2.3.6, and more specifically in his explanation of the 3±1 language outcome approach. The model can be profitably applied to Côte d'Ivoire because the country is linguistically zoned. There are 19 ethnolinguistic regions. In each region, there is at least one regional LWC that is spoken by 100,000 or more. All in all, there are 17 regional languages listed alphabetically as follows: Abey, Abron, Adjoukrou, Anyi, Atie, Baule, Bété, Dida, Diula, Guere, Guro, Kulango, Lobi, Mahou, Malinké, Senoufo and Yacouba. These same languages are broadcast nationally on radio and television. Each is given 15 minutes of air time each week to summarize leading news items. Botau (2004:8) notes that Aburé and Nzema are also broadcast even though they are minority languages. In 1982 a soccer match opposed Ghana and Côte d'Ivoire. Presumably, the Ivorian team and their supporters were brutalized in Ghana. Ivorians responded by brutalizing Ghanaians who lived in Côte d'Ivoire. The Aburé and the Nzema of Côte d'Ivoire live very close to the Ghana border and speak the same language. Many Ivorians mistook them for Ghanaians and brutalized them too. It was as a result of this incident that a political decision was made to broadcast their language on television and radio. Moreover, since 1998, 52 FM regional radio stations called "Radio de Proximité" have broadcast in these languages in their respective areas. It is as though the way has been paved already for the implementation of MM. Under the proposal put forward here, each regional LWC language can be used for mother-tongue education in the area where it is spoken. It is conceivable that more than one language will need to be taught in a couple of regions because of a large influx of immigrants. For instance, now that the Baule constitute a large segment of the population in Bas-Sassandra county, their language should be taught there too, alongside Bété which is still the dominant regional language. For the same reason, Diula could be taught in the Savanes County alongside Senoufo, and in the Vallée du Bandama region alongside Dida. So, if MM is implemented across the country, the linguistic portfolio of a high school graduate will consist of 3±1 languages:

Local language ± (Regional language) + English + French

Some students will graduate from high school being able to speak and read proficiently in at least three languages. If their local language is the same as the regional language, they will have oral and written proficiency in their indigenous language, French, and English. However, if the local language is different from the regional LWC, the student will need to have oral proficiency in four languages: his/her local language, the regional language, French, and English. Being proficient in at least two indigenous languages is not a herculean task because bilingualism is already widespread.

5.5.1 The implementation of MM syllabus

The introduction of Ivorian languages in secondary schools in replacement of German and Spanish fits seamlessly into the present curriculum. No special curriculum change is needed since the indigenous languages will simply take the time slot already allotted to German and Spanish. Currently, about four hour per week is devoted to teaching these two languages in secondary school. The same ratio should be kept for the teaching of the 17 regional LWCs. Critics may complain that this ratio is not enough. However, there is no grounds for such criticism. If it was deemed sufficient for the teaching of German and Spanish, it is certainly sufficient to teach local languages. Parents of secondary students are more likely to throw their support behind this model if it is perceived as not usurping the socio-economic advantages linked to knowing French. German and Spanish are introduced in the curriculum in ninth grade. The same schedule should be kept for the teaching of local languages so as not to disrupt anything. Moreover, since German and Spanish are examinable academic subjects in the 10th and 13th grades, so should be the 17 regional LWCs taught in secondary school. Making them compulsory with the same coefficients will force students to take them seriously.

5.6 Personnel planning

The implementation of MM is likely to face three personnel-related challenges discussed by Kaplan and Baldauf Jr. (1997:130):

> No matter what the duration of instruction, a planning issue that needs to be addressed is the teacher cadre which will deliver the instruction. There is a need for a group of teachers trained in language pedagogy and reasonably fluent in the target language. There are essentially three problems in this context: the source of teachers, the training of teachers, and the reward for teachers.

Issues related to teacher training will be tackled in Chapter 8. For now, let's deal with the first two personnel issues. Teacher supply and teacher qualifications can be dealt with at the same time. Estimates based on student enrollment data (see 8.4.3) show that there were 8,262 German and Spanish language teachers in secondary schools in 2010. They can be retrained to teach one or two of the 17 regional LWCs. Such retraining of teachers is not unheard of. Kaplan and Baldauf Jr. (1997:130) show that it has happened in some parts of the world:

> It is clear that a polity undertaking to introduce a new language into the curriculum will be faced with a shortage of competent teachers, and there may be pressure to use untrained and limited competence teachers as a stop-gap measure. There are several different strategies which can be developed to augment the pool of qualified teachers – some short term, some long term.

For example, market forces may pressure language teachers trained in one language to retrain their teaching positions. This occurred in the People's Republic of China in the 1960s with the switch from Russian to English and is occurring in Australia in the 1990s as teachers of French and German are retraining to teach Japanese or Indonesian.

After the fall of the Berlin Wall, teachers of Russian in the former USSR countries were retrained to be teachers of English. In the short term, one has to deal with the issue of teachers who are not fully proficient in their new language. However, in the context of Côte d'Ivoire, this can be overcome very quickly. Since the teachers are being retrained to teach their own native language or a language in which they already have bilingual abilities, the switch over should not been too arduous. Retraining is only a temporary remedy. In the long term, the Institute of Applied Linguistics and the Department of Linguistics at the leading universities in the country will work cooperatively with secondary teacher training colleges to insure that teachers are fully bilingual and biliterate in the language(s) that they teach.

5.7 Potential obstacles

On June 10th 2004, I was invited by the Institute of Applied Linguistics of the Université de Cocody in Abidjan, Côte d'Ivoire, to present my game-theoretic approach to the faculty and to graduate students. The medium-size auditorium was packed and the audience was eager to learn how the Game theory could be applied to language planning. Though I had been presenting about the Game theory and language planning in linguistic conferences in the United States, it was the first time that I had expounded on it in front of a very knowledgeable home audience. It was the acid test of whether my approach would be laughed at as another "linguist of the diaspora" making claims that have no bearing on reality or whether my proposals would be taken seriously. Though I promised everybody that I would make the presentation available to the participants via e-mail, the participants took extensive notes and were extremely attentive. They were genuinely impressed by the novelty of the approach and agreed that MM was a consensus-building approach that could work. A print journalist later told me that a copy of my presentation made its way to a presidential advisor who promised to follow up after the elections. The participants found the data about the financial payoffs to be particularly compelling (see Chapter 8). Numerous questions were asked; one was expected, but two came as a surprise. The question that I expected had to do with the plight of the 43 or so languages that will not be taught in secondary school. The two that caught me off guard had to do with the diplomatic fallout if German is replaced and possible retaliation by the Spanish Catholic clergy if Spanish is no longer taught in secondary school.

Language planning involves making tough decisions. It is impossible to teach all the languages spoken in Côte d'Ivoire in secondary school. Given limited financial and human resources, it is unrealistic to think that all the languages spoken in any given country can be used in formal education. No highly multilingual country has ever succeeded in doing so. Consequently, it is not a burden that should be put on language planning in Côte d'Ivoire. The criteria for selecting the 17 regional LWCs are based on sound demographic, ethnolinguistic, and administrative mapping. As a result, the dominant language(s) of each one of the 19 administrative counties will be taught in school. Moreover, since all the languages in each county belong to the same family, bilingualism is already widespread. As a result, literacy skills can be transferred very easily from regional LWCs to minority languages in the same county. Additionally, in the language planning model under consideration, all 60 Ivorian languages will be planned. Seventeen will be taught in secondary school, but the remaining 43 or so will be taught in adult literacy classes (see Chapter 7).

The first unexpected question came from a person who was genuinely concerned that the German government would retaliate by curtailing or stopping its foreign aid to Côte d'Ivoire if their language is no longer taught in secondary school. I had not anticipated such a dire diplomatic consequence. I conceded that everything is possible in the shadowy business of international politics, but I also said that it would be extremely doubtful that the German government would condition development assistance to Côte d'Ivoire on the condition that it keep teaching its language in secondary school. The Japanese provide foreign aid to Côte d'Ivoire but Japanese is not taught in the country. I gave the example of foreign governments that provide foreign aid even though their national languages are not part of the Ivorian school curriculum. I also noted that postponing German until college will be more beneficial for the German government because they can send language teachers to provide good quality instruction instead of the watered-down instruction going on in secondary schools. I also added that if the unthinkable were to happen, and the Germans withdrew their development aid, that would not be such a great loss because the twenty-two million dollars that would be generated annually in textbook sales surpasses the foreign aid that Côte d'Ivoire receives from Germany (see Chapter 8). This remark drew thundering applause.

A follow-up question had to do with Spanish, and whether some private Catholic schools founded by Spanish missionaries would be in jeopardy of closing their doors if Spanish were no longer taught in secondary school. Some Catholic schools that are affiliated with Spanish missions have been waging a silent war against German by not including it in their schools. It is feared that if Spanish were replaced by indigenous Ivorian languages, Spanish mission agencies could withhold financial and human resources from these schools. The reality, however, is that in many Catholic schools, the overwhelming majority of the teachers of Spanish are Ivorian priests or laypeople. Moreover, many of the same schools are largely tuition-driven and count on government subsidies for paying a large portion of teachers' salaries. Because of this, if Spanish is replaced by Ivorian languages, whatever retaliatory action that is taken by Spanish missionaries will have an insignificant effect on the operation of these schools. Ivorian parents who can afford it send their children to private Catholic schools not because Spanish is taught there, but because of the excellent reputation of these schools. Priests and nuns enforce a very stringent moral and academic discipline that has served students well. It is quite unlikely that the Catholic clergy would abandon its mission of spiritual and moral formation just because Spanish is no longer taught in secondary school. These two questions were so pertinent that they forced me to include Germans and Spaniards as players in Table 5.4.

5.8 Summary

Ivorian leaders and the population at large have not been very enthusiastic about mother-tongue education for a number of valid reasons. First, unlike in other African countries, there is no indigenous language known by half of the population. Even the speakers of the largely mutually intelligible Anyi-Baule dialect continuum barely make up 30% of the overall population of the country. The lack of a local language that is spoken by the half of the population has been a stumbling block. The fear that ethnolinguistic pluralism is a liability for nation-building has led political leaders to vigorously promote French at the expense of local languages. However, the ever increasing encroachment of French on domains reserved to ancestral languages is causing citizens to look for a solution to their sociolinguistic dilemma. On the one hand, they want to keep French as the language of modernity, national unity, and upward socio-economic mobility. On the other, they want to maintain their indigenous languages and do not want to see them shrivel up and die. The expectations of the general population have not been met by academic linguists and language planners because the mother-tongue education models that have been used elsewhere do not seem to work in Côte d'Ivoire.

After reviewing the sociolinguistic make-up of the country and the various proposals for language of education models, it has been argued on the basis of the Predictioneer's Model that MM is the one that Ivorians can agree on because it matches fairly well with weighted mean score which reflects their preference. More will be said in Chapter 8 to highlight the economic payoffs linked to the implementation of this model. As for now, let us sum up the non-tangible benefits that would make its implementation desirable in the country. It can help alleviate the linguistic anxieties that Ivorian parents have felt for years with regard to their own role in shifting from their ancestral languages to French. It can give Ivorian children the chance not only to speak their ancestral languages, but also to learn to read and write them proficiently at school. Also, parents would feel at ease with implementing MM in secondary school knowing that doing so would not interfere with the continued proficiency in French that they want for their children. Given the fact that German and Spanish are not required for national security interests or for communication with any neighboring African country, parents would not be opposed to their removal from the secondary school curriculum. Last but not least, the implementation of MM will help valorize the linguistic and cultural heritage of the country.

Chapter 6
Game-theoretic assessment of language of education policies in African megacities

Introduction

Urbanization is the proverbial 800 pound gorilla in the room where applied linguists assemble. It can vitiate even the most cleverly designed plans to teach African languages at school. Yet language planners hardly pay attention to it. According to UN figures quoted by Jegede (1995:273), Africa is urbanizing faster than any other continent. A decade or so ago, it was estimated that by 2000, more than 40% of Africans would live in a megacity. Urban planning specialists tell us that African cities triple in size every 15 years. Given this maddening pace of urbanization, the language behavior in African megacities needs to be better understood. This chapter examines language trends in African megalopolises and proposes ways to implement MM in secondary schools in Francophone Africa. However, the chapter does more than that. It provides an overview of urbanization in Africa, addresses such complex issues as ethnolinguistic loyalty and occupation of urban space, urban social network analysis, and language shift and endangerment in megacities. If these ancillary issues are not discussed first, the application of the Repertoire Model and the proposals derived from it will not make a lot of sense. For the purposes of the analyses in the chapter, a three-way distinction is made between megacities with ethnolinguistic hegemony, megacities with ethnolinguistic dominance, and megacities with ethnolinguistic equilibrium. It is argued here that the model of language of education selected should correlate highly with this tripartite differentiation.

6.1 Urbanization in Africa: Historical overview

Reading the contemporary literature on urbanization in Africa, one is left with the uneasy impression that city-dwelling is a new phenomenon on the continent. Nothing could be further from the truth. The ancient cities of Memphis (northern Egypt), Thebes (southern Egypt), Carthage (northern Tunisia), Napata, Meroë, Naga, and Axum, (all in present-day Sudan and Ethiopia), and Timbuktu in (Mali), speak of a continent that was somewhat urbanized centuries before the 15th century. This section provides a brief overview of pre-colonial urbanization trends in Africa and their sociolinguistic impact.

West Africa boasted half a dozen cities, of which Timbuktu is undoubtedly the most famous. Historians tell us that it had as many as 60,000 inhabitants in its heyday, that is, around the 16th century. Next to glamorous Timbuktu, mention is also made of important trading centers such as Agades (in Niger), Gao (in Mali), Kano (in northern Nigeria), Jene (in Mali), and Kumbi Saleh, the capital city of the Ghana empire (south east Mauritania).[41] The latter was reportedly the largest city in Sub-Saharan Africa in the eleventh century. After the fall of Timbuktu, Skattum (2008:101) reports that Gao City in the Gao Kingdom became the biggest city in West Africa in the 15th century. Most of these cities were located in the desert-like areas of Africa known as the Sahel. These were the places where the trans-Saharan commerce thrived. Much of what is known about these Sahel cities comes from the travel accounts written by Arab merchants and missionaries. Since their interactions with West Africans did not extend further south, very little is known about cities in forested areas. However, travel logs by Portuguese explorers in the 15th century make mention of the influential city of Kumasi among the Ashanti (in present-day Ghana) and of other cities. Cole and De Blij (2007:61), for instance, state that Yoruba states had "urban centers of considerable size." It is virtually impossible to know how many people lived in those West African towns, but Lamphear and Falola (1995:85) conjectures that pre-colonial towns were fairly urbanized:

> In most states, the population was divided into two distinct strata. Each state had important urban centers which for their time were very large cities indeed. By as early as the eleventh century, the capital of Ghana had an estimated 30,000 inhabitants, while Gao, the largest city of Songhai, had nearly twice that many by a few centuries later. ... Such was the case, for example,

---

41 At independence, both the countries of Ghana and Mali took the names of ancient African kingdoms. This situation is likely to create confusion for the modern reader. Here are the approximate centuries for the two great kingdoms: Ghana, 8th to 11th centuries, its territory covered present-day Mauritania and Mali. The kingdom of Mali, 13th to 15th centuries, was very large. It encompassed territories from present-day Mauritania to Niger and as far south as portions of present-day Burkina Faso. From the ashes of Mali rose the kingdom of Gao which covered pretty much the same territory as Mali but extended further into parts of Nigeria (Skattum 2008:100–1).

with the Songhai cities of Jenne and Timbuktu, each of which boasted fine Islamic universities by the sixteenth century.

Southern Africa probably had some important cities, but so far the most well-known is the capital of the Great Zimbabwe Kingdom. Archaeological evidence described by O'Toole (2007:38) gives an impression of a highly urbanized city:

> Great Zimbabwe (in the modern country of the same name), the center of extensive and complex archaeological remains, dates back at least 800 years. The impressive stone ruins called Zimbabwe (Great House) were built by people ancestral to modern-day Shona speakers. This complex probably served as a capital for an empire that stretched from the Zambezi to the Limpopo. ... The organization of the necessary labor to build these structures suggests a sophisticated and complex social, economic, and political organization. Oral histories and firsthand descriptions of early Portuguese visitors to the area also confirm the existence of a strong centralized political system.

The eastern seashore of the continent also boasted three important cities: Dar-es-Salaam, Mombasa and Zanzibar, which were thriving commercial hubs. These cities were established by Arab slave traders and their Bantu-speaking intermediaries.

Urbanization in northeastern Africa has more historical depth than in any other area of the continent. First, Napata, the first capital city of the Kushite Empire, was known throughout the ancient world.[42] Secondly, bellicose pressures from enemies near and far forced Kushite authorities to transfer their first capital to a city further south and east known as Meroë. On the ashes of the kingdom of Kush rose the powerful kingdom of Aksum whose capital city bore the same name. Around 100 A.D. Ge'ez became one of the most important ancient languages in the region. As noted by Appleyard and Orwin (2008:270), Ge'ez did not spread because of urbanization, but rather because it was the language of the church. It retained its prestigious role as the sole medium of the Christian empire. Cole and De Blij (2007:520) give us a glimpse of the glory of its capital city:

> Aksum was located against the northern extremity of the Ethiopian massif and extended to the Red Sea coasts. Nowhere else in the region was there the organization, architecture, art, literature, or prosperity of this kingdom.

---

42 Napata is located near the present-day cities of Khartoum and Abtara in Sudan.

The only area of Africa where scholars have not found evidence of significant signs of urbanization is in central Africa. As of now, it is unclear as to why big cities have not been found in this area.

Anachronism, that is, misinterpreting historical events in the light of contemporary realities, is a constant danger in this kind of overview. We need to place a big caveat here lest we are misled into thinking that the cities mentioned are comparable to present-day Sub-Saharan cities such as Abidjan (Côte d'Ivoire), Accra (Ghana), Addis Ababa (Ethiopia), Dakar (Senegal), Dar-es-Salaam (Tanzania), Ibadan (Nigeria), Johannesburg (South Africa), Kinshasa (Congo, DRC), Lagos (Nigeria), or Nairobi (Kenya). In fact, Gordon (2007:207) reminds us that "Sub-Saharan African cities never achieved the great size of the major industrial cities of Europe." Consequently, the expected sociolinguistic impacts that those ancient cities could have had must be kept within proportions. It is my contention that pre-colonial urbanization did not help spread the urban languages spoken in those cities. For instance, even though the Soninke language was spoken in the largest city in Sub-Saharan Africa in the 11th century, it did not spread to all corners of the Mali empire. Similarly, Songhai, the language of the capital city of Gao, did not spread to other parts of the Gao empire in spite of it being an important urban language. Virtually all the cases of language spread in pre-colonial Africa could be accounted for either by the agencies of trade, religion, and/or military conquest. This is certainly the case for the spread of Bambara, Hausa, or Swahili, to mention only three. Thus, we conclude this section by noting that pre-colonial urbanization did not play any significant role in language spread, nor did it bring about language shift or endangerment.

6.2 Colonial and post-colonial urbanization

Urbanization as we know it started timidly between the late 19th century and the third decade of the 20th century. It accelerated in the 1960s, crescendoed in the 1980s, and has been going strong ever since. Burgeoning and vibrant contemporary African cities are by and large the product of European colonization. Since independence, the growth rate of African cities has exploded. Credible sources estimate that African megacities triple their sizes every 15 years. The UN estimates that 40% of Africans resided in an urban area by the end of 2003 (Cole and De Blij 2007:136–7). This figure was 25% in 1975, compared with 19% in 1960, and only 15% in 1950. The population of city dwellers is expected to be 51% by 2030. Gordon (2007:204) observe that "Lagos is growing so fast that by 2015 it will be the third largest city in the world, with a population of over 23 million

6.2 Colonial and post-colonial urbanization

people." Tibaijuka (2004:2–3) contrasts the urban population surge with the overall world population growth as follows:

> By 2030 Africa will no longer be a rural continent as by then 51% of its people will be living in urban areas. In short, irrespective of where we live, our future is urban, and access to urban space will define the quality of that future. ... In terms of numbers, currently about 300 million Africans live in urban settlements. This figure is expected to reach about 500 million by 2015. The UN estimates that in the next 25 years, 400 million people will be added to the African urban population, putting tremendous pressure on cities and towns. ... In 1960, Johannesburg was the only city in Sub-Saharan Africa with a population exceeding 1 million, in 1970 there were four, Cape Town, Johannesburg, Kinshasa and Lagos. By the late 1980s, the list included Abidjan, Accra, Addis Ababa, Dakar, Dar-es-Salaam, Durban, East Rand, Harare, Ibadan, Khartoum, Luanda and Nairobi. By 2010, it is estimated that there will be at least 33 cities of more than 1 million inhabitants.

The tables below provide us with numerical evidence of the post-colonial explosion of population growth in urban Africa.[43] Chaudenson (2008:180) cautions that figures about Africa must always be taken with a grain of salt because census-taking is infrequent and/or unreliable. This means that the number of inhabitants could be considerably more than the actual figures found in various publications.

> Indeed, if individual elements of African development were superimposed on the map as though they were a series of transparencies, a growing and intensifying geographical pattern of inequality would be evident. This series of maps would highlight several prominent 'development islands' surrounded by large "sea" of underdevelopment. ... Areas of major commercial production account for only about 4 percent of the total area of Africa, yet they include nearly all the urban population and more than three-quarter of the value of African products sold on world markets. Through commercial linkages and migration streams, these 'islands' have a profound influence on local economies, social institutions, and cultures in even the most rural areas. Thus, although relatively few in number, the major areas of urban concentration and commercial production play an important role in articulating the overall pattern of African development. This phenomenon has remained relatively unchanged over the past eighty years, and the dominance of these centers in economic and political terms has been accelerating.

---

43 Retrieved from http://esa.un.org/unpd/wup/index.htm, on February 1, 2010.

Table 6.1. Urbanization Rates

No.	Megacities	Country	1960s	2000s	2010	2025[1]
1.	Abidjan	Ivory Coast	1,920,000	3,032,000	4,125,000	6,321,000
2.	Addis Ababa	Ethiopia	519	2,376,000	2,930,000	4,757,000
3.	Accra	Ghana	393	1,674,000	2,342,000	3,497,000
4.	Antananarivo	Madagascar	252	1,361,000	1,879,000	3,148,000
5.	Bamako	Mali	130	910	1,699,000	2,971,000
6.	Brazzaville	Congo	124	986	1,323,000	1,878,000
7.	Conakry	Guinea	112	1,219,000	1,653,000	2,906,000
8.	Cotonou	Benin	73	642	844	1,445,000
9.	Dakar	Senegal	353	2,029,000	2,863,000	4,338,000
10.	Dar es Salaam	Tanzania	162	2,116,000	4,153,000	6,202,000
11.	Douala	Cameroon	153	1,433,000	2,125,000	3,131,000
12.	Freetown	Sierra Leone	119	688	1,046,000	1,420,000
13.	Harare	Zimbabwe	248	1,379,000	1,632,000	2,467,000
14.	Ibadan	Nigeria	570	2,236,000	2,837,000	4,237,000
15.	Johannesburg	South Africa	1,147,000	2,732,000	3,670,000	4,127,000
16.	Khartoum	Sudan	347	3,949,000	5,172,000	7,953,000
17.	Kigali	Rwanda	34	497	939	1,690,000
18.	Lagos	Nigeria	762	7,233,000	10,578,000	15,810,000
19.	Lilongwe	Malawi	8	493	865	1,784,000

(Continued)

6.2 Colonial and post-colonial urbanization

Table 6.1. Urbanization Rates (Cont.)

No.	Megacities	Country	1960s	2000s	2010	2025[1]
20.	Lomé	Togo	95	1,020,000	1,667,000	2,763,000
21.	Luanda	Angola	219	2,591,000	4,772,000	8,077,000
22.	Lusaka	Zambia	91	1,073,000	1,451,000	2,267,000
23.	Kampala	Uganda	137	1,097,000	1,598,000	3,189,000
24.	Kinshasa	Congo, DRC	443	5,611,000	8,754,000	15,041,000
25.	Mogadishu	Somalia	94	1,201,000	1,500,000	2,588,000
26.	Maputo	Mozambique	181	1,096,000	1,655,000	2,722,000
27.	Monrovia	Liberia	75	836	827	932
28.	Nairobi	Kenya	293	2,230,000	3,523,000	6,246,000
29.	Niamey	Niger	58	680	1,048,000	2,105,000
30.	N'Djamena	Chad	71	647	829	1,445,000
31.	Ouagadougou	Burkina Faso	59	921	1,908,000	4,332,000
32.	Port Elizabeth	South Africa	289	958	1,068,000	1,222,000
33.	Pretoria	South Africa	419	1,084,000	1,514,000	1,637,000
34.	Vereeniging	South Africa	187	897	1,1143,000	1,313,000
35.	Yamoussoukro	Côte d'Ivoire	4	348	885	1,797,000
36.	Yaounde	Cameroon	75	1,192,000	1,801,000	2,664,000

Note:
1 Retrieved from www.wikipedia.com, on February 1, 2010.
McNulty (1995:13, 21) has coined the phrase "development island" to refer to the role that megacities in Table 6.1 play in relation to other localities on the continent.

6.3 Rationale of the unprecedented urban growth

Before drawing the sociolinguistic consequences of this urban explosion and its likely impact on formulating language of education policies, we must first try to understand why African megacities are growing and will continue to grow at such a maddening pace. Some have proposed that the surge in urban population is inextricably tied to the concept of development island and to the development model pursued by African countries since independence. Nearly all the African cities that qualify as 'development islands' were created during the colonial era. Moreover, in the decades of the 1970s and 1980s, the prevailing development models were primarily concerned with economic growth, industrial output, exports, imports, GDPs (Gross Development Product), and GNPs (Gross National Product). It was then believed that cities were the engines that would pull Africa towards rapid development. Experts had the European and the North American models as their guide. Indeed, the figures provided by Tibaijuka (2008:16) show convincingly that megacities lead the way in economic growth:

> In terms of contribution to economic output, cities drive national economies in the industrialized countries. For example, in the USA, cities outpace states and even nations in economic output. If treated as nations, US metropolitan areas in 2000 would comprise 47 of the world's largest economies. The combined gross economic output of the top ten metropolitan areas in the USA in 2000 was $2.43 trillion. This is an amount greater than the combined economic output of 31 states in the USA. If the 5 largest metropolitan areas in the USA (New York, Los Angeles, Chicago, Boston and Philadelphia) were treated as a single country, it would rank as the fourth largest economy in the world.

She then goes on to show that African cities lead the economic development of the continent, albeit modestly:

> Already, and in spite of all the difficulties, urban areas in Africa can be credited with producing 60 percent of the GDP. If managed properly, African cities and towns could provide the critical link between the development of rural areas and the larger global economy. ... A city like Abidjan with an estimated population of 3.3 million, which is 40 percent of the total population of the country, accounts for 33 percent of national GDP. Nairobi, with a population of about 2.6 million, has only 5.2 percent of the national population, but accounts for 20.1 percent of the GDP.

The dominant economic role that African megacities play in the development of the continent has earned them the sobriquet of *"development islands."*

This is an appropriate label because it captures very well the importance of African megacities. They are indeed development islands because they enjoy the highest standards of living, the best infrastructures, the best schools, the best hospitals, the best access to telecommunication, the best of everything that the country has to offer in terms of modernity. As a result, they act like magnets and draw to them millions of people every year who are in search of a better future. Blommaert's (2008:216-7) description of Dar es Salaam is representative of all such cities in Sub-Saharan Africa:

> Tanzania is an overwhelmingly rural country with one big urban center: Dar es Salaam. The official state capital is Dodoma, a small city in the geographical center of the country, but all major services are concentrated in Dar es Salaam: the harbor, the international airport, Parliament, ministries, embassies, the University, the most prestigious schools, headquarters of businesses and international organizations, big international hotels, and so forth. Dar es Salaam is, as noted earlier, the most prestigious place in Tanzania.

6.4 Unemployment, underemployment and urbanization

All the megacities in Sub-Saharan Africa promise more than they can deliver. The prospects of finding relatively well-paying jobs in megacities are better than staying in rural or second-tiered towns. DeLancey (2007:138, 219, 222) writes that "millions see migration to the cities as the best hope they have for a better life. Indeed, cities generally offer their inhabitants better incomes, better services, better nutrition, and less poverty than the places they leave behind. Nonetheless, Africa is more urban than it should be based on its current level of economic development." Since the development crisis of the mid-1980s, labor intensive projects that normally employ scores of people are hard to come by. Yet, rural depopulation has continued unabated. Urbanization is seen by many as the engine that drives the development process. But Cheru (2005:2) contends that it has failed to do so in Sub-Saharan Africa:

> Urbanization without development (or limited development) occurs when overall national economic growth and development are inadequate to meet the needs of a growing population. This type of urbanization takes place in Sub-Saharan Africa, low-income Asia and Central America. The key characteristics of *urbanization without development* are: weak agricultural sector; poor national economic performance; lack of national policy that integrates economic and spatial planning; relative absence of intermediate cities and market towns; over migration leading to growth of mega-cities

with poor economic bases and poor municipal capacity to provide minimum basic services.

Urbanization has not produced the expected development dividends because of the weak rate of industrialization. DeLancey (2007:138) notes that the industrial output of Africa's development islands was only 13% in 2003. Stryker and Ndegwa (1995:380) even use the phrase "widespread deindustrialization" to describe what has happened to the industrial base of African countries for the last three decades. The flow of job seekers has not stopped even though there are fewer and fewer factories to hire unskilled workers. Consequently, according to Cheru, Africa is witnessing an instance of "urbanization without development." Excessive rural exodus combined with unemployment or underemployment has exacerbated urban poverty. A UN report quoted by Tibaijuka (2004:9) underscores this point very vividly:

> In 2001, it was estimated that, in Sub-Saharan Africa, in total, about 166 million people were living in slums. In terms of density alone, one can infer the extent of slum conditions. In Nairobi, about 60 percent of the population lives on 5 percent of the land. For example, in Kibera, the largest contiguous area of slum settlements, about 750,000 to a million inhabitants live on less than 225 hectares of land. This makes Kibera the largest most crowded and appalling slum settlement in Africa (UN 2004).

Two aspects in the report need to be underscored and commented on because they are relevant to language planning in megacities. First, the sheer number of people in slums is astounding. Of the 300 million people in megacities, more than 50% lived in slums. These are generally the unemployed, the underemployed, or street vendors who operate in the informal sector of the economy. Their linguistic habits are crucially relevant to language planning. Secondly, megacity slums are overcrowded spaces with a very high population density per square mile. This piece of information too is relevant because it will help us understand how ethnolinguistic social networks operate in a multilingual megalopolis. But first, let's get acquainted with the phrase "*ethnolinguistic loyalty*," how it is manifested in megacities, and how it might inform citywide language of education policies.

6.5 Assessing ethnolinguistic loyalty

Ethnolinguistic vitality and ethnolinguistic loyalty are two terms that may be construed as synonymous. The former has been widely used in the literature but, to the best of my knowledge, the latter has not. However, I contend here that the two terms should be interpreted as having overlapping semantic fields but not entirely synonymous. Ryan et al. (1982:4–5) have identified status, demographic strength, and institutional support as indispensable ingredients of ethnolinguistic vitality. Must all three components be present at once for a group to be ethnolinguistically vital? If two out the three, or if one out of the three apply but the others do not, is the group still ethnolinguistically vital? If all three components must apply at once, then I am afraid no language in Côte d'Ivoire, and indeed no language in francophone Africa, can be said to be ethnolinguistically vital. Even though many languages have appreciable demographic strength, they have neither legal status nor institutional support. Consequently, I find the application of the concept of ethnolinguistic vitality problematic in describing African languages in Sub-Saharan francophone Africa. For this reason, I prefer the concept of ethnolinguistic loyalty. This term does require that the group be large, nor does it require status or institutional support as indispensable ingredients. Ethnolinguistic loyalty is defined simply on a gradable scale which ranges from high to low. We will be concerned here only with the polar extremes on the scale, namely high ethnolinguistic loyalty and low ethnolinguistic loyalty. Speakers of a language are said to have a high level of loyalty to their language if they take pride in it and make it the *sine qua nom* condition for group membership. Crystal (2000:119–22) provides descriptions that can be seen as characteristic of high and low ethnolinguistic loyalties. The former is described as follows:

> The first position asserts that there is a considerable identity between language and the culture of which it is a part. Its supporters accept the arguments that language expresses their identities and their history, and make this the chief consideration. In their view, so much of their culture is expressed in language and it is not possible to be a member of their community if one does not speak its language.

The linguistic literature is replete with the example of the Kurds as the perfect illustration of high ethnolinguistic loyalty. They are willing to endure persecution in order to preserve their culture and their language. Threats of bodily harm, political isolation, or imprisonment have not diminished their zeal to maintain their language. The Greeks, the Jews, the French, the Anyi of Côte d'Ivoire (McWhorter 2003:78), the Mayan, (Grinevald 2007:67), the Malinche of Central Mexico, (Wardhaugh 2010:6–7, 263, 349), the Koreans, (Myers-Scotton 2008:125), the Pulaar of Senegal (McLaughlin 2008:157–8), the Congolese (Bokamba 2008:117), to mention only a few, have all been described as having high ethnolinguistic loyalty to their language. As a result, these peoples are willing to go to great lengths to maintain and protect their language. The example of Koreans and their attitude toward their language is very telling. They are eager and enthusiastic to acquire English as a second language. However, they have a great loyalty towards their language. According to Meyers-Scotton (2006:125–5) they appear to be the only immigrant group in the United States who has avoided "the third generation curse," a process of language loss that afflicts all immigrant communities by the third generation. Throughout Sub-Saharan Africa, there are groups with high ethnolinguistic loyalty but not much has been written about them. Take the Fon of Benin as an example. Their language is mutually intelligible with Gun. However, Fon Christians have refused for almost 100 years to use the Gun Scriptures for worship. After decades of prodding, the Bible Society of Benin relented to make Scriptures available to the Fon in their own language. When a group has a high ethnolinguistic loyalty, its language survives and thrives against all odds. Language planners must be cognizant of the high ethnolinguistic loyalty when formulating language of education policies for megacities.

Low ethnolinguistic loyalty is often associated with a willingness towards language shift because the speakers of the language appear to have no or only a weak attachment to their language. Crystal (2000:119–22) describes it as follows:

> The second position asserts that there is only a limited identity between language and culture. Its supporters see far more elements in culture than language. ... Indeed, not all cultures, according to some reports, seem to have the same regard for language as a potent symbol of ethnic identity. Matthias Brenzinger and his colleagues have reported some instances from Africa. In one paper, they describe the behavior of several Seereer men from Senegal who had replaced their language with Wolof.

In addition to the second hand report about the Seereer, Crystal mentions examples from Scottish Gaelic, Welsh, and Tlingit to exemplify what low ethnolinguistic loyalty can do to a language. McLaughlin (2008:160) provides us with more insight about the Seereer and supplies an important caveat:

> The Seereer, including speakers of Seereer-Siin and Cangin languages, have been the closest neighbors of the Wolof for centuries and have long spoken Wolof. ... Seerer speakers do not hold the same, often militant, prejudices against Wolof, although they are generally proud of their various languages. Possibly because they have been bilingual in various Seereer languages and

Wolof for many centuries, compounded by the fact that they do not form a coherent linguistic group, the Seereer's concept of ethnic identity is not as centrality linked to language as it is for Haalpulaar. ... Notwithstanding the high rates of bilingualism in Seereer and Wolof, the Seereer languages in rural communities appear to be quite healthy.

McLaughlin invokes a long history of bilingualism and a lack of linguistic cohesiveness as possible explanations for why the Seereer have a rather low loyalty to their language. The crucial question that language planners have to address in the context of language of education policy in megacities is the following: What are the levels of ethnolinguistic loyalty of the various groups in the city? One need not be a rocket scientist to find an answer to this question if one is a citizen or a long term resident of the country where language planning is being considered. Of course, the situation is entirely different for an expatriate linguist who might need to resort to survey instruments to understand the attitudes of the various ethnic groups in the country. If an expatriate linguist is doing the research that will lead to language planning decisions, care should be taken so that survey questions uncover the levels of ethnolinguistic loyalty for each of the people groups in the country, and also the attitude that groups have against each other. In general, people's attitudes towards their own language can very easily reveal their level of ethnolinguistic loyalty. Blench (2007:140–162), Connell (2007:163–178), and Brenzinger (2007:179–204) describe some African languages with fairly strong ethnolinguistic loyalties. The second question that one has to answer is the following. Can ethnolinguistic loyalty be an obstacle for the planned course of action? The answer to this question is a resounding yes. This is the reason why I'm recommending MM as the preferred approach to urban language of education planning. It can help find consensual solutions for cases where groups with strong ethnolinguistic loyalty threaten to derail the whole language planning enterprise.

6.6 The ethnolinguistic profile of African megacities

Gordon (2007:219) makes a useful distinction between megacities and "urban villages." She defines the latter as "rural villages that have grown into cities of 200,000 to 400,000, but lack even the most basic services." These urban villages are usually ethnolinguistically homogeneous. They hardly attract migrants because they lack the economic infrastructures found in cosmopolitan metropolises. The secondary cities in many countries are in fact "urban villages." For instance, Côte d'Ivoire has 70 towns, but only Abidjan is truly a megacity. Bouaké, the second largest city of 1.5 million people, is in some respects an urban village. The population consists mainly of two leading ethnic groups: the Baule and the Diula. Yamoussoukro, the political capital, is definitely an urban village in spite of its magnificent infrastructures because it is mostly a Baule town. Language of education policies for urban villages are similar to regional language planning. The solution proposed in Chapter 5 for Côte d'Ivoire holds for urban villages as well. It was proposed that the dominant language of each county be used in secondary school to replace German and Spanish. Similarly, urban villages should teach the dominant language of that town in secondary school.

As for the true megacities of Africa, a three-way ethnolinguistic distinction must be made between them. Some megacities are *ethnolinguistically homogeneous*. Only five megacities in Sub-Saharan African meet this criterion. In Addis Ababa, Ethiopia, Amharic is the dominant language of the city. In Bujumbura, Burundi, the dominant language is Kirundi. Somali is the dominant language spoken in Mogadishu, Somalia. The inhabitants of Kigali, Rwanda, speak Kinyarwanda. Dialectal variations aside, the inhabitants of these cities use the languages mentioned above to communicate with each other. The second defining characteristic of some megacities in Africa is ethnolinguistic dominance. This refers to metropolises in which an indigenous African language is spoken by 50% or more of the urban population. The megacities that fall into this category are Kinshasa with Lingala, Nairobi and Dar-es-Salaam with Swahili, Dakar with Wolof, Bangui with Sango, Ouagadougou with More, Bamako with Bambara, Accra with Akan, Ibadan with Yoruba, Cape Town with IsiXhosa, and Johannesburg IziZulu (Vigouroux 2008:239–240), to mention only a few. The last defining feature of some megacities is ethnolinguistic equilibrium, that is, a megacity where no indigenous African language is spoken by the majority of the urban population. Only a handful of African megacities fall into this category. It goes without saying that the choice of the language to be used for mother-tongue education is easy for megacities with ethnolinguistic homogeneity, somewhat easy for megacities with ethnolinguistic dominance, and very challenging for cosmopolitan areas with ethnolinguistic equilibrium.

6.7 The ethnolinguistic occupation of urban spaces

Another factor that is crucially relevant in fashioning a language of education policy in an African megacity is the settlement patterns of urban space. Most, if not all, African megacities can be divided into four geographical spheres. The first is what is affectionately called *"Old Town."* This is generally the town or village occupied by the original dwellers before the city began growing. Next is the city center or downtown where offices and tall and modern buildings are found. Usually after work hours the city center is quite deserted except for some expatriates who live in expensive high rise apartment complexes. Surrounding the city center are several suburbs. In some cases, the suburbs can be classified according to the socio-economic fortunes of the people who live in them. Working class suburbs usually butt up against the slums and shantytowns of African megacities where the unemployed and the underemployed live. The living conditions in the shantytowns were described in 6.4. Middle class and upper middle class people generally live further away from the city center because they do not depend on taxis and busses to get to work. Though this four-sphere description of African megacities is often the case, there may be cities where this does not hold true. Lomé (Togo) is such a city where there is not really a shantytown. Apart from La Caisse, a residential area built for French expatriate workers, it is not unusual to see a very impressive house next to a shack.

It has been noted that the occupation of urban space follows two ethnolinguistic tendencies. Cole and De Blij (2007:144) report that migrants "typically cluster together in the same neighborhoods for mutual support." This has been described as evidence for the *re-ethnicization* of African megacities.[44] Myers-Scotton (2006:50) gives the example of Bamako, the capital city of Mali, which has "a more traditional pattern of households, with a separate quarter for each major ethnic group, with the quarter often associated with distinct activities such as tailoring or metal work." Mazrui (2008:198) suggests a similar pattern for Mombassa, Kenya's oldest town, which is also its second largest city. Bokamba (2008:113) mentions ethnic enclaves in Mbandaka, the largest city of the Equateur Province in the Democratic Republic of Congo. In Lomé (Togo), the Bé quarter, from Hotel de la Paix to Hotel Sarakawa, is the bastion of the Mina, whereas the Adewi quarter near the University du Bénin is where a large segment of the Kabyes live. It must be emphasized that this is only a tendency. Settlement patterns do not in any way suggest that there is housing segregation in Sub-Saharan Africa. Ethnic enclaves are not off limits to people from other ethnic groups. Indeed, ethnic mingling is found all over Lomé and in many

---

44 Laitin (1992:28) originally used the terms "detribalization" and "retribalization." However, given the negative connotation that the root "tribe" has received, I have coined the words "de-ethninicization" and "re-ethnicization."

African magacities. Nevertheless, Laitin (1992:28) is right in stating that "ethnic ties in some African cities have grown stronger."

The second important tendency in the occupation of urban space is *de-ethnicization*. Myers-Scotton (2006:50) points out rightly that "there are large numbers of speakers of different languages who are mingled together, but largely only in the urban areas." This detribalization tendency is seen everywhere, both in suburbs or in slums. McLaughlin (2008:156) describes Dakar (Senegal) as a place that epitomizes detribalization. The inhabitants of Dakar claim to have forged an "urban ethnic group" despite the multilingual character of the city. Just like "retribalization," "detribalization" does not in any way suggest that the people have lost their ethnic identities, or that Dakar no longer has ethnic neighborhoods. McLaughlin (2008:157) states explicitly that "similar niches are to be found in ethno-linguistic neighborhoods in Dakar, but this environment is unstable because the neighborhoods are never completely homogeneous and are susceptible to constant change in their ethno-linguistic makeup."

Everything being equal, language of education planning will be made easier to the extent that retribalization of urban space is real. However, my experience with many West African cities tells me that this is not the case. The construction of secondary schools in megacities does not follow any ethnolinguistic rationale. Thus, an ethnic group may be dominant in one specific area, but the secondary schools are found elsewhere in the city. So, whether the megacity is re-ethnicized or de-ethnicized, the challenge of formulating a workable language of education policy remains the same, especially for cities where ethnolinguistic equilibrium exists. However, the challenge is less formidable for megacities with ethnolinguistic dominance. Following McLaughlin's description of the attitudes of the inhabitants of Dakar, it can be hypothesized that formulating a language of education policy for Dakar would be fairly easy because of the existence of a common "urban identity." However, I suspect that even in Dakar, the Haalpulaar would be reticent to have Wolof be the only language of instruction in city schools if the MM were to be applied there.

6.8 Urbanization and social network analysis

It appears from the ethnolinguistic sketches given above that constructs such as ethnolinguistic loyalty, de-ethninicization, re-ethnicization, ethnolinguistic homogeneity, ethnolinguistic dominance, and ethnolinguistic equilibrium all play a vital role as one considers which indigenous language(s) to use in megacity schools. However, even before discussing specific recommendations, let us make some general observations regarding the role of urbanization in language spread, language shift, language maintenance, and language endangerment. This quick overview will help us avoid unwarranted generalizations and guide us towards solutions that are in harmony with the ethnolinguistic profile of each megacity.

Sociolinguistics annals are replete with examples of how dominant megacity languages have swallowed up indigenous languages in the periphery. The process is slow but relentless, and the outcome unmistakably leads to language shift. Bloomfield (1933:477) explains how this process applied in Europe in the Middle Ages:

> The important historical process in this leveling is the growth of central speech-forms that spread over wider and wider areas. Suppose, for instance, that in a locally differentiated area, some one town, thanks to the personalities that live in it or thanks to a favorable topographic situation, becomes the seat of recurrent religious rites or political gatherings or markets. The inhabitants of the villages round about now resort at intervals to the central town. On these visits they learn to avoid the strikingly divergent forms of their domestic speech, replacing them by forms that do not call forth misunderstanding or mockery. These favored speech-forms will be such as are current in all or most of the local groups; if no one form is predominant, the choice will fall usually upon the form that is used in the central town. ... At second, third, and later hands, these locutions may pass to still more remote persons and places. The central town becomes a speech-center whose forms of speech, when there is not too much weight against them, become the 'better' forms for a whole area of the surrounding country. As commerce and social organization improve, this process repeats itself on a larger scale. Each center is imitated over a certain area.

Koffi (1997:81) has hypothesized based on the Wave Theory that the spread of Aramaic during the Neo-Babylonian era followed a similar pattern. Given that the Wave Theory is centered on "how people are affected by change" (Wardhaugh 2010:222), it can offer insights as to what is likely to happen to indigenous languages in megacities and those in remote areas. First, we need to pay close attention to how much time is needed for the process to be completed. Laitin (1992:29) states that "smaller minorities required from one hundred years to four hundred years to assimilate linguistically."

Just as urbanization facilitates language spread, it has also become abundantly clear since the last decades of the twentieth century that urbanization is also responsible for language endangerment. McWhorter (2003:273) states categorically that "urbanization is lethal to language diversity." Language endangerment specialists have singled out urbanization as a villain and frequently, loudly and stridently sound the alarm about the negative linguistic consequences of urbanization. Though Myers-Scotton (2006:377) mocks their gloomy forecast, she readily admits that "as individuals and households move to the cities, they lose their languages and switch to dominant speech-systems." McLaughlin (2008:144) has documented this occurrence in Dakar and states that "urbanization is the greatest threat to minority languages in Senegal because it often precipitates generational language (or dialect) shift to urban Wolof." This urban Wolof is, according to her, a hybridized language that borrows and adapts words from French, and other Senegalese languages. It is a lingua franca of sorts, as explained by Laitin (1992:115), "Massive urbanization and government failure to meet the social needs of the people have created an environment conducive to the rapid growth of lingua francas that are far from the standard languages recorded by missionaries." How can the interplay between ethnolinguistic loyalty, de-ethnicization, re-ethnicization, and urbanization inform policy decisions for megacity schools?

6.9 Social network analysis in megacities

The answer to the preceding question calls for an overview and an analysis of social networking patterns in African megacities. Social network analysis is an emergent sub-branch of sociolinguistics that examines how an individual in any given society interacts with others. Applying its concepts to African megacities can help us make language of education policy recommendations that are based on observable linguistic behaviors of city dwellers. Researchers in this field of inquiry answer the following set of questions before understanding patterns of interactions:

1. How frequently do the individuals in the social network interact with each other?
2. How long do the individuals in the social network interact with each other?
3. How intensive is the social network under consideration?
4. How extensive is the social network under consideration?
5. How simplex is the social network?
6. How multiplex is the social network?

The answer to the first two questions has to do with the frequency of contacts between and among the individuals in the network. It quantifies the number of times and the length of time an individual A interacts with individuals B, C, D, and E, and vice versa. The duration of interaction is calculated in minutes per day. In any given network, the relationship between two individuals tends to be more intensive than with others in the same network.

The relationship between A and B is said to be more intensive than the relationship between A and C if and only if A spends more time with B than with C. An extensive network has to do with the number of people involved in a network and the degree to which all the people in the network interact with each other. So, A is involved in an extensive network with B, C, D, and E to the extent that all the individuals know each other. Researchers sometimes use the term "strong" to describe networks that are intensive. An extensive network is also defined as a "dense" network. "You are said to be involved in a dense network if the people you interact with also know and interact with one another" (Wardhaugh 2010:130). If the individuals in a network do not all know each other, the network is said to be loose. This answers questions 3 and 4.

Questions 5 and 6 address the issues of what the individuals do together when they interact. A network is defined as simplex if the people in the network interact with each other in well-defined and predictable activities: church, work, sport, etc. but do not interact with each other outside of these events. If, however, the people in the social network interact with each other in many other venues and events, their network is said to be multiplex. For instance, if A and B play tennis together and attend church services together and are colleagues, it is said that the social network in which A and B find themselves is strong and multiplex. However, if A and B only meet once a week to play tennis after work, their network is weak and simplex. Wardhaugh (2010:130–1) concludes his discussion of social network analysis by making the following correlations:

> People who go to school together, marry each other's siblings, and work and play together participate in dense and multiplex networks. In England these are said to be found at the extremes of the social-class structure. Such networks indicate strong social cohesion, produce feelings of solidarity, and encourage individuals to identify with others within the network. On the other hand, middle-class networks are likely to be loose and simplex, therefore, social cohesion is reduced and there are weaker feelings of solidarity and identity.

I have not yet seen a social network analysis of the inhabitants of any city in Africa. To the best of my knowledge, the work that comes closest to network analysis is *The Languages of Urban Africa*. The volume is not a social network book but rather addresses the distribution of languages in urban space. Consequently, a conclusion such as the one reached by Wardhaugh about network analysis in England is hard to come by for African megacities. However, the concepts used in tandem with those that we have already examined can help provide some general guidelines about social network and linguistic behaviors in African megacities.

African development island cities are multilingual and cosmopolitan. Porto-Novo, the legislative capital of Bénin, had 215,000 inhabitants in 2000. Yet, according to Adeniran (2009:132, 134) there are 11 languages spoken in the city. In bigger agglomerations, such as Abidjan, Accra, Addis Ababa, Dakar, Johannesburg, Kinshasa, Lagos, and Nairobi, one expects to find that all the indigenous languages spoken in the country are represented in the megacity. Moreover, there may be several other non-indigenous languages spoken in a metropolis because of immigration. This notwithstanding, McLaughlin (2009:6) is of the opinion that many African megacities are ethnically-zoned, that is, "African cities are vast heterogeneous and heteroglossic spaces that are frequently made up of smaller, more coherent neighborhoods." If this is true, then this is a perfect example of the re-ethnicization of the urban space. The people who live in such areas have social networks that can be described as dense, strong, and multiplex. To the extent that such ethnic networks exist, McLaughlin (2009:6) anticipates that they would have important sociolinguistic consequences:

> The existence of such neighborhoods has important consequences for how languages fare in the city. Although urban the lingua franca may be used in broader urban networks, the languages of ethnic minorities may be robustly maintained if such neighborhoods are stable.

Adeniran (2009:132) describes Porto Novo as a city without ethnic enclaves: "residence within the city is mixed as no quarter or part of it is reserved for any particular ethnic group." In this case, Porto Novo is an example of a geographically de-ethnicized city. However, this does not entail a complete de-ethnicization of the social network of the Porto Novians. Re-ethnicization is alive and well in many African cities. People from the same village or region meet for a variety of reasons. They get together at weddings, at birthdays, at funerals, at cultural ceremonies, and for many other social events where ethnic solidarity is required. Moreover, various humanitarian associations are informally created for the "development" of the native village or region. As a result, even while living in a megacity, many city dwellers keep abreast of village and regional news through their ethnolinguistically homogeneous social networks. The social networks in which these people participate is dense, loose, and simplex. The network is dense because all the participants know each other. The network is loose especially if the city is large and stretches over dozens of miles in every direction because it may take people several hours to go from one area to another. However, with the advent of mobile phones it is relatively easier to keep in constant contact. The social network in geographically de-ethnicized cities is simplex because people of the same ethnic background do not live next door to each other.

6.10 Language of education policy in megacities with linguistic homogeneity

A very small number of megacities may be regarded as ethnolinguistically homogeneous. In strict sociolinguistic terms, homogeneity does not exist anywhere on planet earth. However, for the purposes of language planning, one can leave sociolinguistic purism aside and venture a claim that the following cities are linguistically homogeneous. In other words, the citizens of the country who live in the megacity speak the same language.

Table 6.2. Ethnolinguistic Homogeneous Cities

No.	Megacities	Country	Dominant LWC	International LWC
1.	Bujumbura	Burundi	Kirundi	French
2.	Mogadishu	Somalia	Somali[1]	Arabic/English[2]
3.	Kigali	Rwanda	Kinyarwanda	French/English
4.	Tananarive	Madagascar	Malagasy	French

Notes:
1 Appleyard and Orwin (2008:285): "… all Somalis understand what is now referred to as Standard Somali."
2 Prior to independence, Somali was divided into two: British Somaliland in the north and Italian Somaliland in the south. Arabic is commonly used. However, Italian is no longer taught in Somali schools.

Der-Houssikian (2009:182–3) contends that for religious reasons, Swahili is also spoken in Bujumbura but he goes on to say that "there may be some among an older generation of Burundians who deny the presence of Swahili and perceive French as the language among the educated and Kirundi as the home language." This caveat is a clear indication that Der-Houssikian is overplaying the importance of Swahili in Bujumbura. By correlating Swahili with Islam, he is simply noting that some Burundians may add Swahili to their linguistic repertoire as a result of religious conversion. However, it is quite unlikely that Swahili will occupy a place in the school curriculum any time soon.

Given the linguistic homogeneity in Bujumbura (Burundi), Tananarive (Madagascar), and Kigali (Rwanda), it is expected that the citizens of these countries will use the commonly shared language for most of their social interactions. Consequently, formulating a language of education policy for these cities is easy. Indeed, in Burundi, Rwanda, Madagascar, and Somalia, the national LWC is already part of the school curriculum. The Repertoire Model forecasts two possible language outcomes for these cities:

1. {1 + 1}
2. {1 + 0}

Educated residents are bilingual and biliterate in their national LWC and the international LWC used for administration and/or for communication with the outside world. In such environments, code-switching or code-mixing is expected to be very common by the participants in various social networks throughout the city, as described by Der-Houssikian (2009:181), "French is the language used for discussing official matters, and for official ceremonies, but Kirundi is often used in those settings where arguments become heated." Uneducated city dwellers have only one language in their speech repertoire.

6.11 Language of education policy in megacities with ethnolinguistic dominance

A large number of African megacities have one dominant language that serves as the urban LWC. Table 6.3 lists a few megacities of this type:

Table 6.3. Some Megacities with Ethnolinguistic Dominance

No.	Megacities	Country	Indigenous LWC	International LWC
1.	Addis Ababa	Ethiopia	Amharic	English
2.	Accra	Ghana	Akan	English
3.	Bamako	Mali	Bambara	French
4.	Brazzaville	Congo	Lingala	French

(*Continued*)

Table 6.3. Some Megacities with Ethnolinguistic Dominance (*Cont.*)

No.	Megacities	Country	Indigenous LWC	International LWC
5.	Conakry	Guinea	Susu	French
6.	Cotonou	Benin	Fon	French
7.	Dakar	Senegal	Wolof	French
8.	Dar es Salaam	Tanzania	Swahili	English
9.	Lomé	Togo	Mina	French
10.	Kampala	Uganda	Luganda	French
11.	Kinshasa	Congo, D.R.C	Lingala	French
12.	Nairobi	Kenya	Swahili	English
13.	Niamey	Niger	Hausa	French
14.	Ouagadougou	Burkina Faso	Moore	French

The speakers whose native languages are different from the LWC of the metropolis feel pressured to add the urban language to their linguistic repertoire. Newcomers have a very strong motivation to integrate so as not to stick out like a sore thumb. Urbanites everywhere express condescension toward rural dwellers. They see themselves as sophisticated, cultured, and modern, while they look down on others as uncultured, stupid, and backward. Newcomers who have not completely assimilated to urban life are often the butt of many unflattering jokes that caricature them in the most grotesque ways. According to Bokamba (2008a:115), the worst insult that can be hurled at somebody in Kinshasa is to call him/her "mouétataé" (outsider) or "campagnard" (rural inhabitant). In Côte d'Ivoire, there are many such nasty epithets for people who do not act urban; the worst is "broussard" (i.e., from the bush). As a result, new immigrants spend a lot of intellectual capital to acquire the urban language, culture, and identity.

The Repertoire Model predicts the following language outcomes:

1. {1 + 0}
2. {1 + 1}
3. {1 + 1 + 1}

Though the one-language outcome is theoretically possible, it is unlikely. It is hard to imagine someone who moves to the city and insists on refusing to learn the LWC of the city. The two-language outcome is widely attested to in African cities with ethnolinguistic dominance. A number of recent studies, including McLaughlin (2008, 2009) for Wolof in Dakar, Bokamba (2008; 2009) for Lingala in Congo DRC, Mazrui (2008) for Nairobi and Mombassa, Blommaert (2008) for Swahili in Tanzania, Bwenge (2009) for Swahili in Dar es Salaam, Myers-Scotton (2006:93) for Nupe in Ibadan, and Essegbey (2009) and Dakubu (2009) for Akan in Accra, have all well-documented this propensity toward bilingualism in African megacities. The first generation of immigrants become imbalanced bilinguals, that is, they may not acquire the city language very well even though they may get by with it. The second generation that grows up in the megacity tends to be fluent in both their parents' language and the urban language. They are said to be balanced bilinguals. By the third generation, there are signs that the ancestral language is undergoing attrition. Gradually but relentlessly, the urban language spreads to more and more people and extends its domination over the urban linguistic marketplace. McLaughlin (2009:10) and Canut (2009:93) have referred to this process as "linguistic homogenization" in urban spaces. The three-language outcome is for people whose native language is different from the LWC for the megacity, and who also are literate in the international LWC used as the official language of the country. It is important to note here that in nearly all French-speaking African countries, people who have a three-language speech repertoire are literate only in the official language. They have only oral proficiency in the two other languages that they know. The language of education policy that is discussed in 6.12 concerns only educated francophones. Its goal is that they will become literate in an indigenous language in addition to their literacy skills in French.

6.12 Language of education policy in megacities with ethnolinguistic dominance

Francophone countries which have a dominant urban LWC and are looking for a model to follow have two models that they can choose from. Kinshasa, Nairobi, and Dar es Salaam constitute one model and Accra offers the second. The first group of megacities offers a one-language outcome model, but Accra presents a two-language outcome model. In the one-language outcome model, megacity schools offer only the urban LWC. In Kinshasa students learn Lingala. In Nairobi and Dar es Salaam, only Swahili is taught even though in all likelihood all the 215 indigenous languages in Congo DRC, all the 69 languages in Kenya, and all the 128 indigenous languages in Tanzania (Ethnologue 2009:34–38) are represented in these megacities.

Accra (Ghana) offers another model of language of education policy for megacities with ethnolinguistic dominance. Accra is a fast growing and fast modernizing megacity with bustling multilingualism. Essegbey (2009:118) quotes Dakubu (1997) as saying that "all the languages along the West African coast from Ivory Coast to Nigeria can be found in Accra." This makes Accra a highly heteroglossic urban environment. Four Ghanaian languages, Akan, Ewe, Ga, and Hausa, are spoken in Accra (Dakubu 2009:28 and Essegbey 2009:120). The most dominant of these languages is Akan, which is spoken by 39.8% of the residents of the city. The second commonly heard language in Accra is Ga with 18.9%. No figures are available for Ewe and Hausa. Furthermore, Accra is located in Ga territory. According to Essegbey (2009:128), Accra city schools teach two local language: "Until recently, Ga was the only Ghanaian language taught in schools in Accra. However, nowadays, Akan is also taught and, in some areas in the city including an area in Osu, one of the Ga townships, only Akan is taught." The most important point in this discussion is that megacity language of education policies do not need to be based only upon the urban LWC. Accra offers a model of the two-language outcome that can benefit francophone megacities in search of models to follow. From McLaughlin (2008; 2009), it can be extrapolated that Wolof could be used in secondary schools in Dakar. Bamako, Cotonou, Lome, and Ouagadougou city schools could get away with using Bambara, Fon, Mina, and Moore respectively as the only languages in secondary school to replace German and Spanish. However, if the citizens of these cities object, two or three indigenous languages can be taught in schools as a good compromise. In Lomé for example, Mina and Kabye can be taught in city schools. Cotonou city schools can teach Fon and Bariba or Ditamari. In Porto Novo, according to Adeniran (2009:132, 134–5), Gun and Yoruba can be taught at school because they are the two demographically dominant languages out of the 11 languages spoken in the city. In Dakar, Wolof and Haalpulaar can be taught in secondary schools. To sum up, francophone countries where an indigenous language serves as the urban LWC can take advantage of the Repertoire Model and MM to teach more than one language in megacity schools.

6.13 Language planning in cities with ethnolinguistic equilibrium

The phrase "ethnolinguistic equilibrium" is an application of the economics concept of "Nash's equilibrium" that was alluded to in 2.3.7. It is used here to describe a stalemate in which the megacity has no indigenously dominant language. At least five African megacities find themselves in this situation: Abidjan (Côte d'Ivoire), Duala (Cameroon), Libreville (Gabon), Luanda (Angola), and Maputo (Mozambique).

Table 6.4. Megacities with Ethnolinguistic Equilibrium

No.	Megacities	Country	Dominant LWC	International LWC
1.	Abidjan	Ivory Coast	none	French
2.	Duala	Cameroon	Pidgin English[1]	French and English
3.	Libreville	Gabon	none[2]	French
4.	Luanda	Angola	none[3]	Portuguese
5.	Maputo	Mozambique	none[4]	Portuguese

Notes:
1 Biola and Echu (2008:199, 206) write that Pidgin English is also spoken in Yaoundé, the second largest city and also the capital city.
2 Fang, the largest language in the country, is spoken by 32% of the population. However, in Libreville, French is the main lingua franca.
3 Stroud (2008:74) notes that Kimbundu is the most dominant language of Angola but is spoken mostly in rural areas.
4 According to Stroud (2008:74) and Batibo (2008:60) XiChangana, Emakhuwa, and Tsonga are the most important languages but they are spoken predominantly in rural areas.

It goes without saying that formulating a language policy for schools in the megacity is extremely challenging. Here again, Abidjan (Côte d'Ivoire) will be taken as an example and the solutions proposed for it will, hopefully, be applicable to cities that have similar ethnolinguistic configurations.

6.14 Abidjan as a case study

According to Botau (2004:5, 24), the urbanization rate in Côte d'Ivoire is 43%, that is, roughly 10 million Ivorians live in the country's 70 urban centers. However, none of the Ivorian cities has the fame, the aura, or the prestige of Abidjan where, according to recent estimates, 33% of the population lives. Kube-Barth (2009:105) also notes that 30% of the approximately 5 million people who live in Abidjan are foreigners. Among these are tens of thousands of French citizens. Laitin (1992:144) describes the city as having "an aura of being a French outpost." The bulk of the 30% "foreigners" who live in Abidjan come from all over West Africa. The 1998 census indicates that

26.59% of the population of the city consists of Beninois, Burkinabes, Ghanaians, Guineans, Malians, Senegalese, and Togolese, not to mention a large number of Lebanese nationals. Abidjan is truly a cosmopolitan city. Additionally, as was noted in Chapter 5, there is no indigenous national LWC in Côte d'Ivoire. Consequently, French is the dominant language of Abidjan (and of Côte d'Ivoire). A lot has been written about the variety of French spoken in Abidjan, and by extension, in the country. Knutsen (2008:167) states that "Ivorian French has undergone linguistic stabilization and appears today as an emerging new variety of French, comparable to Canadian French or, to some extent, creole languages." This variety of French is commonly known in the literature and among Ivorians as the "Ivorian Vernacular French" or "Français Populaire Ivorien" in French. In recent years a youth variety known as "Nouchi" has developed which Kube-Barth (2009:105) describes as follows:

> Nouchi is the most recently developed variety of Ivorian French. The hybrid language form takes its morphosyntactic frame from French (mainly français populaire), whereas its lexicon is highly heterogenous. Nouchi borrows a lot of words from various Ivorian languages such as Diula, Baule, and Bété and from English, and its speakers are especially creative in inventing new terms. ... Nouchi started as a secret language of street children but quickly found more and more speakers among the younger population of Abidjan. Today it has its own website and satirical newspapers and enjoys broader acceptance in all social classes.

French has been so well domesticated in Côte d'Ivoire that Knutsen (2008:163–4, 167) is right in observing that "knowledge of French is now also a prerequisite for participation in urban life, and as such, it is no longer the privilege of the educated elite." How can MM be applied in the secondary schools of megacities such as Abidjan where ethnolinguistic equilibrium is the norm?

6.15 The implementation of MM in Abidjan

Following the discussions in 2.5.2 and 5.4.2 through 5.4.6, it was argued that MM is the best language of education policy for Côte d'Ivoire. It was also argued that indigenous Ivorian languages should be introduced in the school curriculum in secondary school, from ninth grade until 13th grade. However, the proposals that were made in Chapter 5 are inapplicable to the city of Abidjan because there is no indigenous regional LWC in the city. Moreover, logistically, it is impractical to teach all the 17 regional LWCs in city schools. This means that if indigenous Ivorian languages are to be taught in Abidjan, only a small number of them can make it into the curriculum. I propose that the number of languages in Abidjan schools be reduced five. These five languages come from the four language families found in the country.

We learned in Chapter 5 that in the Akan family of languages, Anyi-Baule is the largest group. Together, they represent 30.65% of the Akan group. From the Kru family of languages, the Soubré dialect of the Bété continuum should be chosen. The Kru family represents 11.34% of the general Ivorian population. The Bété alone constitute 4.46% of the Kru family. In the Gur family, Senoufo is demographically the most important language. Gur speakers are 18.07% of the total Ivorian population. The Senoufo are 10.73% of that language family. Furthermore, the mutual intelligibility between Senoufo and the other languages in the Gur family is fairly high. The Mande family comprises two major sub-families: the Northern Mande and the Southern Mande. Given the lack of intelligibility between the two, the dominant language of each sub-family should be taught in Abidjan schools. Diula is the best candidate for the Northern Mande family of languages. Canut (2009:93) notes that "there is substantial mutual intelligibility between varieties" of Northern Mande. Yacouba is best suited to represent the Southern Mande family of languages, because it alone represents 5.70% out of the 10.34% of the people who belong to the Southern Mande family. In a nutshell, Abidjan city schools will offer five languages to secondary students: Anyi-Baule, Bété, Senoufo, Diula, and Yacouba. As it happens, these languages are, according to Leclerc (2010), taught at the University of Abidjan. The Repertoire Model predicts a 3-language outcome in citywide secondary schools:

$$\text{French} + \text{English} + \left\{ \begin{array}{l} \text{Anyi-Baule} \\ \text{Bété} \\ \text{Diula} \\ \text{Senoufo} \\ \text{Yacouba} \end{array} \right\}^{45}$$

It is worth noting that the number of languages in the speech repertoire of secondary school students does not change. The only thing that changes

---

45 The angle brackets are used here in accordance with formal linguistic conventions. Students must select one and only one language to study at school.

is the configuration of languages. According to MM, German and Spanish are replaced by the five Ivorian languages.

6.16 Language endangerment in African megacities

The most vexing problem in language planning is that minority languages face two types of threats in African megacities. They are either in danger of succumbing to an international LWC or to the dominant megacity LWC. The former type of endangerment has been decried by language activists who have nicknamed international LWCs "killer languages." The alleged looming demise of African languages at the hand of former colonial languages is often attributed to globalization and westernization. Mufwene (2008) and most of the contributors to *Globalization and Vitality: Perspectives from Africa* have downplayed the lethality of international LWCs by contending that "languages compete with each other only when they serve the same communicative functions." Mufwene is of the opinion that the threat posed by European languages has been exaggerated because a functional separation of linguistic powers exists between international LWC and the dominant indigenous LWC. Allegedly, this wall of separation prevents the latter from being decimated by the former.

Curiously enough, many African linguists do not seem the least concerned that majority languages are endangering the survival of minority languages in megacities. Bokamba (2008b:118) seems to welcome it, arguing that "From the perspective of national integration, shift from or loss of ethnic/local languages are not in and of themselves bad developments. The reduction of such languages from any country's repertoire potentiates an increase in nationalism against ethnic loyalties." The proposals made in this chapter do not welcome such an outcome. Though it is logistically not feasible for every language spoken in the country to be part of the curriculum of megacity schools, a genuine effort must be made to teach a handful of demographically important languages. The Repertoire Model can be used with the help of statistical and demographic data to select the languages that can be taught in megacity schools.

6.17 Summary

The rapid pace of urbanization across the continent presents a serious challenge for various groups of experts and policymakers. Some are concerned with urban poverty, others with urban criminality, still others with sanitation and water supply. Language planners have for the most part not dwelt on the issue of mother-tongue education in urban centers. Most of the mother-tongue education projects are located in the hinterlands of Africa under the assumption that urban children do not need it. This is a form of linguistic discrimination that has gone unnoticed. If mother-tongue education is indeed good and desirable, it should be so for every student irrespective of where they live. The proposals in this chapter and in the previous chapter make mother-tongue education accessible to all the citizens of the country. Those who live in regional towns or "urban villages" have the opportunity to learn their own language in secondary school in their own county. A large number of those who live in megacities will be presented with the same opportunity. Unfortunately, for logistical reasons, not every indigenous language represented in the city can be part of the school curriculum. However, the secondary school curriculum can accommodate the dominant language of each language family. This is a reasonable solution that can meet the language of education needs of most urban dwellers. Furthermore, this approach gives a fighting chance to other demographically important languages to survive and thrive in megacities.

Chapter 7
Framework and rationale for literacy planning in rural Africa

Introduction

Stryker and Ndegwa (1995:375) begin their chapter in *Africa, 3rd edition*, with this remarkable statement: "Sub-Saharan Africa, a vast region comprising over fifty independent countries with a population surpassing 500 million people, has long been the 'least developed' area of the world, with the lowest levels of industrialization, life expectancy, nutrition, *literacy*,[46] access to medical care, and safe water supplies, and the highest rates of population growth and infant, child, and overall mortality." Djite (2008:118–9) paints a similarly dismal picture of the continent. But some experts believe that a large scale literacy program in rural areas could be one of the solutions to the litany of problems that besieges Sub-Saharan Africa. In this chapter four models of literacy are compared. The Predictioneer's Model is then used to recommend the optimal model of literacy that can help achieve the desired outcome. The answers to Cooper's (1996:31, 58–72) seven language planning questions, namely, *"Who plans what for whom, when, where, how, and why?"* set the stage for our game-theoretic investigations of past and current practices of adult literacy planning.

7.1 The state of adult literacy in Sub-Saharan Africa

First and foremost, a definition of literacy is in order. It is not at all trivial to note that at its inaugural General Conference in 1946, UNESCO's delegates could not agree on a suitable definition of the term "literacy." Instead, they settled on the skills that literacy provides. A literate individual was defined as "a person who has the reading and writing skills needed to participate in one's own society." In 1966 UNESCO expanded

---

46 The italics do not appear in the original document. They are added here for emphasis.

its original definition to include an illiterate person. The revised definition reads as follows: "(a) A person is literate who can with understanding both read and write a short simple statement on his (her) everyday life. (b) A person is illiterate who cannot with understanding both read and write a short simple statement on his (her) everyday life." Twelve years later, at its General Conference of 1978, UNESCO assigned a goal to literacy and redefined a literate person as "someone who is able to engage in all those activities in which literacy is required for effective functioning of his [her] group or community and also for enabling him [her] to continue to use reading, writing and calculation for his [her] own community's development." Bhola (2006:3) reports yet another UNESCO definition which does not so much focus on the literate person but rather on literacy itself:

> The meaning of literacy has changed radically since the World Conference on Education for All in Jomtien in 1990. Conceived now in the plural as 'literacies', and embedded in a range of life and livelihood situations, literacy differs according to purpose, context, use, script and institutional framework. But these conceptual advances have not been matched by the priority accorded to it in policy and resource allocation, in part because many governments perceive the expansion of primary education as the main driver for the eradication of illiteracy (UNESCO 2002).

The definition of literacy or a literate person has evolved since 1946. The most recent definition, that of 1990 no longer sees reading, writing, and arithmetic as the only defining criteria. As a result, the singular "literacy" has been replaced by the plural "literacies." Consequently, it is now not uncommon to hear phrases such as "math literacy," "computer literacy," "Bible literacy," "science literacy," "civic literacy," "financial literacy," "art literacy," "music literacy," "cultural literacy," etc. In academic circles, one is sometimes forced to define what one means by "literacy." Lind (2008:42) laments this expanded definition of literacy. She fears that by equating "literacy" with "competency," social scientists have relativized the meaning of literacy and have created "frequent confusion in the way the term is used." It is therefore imperative for the reader to keep in mind that in this chapter, terms such as "literacy" and "illiteracy" refer back to UNESCO's 1966 definition. It is considered a benchmark definition because both "literacy" and "illiteracy" are used in tandem to describe the condition of millions of people who lack a specific set of skills. Moreover, UNESCO's own Institute for Statistics (2008:37) uses the 1966 definition to compile data such that in Table 7.1 about illiteracy rates in Sub-Saharan Africa:

Table 7.1. Literacy Figures in Sub-Saharan Africa[47]

No.	Year	Illiteracy Rates	Illiteracy Numbers
1.	1970	72.2%	108,000,000
2.	1980	62.2%	120,000,000
3.	1990	50.8%	131,000,000
4.	1995	45.2%	135,000,000
5.	2000	39.7%	136,000,000
6.	2005	34.6%	136,000,000
7.	2010	30.0%	134,000,000
8.	2015	26.1%	133,000,000

For UNESCO, an illiterate adult is a person who is 15 years old or older and does not know how to read or write. There is presently an attempt to define such people as "pre-literates" because some find the term "illiterate" to be offensive (Lind 2008:41, Ong 1987:174). However, no special effort will be made to avoid the term "illiterate" in this book because even in UNESCO-sponsored publications, people who cannot read or write are still referred to as illiterate. However, in the interest of lexical variation, the term "pre-literate" is also used.

Table 7.1 bears some good news about the state of illiteracy in Sub-Saharan Africa. In the space of 30 years, the illiteracy rate has been cut in half. Furthermore, by 2015, only a quarter of the Sub-Saharan adult population will still be classified as illiterate. In spite of these tremendous gains, UNESCO's Institute for Statistics (2008:37) reports that Sub-Saharan Africa is lagging behind other areas of the world and is unlikely to meet the goal of Education for All.

The slow pace of progress toward a world without illiteracy led the United Nations to decree 2002–2013 "the literacy decade." During these ten years, governments, institutions, non-governmental organizations (NGO), and

---

47 Retrieved from UNESCO Institute for Statistics: Literacy and Non-formal Education Sector, Regional Adult Illiteracy and Population by Gender, July 2002 Assessment.

faith-based organizations have been asked to double and even triple their efforts to significantly reduce adult illiteracy and boost formal schooling for boys and girls in the developing world. This urgent call for action against illiteracy comes from the fact that, according to Kaplan and Baldauf (1997:145), now illiteracy is likened to a dreaded disease.

7.2 A framework for literacy planning

The answers to Cooper's seven questions, "Who plans what for whom, when, where, how, and why" provide the basis for the organization of this chapter into four parts. The first section answers the questions "Who plans what, when, and where." The second part answers the "how" question and deals exclusively with the topic of orthography as a prerequisite to literacy planning. The third section answers the question "why." In the fourth part, various approaches are compared, contrasted, and rated. Then the Predictioneer's Model is used to recommend the model that is likely to yield better results.

7.2.1 Who

Cooper (1996:88) answers the question "who" by identifying three main players in the literacy planning game. These three are individuals, institutions, and governments. However, in most of Sub-Saharan Africa, the government's role in adult literacy planning is symbolic and even negligible. The bulk of the work for the documentation of local languages is outsourced to specialized international organizations. Governments still retain a bureaucratic oversight role which consists mainly in issuing visas to foreign nationals involved in adult literacy work or research. For this reason, in the discussions that follow, the agencies that will be discussed are UNESCO and SIL International. Other agencies will be mentioned in passing, but these two are singled out for discussion because of their global influence. The role of individuals in language planning will be delayed until Chapter 9.

UNESCO is a specialized agency of the United Nations that was birthed in 1946. It is charged with designing, implementing, and monitoring policies regarding education, culture, and science. Since the day of the inaugural conference, UNESCO has wasted no time in issuing position papers on literacy in general. It is by far the most powerful literacy advocacy organization in the world. All the countries in the world that are members of the United Nations are automatically members of UNESCO. Its influence is particularly strong in Africa because it provides grants for many adult literacy programs. It oversees two types of adult literacy programs. Bhola (2006) refers to one as "second-chance literacy." It is so named because it targets those who drop out of school without completing a full course of study. It gives them a second chance to complete their education. In many African countries, the medium of instruction in second-chance literacy is usually English, French, or Portuguese, and to a lesser extent Spanish. The other type of adult literacy program for which UNESCO is well known is called "basic literacy." It teaches illiterate adults how to read, write, and do arithmetic in local languages. In francophone Africa, UNESCO's second-chance literacy programs have been more successful. However, our interest in this chapter is in its basic adult literacy programs.

SIL International is the largest and most influential missionary-linguistic organization in the world. It was founded in the 1930s by Townsend and Pike. According to Svelmoe (2009:631, 635), it boasts more than 6,500 Western missionaries. Its linguistic work encompasses more than 1,100 languages. Its ultimate goal in nearly all language planning situations is the translation of the New Testament into an indigenous language. It celebrated its 500th published New Testament a couple of years ago. The mammoth size of SIL International has overshadowed other missionary-linguistic organizations such as the United Bible Societies (UBS), Pioneer Bible Translators, Lutheran Bible Translators, New Tribes Mission, Bibles International, and others with similar goals. SIL International and like-minded organizations achieve their goals by first engaging in corpus planning. Linguists and missionaries in these organizations spend on average two decades on an indigenous language before a New Testament is eventually published. In the meantime, they design orthographies, write reference grammars, and make dictionaries for the languages that they study. There are like-minded organizations but SIL International is the only one discussed here because it is the largest and most visible of all.

In addition to UNESCO and SIL International, some countries have their own non-profit organizations that do work in adult literacy in local languages. Many of these local non-governmental organizations (NGOs) lack the financial resources, the human resources, and the scientific know-how to compete with UNESCO or SIL International. In many cases, African governments bypass such organizations and deal directly with SIL International to which they have outsourced literacy planning in their indigenous languages. Dobrin (2009:624) notes that SIL International has created local affiliates made up of nationals. However, these "sister" organizations are not often regarded as highly as SIL International because they lack qualified personnel and financial resources. More often than not, they rely solely on volunteers. However, Öney and Durgunoğlu (2005:134) report that relying on volunteers is a liability for adult literacy programs because volunteers stay only as long as they do not have offers of a paid position elsewhere.

7.2.2 Who plans what?

Cooper (1996:31) equates "who plans what" with status planning. I will do the same here. The pronoun "what" stands for the language in which literacy instruction is to be offered. Literacy planners have the choice between three types of languages. Instruction can be given in the clients' native language, in a regional/national LWC, or in an international LWC. My experiences in literacy planning in Benin, Côte d'Ivoire, and Togo have shown that rural inhabitants have a preference hierarchy between the three language options. The hierarchy is as follows: *International LWC > Mother tongue > Regional/National LWC*. The mother tongue is preferred to the regional or national LWC generally because of ethnolinguistic loyalty, as discussed in 1.3 and 6.5. If literacy clients in francophone Africa have their way, a fair number of them would prefer French because they believe that knowing it has a better payoff. Apparently, this is not limited to francophone Africa. Grenoble and Whaley (2006:114, 184) have observed a similar preference elsewhere where diglossia exists:

> More frequently we find examples of the second category [the concept of literacy in the language of wider communication is established] where there is no written form of the local language but literacy in the language of wider communication is at least familiar, and perhaps well established. This is not to say that literacy is an integral part of community life or even recognized as valuable, but rather that it is not an alien concept. In such cases the community may associate literacy and writing with the language of wider communication, but not with the local language. This attitude is a commonly reported stumbling block to initiating local literacy programs because it requires people to reset their thinking to conceptualize that local literacy is possible and useful. ... If any segment of the population is already literate, or semi-literate, in any language, this has a profound impact on attitudes toward literacy as a whole.

The data in Table 7.2 underscore the reality of this situation. The lack of success in adult literacy programs in the local languages of Côte d'Ivoire may be in large measure to the hegemony of literacy in French. The official literacy rate vacillates between 49% and 51%. Yet, in spite of decades of trying, the number of adults who can read and write in their native languages is less than 5%.

Table 7.2. Literacy Ranking

No.	Language	Population[1]	Literacy Rate in French[2]	Literacy Rate in Mother Tongue
1.	Baule	2,629,438	49.5%	10–30%
2.	Senoufo	1,185,288	24.5%	Below 1%
3.	Malinke	998,542	30.4%	Not Available
4.	Anyi	755,365	49.5%	1–5%[3]
5.	Yacouba	629,427	42.3%	1–5%
6-.	Diula	505,764	30.4%	Below 1%
7.	Attie	473,298	49.5%	1–5%
8.	Bété	492,089	62.3%	1–5%
9.	Gouro	383,824	42.3%	Not Available
10.	Guéré	294,251	62.3%	Not Available
11.	Koulango	289,338	24.5%	Below 1%
12.	Mahou	215,418	30.4%	Below 1%
13.	Lobi	205,529	24.5%	Below 1%
14.	Abbey	196,012	49.5%	5–10%
15.	Dida	180,307	62.3%	Below 1%
16.	Abron	162,012	49.5%	Not Available
17.	Wobé	143,995	62.3%	1–5%
18.	Adjoukourou	119,519	49.5%	30–60%

Notes:
1 The information in this column is based on the 1998 census data.
2 The information in this column is taken from Botau (2004:13). The literacy rate is broadly based on language family.
3 The information in this column is taken from Ethnologue (2009:100–5). Literacy in Anyi is less than 1%. The figure of 1–5% must be taken with a grain of salt.

A fellow literacy worker started an adult basic literacy program in French among market women in the port city of San Pedro. The program was widely popular even though the women had to pay tuition to attend the classes. He was later approached by the African Development Bank and given a substantial grant to expand his work to more women. However, the only stipulation of the grant was that courses be in Diula, a lingua franca used by illiterate market women. When the change was announced, all the students who used to attend the French courses withdrew. The decision of the bank to make Diula the language of instruction was interpreted differently by different women. Some feared that it was a subtle conspiracy to Islamize them. In the politically and ethnically volatile situation of Côte d'Ivoire, some interpreted the change from French to Diula as a veiled attempt to steer them towards one political party whose leadership comprises predominantly people of this ethnic background. Needless to say, the market women demanded that French be reinstated as the only language of instruction. This incident speaks volumes about people's preference for basic literacy skills in the international LWC. Since the interest is so high in places where diglossia exists, Grenoble and Whaley (2006:112–3) suggest that room be made for *transitional literacy* in the curriculum. Under such a model, literacy in the local language is introduced first, but instruction gradually moves toward the international LWC. The reality, however, is that most basic adult literacy programs in rural areas offer instruction only in the native language. UNESCO's grants for basic adult literacy are for teaching rural inhabitants how to read, write, and do arithmetic in their own native languages, not in an international LWC. Similarly, SIL International and related organizations teach basic literacy to adults in the languages in which Bible translation is being done.

7.2.3 ... for whom?

Inquiring about the clients of literacy planning helps workers gather two important pieces of demographic information: age and gender. For the purposes of literacy planning, UNESCO defines an adult as anybody who is 15 or older. In recent years, UNESCO has provided useful demographic data such as that in Table 7.3 about illiteracy in Sub-Saharan Africa:

Table 7.3. Illiteracy Rates by Age and Gender

| | | | Age | | | |
No.	Year	Gender	15–24	25–64	65+	Total
1	2005	Male	16,089,260	28,457,450	4,243,680	48,790,390
2		Female	17,749,340	44,707,760	7,155,520	69,612,620
3	2010	Male	17,796,870	31,128,320	4,484,230	53,409,420
4		Female	17,514,300	45,874,430	7,920,490	71,309,220
5	2015	Male	19,614,700	34,501,450	4,721,980	58,838,130
6		Female	17,222,910	46,897,000	8,868,800	72,806,730

What stands out from the data is the literacy gap between males and females. Overall, nearly 2/3 of the illiterate population is female. The gap is closing in the 15 to 24 age bracket because governments all over the continent have seriously committed themselves to the goal of equal access to education for boys and girls. The gap may continue to exist for a while because Africans in rural areas prefer sending their little boys rather than their little girls to school. This also explains why one finds more pre-literate adult women in literacy classes than adult men. Many adult women want to avail themselves of the opportunity to learn to read and write that they were denied when they were little girls.

Answering the question "for whom" also gives literacy planners access to cultural information about gender roles which can help predict the success or failure of literacy planning in rural Africa. Öney and Durgunoğlu (2005:132) put it as follows: "Adult literacy programs are effective to the extent that the models on which they are founded allow them to be sensitive to the social and cultural nuances around literacy in particular cultures. ... Adult literacy programs often fail because of a lack of attention to important social factors that eventually lead to student dropout from programs." Since more women than men attend adult literacy classes, understanding gender roles and expectations is helpful in scheduling classes. Here are some typical gender roles and expectations in the household where I grew up in rural Côte d'Ivoire. Wives get up at the crack of dawn to sweep the compound and take care of household chores while husbands sharpen the machetes and hoes that will be needed for the day's work in the farm. By 7:00 a.m. most farming families walk 5 to 10 miles one-way to the farm. While the wife tends to the crops needed for subsistence, the husband clears the tall grass in the cash-crop farm of the previous years. Usually the wife heads back to the village around

3:00 p.m. carrying a 30 to 50 pound load of yam and/or plantain, and firewood on her head. The husband stays at the farm and continues to work until around 5:00 p.m. When the woman gets home, she builds fire, peels off the skin of the yam or the plantain, or pounds the millet to cook dinner. The family eats around 6:30 p.m. If the family has preteen girls, they wash the dishes and give baths to their younger siblings. If not, the wife does these chores. In many Sub-Saharan African cultures, it is still taboo for husbands to do household chores. By 7:00 p.m., it is pitch black because most villages do not have electricity. Most literacy classes begin around 7:30 p.m. After a day of physically demanding labor on the farm, only the most dedicated of rural dwellers have enough energy left to attend literacy classes. However, some manage to do it. Öney and Durgunoğlu (2005:132) have found that willpower alone is not enough to keep attending literacy classes. They argue that the family support system is often the critical element that determines whether a villager will continue in adult literacy classes or not:

> In our work we also found that adult literacy participants experience various obstacles as well as supports for adult literacy participation. Many successful adult literacy participants had spouses and children who were supportive of their education. They also reported various barriers, such as having young children, unsupportive family members, and inflexible jobs, that often were negatively affecting success in literacy acquisition.

They go on to say that obstacles such as the ones enumerated above account for why 50% or more of the adults in literacy classes in Turkey drop out.

7.2.4 ... when?

Cooper (1996:65) limits his discussions of "when" in language planning to "the time of adoption." However, for literacy planning in rural Sub-Saharan Africa, the answer to the question "when" must be broadened to include various aspects of chronological time. We have already alluded to the fact that rural inhabitants get up early to go to their farms and come back in the late afternoon. This means that the ideal time to hold adult literacy classes is in the evening on most days of the week. Holding literacy classes in the evening, however, raises a number of logistical issues. Most villages do not have electricity, so villagers use three or four kerosene lamps to light the classroom. Even with this many kerosene lamps, the luminosity is not enough for people to see well. Increasing the number of kerosene lamps in poorly ventilated rooms is a health hazard because they emit toxic fumes that cause some people to have headaches. At the beginning of the Anyi literacy program, we tried to deal with the luminosity issue by using rechargeable florescent light bulbs. They were charged up in town and brought to the villages. When fully charged, they could last up to three days. However, this solution proved difficult in the long run because sometimes the light bulbs were fully charged but there were no taxis to bring them back to the villages. Other times, the light bulbs would break or malfunction after just a couple of months. Furthermore, as the number of literacy villages increased, so did the number of light bulbs needed. Eventually, it was decided that the most economical and also the most reliable solution was to purchase small portable generators. After several months of continuous usage, the generators also would break down. In the end, we concluded that to avoid disrupting the curriculum, each village needed two generators so that when one would break down, the other would be ready for use. The switch from rechargeable light bulbs to portable generators had an unexpected positive consequence on attendance in literacy classes. Since the school yard is often the only place that is lit, it automatically becomes the place of social encounters. Many young adults who were not interested in literacy classes began enrolling. When the portable generators were introduced, conversations continued long after class hours.

Another way of dealing with the question "when" has to do with syllabus planning, namely how long literacy clients have to undergo training before they are judged to be literate in their mother tongue. Öney and Durgunoğlu (2005:137) report that the adult literacy program that they designed for the Turkish government lasted only three months. This is a rather short period of time, but it is understandable since theirs was a second-chance adult literacy program and the adults "demonstrated significant improvements in their letter and word recognition, spelling, phonological awareness, and reading comprehension levels after only 90 hours of attendance in the program." However, UNESCO usually suggests a time frame of about four years or the equivalent of a fourth grade reading and writing proficiency level (Grenoble and Whaley 2006:111, Calfee 2005:16). If instruction follows a calendar year, it is important to delineate clearly when the literacy season begins and when it ends. Since many of the agricultural activities in rural areas are seasonal, it works very well when literacy classes do not interfere with peak sowing and harvesting periods.

The third aspect of chronological time to be considered has to do with the amount of time it takes for literacy to impact social change (Cooper 1996:83). There is no clarity in the literature as to when participants in an adult literacy program begin to reap the individual and societal benefits associated with literacy. The historical record of literacy in Western Europe shows that it takes quite a long time for literacy to impact individual and social change. Logan (1986:100) notes, for instance, that it took five to six hundred years from the time literacy was introduced to the time when it began to make an imprint on the Greek society:

> The five to six hundred years that followed the transfer of the phonetic alphabet from the Phoenicians to the Greeks was one of the most creative periods in man's existence. Within this *short period* there appeared many of the elements of Western civilization – abstract science, formal logic, axiomatic geometry, rational philosophy, and representational art. It is not an accident that this unparalleled intellectual development occurred *immediately* following the transfer of the phonetic alphabet.[48] [emphasis added]

He also notes that it took about the same amount of time for literacy to be widespread among the Hebrews of ancient Israel (p. 103).

7.2.5 ... where?

There are two aspects to the "where" question. The first has to do with physical location of the literacy classes, while the second focuses on the criterion for selecting a village for literacy instruction. Adult literacy classes can be held in cities, in villages, and in hamlets. In a nutshell, classes can be held anywhere there are adults who are willing to learn to read and write. However, my experiences have shown that literacy classes in indigenous languages are less successful in urban and semi-urban centers than in rural areas (see also Goody 1987:141) because urban illiterate dwellers prefer to be taught in the international LWC.

There seems to be a rule of thumb in selecting the place to experiment with in adult literacy. This rule can be summed up as follows: "The more remote the village is, the greater the chances for success." In selecting a village for instruction, the Anyi Literacy project team has developed the following cultural procedure. Initial contacts for the recruitment of participant villages are made via a courtesy visit paid to the chief of the village. This first visit is a meet and greet visit to village officials. A token gift is brought to the village chiefs and the youth council leaders. The purpose of the visit is to receive permission from village leaders to begin literacy classes.

---

48 It is commonly assumed that the Greeks acquired writing in 700 B.C., Logan (1987:103).

Grenoble and Whaley (2006:126) see "the approval of traditional community leaders" as one of the prerequisites for success in local literacy planning. Öney and Durgunoğlu (2005:132) concur with this assessment by noting that "adult literacy programs are effective to the extent that the models on which they are founded allow them to be sensitive to the social and cultural nuances around literacy in particular cultures." The blessing of the elders of the community means that the elementary school in the village can be used for literacy instruction. However, to avoid unforeseen bureaucratic hurdles, it is good to obtain written permission from the regional superintendent of schools.

7.3 How

Cooper (1996:40) answers the "how" question indirectly by asking the following rhetorical questions: "Should we confine language planning to an activity which approaches management ideal, whereby needs are rationally determined, goals explicitly stated, means carefully tailored to these ends, and results systematically monitored to permit the adjustment of means and ends to one another?" The very fact that these questions are raised tells us that answering the "how" question can take us in many directions. However, let's not be sidetracked; let's limit our inquiry exclusively to matters related to orthography, which is the cornerstone of every literacy enterprise. Without orthography, there is no reading, no writing, no arithmetic. In spite of all the talk about Literacy for All by 2013, Hasselbring (2006:2) has found that the vast majority of Sub-Saharan African languages have not yet been reduced to writing:

> In Africa, the proportions of languages still lacking an initial written standard are comparable to the worldwide averages. Africa has 2092 indigenous languages according to the *Ethnologue* (Gordon, 2005). Because 683 African languages have had some portion of the Bible published in them (United Bible Society, 2006), at least that many languages have written standards. Probably no more than 100 additional languages of Africa also have written standards. Thus, at least 60 percent of the languages of Africa do not have written standards.

This means that 1,409 languages are still waiting for their orthographies to be designed before literacy can be initiated! Goody (1987:215) recommends that if and when these languages are eventually reduced to writing, their orthographies should be designed in such a way that literacy skills are easily acquired.

7.3.1 Steps towards orthographic transparency

Orthographies are said to meet the transparency criterion if they reduce the amount of mental computations needed in decoding what is written or if there is a strong correlation between pronunciation and spelling. English and French orthographies are said to fail the transparency test because considerable mental cogitation is required to read or spell many words accurately. Nineteenth and early twentieth century missionaries who designed the orthographies of many African languages did their best to fulfill the transparency criterion. Under the scholarly tutelage of linguistics giants such as Meinhof, Westermann, and Jones, the International Institute of African Languages and Cultures (hereafter, "Institute"), was created to give practical advice on orthography matters. It published the *Practical Orthography of African Languages*. The demand for such a resource was so high that the 3,500 copies that were initially printed sold out in two years (Institute, p. 1). No less than 50 different languages spoken throughout Sub-Saharan Africa were studied. The Institute provided guidelines on all or nearly all the pertinent issues in orthography. It gave advice on the types of consonant and vowel graphemes to use. It gave examples of how to use diacritics to signal nasalization, length, and tones. It addressed issues related to capitalization and to the alphabetic order. The Institute even went so far as to suggest indigenous names for graphemes. The overriding principle for writing African languages was "the orthography of a given language should be based on the principle of one letter for each phoneme of that language. This means that whenever two words are distinguished in sound, they must also be distinguished in orthography." Most of the early orthographies succeeded at providing a fairly accurate inventory of phonemes. But in spite heroic efforts, the orthographies of African languages designed by early missionaries were (some still are) defective because they missed some linguistic features that are significant for reading and spelling correctly. This has led to defective orthographies which are the source of all sorts of difficulties. Wa Thiong'o (1986:74–5), the well-known Kenyan writer, tells of his frustrations with learning to write in Gikuyu:

> Words and tenses were even more slippery because of the unsatisfactory Gikuyu orthography. Gikuyu language had been reduced to writing by

non-native speakers such as European missionaries and they could not always identify the various lengths of vowels. The distinction between short and long vowels is very important in Gikuyu prose and poetry. But the prevailing orthography often left the reader to guess whether to prolong or shorten the vowel sound. This would be very tiring for an extended piece of prose. This lack of the means of making distinction between the long and short vowel sounds assumed a previous knowledge of all the words on the part of the reader.

At the 31st Annual Conference on African Linguistics in Boston in 2000, wa Thiong'o convened a panel of experts to provide guidance for a Gikuyu orthography reform. Dewees (1977:124–5) reports a similar problem in Luganda orthography for the short /t/ and the long /t:/. Examples such as these which have to do with the misperception and misrepresentation of phonological segments can be multiplied ad infinitum. Fortunately, over the years mild orthography reforms have helped correct these problems. So far the main issue that has frustrated efforts towards designing truly transparent orthographies for Sub-Saharan African languages is tone. This explains why it is the focus of the question "how."

7.3.2 Issues with tones in reading some African languages

The linguists of the "Institute" have been blamed for having ignored the issue of tone altogether. This, however, is an oversimplification of their views on how tone should or should not be represented in the orthography. Here are the actual recommendations that they made about tone:

> In books for Africans, tones, generally speaking, need only be marked when they have a grammatical function, or when they serve to distinguish words alike in every other respect; and even then they may be sometimes omitted when the context makes it quite clear which word is intended. As a rule, it will suffice to mark the high tone or the low tone only (page 13).

These recommendations are rather insightful. However, because they were not stated forcefully, they were interpreted as though writing tone was not necessary. So, nearly all 19th and early 20th century missionaries interpreted these recommendations as permission for not writing tone in the orthography. However, Welmers (1973:77) contends that the real reason for avoiding writing tones in the orthography of African languages was fear!

A missionary candidate and his wife admitted that, when they learned that the language that their African field was a tone language, they seriously questioned whether the Lord had actually called them to missionary service. Writers of grammars have commonly neglected to describe and write distinctions in tone on the theory that "tone can be learned only by observation and practice." Leonard Bloomfield aptly commented on this (1942), "such a statement is nothing less than downright swindle, for of course observation and practice are the only way anything can be learned." Others dismiss the entire topic of tone with only a brief statement of this sort: "Tone is important, as will be seen from the following examples [two or three examples follow]; however, tone will not be marked in this grammar. One grammar does discuss tone fairly fully but relegates it to an appendix explicitly added for the benefit of those who are particularly interested and who consider themselves especially gifted. Many more grammars – more than half of over a hundred grammars of African languages examined – omit all mention of tone; some go so far as to assert that the language being treated is definitely not a tone language, though a little investigation readily proves that it is. A shocking number of people concerned with African languages still seem to think of tone as a species of esoteric, inscrutable, and utterly unfortunate accretion characteristic of underprivileged languages – a sort of cancerous malignancy afflicting an otherwise normal linguistic organism. Since there is thought to be no cure – or even reliable diagnosis – for this regrettable malady, the usual treatment is to ignore it, in hope that it will go away of itself.

In order for readers of English to empathize with readers of tone languages when tone is not indicated in the orthography of their language, I often ask my audience to read the two texts below out loud:

Text 1
"The offense in this whole thing is that the offense did not play offense and the defense did not play defense. There is absolutely no defense for this loss."

Text 2
"Every Sunday I read the weekend paper faithfully with my morning coffee until an unscrupulous reporter misquoted me in a story."

If you are like most Americans who have been asked to read these two texts, you probably hesitated more than once in reading Text 1 because you did not know which stress to assign to the words <*offense*> and <*defense*>. Readers frequently stumble over how to pronounce <*offense*> and <*defense*> correctly because they are unsure of where to place stress. As for Text 2, you probably pronounced <*read*> as *[ɹi:d]*. However, when you got to the end of the sentence, you realized that it should have been read as *[ɹɛd]* because of the syntactic clues found further down in the sentence. So, you probably, re-read the sentence again so as to pronounce <read> correctly. Words such as <offense>, <defense> and <read> are called homographs.

These are words that have the same spelling but different pronunciations. Homographs are a vexing issue in the orthography of English, but fortunately homographic words rarely co-occur in the same sentence. However, this is not the case for the orthography of many Africa languages that have lexical or grammatical tones. The phonemic principle proposed by the linguists of the Institute to write these languages has had the unintended consequence of introducing many homographs into the orthography. Since tone is not indicated in the orthography, homographic words occur fairly frequently, causing all kinds of reading difficulties, as shown by the examples below:

> An intelligent, educated native speaker of a tone language of West Africa was asked to read a page from a primer in his own language. He remained staring at the page without speaking for so long that the people around him became embarrassed. Finally they said, 'Never mind. It's quite all right if you don't want to read it.' The African replied, 'Oh, no, … no. I'll be ready in a minute. It's just that I haven't figured out yet what it is supposed to say, so I don't know what tone to read it with (Gudschinsky 1970:23).

> It is because of tone that I've had to go back and reread several times what I wrote the day before in order to know what I meant on this translation work I've been doing. We all have to do something about it. What shall we do? (Lucht 1978:26).

Coulmas (1989:173) notes that the designers of the orthographies of many languages try very hard to avoid homographs "in the interest of direct lexical access."

7.3.3 Issues with tones in writing some African languages

Toneless orthographies cause problems not only for reading aloud. They are also the source of spelling difficulties. Wa Thiong'o (1986:74–5) shares his frustrations when he decided to begin writing in his native language:

> Gikuyu is also a tonal language but the prevailing orthography did not indicate tonal variations. So for all these reasons, I would write a paragraph in the evening sure of how it read, only later to find it could be read in a

different way which completely altered the meaning. I could only solve the problem by severely controlling the context of words in a sentence, and that of sentences in a paragraph, and that of the paragraph within the entire situation of the occurrence of the action in time and space. Yes, words did slip and slide under my eyes. They would not stay in place. They would not stay still. And this was often a matter of great frustration.

Many others (including me) who have written book-length texts in African languages have experienced similar frustrations. The translators of the Bible in Ditammari and Lokpa, two languages in northern Benin, faced similar challenges. They told me how much they had agonized over the writing of tones for decades. The two decades that they spent translating the New Testament into their respective native languages were nothing but frustration. In the end they decided not to write any tone at all. So, their New Testaments were published without indicating the tone of words. Soon after the distribution of the New Testaments, they realized that people could not read them. They would spend a very long time deciphering the context before being able to arrive at the meaning of the text. Moreover, the translators realized that people were embarrassed when called on to read spontaneously in front of the congregation without a few days' notice. So, for Sunday morning readings, the translators (they were also pastors) would go to church leaders as early as Friday night and tell them what their portion was. People would prepare well before Sunday so that they could read the texts with as few false starts and repairs as possible. When it came time to translate the Old Testament, they were determined to write tone. However, they were assailed with the same difficulties that led them to avoid writing tone in the New Testament in the first place. The problems that they encountered are the following. First, their perception of the tone of the same word changed from syntactic context to syntactic context. Second, translators on the same team never quite agreed on the tone of many words. Where one person perceived a high tone another heard a mid tone. Third, on subsequent re-readings of the same passage, the translators often changed their minds over the accuracy of the tone that they had written previously. They were completely demoralized by the time I was given oversight of their Old Testament translation project. I shared with them my approach to tone marking, which revolutionized their understanding of tone and how to write it. However, before revealing my optimal tone marking solution, let's review briefly the conflicting proposals that have been made regarding the issue of writing tone in the orthography of African languages.

7.3.4 Proposals and counter proposals

Over the years, various proposals for writing tone have been put forth, but to date no consensus has been reached. The following is a quick summary of the main ones followed by my own recommendation in 7.3.5. Pike (1946:255) made the following recommendation:

> Symbols for tone and stress should reflect an adequate analysis of the language. Where tone and stress are phonemic and affect the meaning of words, they should be symbolized *at each occurrence of the units*. One should not content oneself with writing tone merely on those words which may be misunderstood if the tone is given inaccurately. *Tone should be written on each of the words of the tone language, wherever the tones occur*. In this way the native learns the meaning of the tone symbols and how to read them within the words where the consonant and the vowels and the context make these particular words unambiguous. Once he has learned the meaning of the tone symbols in unambiguous contexts of this type, he should then be able to utilize these symbols to distinguish words where the tone is the only distinctive characteristic. [Italics added for emphasis]

This recommendation was ignored because it was feared that too many tone diacritics would overcrowd the text and slow down the reading process. Instead, some orthographers began advocating a return to the selective tone marking scheme proposed by the "Institute", namely, "they [tones] may be sometimes omitted when the context makes it quite clear which word is intended." However, Smalley (1964:41) rejected this approach categorically because "it represents the speech system of the language in such an inconsistent way, it compounds the learning problem seriously and, in many cases, means that the reader never learns to use the tone symbols at all because he meets them in such an inconsistent fashion." Longacre (1964:133) published an influential paper in which he argued strongly against writing tone only on lexical minimal pairs. He insisted that writing tone selectively is not a good solution to the problem of toneless orthographies because "[it] presupposes that one has already made a list of all the words in the language to see which ones are minimal pairs. Such a claim is pretentious since most newly written languages do not have good dictionaries." The assumption underlying Longacre's position is that lexical minimal pairs distinguished only by tones are in abundant supply and in the absence of a dictionary one cannot be sure that all the minimal pairs are accounted for. This cautious attitude was completely understandable in the 1960s. However, research by Welmers and others has found that the number of lexical and grammatical minimal pairs in many tone languages is far smaller than had been anticipated.

Nearly 40 years had passed since Pike's call for a systematic representation of tone. In the decade of the 1980s, Wiesemann (1989:16) revived Pike's original proposal and gave it a new twist. She managed to persuade many of her SIL International colleagues and teams that tone should be marked fully in the orthography. She organized several important workshops and seminars to this effect in Central and West Africa. Translators and literacy workers ministering under the auspices of SIL International began writing tones fully. This led to another set of reading and spelling difficulties that have been widely reported in Bird (1998a), (1998b), and (2001). He led a series of experimental studies on Dschang, a language of Cameroon in which tone was marked fully. From these studies, Bird (2001:18–20) concluded that writing tone fully was worse than not writing tones at all:

> Although each of the three experiments uses different methods, different kinds of subjects and different languages, *all agree that full surface tone marking is not optimal*. The high tone density which results from surface tone marking imposes too great a cognitive load on readers, and they are unable to use the information conveyed by the tone marks effectively. [emphasis added]

This conclusion was more of a surprise to "armchair" linguists than to seasoned field linguists and orthographers. However, Bird's recommendation for a return to a toneless orthography for Dschang was soundly rejected by literacy workers and by SIL linguists. He did not take the rejection of his recommendation well. He accused the Dschang literacy workers for being stubborn. He blamed the members of the language committee for summoning "naïve linguistic arguments to rationalize their position." He also jabbed expatriate linguists for wanting to write phonemic tone because "they can give fluent reading performances, with correct production of the tone" (2001:18–9).

7.3.5 The advent of the Tone Optimality Model

The examples in the previous sections have shown that not representing tones at all in the orthographies of African languages is not a sound decision because toneless orthographies lead to too many reading difficulties. Bird's experimental findings have also shown that writing tones fully lead to too many reading and spelling difficulties. There did not seem to be any middle-of-the road solution because a number of experienced linguists had spoken out clearly against writing tone selectively. In 1992, I began my work in West Africa as a consultant for the United Bible Societies in the midst of this tone and orthography conundrum. Fortunately, I had just finished a Ph.D. dissertation dealing with the interface between phonology and morphology in making decision for optimal orthographies. It was the perfect opportunity for me to put my training in theoretical linguistics to practical use. I began an experiment which is now known as the Tone Optimality Model (TOM). Readers who are interested in the details of this proposal can find the relevant information at www.orthographyclearinghouse.org. For now, suffice it for me to give a quick summary of the insights that led to this proposal.

I started training my teams on the supradialectal benefits of an optimal orthography, as discussed in *Sound Patterns of English* by Chomsky and Halle (1991). On the subject of tone, I proposed that phonemic tones be represented in the orthography *if and only if* they have semantic and/or grammatical functions in the language. The point of this proposal was to write the least number of tones possible, but to write them systematically and exhaustively. I began organizing week-long tone seminars for translators, literacy workers, and reviewers. Participants were grouped by language and were asked to come up with as many tone-induced lexical minimal pairs and grammatical pairs in their languages as possible. At the end of a mentally taxing week of intense brainstorming about tones, the participants shared their preliminary lists of words and tone-induced grammatical minimal pairs. Teams were sent home with their list and were charged to engage in a three-month research on the same topic. We met again at the appointed time and went over the list of words and grammatical constructions that they had collected since the last meeting. These sessions led to three surprising findings. First, I had expected to find a long list of tone-induced lexical and grammatical minimal pairs, but no language came up with more than 100 lexical minimal pairs, that is, 200 words that contrasted only by tone. Second, more surprising was the fact that the list of lexical minimal pairs did not grow appreciably longer during the three months devoted to this research. This showed me that even for languages that do not have a dictionary (the overwhelming majority of African languages are in this category), the list of lexical minimal pairs is not as long as had been previously extrapolated. Third, grammatical constructions distinguished by tone contrasts do not amount to more than half a dozen. They are most often associated with tense-aspect and mood in the conjugation of verbs. In some cases, tense-aspect and mood information is not even carried by the verb, but by the subject pronoun in the vicinity of the verb. My findings during these sessions confirmed what Welmers (1973:117) had previously discovered about the low frequency of lexical minimal pairs in many West African languages:

> Perhaps there is no tone language which is completely devoid of minimal contrasts in tone at the lexical level. There are, however, many languages in which such minimal contrasts are far from numerous. Minimal pairs are uncommon in many Bantu languages, in Akan, and in Hausa. In Baule, hundreds of words were transcribed before the first minimal contrast in tone was found, although tonemic contrasts had been established long before.[49]

In fact, after nearly twenty years of research on Anyi, I have not yet come across more than eighty tone-induced minimal pairs. Bird (1998a:17) reports that out of more than 3,000 words in Komo (language spoken in the Democratic Republic of Congo) studied by Thomas, only 28 lexical minimal pairs were found. This suggests that with some basic memory effort, speakers can recall the most common lexical minimal pairs of their language. In Bird (1998a:11), we also read that "if there are high frequency minimal pairs in close association, they will come to the mind of the writers, or else writers will learn from experience which words to mark for tone." It is on the basis of these findings that I made the following tone marking recommendations:

1. List exhaustively the tone-induced lexical and grammatical minimal pairs in the language.
2. Write tone systematically on all lexical and grammatical minimal pairs everywhere they occur in the text irrespective of context.
3. Write only phonemic tone, i.e., the tone of the word in its citation form. Do not write surface tone (phonetic realizations) because such tones are conditioned by various linguistic and paralinguistic factors which are still not completely understood.
4. Vowels bearing rising tones or falling tones should be written in the orthography as a sequence of two identical vowels.

---

49 Of all the languages that Welmers (1973:117) studied, he mentioned only Yoruba and Junkun as examples of languages where lexical minimal pairs are abundant. Glenn Kerr and his colleagues at Bibles International have given me a list of 200 lexical minimal pairs in Sango, a pidgin spoken in the Central African Republic.

5. In the interest of economy, write only the high tone in the orthography. Leave the low tone unmarked.[50] This reduces the overall tone density and prevents overloading the text with tonal diacritics.

The readers and writers of the languages in Benin, Cote d'Ivoire, and Togo who have adopted this method of representing tone have been satisfied. Writing tone only on lexical and grammatical minimal pairs has improved reading fluency. Marking tone strategically, systematically, and exhaustively to signal the meaning or grammatical function of words that would otherwise cause the reader to hesitate is comparable to road signs that help navigate through treacherous terrains. Writing only the high tone on these aforementioned items also reduces the overall diacritical tonal density in texts.

7.4 Why

Cooper (1996:68) proposes to answer the "why" question by examining two types of incentives: the incentives that lead policymakers to plan languages and the incentives that induce the adopters to adopt the products of language planning. The bottom line for both types of payoffs is that literacy and development go hand in hand, "It is a rule," Laubach (1947:11) contends, "that with literacy comes a rising level of economic development." The converse is also true, namely that illiteracy and poverty are bedfellows. Laubach (1947:21) puts this correlation succinctly as follows: "Poverty and ignorance (illiteracy) form a vicious circle. People are poor because they are ignorant, and they are ignorant because they are poor." Bhola (1984:11) is more blunt: "The world map of illiteracy is also the map of poverty." Cipro (1980:5) adds that there is no shortage of evidence correlating illiteracy with underdevelopment. Ong (1982:105) concurs with these assessments and provides historical evidence to support the claim that literacy is the surest pathway to development: "The ancient Greeks and Romans knew writing and used it, particularly the Greeks, to elaborate philosophical and scientific knowledge."

---

50 This recommendation is based on numerous studies which show that in languages that have a high tone or a low tone, the low tone tends to occur more frequently than the high tone. This is a universal tendency. The proposal also works for a language where high tones are more frequent than low tones. In that case, only the low tone would be indicated in the orthography.

This broad consensus on the virtue of literacy as a catalyst for development is the thrust behind the push of the United Nations to eliminate illiteracy worldwide. The United Nations Development Programme (UNDP) has provided data that convincingly correlate illiteracy and poverty. Of the 169 countries or territories ranked by the UNDP in 2010, African countries rank the lowest on the Human Development Index (HDI). The HDI was introduced by economists in the 1990 to provide both non-monetary and monetary indices to measure development. The non-monetary index includes "the long and healthy life index" and "the education index." The monetary index still measures the gross development product (GDP). In 2010 the UNDP began using these indices to classify countries into four categories: Very High Human Development, High Human Development, Medium Human Development, and Low Human Development.[51] Nearly all Sub-Saharan African countries with the exception of Congo, Gabon, Botswana, Namibia, South Africa, Equatorial Guinea, and Cape Verde, are classified as Low Human Development countries, as seen in Table 7.4:

Table 7.4. Literacy Ranking[52]

No.	Country	Literacy Rate	Literacy Ranking	HDI Ranking
1.	Algeria	77.6%	132	84
2.	Angola	67.4%	146	146
3.	Benin	43.0%	173	134
4.	Botswana	98%	120	84.8
5.	Burkina Faso	28.7%	178	161
6.	Burundi	59.3%	157	166
7.	Cameroon	67.9%	145	131
8.	Cape Verde	85.9%	117	118
9.	Central African Republic	48.6%	169	159
10.	Chad	31.8%	176	163
11.	Comoros	77.5%	133	149

(*Continued*)

---

51 The information in this section was retrieved from http://hdr.undp.org/en/statistics/ on March 25, 2011.

52 Retrieved from http://hdrstats.undp.org/en/indicators/6.html and http://en.wikipedia.org/wiki/List_of_countries_by_literacy_rate on March 4h, 2011.

Table 7.4. Literacy Ranking[52] (*Cont.*)

No.	Country	Literacy Rate	Literacy Ranking	HDI Ranking
12.	Congo, DRC	67.2%	147	168
13.	Congo, Republic	81.1%	125	126
14.	Côte d'Ivoire	48.7%	168	149
15.	Djibouti	70.3	143	NA
16.	Egypt	66.4%	148	101
17.	Equatorial Guinea	67.9%	112	117
18.	Eritrea	67.7%	153	117
19.	Ethiopia	35.9%	175	157
20.	Gabon	88.2%	114	83
21.	(The) Gambia	NA	171	NA
22.	Ghana	67.3%	150	130
23.	Guinea, French	29.5%	177	156
24.	Guinea-Bissau	69.5%	152	164
25.	Kenya	73.6%	135	128
26.	Lesotho	82.2%	122	141
27.	Liberia	58.9%	NA	162
28.	Libya	88.0%	113	53
29.	Madagascar	70.7%	141	135
30.	Malawi	74.5%	140	153
31.	Mali	26.2%	180	160
32.	Mauritania	57.6%	161	136
33.	Mauritius	88.6%	111	72
34.	Morocco	58.2%	162	114
35.	Mozambique	46.2%	170	165
36.	Namibia	88.9%	107	105
37.	Niger	28.7%	178	167
38.	Nigeria	74.8%	139	142
39.	Rwanda	64.9%	151	152
40.	Sao Tome y Principe	89.2%	110	127

(*Continued*)

Table 7.4. Literacy Ranking[52] (Cont.)

No.	Country	Literacy Rate	Literacy Ranking	HDI Ranking
41.	Senegal	41.9%	172	144
42.	Seychelles	91.8%	90	60
43.	Sierra Leone	41.4%	174	168
44.	Somalia	NA	NA	NA
45.	South Africa	89.3%	107	110
46.	Sudan	60.9%	156	154
47.	Swaziland	79.6%	126	121
48.	Tanzania	73.2%	138	148
49.	Togo	54.2%	165	139
50.	Tunisia	80.0%	128	81
51.	Uganda	76.4%	135	143
52.	Zambia	71.4%	142	150
53.	Zimbabwe	92.6%	91	169

The correlation between literacy and development is uncontroversial. Worldwide, four main models of literacy are commonly used. However, to the best of my knowledge, they have not been compared and contrasted to see which of the four meets the needs and expectations of illiterate adults in rural Africa. In the remaining section, the Predictioneer's Model will be used to determine which of the four literacy models – Autonomous Literacy, Functional Literacy, Faith-based Literacy, and Advocacy Literacy – can be most effective in this endeavor.

7.4.1 The contributions of Autonomous Literacy

Autonomous Literacy can be described as the view according to which literacy is the agency that sets in motion social and cognitive change. Grenoble and Whaley (2006:104) claim that "[Autonomous Literacy] has been enormously influential in shaping views of literacy, education, and cognitive development." They name Goody and Ong among the leading proponents of this view. I suspect that if Grenoble and Whaley had been aware of Logan's work, his name would have figured prominently among the proponents of autonomous literacy. The title of his book alone, *The Alphabetic*

Effect: The Impact of the Phonetic Alphabet on the Development of Western Civilization, is a celebration of the payoffs of autonomous literacy. Logan (1986:65, 68, 107, 123) describes how literacy propelled the Hellenistic world, and subsequently Western societies, toward development. He contends that alphabetic literacy first led to abstract thinking, then to the atomization of knowledge, to the development of theoretical sciences, and ultimately to the emergence of applied sciences. He describes the role of atomization in the overall process as follows:

> With the alphabet every word is fragmented into its constituent sounds and constituent letters. The Greeks' idea of atomicity, that all matter can be divided up into individual distinct tiny atoms, is related to their alphabet: 'Atomism and the alphabet alike were theoretical constructs, manifestations of a capacity for abstract analysis, an ability to translate objects of perception into mental entities. … The capacity for fragmentation and separation extends far beyond the Greek concept of atomicity of matter. With writing, what is recorded or remembered becomes separate from the writer. It stands alone in a book or a scroll independent of the context of the person who originated the ideas or the information. Knowledge begins to take on an identity separate from the knower. The Greeks through writing developed a notion of objectivity – the separation of the knower from the object of his study. This is the beginning of the scientific method and the source of the dichotomy the Greeks created between subjective and objective thinking (Logan 1987:107).

For Goody (1987:239), the key transformative power of literacy resides in its capacity to store, retrieve, and pass on knowledge to the next generation. If only more Africans in rural areas could be taught to read and write, so the proponents of autonomous literacy would argue, they would write down their vast ethnoscientific knowledge, store it so that succeeding generations could learn from it, and improve on it for the good of their societies as a whole. Instead, the oral traditions in which many rural communities live are not conducive to development because, according to Lestage (1983:3), "the objective transformation wrought by the development process cannot come about as long as one is exclusively confined to oral communication. Such communication, although functional in static contexts, does not allow sufficient accumulation and use of knowledge in changing societies." The one domain where the lack of literacy thwarts progress the most in rural Africa is in the area of medical science. Scores of illnesses that the elders were able to cure easily with local plants are playing havoc on the populations because that knowledge was not passed down when elders passed away accidentally. Logan (1986:66–7) argues that if the people were literate this would not happen because they would write their knowledge down and this body of knowledge could be referred to centuries later.

A great deal of energy and time on the part of the proponents of autonomous literacy went into testing some of the postulates. Many of them were greatly disillusioned to know that literacy for the sake of literacy could not achieve the expected results of social and cognitive transformation. The results of several studies done by Scribner and Cole (1973), Ong (1986), and Goody (1987) among the Vai of Sierra Leone laid to rest the claims of autonomous literacy. Contrary to the prevailing ideas of the time, Scribner and Cole (1973) argued that not all types of literacy are conducive to cognitive and social development. They concluded from another study that "literacy in Vai has not set off a dramatic modernizing sequence; it has not been accompanied by rapid developments in technology, art and science, it has not led to the growth of intellectual disciplines" (Scribner and Cole 1981:239). Goody (1987:216) grudgingly agreed that "The Vai material does not fulfill the expectations of those social scientists who consider literacy a prime mover of social change." In light of this finding, Cooper's (1996:130) statement that "the Vai enjoyed an economic status superior to that of neighboring African peoples as well as enhanced prestige, owing at least partly to their possession of a unique script" has to be taken with a grain of salt. Various attempts have been made to explain why Autonomous Literacy has not yielded the expected payoffs. Recently, Grenoble and Whaley (2006:106) have suggested that "It is not literacy per se but rather formal education which affects thought processes."

7.4.2 The contributions of Functional Literacy

The realization that autonomous literacy was not capable of bringing about societal change led UNESCO to look for a different model of literacy. It found what is commonly referred to as "functional literacy." Proponents of this approach train illiterate populations for specific and well-defined skills. Some agro-industries in West Africa provide literacy training to cotton and sugar cane factory workers. Some NGOs working in the fishery business have provided basic literacy skills to fishermen in coastal areas of the Gulf of Guinea so that they can prepare and conserve their catch. In the majority of cases, functional literacy skills are provided as an economic incentive. Pre-literate people are lured by the promise that knowing how to read and write will accrue financial benefits for them. Grenoble and Whaley (2006:112) write that many people are now taking issue with this model:

UNESCO has been criticized for placing too great an emphasis on the economic development and failing to recognize the complexities of literacy. Critics point out that literacy is a complex cultural dynamic; attempts to single out economic functionality and give it primacy lead to a false dichotomy between economics and life as a whole.

This criticism notwithstanding, Grenoble and Whaley (2006:112) note that UNESCO's programs "continue to flourish because it promises comparatively substantial gains by equipping individuals with an ill-defined but relatively modest level of competence." Generally, functional literacy programs work very well for second-chance literacy programs where instruction is done in an international LWC (Bhola 2006). People who live in urban or semi-urban areas have taken advantage of UNESCO's second-chance literacy classes to increase their marketable skills. Such programs were wildly popular in Côte d'Ivoire in the 1980s. I taught adults middle school French and English in one UNESCO school in a suburb of Abidjan so that drop-outs could take their junior high school exam.

Functional literacy programs in indigenous African languages are far less successful for a variety of reasons. First, the incentive structure is not sufficiently appealing. Many cash crop farmers do not see the need to be literate before using fertilizers to get a better yield for their cotton, coffee, or cocoa. They just need to be shown how to use the modern farming techniques and technologies. Even if they do become functionally literate, they do not expand their skills beyond the task at hand. Once they become good at what they are doing, they become complacent. Secondly, there is often a lack of new material to sustain literacy. Printing one or two booklets to teach how to grow cotton, for instance, will not do. Logan (1986:119–20, 131) states that new reading materials must be continuously printed to keep newly literate people interested in reading. The third major obstacle is funding. UNESCO and many agencies are eager to start literacy projects with a five year grant. As soon as the funding stops, the literacy program also stops because African governments do not continue funding the project even though they may have said they would to get the grant. The fourth weakness of functional literacy is the lopsided attention it gives to reading at the expense of writing. As a result, graduates of such programs are less inclined to write in their native languages. If Goody is right that development is fostered by accumulating, retrieving, and passing on indigenous knowledge, the lack of emphasis on writing is a serious handicap.

7.4.3 Contributions of Advocacy Literacy

The name Paulo Freire is often associated with literacy advocacy. Inspired by Marxist ideology, Freire vigorously promoted literacy as a way of helping the politically and the economically disenfranchised in his native Brazil. He hoped to use literacy to affect social change from the bottom-up. Freire believes that the powerful elite often keep the masses illiterate so that they can control them better. Two Brazilian peasants who were his students expressed very eloquently why they wanted to be literate. One said, "I want to learn to read and write so that I can stop being the shadow of other people." The other added, "I am not angry at being poor, but at not knowing how to read" (Freire 1972:50). African countries that embraced the Marxist ideology made more progress in indigenous adult literacy than those that remained staunchly capitalistic. The case of Tanzania under Julius Nyerere has been well documented. Less known, however, are the cases of Ethiopia and Somalia. Cooper (1996:21, 24) reports that indigenous adult literacy programs were established throughout Ethiopia when the Communists took over:

> Within a few months more than 50,000 students were to be sent into the countryside on a rural development campaign, which included teaching the peasants, almost all of whom were illiterate, how to read and write. ... Like the Emperor [Haile Selassie], the Derg saw the importance of language in social control. Shortly after taking power, the Derg announced a multilingual mass-literacy campaign.

Laitin (1992:108, 151) reports similar progress in Somalia. Before the advent of Mohamed Siad Barre's Communist government, Somali scholars had been engaged in a twenty-year dispute about which script to use to write their language. He writes that "It took a revolutionary regime to compel the society to adopt a script for its language and to employ that language in administration." Once the debate over the script was forcefully resolved, Somali leaders sent college students all over the country to conduct literacy classes for adults. Laitin (1992:158) notes that "adult literacy programs immediately became feasible, and national literacy rates soared." In 22 years of rule over Somalia (1969–1991), Mohamed Siad Barre and his Marxist Supreme Revolutionary Council succeeded in spreading literacy in urban and rural areas across Somalia. He accomplished more for mass literacy in two short decades than all of UNESCO's fifty years of advocacy for adult literacy.

With the fall of the Berlin Wall, Communism is no more a dominant ideology. But a new form of literacy advocacy has emerged. This approach has been labeled "Humanitarian Literacy" by Grenoble and Whaley (2006:122).

It may be seen as part of the strategy employed by the Linguistic Rights movement. Since the landmark World Congress on Linguistic Rights of June 6–9 in Barcelona in 1996 which produced the Universal Declaration of Linguistic Rights document,[53] groups of linguists have been agitating for the preservation, maintenance, codification, and documentation of minority languages. Language rights advocates see literacy in local languages as a way of revitalizing moribund languages.

7.4.4 The contributions of faith-based literacy

Religion and literacy have been bedfellows for a very long time. The interconnection between the two goes back more than 5,000 years. Ancient societies often attribute the origin of their writing systems to a divine agency, as is the case of ancient Egyptian writing:

> Later writing was used to keep a calendar for calculating the annual flood of the Nile and to give permanent form to the spells and prayers necessary to ensure a plentiful harvest year after year and to transmit them in the correct form to future generations. While the stimulus was apparently economic in both countries [i.e., Mesopotamia and Egypt], it was priests and administrators who devoted themselves to the leisured exploitation of this complex system of writing. The complexity of the writing confined its systematic use to a well-trained set of scribes, whose training was at times carried out by priests (Goody 1987:3–56).

Logan (1986:164–5) explains that wherever Judaism, Christianity, and Islam spread, literacy also spread because these three religions are known euphemistically as the "Religions of the Book." This is certainly the case for Europe, Africa, and several other places in the world. Koffi (2010:35–38) writes that literacy spread into Europe through the agency of the church. Beginning around the sixth century, Christian missionaries taught Europeans how to read, write, and do arithmetic in their various languages. Similarly, everywhere in Africa where literacy in indigenous languages exists, its roots can be traced back either to Islam or to Christianity (Goody 1987:141). Frazer (2006:103) attributes the introduction of literacy to Native American communities in the Midwest to Christianity: "Believing that salvation lay in

---

53 Retrieved from http://www.linguistic-declaration.org/index-gb.htm and http://www.linguistic-declaration.org/versions/angles.pdfhttp://www.unesco.org/cpp/uk/declarations/linguistic.pdf on April 25, 2011.

the ability to read the Bible, they [Puritans] promoted literacy." In light of this long and successful association between literacy and religion, Grenoble and Whaley (2006:41) find it ironic that contemporary academic discussions of literacy often overlook religion as a facilitating agency.

7.5 The quest for an optimal model of literacy planning

Let's now apply the Predictioneer's Model to these four approaches to literacy planning to see which one is most likely to be successful in rural Africa. Each model is assigned a numerical value. The Autonomous Literacy Model is rated at 100 because it is the most widely used and practiced literacy model. It is used in all kinds of educational settings and in nearly all countries. Next is the Faith-based Literacy Model. As the second best-known model, it has been used for hundreds of years and by hundreds of faith-based organizations all over the world. Functional Literacy is relatively new since it is generally associated with UNESCO. It is rated at 50. The Advocacy Literacy Model is rated 25 because it carries ideological baggage that turns some communities off. Finally, room has been made for language groups or communities that, for cultural reasons, do not want their local languages to be reduced to writing. Grenoble and Whaley (2006:116) and Grenoble et al. (2009:197) mention some Latin American Indian communities who oppose literacy in their indigenous languages. The position of not allowing indigenous literacy is rated 0.

Table 7.5. Preferred Literacy Models

No.	Models of Literacy Planning	Ranking of Models
1.	Autonomous Literacy Model	100
2.	Faith-based Literacy Model	75
3.	Functional Literacy Model	50
4.	Advocacy Literacy Model	25
5.	No literacy in Indigenous Languages	0

Table 7.6 rates players with regard to the medium of instruction. A rating of 100 means that the player wants the medium of instruction to be the indigenous language. A rating of 0 means that he/she favors the international LWC. The rating of the position held by players is based on the information presented in 7.2.1 and 7.2.3. All in all, 21 players have been identified. The acronym FBO stands for faith-based organizations, NGO for non-governmental organizations, and GO means governmental organizations.

Table 7.6. Position Scale

No.	Rural Literacy Players	Position Scale
1.	UNESCO on Literacy in Indigenous Languages	100
2.	UNESCO on Literacy in International LWCs	0
3.	UNESCO on Literacy in Regional/National LWCs	50[1]
4.	FBO on Literacy in Indigenous Languages	100
5.	FBO on Literacy in International LWCs	0
6.	FBO on Literacy in Regional/National LWCs	0
7.	NGO on Literacy in Indigenous Languages	100
8.	NGO on Literacy in International LWCs	0
9.	NGO on Literacy in Regional/National LWCs	0[2]
10.	Individuals on Literacy in Indigenous Languages	100
11.	Individuals on Literacy in International LWCs	10
12.	Individuals on Literacy in Regional/National LWCs	10
13.	GO on Literacy in Indigenous Languages	50
14.	GO on Literacy in International LWCs	70
15.	GO on Literacy in Regional/National LWCs	80
16.	Males on Literacy in Indigenous Languages	80
17.	Males on Literacy in International LWCs	100
18.	Males on Literacy in Regional/National LWCs	0[3]
19.	Females on Literacy in Indigenous Languages	80
20.	Females on Literacy in International LWCs	100
21.	Females on Literacy in Regional/National LWCs	0

Notes:
1 As the example in San Pedro, see sections 3.5 and 7.2.2 UNESCO and other funding agencies would rather spend money planning literacy in a regional or national LWC than in individual languages. Most of UNESCO projects are large scale projects aimed at languages with hundreds of thousands of speakers.
2 Some NGOs target specific languages for maintenance or revitalization, they are not interested in regional or national LWCs per se.
3 When the speakers have a strong ethnolinguistic identity, they reject this form of literacy. They are willing to be literate in their own language or an international lingua franca. The example of Diula in San Pedro lends support to this claim. Naturally, if literacy is being planned for a group with low ethnolinguistic loyalty, these figures may have to be adjusted.

Table 7.7 rates the salience (level of interest) of each of the 21 players. In the Predictioneer's Model, the highest level of interest is rated at 95 because one cannot be absolutely sure, and the lowest level of interest is rated at 10.

Table 7.8 assigns numerical values to the players according to their influence. UNESCO is rated 100 on the basis of the information discussed in 7.2.1. SIL International is rated 80 because the decision to allow its members to stay in a country is based on the good will of local officials. The country's own agency that supervises literacy is rated 70 because those agencies are often staffed with people who have very little expertise in the field of literacy. The influence of local NGOs is rated 60. International language rights NGOs that seek to revitalize moribund languages are rated 50. Influential individuals who initiate indigenous literacy programs are rated 40.

Table 7.7. Salience Scale

No.	Salience	Salience Scale
1.	UNESCO on Literacy in Indigenous Languages	95
2.	UNESCO on Literacy in the International LWCs	50^1
3.	UNESCO on Literacy in a Regional/National LWCs	80
4.	FBO on Literacy in Indigenous Languages	95
5.	FBO on Literacy in the International LWCs	10
6.	FBO on Literacy in Regional/National LWCs	10^2
7.	NGO on Literacy in Indigenous Languages	95
8.	NGO on Literacy in International LWCs	10
9.	NGO on Literacy in Regional/National LWCs	10^3
10.	Individuals on Literacy in Indigenous Languages	95
11.	Individuals on Literacy in International LWCs	10^4
12.	Individuals on Literacy in Regional/National LWCs	10^5
13.	GO on Literacy in Indigenous Languages	60
14.	GO on Literacy in International LWCs	70
15.	GO on Literacy in Regional/National LWCs	70
16.	Males on Literacy in Indigenous Languages	70
17.	Males on Literacy in the International LWCs	95
18.	Males on Literacy in Regional/National LWCs	10

(*Continued*)

7.5 The quest for an optimal model of literacy planning 245

Table 7.7. Salience Scale (*Cont.*)

No.	Salience	Salience Scale
19.	Females on Literacy in Indigenous Languages	90
20.	Females on Literacy in the International LWCs	95
21.	Females on Literacy in Regional/National LWCs	10

Notes:
1 UNESCO does not favor literacy in international LWCs except in the case of second-chance literacy projects. This research is not interested in such projects.
2 Faith-based organizations during the colonial period were more interested in literacy in regional languages. There are many examples of this, including the promotion of Ewe in Ghana and Togo, and Swahili in eastern Africa, as discussed in 4.25, 4.2.6, and 4.4.1. However, mission organizations are now focusing on individual people groups. As a result, they are no longer interested in regional literacy planning.
3 Most NGOs are now driven by language maintenance and revitalization. As such, they tend to focus on individual languages, not regional or national LWCs.
4 It is quite unlikely that an individual who speaks a specific African language would leave his/her native language on the side and promote a language that is different from his/her own. If the individual is a contemporary foreign missionary, he/she is likely to plan the language for the specific group among whom he/she is ministering.
5 Individuals are often driven by language planning to benefit a specific community, they have very little interest in planning regional/national LWCs.

The influence that men have is rated at 20 and that of women is rated 10. Though women are more likely to attend literacy classes, the gender roles discussed in 7.2.3 show that they have a lesser influence than men in many traditional African societies.

Table 7.8. Influence Scale

No.	Rural Literacy Players	Influence Scale
1.	UNESCO	100
2.	International Faith-based Organizations	80
3.	Governmental Organizations	70
4.	Local Non-Governmental Organizations	60
5.	International Non-Governmental Organizations	50
6.	Individual Agencies	40

(*Continued*)

Table 7.8. Influence Scale (*Cont.*)

No.	Rural Literacy Players	Influence Scale
7.	Male Literacy Clients	20[1]
8.	Female Literacy Clients	10

Notes:
1 Generally, literacy clients in rural areas do not have much say on how literacy projects are run. However, men tend to have a little more say than women because of the gender roles discussed in 7.2.3.

The preceding pieces of information can now allow us to calculate the weighted mean score which is shown in Table 7.9.

Table 7.9. Weighted Mean

No.	Rural Literacy Players	Influence Scale	Salience Scale	Position Scale	I × S × P	I × S
1.	UNESCO on Literacy in Indigenous Languages	100	95	100	950	9,5
2.	UNESCO on Literacy in International LWCs	100	50	0	0	5
3.	UNESCO on Literacy in Regional/National LWCs	100	80	50	400	8
4.	FBO on Literacy in Indigenous Languages	80	95	100	760	7,6
5.	FBO on Literacy in International LWCs	80	10	0	0	800
6.	FBO on Literacy in Regional/National LWCs	80	10	0	0	800

(*Continued*)

Table 7.9. Weighted Mean (*Cont.*)

No.	Rural Literacy Players	Influence Scale	Salience Scale	Position Scale	I × S × P	I × S
7.	NGO on Literacy in Indigenous Languages	50	95	100	475	4,75
8.	NGO on Literacy in International LWCs	50	10	0	0	500
9.	NGO on Literacy in Regional/National LWCs	50	10	0	0	500
10.	Individuals on Literacy in Indigenous Languages	40	95	100	380	3,8
11.	Individuals on Literacy in International LWCs	40	10	10	4	400
12.	Individuals on Literacy in Regional/National LWCs	40	10	10	4	400
13.	GO on Literacy in Indigenous Languages	70	60	50	210	4,2
14.	GO on Literacy in International LWCs	70	70	70	343	4,9
15.	GO on Literacy in Regional/National LWCs	70	70	80	392	4,9
16.	Males on Literacy in Indigenous Languages	20	70	80	112	1,4
17.	Males on Literacy in the International LWCs	20	95	100	190	1,9

(*Continued*)

Table 7.9. Weighted Mean (*Cont.*)

No.	Rural Literacy Players	Influence Scale	Salience Scale	Position Scale	I × S × P	I × S
18.	Males on Literacy in Regional/National LWCs	20	10	0	0	200
19.	Females on Literacy in Indigenous Languages	10	90	80	72	900
20.	Females on Literacy in the International LWCs	10	95	100	95	950
21.	Females on Literacy in Regional/National LWCs	10	10	0	0	100
22.	Total				4,387,000	61,5
23.	Weighted Means				71.33%	

7.5.1 The ingredients of an optimal model

The weighted mean score of 71.33% suggests that the Faith-Based Model is the one that is most likely to succeed in rural Africa. What if, for one reason or another, proselytism is not allowed in the society in need of literacy? Faith-based literacy programs have four key ingredients that can be secularized. These four indispensable ingredients are long-term commitment, proximity, sustainability, and payoff. Literacy requires a commitment that spans across several decades. UNESCO and many granting agencies provide funding for three to five years. The late Dr. Fagerberg Diallo told me over lunch at the 38th Annual Conference on African Linguistics at the University of Florida that a rural literacy project begins bearing fruit after 20 to 30 years of toil. The Faith-based Model of indigenous literacy is more successful than other models because Christian organizations are committed for the long term. The literacy project of the Christian and Missionary Alliance among the Baule of Côte d'Ivoire has been going for nearly 100 years.

Proximity is another important ingredient that secular sponsors of literacy projects should take seriously. Christian missionaries live and work in the rural communities where they are ministering. As a result, they know their clients (see 7.2.3). They understand the important issues related to where and when literacy classes are held, as discussed in 7.2.4 and 7.2.5. Because of proximity, they can respond to the various needs that can hamper the progress of the literacy project. However, this is not so for UNESCO's projects or secular projects funded by governments or NGOs. Most of these projects have a top-down management structure. More often than not, project managers are in an air-conditioned office in the capital city. They seldom visit projects. They rely on second-hand reports. Yet they manage to produce flattering project evaluations that they pass on from supervisor to supervisor until they reach the head office. In the end, reports that are too good to be true are compiled and disseminated worldwide. Bhola (2006) notes that UNESCO is experimenting with a better way to evaluate literacy projects. He, however, acknowledges that it would be hard to implement such an instrument because reports from member countries have to clear national and administrative red tape.

The third key ingredient in gauging the success of a literacy program and its long time viability is sustainability. Sustainability means availability of resources in the indigenous language that encourage people to keep on reading. As noted in 7.4.2, functional literacy programs do not often produce enough reading materials to entice the newly literate person to keep reading. As a result, when a person is trained under the Functional Literacy Model and has finished going through the course syllabus, there is nothing more to read. Many stagnate and revert back to near illiteracy. Faith-based literacy projects, on the other hand, have a variety of texts that they make available to readers. In addition to primers, they make different books of Scripture available to readers so that the newly literate person can get hold of new reading materials. German missionaries in Ewe published a large variety of reading materials, some of which had nothing to do with promoting the faith. Granting organizations should do everything within their power to produce at least 20 titles on topics of interest to the community. Reading materials dealing with environmental concerns, maternal and infant care, hygiene and nutrition, democratic citizenship, history, etc. should be planned. Moreover, some grant money should be set aside to publish works written by indigenous writers. Doing so will foster the accumulation of ethnoscientific knowledge that seems to be a prerequisite to development.

The last ingredient is payoff. This is another area where secular literacy organizations may be at a disadvantage in comparison with faith-based organizations. The former usually has to entice rural communities with various types of incentives to win them over to literacy. Appealing to their ethnolinguistic loyalty or issuing doomsday prophecies about the impending demise of their languages have not convinced many to embrace adult literacy in indigenous languages. Many Sub-Saharan Africans have come to equate literacy with a job that pays a salary. Anything short of that is, according to Kaplan (1998:421), "an activity that promises a vague good in the distant future." The lack of marketable skills after training in an indigenous language makes secular literacy projects unappealing to most. This is not so for faith-based literacy projects. Those who enroll in them expect spiritual payoffs. And they are not disappointed. They acquire literacy skills which they use throughout their terrestrial lives to enrich themselves spiritually. Looking back at over the five thousand years since Homo Sapiens have been acquainted with literacy, religion has been the surest pathway through which it has spread. From religious instruction, literacy has overflowed into other areas of secular life and led to all kinds of scientific, cognitive, and societal transformations.

7.6 Summary

The answers to the questions, *"Who plans what for whom, when, where, how, and why?"* have provided us with insight about the players in the literacy planning game and the logistics of literacy planning in rural areas. The answer to the "how" question in particular brought into focus how corpus planning decisions can hamper or facilitate reading and writing skills in tone languages. The comparative analysis of the four major models, each with its strengths and its weaknesses, led to the Predictioneer's Model. The weighted mean score of 71.33% points to the Faith-Based Model as the one most likely to succeed in Africa. The four indispensable ingredients of the Faith-Based Model that make it so efficient – commitment, proximity, sustainability, and payoff – can all be secularized. According to UNESCO's own assessment, adult literacy planning in local African languages is not going as well as expected in spite of very important gains since independence. It is perhaps time to experiment with a secularized version of the Faith-Based Model.

Chapter 8
Planning multiple languages on a shoestring budget for profit

Introduction

Most of the literature on planning for mother-tongue education has assumed that planning for multiple languages would be prohibitively expensive and it would play havoc on the budgets of cash-strapped countries in Sub-Saharan Africa. Because of this assumption, most of the emphasis has been placed on planning for a single national LWC instead of planning for multiple languages. This chapter shows that it is not more expensive to plan for multiple mother tongues for use in schools than it is to plan for a single national LWC. Under the game-theoretic model of language planning model, many African countries can turn their vast linguistic resources into an economic bonanza. For game theorists, planning languages is like planning any other resources. Before economic gains can be made, capital must be invested first. This is the commonsensical view that is taken in this chapter. It will be shown that the initial capital needed to turn the vast multilingual resources of the continent into economic manna is within the reach of even the poorest country in Africa.

The data in support of this analysis is drawn from Côte d'Ivoire, but similar information is found elsewhere that can validate the claim that teaching multiple languages in secondary school is not significantly more expensive than teaching a single LWC. Two reasons justify my choice of Côte d'Ivoire. First, I know this country far better than any other country on the continent for having been born and raised there. Moreover, the data that constitute the basis of this chapter has been collected over a long period. Government data, newspaper articles, and multiple sources have provided me with information that is verifiable. The second reason for choosing Côte d'Ivoire is that the analyses in Chapter 5 showed that it presents an extremely difficult case of language planning. According to Bamgbose (1991:56), Côte d'Ivoire is one African country for which language planning is a very low priority because it is "happy with French." I contend in this chapter that if Ivorian languages can be turned into economic assets despite their perceived low market values, any other Sub-Saharan country can easily turn its linguistic resources into economic manna. However, before delving into the arguments that prove the above-mentioned points, we must first review some basic notions about the economics of language.

8.1 An overview of the economics of language

Since this chapter deals with cost-benefit analysis, it falls within the province of the sub-discipline of economics known as the "economics of language." In a brief review of the literature, Vaillancourt (1983:168) credits economists from Quebec with having played a leading role in the development of this academic sub-discipline. In a statement that may be construed as scornful, albeit candid, he describes the new discipline as a "fledgling branch of the dismal science." Presumably, the phrase "economics of language" appeared in the literature for the first time in the 1950s. Back then, it was mainly concerned with the relationship between language, economics, and ethnicity. Vaillancourt's (2009) contribution to *Language and Poverty* shows that the economics of language has not strayed too far away from its original focus. However, over the years, the scope of the new discipline has been broadened to include topics of interest such as the correlation between language skills and earnings, the economic rationales for second language acquisition, language use in the workplace, and the language policies of multinational corporations, to name only a few. Vaillancourt (1983:172) notes that language economists have spent more time on microeconomic issues than on macroeconomic ones. For instance, he contends on page 168 that such an important question "What is the economic effect of language planning on society?" has gone unanswered. This chapter seeks to provide an answer to the aspect of this question that touches on the language of education policy. For this reason, let's examine two metaphors commonly found in the economics of language literature. Both figures of speech liken language and time to money.

8.1.1 Language is money

The metaphor that compares language to wealth or treasure has been made repeatedly since the 15th century (Koffi 2010:37–8). However, when the terms "wealth" or "treasure" were equated with language, the emphasis was on the non-monetary value of language. Usually when the metaphor is used, it highlights the cultural worth and the intrinsic values that a mother tongue represents for a given speech community. However, when contemporary economists compare language with money, they have in mind the aspects of language that are quantifiable into financial gains. They do not hesitate to view language as a resource on par with natural resources. For this reason, language is being increasingly referred to as a "capital," "an investment portfolio," or "an asset." This shift in the way language is talked about among economists of language is having an impact on language planners. Language planning is no longer being viewed merely as a sociolinguistic or a political decision, but also as an economic one. Language planners are now beginning to understand that decisions about which language to learn at school are in fact economic investment decisions. It is precisely because language consumers see language as an economic good that individuals and communities tend to acquire high-yield languages. They gravitate toward languages that accrue more economic returns for their investment of time and intellectual efforts. This age-old linguistic behavior is in line with Mohanty's (2009:119) hypothesis of the "hierarchical competitive relationship" among languages. Under normal circumstances, language consumers will invest their talents in learning a language that is economically or politically profitable for them. Viewed from this perspective, the linguistic behavior of Africans as described by Alexander (2009:56) makes perfect sense. He argues that for Africans, investing in French, English, or Portuguese is a wise portfolio management strategy because "their acquisition represents truly a form of capital accumulation." Kamwangamalu (1997:243) uses essentially the same marketability rationale in explaining why South African parents are more eager for their children to learn English than their own native tongues at school. Alexander (2009:62) warns that if the marketability of African languages does not become obvious, mother-tongue education is bound to fail. The age of Globalization in which we live has presented a serious challenge for language planners. They can no longer count on guilt-laced emotive arguments such as "let's not let our mother tongue die" or "if our language dies, that's the death of our culture" to guilt people into choosing to learn their mother tongue at school. Sound marketability arguments should be made to show to language consumers and policymakers that mother-tongue education in indigenous languages is economically profitable.

This has been a tall order for the past fifty years or so because policymakers and experts have led Africans to believe that planning multiple languages for use at school is ruinous economically. The metaphor that language is money has also suggested, maybe inadvertently, that planning for multiple languages leads to poverty. Vaillancourt (1983:171) explains it as follows:

One approach is to treat language as money. In that case, the greater the acceptance of a given language, the greater is its usefulness. Another approach is to treat language as a cost of trade; the wider the use of a language, the lower the barriers to trade and the greater the gains. Both theoretical models lead to the conclusion that the emergence of a lingua franca within a society, or between societies, is to be desired

Bamgbose (1991:36–7) has decried this correlation and has argued that "there is no necessary correlation between linguistic homogeneity and low economic status or vice versa." Unfortunately, this belief is still widespread among linguists, politicians, and the citizenry of many African nations. Multilingualism is viewed more as an economic curse than a blessing. The goal in this chapter is to prove based on solid data that this need not be so. It will be argued in 8.5 that linguistic diversity with the right type of language of education policy can be an economic bonanza for African countries.

8.1.2 Time is money

"Time is money," goes the popular adage. Vaillancourt (1981:165) describes time as both "a scarce and valuable resource." If language is money and time is money, it goes without saying that neither of the two should be wasted. It also means that the longer African languages go unplanned, the more time and money are being wasted. Fifty years after independence, African languages in francophone countries are woefully absent from the formal linguistic marketplace. It is true that some of them are used daily in the exchange of goods and services, but the informality of these transactions makes it hard to quantify in monetary terms the worth of these languages. Worse, the widespread use of some of these languages in the informal sector have convinced some decision makers that nothing further needs to be done to maximize the profitability of these languages. Nothing could be further from the truth. The thesis that is being defended in this chapter is that the more African languages are used in the educational system, especially at the secondary level, the more their market value will increase.

The adage "Time is money" is also true with respect to "time-horizon planning" (Thorburn 1972:512, 516). The longer a language goes unplanned, the more accentuated is the loss of revenue that it could have generated if it had been planned sooner. To prove this point, we will examine how much revenue can be generated by planning multiple Ivorian languages over a fifteen-year period. Normally, Thorburn (1972:516) recommends a twenty-five year time frame, but it will be shown that fifteen years is plenty for planned languages to start generating multimillion dollar revenues.

8.2 Paradigm shift in language planning

It has been said in the previous chapters, but it is worth repeating, that language planning is a relatively new academic discipline. Its history cannot be traced back further than the 1960s. For most of that history, that is, until the mid-1990s, language planning was characterized by a monolithic strategy geared towards selecting an indigenous LWC as the national language. Alexander (2009:57) has used the phrase "Old Dispensation" to describe this historical period. I will contrast this period with an emerging model of language planning which began from the mid-1990s. This period will be referred to as the "New Dispensation."

8.2.1 Language planning in the Old Dispensation

Language planning in the Old Dispensation was dominated by the hegemonic model. For nearly 50 years, experts operated under the language planning equation of One Nation = One Language. Cooper (1996:3–11) contends that many European nations followed the French model and elevated one language above all others as their "national" language. The language that achieved that higher status also became the "official" language by virtue of being used to carry out official state functions. Legal provisions were made which enshrined that language in the Constitution. When the formerly colonized countries of Africa, Asia, and Latin America gained their independence, they kept the colonial language as their official language because it was already used throughout the colony to conduct state business. As a symbol of true independence, attempts were made here and there to elevate an indigenous LWC to the status of "national" language in an imitation of the European model of One Nation = One Language. Kaplan and Baldauf (1997:153) describe the main focus of language planning in the Old Dispensation as follows:

> Thus, much of the motivation for language planning, during its early development as a discipline in the 1960s and 1970s, was sociopolitical and focused on nation building, primarily using the nineteenth century European model of one state, one language, one culture, regardless of how inappropriate such a model might have been for the new emerging multilingual polities.

With hindsight, we now understand why this model could not have worked in multilingual Africa. With the exception of Congo (in 4.3), Kenya (in 4.2.7), and Tanzania (in 4.4 and 4.4.1), the hegemonic model has been a catastrophic failure. No country in French-speaking Africa that is highly multilingual has been successful in imposing an indigenous LWC as its national language. The reasons for this have been discussed in depth in various parts of the book, but it is worth summarizing them again quickly. The hegemonic model has failed in some countries because there is no dominant indigenous language. The search for an indigenous national language has been fruitless in other countries because the political elite, even though they speak a minority language, have sought to impose their language on the rest of the citizenry. There are also countries where, though the political elite belong to the majority language, they are afraid that if they select their own language as the national LWC, the choice might backfire because it would be perceived as a case of linguistic dictatorship. In other cases, strong ethnolinguistic loyalty has forestalled any attempt at language planning. In many French-speaking and Portuguese-speaking portions of Africa, elite apathy and ambivalence towards local languages has not led to the choice of a national LWC. Parental opposition, due in large part to the low marketability value of indigenous languages, has also derailed attempts at the hegemonic model of language planning. The failure has also been blamed on astronomical cost-benefit ratio estimates. Faced with many urgent and multi-dimensional crises that are all clamoring for attention, many African leaders see language planning as a luxurious expense that Africa can ill-afford. These are the reasons that explain the failure of language planning in the Old Dispensation.

8.2.2 Language planning in the New Dispensation

The winds of change in the world of language planning began blowing in the second half of the 1990s. The lack of enthusiasm for the hegemonic model is clearly seen in the last pages of Kaplan and Baldauf's (1996:321) book where they seem to distance themselves from the hegemonic model:

> We have tried to argue that language planning cannot any longer be conceived in terms of the one-language/one-nation myth, since – in any case – there are virtually no monolingual nations, and since any given language is likely to occur simultaneously in more than one polity.

8.2 Paradigm shift in language planning

Perhaps the single most important event that ushered in the New Dispensation came as a result of the 52-artcile document produced by the World Conference on Linguistic Rights held in Barcelona, Spain, in June 1996.[54] This document is now known as the Universal Declaration of Linguistic Rights. This Declaration has emboldened language activists in many parts of the world who have been agitating against the hegemonic model because it was endangering minority languages everywhere. This, along with the widespread press coverage of the unenviable plight of minority languages, has helped shift the focus of language planning from the One Nation = One Language formula towards a pluralistic model. Grenoble et al. (2009:188) echo the sentiments that have led to this paradigm shift by saying that "people around the world are increasingly aware of language as a marker of identity." The tacit recognition and celebration of ethnolinguistic pride is shifting attitudes and priorities in language planning in general and mother-tongue education in particular. The new language planning slogan seems to be "*e pluribus unum*" which can be loosely translated as "Many Languages, One Nation." It is now believed that nationhood can be achieved in the absence of a single national LWC. Simpson (2008:12), for example, contends that other indexical features of identity can contribute to a "national identity" even in the absence of a national LWC. He argues that "there are various other indexes of identity which may have a stronger binding force for the populations than language, when promoted in a vigorous way, and these may sometimes either override or alternatively obscure the potential that language has to establish cohesion and loyalty across large populations." In other words, one does not need to speak the same indigenous language before one feels that one shares a national identity with others who have experienced the same colonial or post-colonial legacy. The myth of One Nation = One Language has now been laid to rest. It is time to embrace a pluralistic model of language planning whose benefits Brenzinger (2009:40) highlights as follows:

> In order to achieve economic integration and ethnic stabilization, which is the only way to overcome poverty, educational policies must reach the majorities. For this goal to be reached, the choice of African languages as media of instruction is crucial. The most promising strategies are to promote stable multilingualism: spread of proficiency in European languages among all people *in addition to use of African languages*. [Emphasis added]

---

54 Retrieved from http://www.unesco.org/cpp/uk/declarations/linguistic.pdf on May 30, 2011.

The phrase *"in addition to use of African languages"* is the key to understanding language planning in the New Dispensation. The remaining sections will answer two vexing questions: How can multiple languages be planned for a single country? What is the cost-benefit ratio for doing so?

8.2.3 Pluralistic language planning in the New Dispensation

The new buzz in the social sciences in the beginning decades of the 21st century is "diversity." There is no indication that this trend is going to be discontinued anytime soon. Curricula are being designed for schools, for the workplace, and for many other aspects of society with "diversity" at their core. Diversity is being timidly championed in language planning. Batibo (2009:29) writes that "it is important to design language policies which ensure that the linguistic diversity becomes a development asset rather than a liability." Blommaert (1996:211) has gone so far as to accuse European linguists and scholars of duplicity because they now praise multilingualism in Europe "as part of the unique European heritage, while it is despised in Africa as one of the causes of underdevelopment and chaos." A significant portion of language planners are openly speaking in favor of the pluralistic model, but this new model faces serious challenges. Bloommaert (1996:202) summarizes them as follows:

> Selecting a handful of languages while deleting others, might be interpreted as ethnic favoritism; education in one's ethnic language might trigger an increased awareness of ethnic, sub-state identities and threaten the ideal of national unity so strongly advocated by the new political leaders. And allowing all local languages to be used as media of instruction in education would bump into the same feasibility argument: it would mean that teaching materials would have to be created in all these languages, that a plethora of local teaching programs would have to be developed and implemented and so on, and there wasn't time and money for that.

The challenges are daunting, but India provides us with a roadmap for selecting which languages should be taught at school and which ones should not. Mohanty (2009:103–4, 107) reports that 300–400 languages are spoken in India. He also notes that only 41 languages are used in schools as either media of instruction or as school subjects. An additional 104 languages are used in adult literacy programs. This is the 3±1 model that many people are now talking about. Its use in India ensures that many educated citizens can read at least three languages: a minority language, a majority language, the national language (Hindi), and English. Indian authorities relied on demographic data for selecting which language is to be taught in formal education and which is to be taught in literacy classes. Ladefoged (1992:811) reports that he used a similar approach when he advised the Ugandan government about language of education policy. Of the 43 local languages, 20 were considered "major" on the basis of demographic data. Six of twenty were recommended for use in schools because they were the most widely spoken. When a similar approach is used in Cote d'Ivoire, we will see in 8.6 that 28% of its languages can be taught at school while 72% can be taught in literacy classes. The pluralistic model does not require that all the languages spoken in any given country be taught in formal education. However, it calls for a substantial number of them to be used for mother-tongue education. Even Brenzinger (2009:40), a strong advocate for minority languages in Africa, concedes that it is not feasible to use all languages for mother-tongue education. Kamwangamalu (1997:240–1) uses an economic rationale for explaining why this is not possible:

> Those who argue against mother-tongue education maintain that it is not possible to provide *every single child with education in his or her own language. This is not practically possible as it will be cost-prohibitive.* Resources would have to be committed toward the production of curricular materials, the training of teachers, the launching of campaigns, etc. to promote the use of these languages. *The cost would be unbearable, especially as language problems are not the only problems that require the attention of the state.* [Italics added for emphasis]

Cost is a formidable obstacle, but it is not the only impediment. Even if money were available, some 1,409 of Africa's 2,013 languages are not ready to be used for instruction because they have not yet been reduced to writing. In a case like this, Grenoble et al. (2009:184) suggest that "intellectual poverty," that is, the lack of local expertise in corpus planning, is another obstacle with which one has to contend.

8.3 Application to Côte d'Ivoire

It is now time to apply the preceding information to design a language of education policy for Côte d'Ivoire. It should be recalled, as noted in Chapter 5, that there are more than 60 ethnolinguistic groups in the country and that, according to the National Institute of Statistics, there are 17 major regional languages spoken in the 19 administrative counties in the country. The administrative zoning coincides with the ethnolinguistic make-up, except in the case of Baule, the largest ethnic group, whose speakers are spread over two other counties. The Predictioneer's Model discussed in Chapter 5 led me to conclude that if Ivorians were given the choice between models of mother-tongue education, they would choose MM over TIM as reflected in the weighted mean score of 68.75%. Even though this is the case, cost analyses will be done for TIM, MM, and AIM in order to prove that planning for multiple languages is not significantly more expensive than planning for a single national LWC.

8.3.1 Quick review of TIM

If Côte d'Ivoire were to implement TIM as a language of education policy, it would have to budget for four sub-varieties of the policy and determine which sub-type is economically feasible on the basis of how its elementary school system is structured (see 5.3.1). The four are represented in Table 8.1.

Table 8.1. Four Models of TIM

No.	Four Sub-types of TIM
1.	NLWC in 1st–3rd grades as Medium of Instruction (NLWC 1–3)
2.	NLWC in 1st–6th grades as Academic Subject (NLWC 1–6)
3.	RLWC in 1st–3rd grades as a Medium of Instruction (RLWC 1–3)
4.	RLWC in 1st–6th grades as Academic Subject (RLWC 1–6)

The prefix "N" in NLWC stands for "national" while the "R" stands for "Regional." The acronym NLWC 1–3 means that instruction is given in a single national LWC for the first three years of elementary school. NLWC means that the national LWC is taught as an academic subject throughout the six years of elementary school. RLWC 1–3 means that the 17 regional languages are used in lower elementary as the media of instruction, while RLWC 1–6 means that the 17 major regional languages are taught only as academic subjects. The cost-benefit analysis of implementing TIM takes into account these four versions.

8.3.2 The cost analysis of status planning

For status planning, Kaplan and Baldauf (1997:98) recommend a small army of experts which includes a historian, an economist, a political scientist, an anthropologist, and a computer scientist. Their job is to do the sociolinguistic survey which serves as the basis for selecting the national LWC. Such a survey is meant to collect information about the opinions and attitudes of the citizenry over the choice of this or that language as a national language. Kaplan and Baldauf (1997:98, 103) provide the blueprint for estimating the expenses associated with status planning. This form is adopted and is adapted here to provide a realistic budget as though Côte d'Ivoire had decided to plan for mother-tongue education in 2010. Three budgeting scenarios are played out. In one case, expatriate experts are hired to do status planning for a national LWC. In the second scenario, local experts are in charge of status planning. In the third scenario, 17 regional LWCs are selected for mother-tongue education.

For the expenses to appear as realistic as possible, the consulting fees under the first scenario are based on the per diem rate established by the State Department's Foreign Service Division for the year 2010. Information obtained from the US government indicates that maximum per diem allowed for a US diplomat in Abidjan was $281.[55] We make three additional assumptions about the four expatriate experts. First, we assume that they are university professors from the United States. Second, we hypothesize that they would spend a total of 45 days on all the sociolinguistic survey activities. Third, we assume that they advocate the maintenance of African languages. Therefore, they do not charge more than the per diem for their language planning services. In addition to the per diem, plane tickets, hotel accommodations, taxi rental fees, and other amenities are provided for expatriate consultants.

The survey work requires local expertise. The national staff would include a national survey coordinator, four regional survey coordinators, 25 fieldworkers, and 10 secretarial support staff. We estimate further that the local personnel will be compensated for a period of 12 months. The compensation of the national workers is calculated on the basis of high school, middle school, and elementary school teachers' salaries. By Ivorian standards, school teachers are well remunerated for their qualifications. Therefore, the national survey coordinator and the regional survey coordinators would make $1,038 a month.[56] The monthly salary of a fieldworker is

---

55 Retrieved from http://aoprals.state.gov/web920/per_diem_action.asp?MenuHide =1&PostCode=10724 on May 2, 2011.
56 Retrieved from http://www.xe.com/ucc/convert/?Amount=1&From=USD& To=XOF on May 3, 2011.

estimated to be the same for a middle school teacher, that is, $888. Each secretary makes $463 a month. Other expenses considered by Kaplan and Baldauf (1997:98) include transportation, materials and supplies for the survey, equipment, the cost of maintaining the equipment, publications, and other miscellaneous expenses. All the itemized expenses pertaining to status planning are found in Table 8.2:

Table 8.2. Status Planning Expenses

No.	Status Planning Costs	Estimated Costs
1.	Four Expatriate Consultants' per diem for 45 days	$50,580
2.	Expatriate personnel's plane tickets x 4[1] $2,400/person	$9,600
3.	Hotel accommodation for 4 consultants for 45 days at a rate of $100.00 per room, per day, per consultant.	$18,000
4.	Expatriate fringe benefits	$0.00
5.	Taxi rental fee for consultants for 100$ per day for 45days	$4,500
6.	One National Survey Coordinator and four Regional Survey Supervisors	$62,280
7.	25 survey fieldworkers salaries	$266,400
8.	10 support staff	$55,560
9.	Material and supplies	$10,000
10.	Equipment (10 computers and printers). Cost per computer and printer = $1,200.	$12,000
11.	Equipment maintenance	$2,000
12.	Transportation for survey team for one year	$15,000
13.	Publication	$3,000
14.	Miscellaneous/unexpected expenses	$5,000
15.	Estimated total expenses	$513,920

Note:
1 Round trip ticket price retrieved http://www.delta.com/booking/ on May 3, 2011.

If expatriate consultants are not needed, and Ivorian professors are in charge of status planning, they too would work for 45 days. On average, a college professor made $3,500 a month in 2010; each professor would make $5,250.00. Collectively, the four national expert consultants would make

$21,000.00. We assume that all other expenses in Table 8.2 except plane tickets and accommodation expenses would remain identical. If everything else remains identical, the Ivorian government would spend $466,340 instead of $513,920 by using its citizens. However, the estimated savings of $47,589 is really not a huge amount. Doing status planning for 17 regional languages does not cost anything because the government has already carved up the country into 19 counties purely on an ethnolinguistic basis.

8.3.3 The cost analysis of corpus planning and curriculum development

Corpus planning is the area of language planning where descriptive linguistic analyses are done. The following activities are subsumed under corpus planning:

1. The phonetic and phonological analyses lead to the development of a practical orthography for the language.
2. The morphological and syntactic analyses lead to the writing of a reference grammar or a pedagogical grammar of the language.
3. The analysis of word formation processes and lexical analyses lead to the elaboration of word lists and/or the making of the dictionary of the language.
4. The terminology management of the language leads to the modernization of the lexicon.
5. The study of the discursive strategies of the language brings about a heightened awareness of the rhetorical devices used by the language. This, in turn, leads to the writing of texts that reflect the different genres used in the language.

The cost estimate for corpus planning is based on a grant in the amount of $22,574 (10,000,000 CFA) that was given by a benefactor to a team of linguists in Côte d'Ivoire to cover the expenses involved in the research leading to the publication of a dictionary. We assume that for a comprehensive coverage of corpus planning, the same amount would be needed in each of the five areas of corpus planning mentioned above. Therefore, the amount of money that one would need to do corpus planning for one Ivorian language is $112,870. However, this price tag differs according to the model of language planning that one chooses. If a single national LWC is chosen, one would need only $112,870. However, if all 17 regional LWCs are selected for mother-tongue education, then corpus planning would cost $1,918,790. Corpus planning for multiple languages is definitely more expensive than corpus planning for a single LWC. It should, however, be noted that this is the only area where planning for multiple languages is more expensive than planning for a single language.

8.3.4 The cost analysis of acquisition planning

Acquisition planning is a comprehensive area which includes planning for the medium of instruction and planning for the curriculum. The mother tongue can be used in one of two ways at school. It can be planned in such a way that it is taught as an academic subject. It can also be planned as a medium of instruction. This means that all instructions are carried out in the language itself. Acquisition planning also addresses the issue of curriculum planning, syllabus planning, and even personnel planning. As should be expected, the cost of acquisition planning is inextricably bound to the medium of instruction and to the model of mother-tongue education under consideration. If a single national LWC (NLWC 1–3) or 17 regional LWCs (RLWC 1–3) are used as media of instruction in first through third grades, at least three separate textbooks are required: one for reading, one for spelling, and one for arithmetic. On the other hand, if a single national LWC is used or if 17 regional LWCs are used as academic subjects, only one textbook is needed.

Now, let's calculate how much the government of Côte d'Ivoire would have spent on textbook purchase if Ivorian languages had been taught in elementary school in 2010. It should be borne in mind that the government provides elementary school textbooks free of charge. The government also has strong purchasing power because it would buy books in large quantities. For this reason, let's assume that each textbook is sold to the government at the discounted price of $2.00. In the academic year 2010, the figures from the Department of Primary Education reported by the newspapers, *Le Nouveau Réveil* of July 6, 2010 and *Fraternité Matin* of July 7, 2010, indicate that 397,979 students took the Seventh Grade Entrance Exam. Even though there are more students in grades 1 through 5 than there are in sixth grade, we will keep the same figure for each grade level, from first through sixth grades. As a result, we estimate the elementary student population of 2010 to be 2,387,874 nationwide. This figure is more than twice the figure of 1,025,000 primary students reported by Loucou et al. (1987:288) for the 1980–1 academic year.

If a mother tongue had been used as a medium of instruction under NLWC 1–3 or RLWC 1–3 in 2010, half of the elementary student body, that is, 1,193,937 students, would be affected. Since each lower elementary student has three textbooks: a reading textbook, a spelling textbook, and an arithmetic textbook, this means that the government would have provided a total of 3,581,811 books free of charge. This amounts to some $7,163,622 for textbooks. After third grade, the mother tongue is taught only as an academic subject. This means that each fourth, fifth, and sixth grader requires only one textbook per grade. Since there were 1,193,937 in these three grades and a textbook costs only $2.00, textbook expenditures for upper elementary students would amount to $3,581,811. In the end, the implementation of NLWC 1–3 or RLWC 1–3 would have cost $10,745,433 for all elementary students. However, if NLWC 1–6 or RLWC 1–6 were implemented, that is, if a national LWC or the 17 regional LWCs were taught as academic subjects the government would have spent only $4,775,748 because in this model, students require only one textbook.

It is important to note here that the cost of textbooks does not change whether one language is taught or several languages are taught. Expenditures for textbooks are affected only by how the mother tongue is taught. Using it as a medium of instruction requires more investment because each student would need at least three different textbooks, one per academic subject. However, if the language is taught as an academic subject, a single textbook would suffice. An experiment reported by Bamgbose (2004:15) shows that the cost of publishing textbooks in multiple African languages could be kept relatively low. In that experiment 40 publications were produced in 15 languages/dialects between 1970 and 1972 at a cost of only $20,000. Bamgbose explained that this was achieved by minimizing the cost "through the use of uniform formats and illustrations for primers as well as well as cheaper methods for producing reading materials." The Ivorian school system has a top-down structure. All curricular decisions are made at the highest level of government under the Ministry of Elementary Education or the Ministry of Secondary and Technical Education. This highly centralized system would allow for the creation of "a master curriculum" in French which would then be translated into the one national LWC or the 17 regional LWCs. The centralization of the curriculum would reduce the cost of printing textbooks.

8.3.5 The cost analysis of personnel planning

Kaplan and Baldauf (1997:113–7) include personnel planning under the umbrella of acquisition planning. Available data on the number of elementary teachers in Côte d'Ivoire date back to 1971. Loucou et al. (1987:290) note that in 1971 there were 8,503 elementary school teachers. The number climbed to 12,400 in 1975. In the space of four years, that is, from 1975 to 1979, the number of teachers almost doubled to 21,000. In spite my best efforts, I have not been able to find recent data on the number of teachers. However, during the 2010 presidential debate, incumbent president Laurent Gbagbo promised to hire 11,000 more teachers if he were re-elected because the current staffing levels are woefully inadequate. His challenger, Alassane Ouattara, talked about the need to hire 60,000 new teachers to meet the population growth of the next 5 years.[57] In the absence of reliable data from governmental sources, I have calculated the approximate number of teachers by using data from the Seventh Grade Entrance Exam and class sizes. It was stated in 8.3.4 that the elementary student body nationwide was 2,387,874. If we assume that there were on average 60 students per classroom, as mentioned in Loucou et al. (1987:290), we arrive at the figure of 39,798 teachers for elementary schools throughout the country.

Under NLWC 1–3 or RLWC 1–3, approximately half of the teachers, that is, 19,899 would be needed to teach in lower elementary. This also means that an additional 110 teachers would be needed to teach the national LWC or the regional LWCs in upper elementary as academic subjects. We arrive at the figure of 110 by dividing the total number of mother-tongue teachers by 180 because an upper elementary teacher would be required to teach fourth through sixth grades and each class has 60 students. So, the total number of teachers needed to teach the mother tongue would be 20,009. However, under NLWC 1–6 or RLWC 1–6, that is, if Ivorian languages were taught as academic subjects, only 6,633 teachers would be needed because a single teacher could teach all six grade levels, that is, approximately 360 students. The average salary of an elementary school teacher in Côte d'Ivoire as of 2010 was $463 a month. It is important to keep in mind that teachers have a twelve month contract; therefore they are paid in the summer months even when they are not teaching. Using a single Ivorian language as a national LWC or 17 regional LWCs as media of instruction would necessitate hiring 20,009 teachers for an annual compensation package of $111,170,004. However, if the national LWC or the 17 regional LWCs are taught as academic subjects, the annual salary of the 6,633 teachers would be $36,852,948.

---

57 *Le Patriote* of November 26th, 2010. The two leaders were using data from the same source. One focused on the immediate need while the other stated the need over a five-year period.

To summarize, if the Ivorian government in 2010 had planned and used its linguistic resources to educate its citizens in elementary schools, it would have incurred the following expenses. Promoting NWLC 1–3 would have cost $466,340 for status planning, $112,870 for corpus planning, $10,745,433 for textbooks, and $111,170,004 in teacher salaries, for a total of $122,494,647. If RLWC 1–3 had been selected as media of instruction in lower elementary, status planning would not have cost anything, corpus planning expenses would have amounted to $1,918,790, textbooks would have cost $10,745,433, and teachers' compensation would have been $111,170,004, for a total of $123,834,227. If, on the other hand, NWLC 1–6 had been chosen as the model of mother-tongue education throughout the country, the expenses would have been, $466,340 for status planning, $112,870 for corpus planning, $4,775,748 for textbook, and $36,852,948 in teacher salaries, for a total of $42,207,906. Finally, for RLWC 1–6, status planning does not cost anything. The cost of corpus planning would have been $1,918,790; the expenditure for textbooks would have amounted to $4,775,748. The personnel needed to teach would have been paid $36,852,948. The cost of teaching RLWCs as academic subjects would have amounted to a total of $43,547,486. The various costs are summarized below:

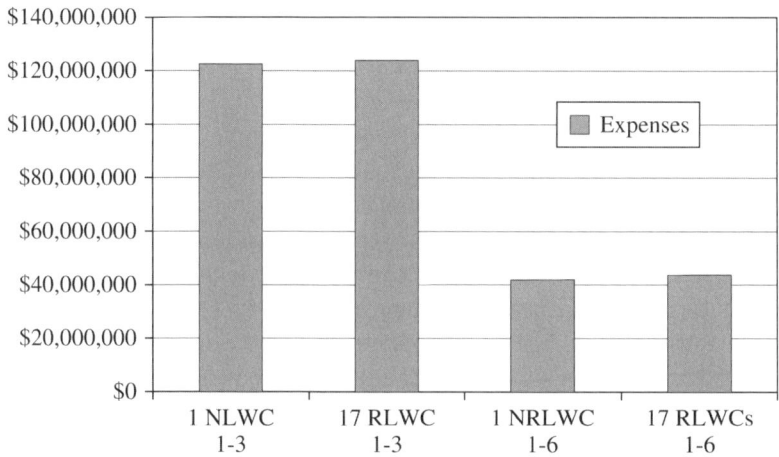

Figure 8.1. Overall Expenses in Implementing TIM

Two important observations can be made on the basis of the information provided in the chart. First, the data from Côte d'Ivoire refutes the claim that it would be prohibitively expensive to plan multiple languages. The expenses involved in using one national LWC as opposed to 17 regional LWCs as media of instruction in lower elementary are virtually the same. Planning for RLWC 1–3 is only $1,339,580 more expensive than planning for NLWC 1–3. The same amount constitutes the difference between planning for NLWC 1–6 and RLWC 1–6. Second, the only noticeable difference as far as cost is concerned is between how the mother tongue is taught. If it is taught as an academic subject throughout elementary school, it costs only a third of what it would cost to use it as a medium of instruction. This option has not been given serious consideration by mother-tongue planners, but it is worth taking seriously because it is economically more feasible.

8.4 A quick overview of MM

The game-theoretic analysis of the various models of mother-tongue education was first introduced in 2.5.2 and later discussed in sections 5.4.1 through 5.4.3. The weighted mean score of 68.75% led me to the conclusion that MM was the model of language planning that would meet the needs of Ivorians. In a nutshell, MM calls for the postponement of Spanish and German until college and their replacement in secondary school by one national LWC or by 17 regional LWCs. It was argued in 5.5 and 5.5.1 that since the overwhelming majority of Ivorians did not use German and Spanish in their daily and professional lives, continuing this colonial tradition was a waste of financial resources. Generation after generation and thousands upon thousands of Ivorians have dutifully studied these two languages from 9th grade through 13th grade, and yet the overwhelming majority of them do absolutely nothing with them. Worse, no sooner do students graduate from secondary school than they forget them. Consequently, I argued in Chapter 5 that the country would be best served if its scanty financial resources were used to teach Ivorian languages. The choice of secondary school as the optimal grades to introduce local languages in the curriculum is further confirmed by Bamgbose's (2004:11) observation that "the use of an African language as a medium of instruction at secondary school level is very rare." This statement is additional proof that the Predictioneer's Model predicted accurately that secondary school is the best grade level to implement MM. So, in the following section, a cost analysis of using one national LWC or 17 regional LWCs in secondary school will be discussed.

8.4.1 The cost analysis of status planning

The cost of status planning under MM is exactly the same as under TIM. If a national LWC is envisaged, the cost analysis of status planning amounts to

$466,340. However, if 17 regional LWCs are chosen to be taught in secondary schools, it does not cost anything for reasons that have been already discussed, namely that the administrative and ethnolinguistic maps of the country are based on the principle of one major regional language per county. This, however, does not mean that other status planning decisions do not need to be made. Legislative action is needed to officially remove German and Spanish from the secondary curriculum. Separate legislation may be needed to replace them with either a national LWC or 17 regional LWCs. If strong legislation is not passed, some parents may find clever ways to exempt their children from learning Ivorian languages at school. Bamgbose (1991:117–8) laments the fact that caveats and loopholes in the Nigerian official language policy have made it hard to implement it effectively:

> The first thing to note about the policy is the way in which escape clauses are built into the formulation: "when adequate arrangements have been made therefore", "may", "as the House resolution may approve". Although one can argue that such clauses are necessary in a legal document (for example to prevent someone going to court to seek premature enforcement), the net result is to maintain the status quo as represented in the earlier policy, which is that the 'business of Parliament shall be conducted in English'.

The attempt to circumvent national language policies is well-known and widely attested in the language planning literature. Laitin (1992:152, 163) uses the phrase "private subversion of a public good" to describe such behaviors. To counter this tendency, a binding language law should be passed. The exact language of the law is to be determined, but legislation stating that every Ivorian national attending secondary school (grades 9th–13th) within the territorial borders of Côte d'Ivoire must study and demonstrate proficiency in at least one ancestral Ivorian language as a precondition for graduation would be welcomed. With such stringent legal language, private schools will feel compelled to teach Ivorian languages so long as they enroll a single Ivorian national. Section 6.15 explains how planning multiple languages can work in cosmopolitan megacities. In the economic capital city of Abidjan and in the political capital of Yamoussoukro, each secondary school will offer five languages. The legislation should also take care to state that, just as German and Spanish are currently examinable school subjects for the O Level, the A Level, and the 11th Grade Entrance Exams; so should be the Ivorian languages taught in secondary school. Failure to make the local languages compulsory examinable subjects with the same coefficients that German and Spanish now have will encourage students not to take local languages seriously even if they are taught at school. To summarize, all the requirements that students must presently fulfill with regard to German and Spanish should be identical when Ivorian languages are taught in secondary school. German and Spanish are taught as academic subjects; Ivorian languages should also be taught as academic subjects.

8.4.2 The cost analysis of corpus planning and curriculum development

The costs involved in corpus planning and curriculum development are exactly the same in MM as those needed for corpus planning under TIM. If a national LWC is chosen, the cost would be $112,870. However, if 17 regional languages are chosen, the expenses would amount to $1,918,790. The cost of curriculum development can be minimized if the textbooks in the 17 regional LWCs are translated from a master copy written in French. Curriculum developers should try to kill two birds with a single stone. This means that books should help modernize the lexicon and also reinforce instruction in core content areas. For these reasons, I suggest that textbooks in local languages be written in the format of "Advanced Review" books. Such books should adopt the same curricular philosophy as the publishers of Cliff's Notes. The topics discussed in the books should be relevant for each grade. They should contain abbreviated coverage of key academic subjects such as Language Arts, Social Studies, Natural Sciences, Mathematics, etc. Advanced Review books of this type would have the advantage of helping students encounter the same concepts at least twice: once in their French textbooks, and a second time in the local language that they are studying. There is also an added advantage in that the "Advanced Review" format will force the authors of texts in indigenous languages to engage in terminology management so as to create new terms to cover key concepts in the core academic areas. The textbook for 9th graders should follow the same format as "New Reader" books because under MM Ivorian languages are introduced into the school system in 9th grade. Such a book should devote a considerable amount of time to the orthography of the language(s) under consideration. The textbook should be written in such a way that by the end of 9th grade, students will have developed the skills necessary to read, write, and do basic math, science, geography, etc. in the local languages.

8.4.3 The cost of personnel planning

We learn from Loucou et al. (1987:290) that there were 4,600 secondary teachers in Côte d'Ivoire in 1980. We also learn that in 1971, there were 35 students per classroom in secondary school. The latter figure increased to 44 in 1976, and to 55 in 1980. The severe economic crises of the 1990s have prevented the government from building as many secondary schools as the demographic explosion has called for. As a result, secondary private schools of dubious reputation have mushroomed here and there with government subsidy. Though there may be as many as 70 students per classroom in some cases, a national average of 60 per classroom will be used for all calculations. A secondary school teacher teaches four classes a day. This means that he/she encounters on average 240 students a day. According to the newspapers, *Le Mandat* of July 7, 2010 and in the *L'intelligent d'Abidjan* of July 8, 2010, a total of 644,518 students took the O Level exam in In 2010. If we keep this figure the same for both 9th and 10th grades, then there were 1,289,036 lower secondary students. Since each teacher teaches on average 240 students a day, we can estimate the total number of German and Spanish language teachers to be 5,371. The median salary of lower secondary teachers is $888 a month. If the teaching of local languages in lower secondary school had been implemented in 2010, the government would have needed 5,371 teachers. Their annual salary would have amounted to $57,233,376.

According to the newspaper, *Le Quotidien* of June 29, 2010, a total of 192,704 students in 13th grade took the A Level exam in 2010. If we keep the same numbers for 11th and 12th grades, then the total number of students in upper secondary is 587,122. Let's assume that in upper secondary there are only 50 students per class. Since each teacher teaches during four class periods, he/she would then teach 200 students per day. On the basis of this calculation, we can estimate the number of upper secondary German and Spanish language teachers to be at 2,891. The median monthly salary of an upper secondary language teacher is $1,038. Therefore, the amount of money spent on the salary of upper secondary teachers is $36,010,296. According to my calculations, there were approximately 8,262 people who taught German and Spanish in lower and upper secondary school. Collectively, they earned $93,243,672 in salaries.

8.4.4 The cost analysis of maintaining the status quo

The status quo corresponds to AIM as discussed in 2.5.2 and in 5.2, and 5.2.1. Under this approach, the Ivorian government would continue to not teach Ivorian languages in elementary school or in secondary school. If absolutely nothing is done to change the status quo, the Ivorian government will still spend $93,243,672 annually for the financial compensation of German and Spanish language teachers. However, as has been argued in this chapter, since the teaching of these two languages does not benefit the students or the nation directly, continuing to do so is tantamount to squandering national financial resources. The government would have a better return on its educational investment by retraining the 8,262 German and Spanish language teachers to teach Ivorian mother tongues in secondary schools. Retraining foreign language teachers to teach another language is not unheard of, as discussed in 5.6. If MM is implemented, in the short term, there will be a shortage of competent teachers to teach Ivorian languages. However, this situation can be remedied if the introduction of mother tongues in the secondary curriculum is planned carefully over a period of three years prior to implementation. Since German and Spanish language teachers are already trained in pedagogy courses as part of their certification requirements, they would only need basic courses in descriptive linguistics. This can be done over a period of three years in intensive summer institutes. Ivorian teachers are paid all through the summer even if they are not teaching, so the government does not need to worry about incurring additional expenses for salaries. However, it would be wise to budget to pay the salaries of 20 college professors who would be retraining the teachers. As noted before, college professors make on average $3,500 a month. If they can commit to two months each summer for a period of three years to retrain former German and Spanish language teachers, $420,000 could be budgeted for their salaries. An additional $600,000 should be budgeted for course-related materials. So, a total of $1,000,000 should be budgeted over three years to cover all retraining expenses.

A word of caution is in order regarding teacher qualifications: Every effort should be made to avoid lowering the quality of the training for the teachers of Ivorian languages. Experience in other parts of Africa has shown that teachers of African languages tend to be regarded as less qualified compared to their colleagues who teach European languages. Bamgbose (1991:94) sees this as a serious problem that must be carefully addressed:

> Perhaps the most serious obstacle in the teaching of African languages in secondary schools is the low prestige attached to it. Teachers of such languages are not much sought after and quite often, students do not consider them as proficient academically as teachers of other subjects.

Another temptation that is to be avoided at all costs is the inclination to pay teachers of indigenous languages less than those who teach European languages. Grenoble and Whaley (2006:95) report that a long time ago in Hawaii, the government paid English-speaking teachers more than their Hawaiian-speaking counterparts. Paying teachers of indigenous languages exactly the same wages and benefits as they earned when they were teaching German and Spanish will go a long way towards raising the market value of these languages. Ivorian parents will be less likely to discourage their children from studying and teaching these languages if the salaries and other benefits can help them meet their existential needs.

8.4.5 Summary of cost analyses

In summary, if a national LWC had been chosen in 2010 as an academic subject for secondary school, the total expenditure would have been $94,822,882, that is, $466,340 for status planning, $112,870 for corpus planning, $93,243,672 for teachers' salaries, and $1,000,000 for teacher retraining costs. If 17 regional languages had been selected for the same purposes, the government would have spent no money on status planning, $1,918,790 for corpus planning, $93,243,672 for teacher's salaries, and $1,000,000 for retraining former German and Spanish language teachers, for a total expenditure of $96,162,462. If, on the other hand, the government did not implement any changes at all and kept the status quo, it would spend $93,243,672. Chart 2 is a summary of the cost analysis:

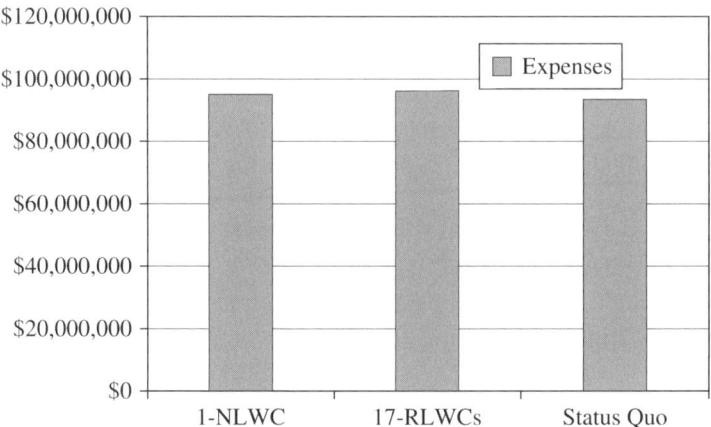

Figure 8.2. Cost Summary of MM

The observations here are similar to those already made in relation to Chart 1, namely that teaching a national LWC in secondary school costs just about the same as teaching 17 regional LWCs. This puts to rest the claim that it is not cost effective to plan multiple mother tongues for education. The second observation that is worth drawing attention to is that if the government had decided to introduce Ivorian languages in 2010, it would have spent less than $3,000,000 in new money. Teaching German and Spanish costs the government $93,243,672. Teaching 17 regional LWCs would cost $96,162,462. So, replacing German and Spanish in secondary school with local languages is not that expensive because the personnel cost is the same. Only $2,918,790 in new money would need to be spent on status planning and/or corpus planning.

8.5 Overall cost comparisons and cost-benefit analyses

The overall cost analyses done in the previous sections allow us to make the following comparisons: On the face of it, the least expensive way of planning mother-tongue education in Côte d'Ivoire is to introduce it in elementary schools throughout the country as an academic subject in grades 1–6. Doing so for a single national LWC would have cost $42,905,036 in 2010. If 17 regional LWCs were used instead of a single national LWC, the cost would have been $43,775,748. These expenses would triple to $121,187,840 if a national LWC were taught in lower elementary as a medium of instruction, or to $122,640,290 if 17 regional LWCs were used in the same way.

If a single national Ivorian language had been introduced in secondary schools nationwide to replace German and Spanish in 2010, the cost would have been $94,822,882. If the same had been done for 17 regional LWCs, it would have cost $96,162,462. In 2010, the government spent $93,243,672 just paying the salaries of German and Spanish language teachers. Chart 3 summarizes all the information presented so far and provides a display of cost comparisons:

There is something deceptive about this chart. It misleads the reader into believing that planning NLWC 1–6 or RLWC 1–6, that is, when local languages are taught as academic subjects in elementary school, is the cheapest model of language planning for Côte d'Ivoire. Actually, this is not the case because the government would still have to disburse new money year after year to implement such a policy because, as explained earlier, the government provides textbooks free of charge to elementary school students. As long as there are elementary students, the government would continue

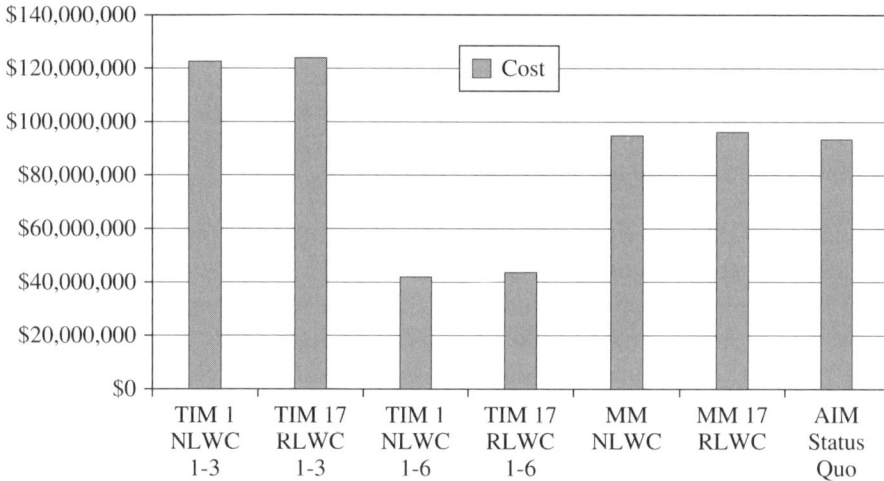

Figure 8.3. Cost Comparison Analyses

year after year to provide them with textbooks in local languages. In reality, the cheapest approach to language planning is teaching a single LWC or teaching all 17 regional languages in upper secondary school because in those upper grades, textbooks are purchased by parents, not by the government. How much the government stands to benefit if MM is implemented is discussed in 8.5.2.

8.5.1 Cost-benefit analyses

The concept of cost-benefit analysis is near and dear to the hearts of economists. They use it to determine whether or not a project is monetarily feasible. Kaplan and Baldauf (1996:94, 95) define cost-benefit analysis simply as "a comparison of costs (inputs) and benefits (outcomes) where each is measured in monetary terms." They, however, complain that "very few cost benefit analyses have been done or are available for scrutiny." This oversight is, I hope, corrected by the information provided here. Thorburn (1972:512) stresses the importance of comparing real costs with potential benefits. However, he also warns that it should not be the single most important determining factor in making a decision about language planning:

> It is thus evident that a cost-benefit analysis is not intended to be a complete and absolutely reliable foundation for language planning. There are many consequences that are extremely difficult to identify, quantify, and evaluate;

they must, nevertheless be taken into account in any final political decision. A cost-benefit calculation ought to assemble all relevant scientific knowledge pertaining to the problem in question (description and relations), which ought to be presented to the politicians in an impartial and clear way. How to weigh the advantages and disadvantages and to judge the uncertainties is up to the politician (p. 515).

Ivorian political authorities have been leery about the ethnolinguistic and the sociological atmosphere of the country since its independence from France in 1960. The recent political and ethnic clashes seem to suggest that they were right in being cautious about imposing a single LWC on the citizenry. In 1999 a military coup unseated the democratically elected government. In 2002, an ethnically motivated coup failed to remove the democratically elected president. However, it led to the partitioning of the country into two sections: the speakers of the Gur and the North Mande families of languages found themselves in rebel controlled areas of the country, while the South Mande group, the Kru group and the Akan group were in the government controlled areas. Poorly organized elections in 2010 have led to post-election carnage along ethnic lines.[58] The towns of Douekoue in the western part of the country, and Yopougon (the most populous suburb of Abidjan) have felt the weight of this barbaric form of ethnic cleansing.[59] In light of such an ethnolinguistically poisoned atmosphere, it would be unthinkable that the population will accept a hegemonic model whereby a national LWC is imposed on them. In these circumstances, the pluralistic model of using 17 regional LWCs appears to be the least objectionable solution.

Selecting 17 regional LWCs does not, however, answer the fundamental question of which language of education policy is to be adopted. Should it be RLWC 1–3, according to which multiple languages are used in lower elementary grades as media of instruction while French takes over in upper elementary? Or should it be RLWC 1–6, according to which multiple local languages are taught throughout elementary school as academic subjects? Or should it be MM which recommends using all 17 regional LWCs in secondary school? The answer to the first two questions is most likely "no" because, as noted in this chapter and elsewhere in the book, parental

---

58 Retrieved from http://www.amnesty.org/en/region/cote-divoire/report-2011 on June 3, 2011.
59 Retrieved from http://www.hrw.org/en/news/2011/06/02/c-te-d-ivoire-gbagbo-supporters-tortured-killed-abidjanon June 3, 2011.

opposition is strong all over French-speaking Africa and particularly in Côte d'Ivoire. This leaves MM as the most workable approach to language planning in Côte d'Ivoire. The weighted mean score of 68.75% discussed in 5.4 supports it as the consensus building model. We will also see in 8.5.2 that it is economically the most profitable model.

8.5.2 The feasibility and profitability of MM

Thorburn (1972:512, 516) suggests that the normal time-horizon planning is 25 years. However, we do not need to wait this long to see that MM is economically profitable. We see the economic payoffs accrue in only 15 years. The 15 year time-horizon can be divided into two phases: the first three years are devoted to the initial planning while the next 12 years deal with the full implementation of the language plan. Planning for 17 regional LWCs under MM means that the government must invest an initial capital of $1,918,790 for corpus planning expenses. This money will be used to develop the five critical areas of corpus planning in all 17 languages as discussed in 8.3.3. Some of the money will also be used to write the master curriculum in French from which the New Reader book and the Advanced Review books will be translated. Additionally, the government will invest $1,000,000 over three years for personnel retraining and workshop expenses. All in all, an initial capital outlay of nearly $3,000,000 is expected.[60] Donnacha (2000:17) is right in saying that "anyone who thinks language survival (i.e., planning) can be got for nothing is under an illusion."

The three years of planning will be followed by 12 continuous years of implementation of the language plan. The demographic changes during the next 15 years are expected to be important given the present birthrate of 700,000 babies a year. However, for the sake of simplicity, we will calculate the potential return on investment on the basis of the 2010 secondary students population. We learned from 8.4.3 that there were 1,289,036 students in lower secondary and 587,122 students in upper secondary, for a total of 1,876,158 students. In the same year, German and Spanish textbooks sold for $12.00 each. This means that in 2010, students spent $22,513,896 on textbooks. Let's remember that the Ivorian government

---

60 By way of comparison, the Ivorian government spent $97,065,462 (43 billion CFA) in preparation for the soccer World Cup tournament in South Africa in 2010. The team was eliminated in the first round!

provides free textbooks only to elementary school students. Parents must purchase textbooks for their secondary students. If we project the textbook sales forward over 12 years, it means that textbook revenues will amount to approximately $270,166,752. This is, without a doubt, a handsome profit for an initial investment of only $3,000,000! By contrast, according to the information summarized in 8.3.5, if NWLC 1–6 or RLWC 1–6 were implemented in elementary school, the government would have to spend at least $57,308,976 in new money over 12 years. If NLWC 1–3 or RLWC 1–3 were implemented, textbook expenditures alone would rise to at least $128,945,196 over 12 years. The projection of cost-benefit over 12 years is summarized in Chart 4 below:

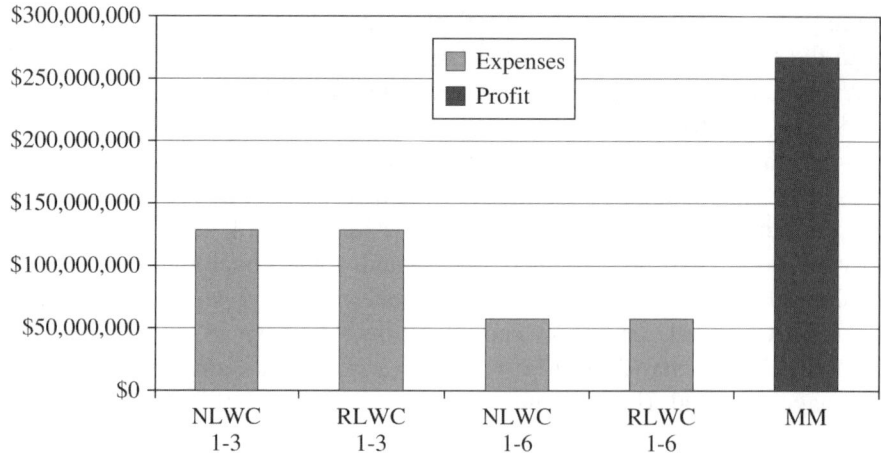

Figure 8.4. Cost-Benefit Analysis Comparison

When one subtracts the $3,000,000 initial investment from the $270,166,752 revenue from textbook sales, the profit margin is $267,166,752. Therefore, the implementation of MM can turn the linguistic resources of the country into an economic manna for the government.

8.5.3 Non-monetary benefits

The discussions in the preceding sections have highlighted the monetary benefits of language planning. But we should not lose sight of the fact that there are many other intangible benefits of developing one's own linguistic resources for use in formal education. There are undeniable psychological and cultural benefits that can accrue in a society that revalorizes its linguistic treasures. The language shift that Ivorians are experiencing now is due in large part to the fact that parents do not see the profitability of their children learning their indigenous languages at school. However, as soon as the market value of local languages becomes obvious, parents would take great pride in their children when they go to college, major in local languages, and get a job teaching them in secondary schools or in college. In reality, many parents do not object to what their children study in college. What they care about is that after graduation their son or daughter has acquired marketable skills that afford them a decent living. So, the negative or ambivalent attitudes that Ivorians have about their languages will change positively if they know that they can make a living from their linguistic resources. Once this happens, the increased market value of the local languages will spill over into other economic and employment sectors. Publishing companies, for instance, will expand their facilities and hire more people. Other jobs such as mother-tongue editors, writers, and proofreaders that did not exist before will also be created. Once the economic wheels start turning, entrepreneurs will find additional ways to make money and to continue increasing the marketability value of the linguistic resources of the country.

8.5.4 Merging TIM and MM

When these iconoclastic ideas were presented for the first time in 2004 at the University of Abidjan, Cocody Campus, they were warmly received. In the discussions that followed the plenary address, it was suggested that the TIM and MM could be merged during the first 25 years. It was proposed that the first 15 years be devoted to MM. After this period of implementation, and while MM is continuing to be used as the model of mother-tongue education in secondary school, the country may begin the implementation the RLWC 1–6 version of TIM. Here, the 17 main local languages would be taught as academic subjects throughout elementary school. As noted in 8.3.5, the implementation of RLWC 1–6 calls for only 6,633 teachers as opposed to the 20,009 that NLWC 1–3 or RLWC 1–3 would require. The reason for suggesting the merger of MM and TIM is that the financial profits accrued by MM over 12 years could help support the cost of TIM even if the government were reticent to pour new money into implementing mother-tongue education in elementary schools. If mother-tongue education is to be extended to elementary school, it also means that it should be extended to 7th and 8th graders first. Otherwise, there would be a two-year hiatus between the end of 6th grade and the beginning of mother-tongue education in 9th grade. All this shows that if MM is implemented, mother-tongue education can gradually permeate the whole educational system of Côte d'Ivoire without bringing about strong parental opposition. Furthermore, since the gradual implementation of MM is financially self-sustainable, it is less likely to be rejected for being too expensive. Last but not least, the implementation of MM is unlikely to exacerbate ethnolinguistic rivalry and cause unnecessary conflicts because each of the 19 administrative counties will teach its own major language and, if necessary, accommodate the language(s) of the largest immigrant community in its midst.

8.6 Language planning for all

The position taken in this book is that the 3±1 model of the Game theory makes it possible to plan all the languages of Côte d'Ivoire. Here is how the model would work to achieve the goal of language planning for all: Every Ivorian who graduates from secondary school will be literate in two languages: French and his/her regional language. If his/her native language is different from the 17 regional LWCs, he/she can very easily transfer the literacy skills of the regional LWC into his/her native language. This is possible because of the orthographic strategies used in reducing Ivorian languages to writing. These strategies were first employed by the African Institute in designing the orthographies of African languages. They allow for maximum transferability of literacy skills between related African languages. They are explained in the introduction of *Practical Orthography of African Languages* as follows:

> The aim of the recommendations of the Institute has been, and is, the unification and simplification of the orthography of African languages. Over large areas which have political, geographical, or linguistic unity an unsatisfactory state of affairs is found to exist at the present time owing to lack of agreement as to the general principles of writing down the languages, and as to the letters to be used and the meanings attached to them. In Africa today conditions of life are such that many thousands of natives leave their home districts and, either with or without their families, settle temporarily or permanently in districts where their mother tongue is not understood. Thus, for everyday intercourse, for church and school life, or in order to read a newspaper, they are obliged to learn another language. It would obviously be a great advantage if in the orthography of the new language, the

value of the letters were the same, or as nearly as possible the same, as those they have already learnt for their mother tongue. Moreover, in many parts of Africa, children in the early stages of school life receive instruction through the medium of the mother tongue, and later in a language which is used over a wider area. The change from mother tongue to another language may not be very difficult for the Negro, because of his linguistic ability and because the two languages are generally closely related, and their construction, grammar, idiom, and vocabulary are often very similar. But if the two languages are written with two different systems of orthography, confusion is likely to arise, and unnecessary difficulty is placed in the path of the learner. In such cases the promotion of uniformity is clearly an important need of the moment (Institute 1930:1–2).

The same principle of transferability from one African language to another within the same language family, and from French to Ivorian languages, is clearly stated in the *Practical Guide to the Orthography of Ivorian Languages*. This fact alone combined with widespread oral bilingualism makes it very easy to transfer skills from one language into another. Here are two firsthand examples to illustrate how this can be done. Though my native language is Anyi, I learned to read Baule almost effortlessly. In 2008, I trained some Catholic nuns to read Anyi. One of the nuns is a native speaker of Attie, a language of the Akan family. The Attie-speaking nun caught on to reading Anyi faster than, or as fast as, the native Anyi-speaking nuns because she was already a proficient reader of Attie. So, the uniformity of script and the phonemic principle underlying most Ivorian orthographies make the transfer of literacy skills fairly easy.

The example of language planning in India mentioned in 8.2.3 shows how Côte d'Ivoire can achieve the goal of language planning for all. Mohanty (2009:103, 107) informs us that there is a three-tiered mother-tongue education model. The first tier is represented by English and Hindi that children learn at school. The second tier is the 41 regional majority languages that are used in formal education. The third tier is represented by the 104 languages that are not used for formal schooling but are used in adult literacy classes. Statistically speaking, India uses little over 10% of its languages in formal education and 26% in adult literacy programs. India has not been able to achieve language planning for all. However, if MM is adopted, and Côte d'Ivoire teaches 17 regional LWCs in secondary school, that would amount to using 28% of its languages in formal education. The remaining 43 languages (72%) can be planned for adult literacy programs. So, the goal of language planning for all is achievable, as shown by the discussion below.

8.6.1 Cost analysis of informal adult literacy programs for all

Two decades of adult literacy programs in rural eastern Côte d'Ivoire have provided me with accumulated data that show that a literacy classroom can be run effectively with about $1,000.00 per year after an initial set-up cost of $1,000.00. The set-up cost is for the purchase of two portable generators and the wiring that is needed to prepare the classroom for electricity, as discussed in 7.2.4 and 7.2.5. The cost of running a normal literacy classroom is broken up as follows: About $300 goes directly towards a teacher's stipend. This is equivalent to the amount of money that a sharecropper makes for working on a cocoa or coffee farm for a year. When the Anyi Literacy program began in 1997, it depended solidly on volunteer teachers. However, we learned, much to our disappointment, that volunteers leave for seasonal farm employment. We then decided to match what they would make sharecropping. This has brought great stability in the teaching staff. Approximately $300.00 is spent for training, room and board, and transportation for teachers. Teachers meet quarterly for refresher courses. Students receive pencils and literacy booklets free of charge. This amounts to about $200.00. The remaining $200.00 is used for paying the utility bills and the upkeep of the literacy center.

8.6.2 Funding adult literacy programs

If the Ivorian government spends a fourth of the $267,166,752 profit that it stands to make from textbooks sales, that is, $66,791,688, it can fund about 66,791 literacy classes throughout the nation. This would be literacy program on a large scale such as has never been seen since the Somali experiment alluded to in 7.4.3. However, since African governments have been notoriously delinquent in fulfilling their adult literacy obligations, Côte d'Ivoire should grant publishing rights of secondary textbooks to a reputable textbook publishing company. The contract then would charge the company to re-invest 10% of its profits into adult literacy programs every year. The privatization of adult literacy programs is likely to work better than turning it over to the government. It could still promote its strategic partnership with specialized faith-based organizations while staffing its own linguistics departments. It could assign to these organizations the responsibility of corpus planning and literacy material development in minority languages. It could incentivize these organizations by granting them tax-exempt status because of their language revalorization efforts. The government could continue to attract funds from UNESCO and other donor agencies. If some of the proceeds of textbook sales are reinvested into adult literacy planning, the risk of endangering the 43 minority languages that have not been selected for mother-tongue education can be reduced, though not entirely eliminated.

8.7 Summary

This chapter has led to three iconoclastic conclusions. The claim that the cost of language planning rises proportionately with the number of languages planned has been disproved. We now know that planning for multiple languages is not significantly more expensive than planning for a single language. The second iconoclastic conclusion is that it does not take much to raise the marketability value of African languages. Postponing German and Spanish until college and teaching regional Ivorian languages in their stead immediately increases their marketability values. Essegbey (2009: 126–8) shows that the marketability value of Akan is on the rise in Ghana because multinational companies are now advertising in it. Bwenge's (2009) article on Language Choice on Dar es Salaam's billboards attests to the same phenomenon of an increasing use of African language in advertisement. The third iconoclastic conclusion is that it is economically more feasible and profitable to introduce Ivorian languages in upper secondary school than to do so in elementary school. Moreover, the revenue made from textbook sales can help spread adult literacy classes all over the country. Ultimately, I agree with Thorburn (1972:515) that the ball is in the policymakers' corner because, as he puts it,

> A cost-benefit analysis is not intended to be a complete and absolutely reliable foundation for language planning. There are many consequences that are extremely difficult to identify, quantify, and evaluate; they must, nevertheless be taken into account in any final political decision. A cost-benefit analysis calculation ought to assemble all relevant scientific knowledge pertaining to the problem in question (description and relations), which ought to be presented to the politicians in an impartial and clear way. How to weigh the advantages and disadvantages and to judge the uncertainties is up to the politician. In my opinion, such a cost-benefit analysis can be extremely valuable in language planning.

Chapter 9
Individual efforts in language planning

Introduction

Applied linguists have been so influenced by the model offered by the French Revolution that many have come to believe that language planning is the prerogative of big governments. This fallacy was reinforced in the 1960s by the examples of Indonesia, Malaysia, and the Philippines. Historically though, successful language planning has been carried out by individuals. If a museum of language planners existed, its walls would be filled with superstars such as St. Cyril, Martin Luther, Noah Webster, and Eliezer Ben Yehuda. Next to them would be stars such as Alfred Saker, Alexander Mackay, Diedrich Westermann, Johann Ludwig Krapf, Johannes Rebmann, Robert Moffat, Samuel Ajayi Crowther, and St. Stefan of Perm, to name only a few.[61] On another wall not too far away, there should be a plaque dedicated to the Unknown Language Planners. These are countless individuals who labored (some are still laboring) long and hard, sometimes in obscurity, to plan the future course of a language. The superstars, the stars, and the anonymous language planners, past or present, are united by a common bond. They all seek to breathe new life into a language in distress or to chart a new course for a language. The goal of this chapter is to review the strategies used by three distinguished language planners of past centuries so as to discover the secrets of their success. The three who will occupy center stage in this chapter are St. Stefan of Perm, Eliezer Ben Yehuda, and Bishop Samuel Ajayi Crowther. The

---

61 Sigusmund Wihelm Koelle (1823–1902) of the Church Missionary Society worked on Kanuri, a Chadic language; and Johann G. Christaller of the Evangelical Missionary Society worked on Twi, an Akan language. These two eminent German linguists did important work on their respective languages. However, they are not included in this discussion because not much is known about their approach to language planning even though they produced linguistic work of great theoretical importance (Welmers 1974:197–99).

achievements of six others, Alfred Saker, Alexander Mackay, Dieedrich Westermann, Johann Ludwig Krapf, Johannes Rebmann, and Robert Moffat, will be highlighted along the way.

9.1 Genre, organization, and selection

The writings about the heroes of language planning constitute a special literacy genre. They are not the normal biographical genres that deal with major rites of passage in the life of the individual being written about. Instead, linguists who have written about the language planning accomplishments of these legendary figures bypass most of the human interest stories and focus primarily on their linguistics achievements, unless the human interest story enhances the overall narrative. This genre is hard to write because the researcher has to comb through the person's life to find nuggets of information that are relevant to language planning. More challenging is the fact that the language planner himself may not have had a clue as to the linguistic significance of some of his/her actions. So, the linguist is forced to interpret on his/her own such actions and compose a coherent language planning narrative. Such was the challenge that Fellman (1974:454–5) faced when writing about the language planning achievements of Ben Yehuda:

> Ben Yehuda had in mind almost no real plan of action for the revival of the Hebrew language when he arrived in Palestine, except a firm decision based, as he admits, on the 'rashness of youth' to speak only Hebrew himself, to set up a Hebrew-speaking home with a wife who did not herself know Hebrew, ... Ben Yehuda was not a methodological planner or thinker. Rather, as Tur-Sinai notes, his actions were based 'not on scientific reasoning but on inspired feeling.'

To my knowledge only two scholarly articles have been written in this style with a focus on language planning. The first was written by Ferguson (1968) about the language planning genius of St. Stefan of Perm. The second was by Fellman (1974) about the seven initiatives used by Ben Yehuda in the revitalization of Hebrew. I have reanalyzed their articles and drawn from them only information relevant to the status planning, the corpus planning, and the acquisition planning strategies used by the language planning heroes that they wrote about. I imitate the style of these two articles as I write about the language planning strategies used by Bishop Samuel Ajayi Crowther in 9.5 through 9.5.3. In each case, I begin with a short paragraph to introduce the three language planners who are the focus of this chapter.

9.2 St. Stefan of Perm

Ferguson (1968:253–65) introduces St. Stefan of Perm as an unusual man who was born in 1335 and died in 1396. Sixteen of his sixty-one years were spent in a monastery where he studied Latin and Greek. He was a Russian-born priest who spent most of his life among the Komi people. His parents moved to the Komi-speaking area when he was very young. So, he grew up as a Russian-Komi bilingual. Komi is a language currently spoken in northeastern Russia by 496,000 people according to a 2002 census. Seventy-one percent of the responders consider it to be their native language, while 29% speak it as a second language.[62] The latter group is made up of Komi-Russian bilinguals. Komi belongs to the Uralic family of languages. The language game that St. Stefan and the Komi played can be described as a two-person cooperative game. He orthographed their language, and in return, they loved him and adored him. However, it did not begin as a cooperative game but rather as a competitive game because the Komi opposed him. Ferguson writes that St. Stefan met considerable resistance from them because they were predominantly shamanistic. As for language planning proper, he was faced with three important challenges: "What variety of the language shall be chosen as the standard? What kind of writing system shall be used? What kind of literature shall be produced?" (Ferguson, p. 255). In other words, St. Stefan was faced with problems related to status planning, corpus planning, and acquisition planning. Let's find out the strategies he used in solving these problems.

9.2.1 St. Stefan's status planning strategies

Status planning generally deals with choosing one dialect out of many to serve as the written standard. In contemporary linguistics, this decision is often made after several months of dialect survey studies during which data is collected from among various dialects of the same language. The data is used for mutual intelligibility testing. Additionally, census data (when available) and issues of prestige are taken into account before issuing a final decision about which dialect should serve as the written standard. St. Stefan did not have the benefits of all these sociolinguistic insights. Ferguson (pp. 257–8) indicates that he based his decision on a second language acquisition criterion. St. Stefan reasoned that "the dialect at the point of entry," that is, "the one used by bilingual and bicultural individuals" is to

---

62 Retrieved from http://www.phrasebase.com/languages/komi/ on July 14, 2011.

serve as the standard for writing Komi. Ferguson describes St. Stefan's choice as brilliant because the dialect of a language that is commonly learned as a second language is generally less complex phonologically, morphologically, and syntactically. So, St. Stefan chose the dialect "spoken along the lower course of the Vyčegda River" because it met that criterion. It was the dialect that he himself learned in his childhood in the Russian settlement. It was also the dialect that most Russians learned when they moved to the Komi-speaking area.

9.2.2 St. Stefan's corpus planning strategies

St. Stefan had to make a decision about graphization, i.e., the choice of the symbols to be used in the orthography. In the world in which he lived, there were basically two types of orthographic symbols to choose from: the Cyrillic alphabet and the Roman alphabet. St. Stefan was a creative man. So, he designed a writing system that combines both alphabets and more. Here is how Ferguson (p. 259) describes his alphabet:

> Stefan's choice of writing system is of special interest. He invented an alphabet, called Abur, which was clearly based on his knowledge of Greek and Church Slavonic, but he deliberately made the forms of the letters sufficiently different from either so the Komi could regard the writing system as distinctly theirs and not an alphabet used for another language. It seems likely that he gave some of the letters an appearance suggestive of the Tamga signs in use among the Komi as property markers and decorations.

It is noteworthy that as far back as the 14th century, St. Stefan was acutely aware of the political significance of orthographic symbols. This led him to design a system that was uniquely tailored to meet the ethnolinguistic pride of the Komi people. As laudable as this strategy was, it has been strongly discouraged by the International African Institute for reasons given in 8.6. However, following St. Stefan's example, orthographers for African languages can meet the ethnolinguistic needs of the speakers for whom they are designing an orthography by finding ways to coin metalinguistic terms and to indigenize punctuation marks for local languages, as Koffi (1995) suggests in his paper about *Indigenizing Punctuation Marks*. Another aspect of St. Stefan's corpus planning activities included his modernization of the Komi lexicon through the translation of major parts of the liturgy of the Orthodox Church. Because of this work, Komi became the second among Uralic languages to have a vibrant literary life: "[St. Stefan] gave Komi the oldest literacy monuments in any Uralic language except Hungarian, and he introduced Komi in public worship and in the schools he established" (Ferguson p. 254).

9.2.3 St. Stefan's acquisition planning strategies

Ferguson failed to say much about St. Stefan's acquisition planning strategies except for the fragment of a sentence in which he wrote that "he introduced Komi in public worship and in the schools he established." This is the only clue in the entire twelve-page article that tells us how the Komi learned to read and write their language. This fragment of a sentence unlocks for us the secrets of St. Stefan's tremendous language planning success among the Komi. He may not have lived long enough to see how much fruit his labor bore, but Ferguson (p. 254) tells us that he had tremendous success: "With the death of St. Stefan the Komi people began their history of five centuries of loyalty to the Orthodox Church, love and reverence for the name of St. Stefan, and pride in the early possession of a literary language of their own." St. Stefan's language planning successes did not go unrecognized. His fame spread so far and wide that he received the greatest payoff he could have dreamed off: he was beatified as a saint; not an ordinary saint, because his sainthood was "recognized by the Roman Catholic Church, even though he lived after the great schism between East and West" (p. 254). Ferguson (p. 262) concludes his article with the following tribute in recognition of St. Stefan's applied linguistic genius:

> In all these decisions the good saint acted without benefit of a sociolinguistic theory or frame of reference, and without any recorded body of previous experience he could consult. One must admire St. Stefan's clear-cut decisions and successful implementations of them, but equally one must bewail the fact that a present-day agent of culture change faced with the language problems in a nonliterate society still has no sociolinguistic theory and very little in the way of recorded and analyzed case histories to give guidance. We have not progressed much beyond St. Stefan's competence five centuries ago.

Ferguson (p. 253) suggests that the solutions that St. Stefan devised for Komi are still applicable today, and that applied linguists facing similar problems in Asia, Africa, and Latin America could benefit from his language planning strategies.

9.3 Eliezer Ben Yehuda[63]

Eliezer Ben Yehuda (1858–1922) is a household name in language planning circles. The short biographical sketch presented here highlights aspects of his life that are relevant to his language planning career. He graduated from high school in 1877. Thereafter, he devoted 45 years of the 64 that he lived charting the future course of the Hebrew language. His desire to resurrect Hebrew took him on a tortuous journey. One year after graduation, he left for Paris where he intended to study medicine at the Sorbonne University. However, three years into his studies, he had to stop because he fell sick with tuberculosis. French doctors did not give him long to live. So, he made two vows: the first was to immigrate to Israel and the second was to break up with Deborah Jonas, his high school sweetheart, because he did not want to infect her with tuberculosis. However, Deborah refused to break up with him. They got married in 1881 and left for Israel. They arrived in Jaffa in October, settled there briefly and then moved to Jerusalem. A year later, their son Ben-Avi was born. His birth set off a unique experiment in the annals of child language acquisition. Both Ben Yehuda and Deborah lacked oral proficiency in Hebrew and yet they agreed to speak only Hebrew in their home. This turned out to be a monumental task. They had to coin all kinds of words to keep up with the communicative needs of a growing family. Gradually, the experiment paid off and more and more families joined in.

In 1884, Ben Yehuda began to publish a weekly newspaper in Hebrew. Ten years after they arrived in Israel, Deborah passed away. However, before she died from tuberculosis, she wrote to her younger sister Paula and urged her to marry her husband. Paula agreed, immigrated to Israel and married Ben Yehuda. Upon marriage, she changed her name to Hemdah. She proved herself to be a strong woman on two counts. First, in 1900 she became the editor of the newspaper that Ben Yehuda began. Secondly, she mounted an international campaign to free her husband from jail in 1904. He had used his newspaper as a platform to launch vitriolic attacks and charges of corruption against some elements of the religious establishment. So, they conspired against him, twisted a sentence that he had written, and reported him to the Ottoman government for planning a revolt. He was arbitrarily charged with conspiracy and sentenced to one year in jail. Hemdah's efforts led to an international outcry over Ben Yehuda's imprisonment.

---

63 Retrieved from http://www.zionism-israel.com/bio/E_Ben_Yehuda_biography. htm, http://www.levsoftware.com/history, http://en.wikipedia.org/wiki/Eliezer_Ben_Yehuda on June 30, 2011.

Pressured mounted from everywhere, so the Ottoman authorities had no choice but to free him. Hemdah's work on the newspaper also freed him to focus on a gargantuan lexicography project on which he had embarked. He devoted up to 18 hours a day to this project until his death in December 1922 (Fellman 1974:441). The coronation of his life's work came one month before his death when British authorities, who had mandate over Palestine, proclaimed Hebrew the official language of Israel.

Fellman (1974:427–55) uses the term "initiative" to summarize Ben Yehuda's life work in the revival of Hebrew:

1. The setting up of the first Hebrew-speaking household in his own home
2. A call to the Diaspora and to the local population for assistance and advice
3. The creation of Hebrew-speaking societies
4. The establishment of Hebrew through Hebrew classes in the schools
5. The publishing of a modern Hebrew newspaper
6. The compiling of a dictionary of the Hebrew language, ancient and modern
7. The forming of a Language Council

In a short online article, Fellman (2010) reduces these seven initiatives to three phrases: "Hebrew in the Home," "Hebrew in the School," and "Words, Words, Words." They correspond roughly to status planning, corpus planning, and acquisition planning.

9.3.1 Ben Yehuda's status planning strategies

Ben Yehuda's dialect is hard to determine; it cannot be said that Modern Hebrew is based on his own dialect. The problem is compounded by the fact that, according Fellman (1974:430), "he [Ben Yehuda] would struggle with the pronunciation. His conversation was not the conversation of the great." He was so aware of the deficiencies in his own pronunciation that he refused to vocalize the new words that he coined in his newspaper. The readers of his newspaper complained that they did not know how to pronounce the new words (p. 438). The aspect of Ben Yehuda's status planning that is of interest to us is his creation of two language bodies to oversee the development of Hebrew. The first was the "Clear Language Society" (p. 432) and the second was the "Language Council," (pp. 450–2). The model the Académie Française may have lurked in the back of Ben Yehuda's mind when he created these two languages bodies. The language Council had four functions: "The creation of a unified Hebrew terminology, the unification of pronunciation, the unification of the spelling system, and the fixing of grammatical forms" (p. 451). The creation of the Language Council in particular was a brilliant idea because it helped Ben Yehuda to base his spelling and pronunciation decisions on the recommendations made by the committee, in spite of Fellman's (pp. 451–3) skepticism about the relevance of the two language bodies in the overall Hebrew revitalization efforts.

9.3.2 Ben Yehuda's corpus planning strategies

Two strategies stand out when we examine how Ben Yehuda planned the Hebrew corpus. Fellman (2010)[64] sums both up with "Words, Words, Words." He inundated the Hebrew lexicon with the hundreds and hundreds of words that he coined in his newspaper. He and his editorial staff were forced to come up every week with words to describe every aspect of modern life, from entertainment to science, to politics, to cuisine, to pop culture. The second way by which Ben Yehuda "immortalized" the thousands of new words was through his mammoth lexicography project. He decided in 1900 to write an alphabetical dictionary of Hebrew. He spent 22 years on the project. His efforts culminated in a 17-volume entitled, *A Complete Dictionary of Ancient and Modern Hebrew*, the latter part of which was completed postmortem. Ben Yehuda was a polyglot who spoke Russian, German, French, Yiddish fluently. He had earlier published a pocket-size Russian-Hebrew bilingual dictionary and a pocket-size trilingual Hebrew-Russian-Yiddish dictionary. However, he was not prepared for the mountain of difficulties that awaited him when he embarked on the Hebrew lexicography project. The work drained every ounce of mental energy from him to the point that he saw it as a divine punishment: "If God wishes to severely punish someone, he decrees upon him to be a dictionary compiler. ... The life of the compiler is like living in Hell" (Fellman 1974:442).

9.3.3 Ben Yehuda's acquisition planning strategies

The acquisition planning strategy that Ben Yehuda adopted could be aptly summarized by the phrase "Hebrew in the School." He envisioned Hebrew

---

64 Retrieved from http://www.jewishvirtuallibrary.org/jsource/biography/ben_yehuda.html on June 30, 2011.

being used at school, in the synagogues, and at home, because he believed that "the revival could succeed especially, and perhaps only, if the younger generation would begin to speak it freely" (Fellman 2010). FIM was the language of education model that was chosen to teach Hebrew at school. This meant that every academic subject, every discussion, every explanation had to be given in Hebrew. This put tremendous pressure on teachers who were themselves barely fluent in the language. The manner in which the teachers rose to the challenge is described by Fellman (2010):

> True, teaching in Hebrew involved many problems: lack of trained teachers, lack of textbooks, lack of materials such as games or songs, lack of terminologies and so on. David Yudeleviz, an early teacher, wrote in 1928: "In a heavy atmosphere, without books, expressions, words, verbs and hundreds of nouns, we had to begin… teaching. It is impossible to describe or imagine under what pressure the first seeds were planted … Hebrew teaching materials for elementary education were limited … We were half-mute, stuttering, we spoke with our hands and eyes." Another prominent teacher, David Yellin, wrote in the same vein: "Every teacher had a French or Russian teaching book of his own, and he organized his Hebrew work according to it … Terms for teaching did not exist. Every village teacher was an Academy (of the Hebrew Language) member with respect to creating words according to his taste, and everyone, of course, used his own creations." However, as time went on, all these linguistic problems were ultimately solved, and a young all-Hebrew speaking generation did emerge and develop, thus ensuring beyond anything else that the revival would be a success.

Fellman (1974:433) comments that teachers "formed the spearhead of revival," especially since Ben Yehuda himself did not teach very much.

9.4 The Reformation interlude

An interlude is inserted between St. Stefan and Ben Yehuda and the remaining sections because it provides the necessary background to understand the context in which Bishop Crowther and the other 19th century missionaries carried out their language planning duties in Africa. Their work was a continuation of the Reformation Movement that Martin Luther launched in Germany on October 31st, 1517, when he posted his 95 theses on the door of his church in Wittenberg. This event launched an evangelization campaign that has resulted in a vast language planning movement around the globe. In his book, *6,000 Years of the Bible*, Wegener (1958) provides a detailed account of how the passion for the "Written Word of God" transformed Europe through church-based literacy. He contends that "without the Bible the Middles Ages might well indeed have been the Dark Ages. When Christianity had once struggled its way into Europe, it became the driving force of the people. It reached its highest peak in monasteries. The monasteries existed to pray and to work, to study and to teach" (p. 174). Literacy spread because the speakers of major European languages strived to have the Bible translated into their own tongues even at a time when "the general level of education was very low, and more than one reigning monarch could neither read nor write" (p. 174). Literate monks copied the Bible, translated it, and taught it to laypeople in the parishes. Some of the converts joined the established church as priests. Others used their knowledge to create schools. The pattern repeated itself in many villages and cities near monasteries. Little by little, the movement spread outward to other localities. Wegener, however, notes that the momentum was slow but steady. Greater access to Scriptures was made possible after Gutenberg invented the printing press in 1454. After that, Bibles became "cheap enough to be bought by the ordinary man who had never before been able to afford books" (pp. 212–4).

Literacy began to spread even further and deeper with the advent of the Reformation. It was a movement with the Bible as its centerpiece. Martin Luther's translation was so influential that it ushered in a new era of Bible-based language planning. Wegener (1958:211) writes that by the time Luther died on February 18, 1546, he was recognized as "the greatest German who had ever lived." This credit is due in large part to his Bible translation work which provided a common written standard to many more or less mutually intelligible dialects of German. His translation was an overwhelming success because it spread literacy in Germany as never before. It has been estimated that by 1524, as many as 128,000 copies of his New Testament were in circulation. Wegener (1958:206, 209) may have used a hyperbole in saying that Luther's translation was carried "from professor to student, from townsman to farmer. According to a contemporary account, many people carried it around like a talisman and learnt it by heart."

Luther's example had a tremendous impact on English intellectuals such as William Tyndale, Miles Coverdale, John Rogers, and others who translated the Bible into English, sometimes at the risk of their lives. Missionaries from Germany and England carried the Reformation ideals with them as they fanned across the globe. They went with the firm conviction that what Christianity did for Germany and England through Bible translation, it could do for any given culture, provided that the Bible is translated into the "heart language" of the people. They set out to experiment with this belief in Nepomuk, a Native American language of Massachusetts into which John Eliot translated Scriptures in 1661. This experiment was later followed by the translation of the Bible into Tamil in 1728, then into Sinhalese in 1739, and into Eskimo in 1744 (p. 259). In the 18th and 19th centuries, Bible translation topped the agenda of many missionary organizations:

> Missionary after missionary, whether he had a gift for languages or not, forced himself to undertake the wearing task of translating into hitherto entirely undocumented languages, languages without dictionaries, often without books at all. One of these men was William Carey, who rose from being a village cobbler to a Baptist benefice and later the Chair of Theology at Fort William College, Calcutta. Carey founded a school of translation which produced no fewer than forty different versions of the Bible within twenty years (Wegner 1958:259).

By ricochet, the Reformation ideals and experimentations reached the shores of the African continent, especially in areas that were colonized by the Belgians, the British, and the Germans. Wegner (p. 214) writes that "France, Spain, and Italy remained outside this widespread movement which Luther had begun." Concerning Portugal, he said "Portugal had to wait another one hundred years for her first New Testament, and the full Bible did not come out until 1719." This information explains why francophone and lusophone countries in Africa still lag far behind their Belgian and British counterparts in literacy in their local languages. Missionaries from these Reformation-minded countries left for Africa with the firm conviction that the best way to evangelize was to translate the Bible into the peoples'"heart languages."

9.5 Samuel Ajayi Crowther

Bishop Samuel Ajayi Crowther (see 4.2.3) was undoubtedly the most famous and the most influential clergyman in Africa in the 19th Century. His accomplishments are long and impressive. Just a few would be enough to start with. In 1851 when Crowther went to London, "he saw government ministers, he had an interview with the Queen and Prince Albert, he spoke at meetings all over the country, invariably to great effect. This grave, eloquent, well-informed black clergyman was the most impressive tribute to the effect of the missionary movement that most British people had seen"

(Walls 1978).[65] Thirteen years later, he went back to London to be awarded an honorary Doctor of Divinity from Oxford University. That same year, he was ordained Bishop of the Anglican Church. He was the first African to be recipient of both honors in the same year! However, nothing in his birth or his growing up years could have predicted that he would attain such prominence. He was born around 1809 and was barely 12 years old when his world of Osogun in Yorubaland fell apart. He was eating breakfast one morning when slave raiders descended on his little town of approximately 3,000 people. This catastrophic event took place in 1821. He was captured, along with his mother, his toddler brother, and two sisters. He was bought and sold six different times by the time he boarded the Portuguese slave ship *Esperanza Felix* (Olsen 2003:10). These repeated commercial transactions caused him and his family members to be separated. He was placed on a ship with 190 others captives. However, two years prior to his capture, the British Parliament had abolished slavery. The British Navy strictly enforced the antislavery legislation. British armed forces patrolled the West African coasts and intercepted slave-carrying ships. The crew of two navy vessels, the *Myrmidon* and the *Iphigenia*, intercepted the Portuguese ship. The rescue efforts resulted in the death of 100 slaves. Young Ajayi counted himself blessed to have survived the shipwreck of the *Esperanza Felix*. The survivors were resettled in Freetown, in Sierra Leone. The city had been chosen as the headquarters of the British Navy ships and also the home of freed slaves.

The antislavery forces that were associated with William Wilberforce and the Anglican Church came together to create the Church Missionary Society (CMS). Freed slaves were evangelized and many accepted the Christian faith. Young Ajayi also became a Christian in 1825. He was baptized by Rev. J. C. Raban. Upon baptism, he chose to be named after Samuel Crowther, Vicar of Christ's Church in London. CMS created Fourah Bay College in 1828 to train freed slaves. The school graduated eminent African missionaries, architects, and doctors. Walls (1978) writes that Fourah Bay College became a "great language laboratory." Rev. Raban, who was teaching at the school believed that evangelism would be more effective if freed slaves could be reached in their native languages instead of English. Since there was a large contingent of Yorubas among the freed slaves, he began to do basic lexicographic work on Yoruba in order to

---

65 Retrieved from http://www.dacb.org/stories/nigeria/legacy_crowther.html on July 3, 2011.

evangelize them in their native tongue. He chose his understudy Samuel Crowther as his language assistant. Right away he discovered that Crowther was brilliant, a linguistic genius, so he arranged for him to study abroad in England for one year. He came back in 1827 with an admirable command of English. When Fourah Bay College opened its doors in 1828, he was among the very first students to enroll for courses. Again, Crowther excelled in Greek, Hebrew, and Latin to the point that he was later hired to teach Greek and Latin at the college. Crowther's linguistic repertoire included Yoruba, English, and Temme which he spoke fluently. He had scholarly abilities in Greek, Hebrew, and Latin. From 1865 onward, he added Igbo and Nupe to the list of languages that he knew.

In 1841 tragedy almost visited him again. He was part of an ill-fated Niger Expedition. One hundred forty-five people took part in the expedition. Of the 45 Europeans, it is reported that 40 died of malaria (Olsen 2003:11). Two months into the expedition, the two ships had to turn back to Freetown. Samuel Crowther chronicled in great detail their misadventure. Excerpts from his travelogue were published and became an overnight sensation in England. He became a celebrity of sorts. His leadership skills and his composure in the face of danger convinced CMS authorities that he would be a fine clergyman. He was summoned to England where he took courses to be ordained as a minister of the Anglican Church in 1843. Upon his return, he preached, taught, planted churches, and was part of two other successful expeditions. He continued to excel in his pastoral duties, so much so that he was made bishop in 1864. Crowther's ministerial achievements are long and impressive. He labored tirelessly to grow the church in Nigeria. Akinwumi (2002)[66] writes that he was also a formidable social reformer. He battled against twin infanticide, human sacrifice, human trafficking, women abuse, alligator worship, drunkenness, and many other evils in the vast area under his ministerial care.

9.5.1 Crowther's status planning strategies

It is hard to discern with accuracy what Crowther's status planning strategies might have been. All that can be said with certainty is that the Yoruba orthography was most likely based on his own dialect. There are a few

---

66 Retrieved from http://www.transparencyng.com/index.php?option=com_content& view=article&id=1755:samuel-ajayi-crowther-by-reverend-dr-elijah-olu-akinwumi& catid=59:guest&Itemid=37 on July 3, 2011.

facts that point us in this direction. First, he was Rev. Raban's language informant. Walls (1978) writes that Crwother was also the informant for the Quaker educationalist Hannah Kilham. In all likelihood she based her writings about Yoruba on his dialect. As a result, it is quite likely that "the three books about Yoruba" that Rev. Raban published between 1828 and 1830 were based on Crowther's dialect (Walls 1978). Another important piece of evidence comes from the fact that Crowther wrote much of his *Yoruba Grammar and Vocabulary* during the first Niger Expedition of 1841. It is also likely that he completed his work while he was studying for the ministry in England. Olsen (2003:12) writes that "he returned to Sierra Leone and began preaching in both English and a language on which he had begun to write linguistic texts – his own Yoruba." That Crowther should base the written version of Yoruba on his own dialect is not at all surprising.

9.5.2 Crowther's corpus planning strategies

Crowther got his first corpus planning experience under the tutelage of Rev. Raban. He has also been credited with designing the Yoruba orthography, but this may be an overstatement. There may have been an existing orthography that Rev. Raban used for his lexicographic research. Regardless, Crowther played a crucial role in making the orthography more user-friendly. He wrote primers to teach how to read and write Yoruba. Walls (1978) credits him with insisting "that the translation should indicate tone." Versions of his *Yoruba Grammar and Vocabulary* were available as early as 1843. In 1852, he revised and expanded it. The aspect of Crowther's corpus planning that has earned him respect and admiration was his translation of the Bible into Yoruba. Schaaf (1994:64) states that he is widely regarded as "the first African who translated the Bible himself for his own people." He certainly deserves this honor, but he did not do the work alone, nor did he do much for the Old Testament. He may have been the main translator of the Yoruba New Testament. It is known for sure that he translated the Epistle to the Romans, the Gospel of Luke, the Acts of the Apostles, the Epistle of James, and the Epistle of Peter. It is also known that he made extensive notes on the Gospel of Matthew which his fellow Yoruba speaker and Fourah Bay graduate, Thomas King, had translated (Schaaf 1994:65). Walls (1978) indicates that Crowther did extensive field linguistics work but that a lot of it was destroyed by fire when his residence burned down in 1862: "Over the years, wherever he was, he noted words, proverbs, forms of speech. One of his hardest blows was the loss of the notes of eleven years of such observations, and some manuscript translations, when his house burned down in 1862." As for the Old Testament, after translating Genesis and Exodus, his ministerial duties led him to take up residence in Igboland in 1865. This and other church administration duties left him with little time for translation.

9.5.3 Crowther's acquisition planning strategies

How did Crowther go from writing primers, a reference grammar, and translating Scriptures in Yoruba to teaching the Yoruba people how to read and write in their own language? Some 500 Yoruba speakers left Freetown and re-immigrated to Yorubaland around the same time as Crowther was doing church planting there. A fair number of them were already literate, and some joined him as catechists and school teachers. Among them was the distinguished Thomas King, a catechist who became well-known for translating the Gospel of Matthew. Three other individuals were part of the Yoruba leadership team: T.B. Macaulay, another Yoruba speaker, Henry Townsend, a British missionary, and C.A. Gollmer, a German missionary. They were all commissioned by CMS to go to Abeokuta to start churches. It is said that Henry Townsend and C.A. Gollmer were very good Yoruba linguists.

The team that Crowther led from Sierra Leone to Yorubaland had a three-pronged acquisition planning strategy. The first one was based on teaching Yoruba to children through mission schools. For this, the FIM approach to language of education was adopted. Akinwumi (2002) alludes to this by saying that "the main weapon of Bishop Crowther's evangelization was school. He regarded education as a means of enlightening the future generations, especially where the texts used to educate were from the Holy Scriptures." He established schools in many areas under his control. He is also credited with pioneering the system of self-supporting schools. Each village was asked to raise the 36 to 62 pounds needed per year to pay an elementary teacher's salary. Villages that could not afford it were helped by funds donated by Bishop Crowther's overseas contributors. Crowther insured that students were taught literacy skills and useful trades such as carpentry and masonry. Teachers were selected from among the best catechists. The second literacy strategy was carried out through catechism. When people became Christians, they were taught to read. The Anglican *Book of Common Prayer* was used extensively by the missionary team in adult literacy education. It is said that there were as many catechists as school teachers. Some of the 500 Yoruba men and women became businessmen and women. However, many more joined Crowther in evangelism and in teaching.

The third strategy used by the Yoruba ministry team was the newspaper. Townsend, whom Walls (1978) describes as a good practical linguist, was the editor-in-chief of the first Yoruba newspaper. The importance of the newspaper cannot be overstated, as noted by Ajayi (2011)[67]

> To enhance his missionary work and widening the literacy environment, a Missionary, Bishop Henry Townsend of the Church Missionary Society, CMS, Abeokuta (now capital of Ogun State) established a printing press from which he was publishing the first newspaper in Nigeria. The newspaper was called *Iwe Iroyin fun awon Egba ati Yoruba* and was established in 1859. The emergence of this medium sort of democratized written words among the people for whom such was, up till then, unknown.

In summary, the Yoruba ministry led by Bishop Crowther used the FIM approach to language education to teach Yoruba in primary school. Adult literacy programs were taught in Yoruba. A Yoruba newspaper began appearing, which helped modernize the lexicon and spread literacy even further.

9.6 Europeans missionaries' language planning strategies in Africa

Nineteenth century European missionary-linguists who came to Africa did corpus planning in some 20 languages. Their efforts culminated in orthographing languages, writing primers, making dictionaries, and providing reference grammars. Their ultimate goal in all this was Bible translation. We learn from Schaaf (1994:55, 108–9) that before 1885, they had translated the Bible into seven African languages, the New Testament into 15 languages, and portions of the Gospels into 23 languages. These "ancient" translations were done in former Belgian, British, and German colonies. Bibles were not translated into indigenous languages of francophone or lusophone Africa because, according to Wegener (1958:214) the French, the Spaniards, and the Portuguese remained outside of the Reformation

---

67 Retrieved from http://234next.com/csp/cms/sites/Next/ArtsandCulture/Books/5655127-147/story.cspon July 2, 2011.

Movement. The language planning strategies used by five prominent missionary-linguists will be highlighted below because their work resulted in important gains in literacy for the languages in which they worked.

9.6.1 Krapf and Rebmann's legacy on Swahili literacy

Schaaf (1994:76–7, 86–8) and Topan (2008:254) credit Johann Ludwig Krapf and Johann Rebmann, two German missionaries, with pioneering work on Swahili. The two are also famous for being the first Europeans to have seen the snowcapped peaks of Kilimanjaro. However, their report was dismissed by European geographers as "missionary reveries." Rebmann's efforts need to be singled out for special mention because he worked continuously on Swahili for 29 years without ever taking a break to go back to Germany! He was later found almost blind. The pioneer work that Krapf and Rebmann produced is described by Topan (2008:254) as the launching pad from which Swahili took off. Their work was already bearing fruit by the time Tanzania was put under British colonial authority. Literacy in Swahili spread even further when the British took over. Schaaf (1994:77) writes that Bishop Edward Steere (1828–1882) helped to spread literacy in Swahili by building additional schools where it was used as the only medium of instruction. Newspapers were also used to modernize the lexicon and to spread literacy. Topan (2008:256) writes that there were three newspapers published in Swahili by 1905. The availability of church-owned printing presses in Zanzibar made it easy to print large quantities of materials in Swahili and helped to spread literacy in Swahili even among non-Swahili speakers.

9.6.2 Mackay's legacy on Luganda literacy

According to Schaaf (1994:78, 121–2), Alexander Murdock Mackay followed the same strategies as other pioneer missionary-linguists. Mackay was a Scottish engineer by training, so in addition to following the conventional path, he did a few things differently. He learned Luganda and became very fluent in it. He translated the Ten Commandments, some Psalms, and the Gospel of Matthew to get a feel for what it meant to translate into Luganda. However, Mackay believed that native speakers ought to be the main translators. So, he recruited and trained three Luganda speakers: Henry Wright Duta, Sembera Mackay, and Mika Semiotimba. He also recruited a missionary by the name of Pilkington who was very proficient in

Greek. The latter served as the exegete of the Luganda translation project. As a result, it took only nine years to complete the Luganda Bible, that is, from 1887–1896. While the translation was proceeding, Mackay pioneered a new literacy approach. Anybody who wanted to be baptized had to be able to read Luganda first. This daring strategy paid off. By 1904, Mackay and his associates had baptized 9,000 people. The demand for reading materials in Luganda skyrocketed. When the New Testament was completed in 1893, 6,400 copies were printed (Schaaf, pp. 109, 122). Sixteen thousand copies of the Bible were printed in 1896. Between 1887 and 1913, more than 213,290 literacy materials had been printed in Luganda. Literacy on such a large scale had not been seen in Africa before. This extraordinary achievement is to be credited to Mackay's unconventional ideas.

9.6.3 Moffat's legacy on Setswana literacy

Robert Moffat (1795–1883) was a gardener by trade. He converted to Methodism, a movement that grew out of the Anglican Church. This branch of Christianity was created by the Wesley brothers. Seized with the Methodist zeal for "lost souls," Moffat applied to be a missionary with the London Missionary Society (LMS). He was accepted even though he was not highly trained in theology. He arrived in Cape Town (South Africa) in 1817 at age 23. He was appointed to work among the Naquama, but when he married Mary in 1819, they moved to Botswana to start planting churches among the Bechuana. They were not making progress in evangelizing the local population. One morning Moffat was complaining about it to his wife. As the story goes, Mary retorted, "How will you reach people with the gospel without speaking the language of the Bechuana?" This set him on a two-month sociolinguistic survey trip, presumably to discover the dialect of Setswana which was most widely understood. Later he and Mary moved from Lattakoo to the River Kuruman region. After six long years spent learning the language, he preached his first sermon in Setswana in 1825 (Schaaf 1994:98).

Moffat wrote his first book on Setswana in 1825. In 1830, he completed the translation of Gospel of Luke and printed it. In 1833 he published and printed several primers to teach literacy. By 1834, his small congregation had grown from 9 people to 350 people. He built a small school and a church where he taught people how to read and write Setswana. He completed the New Testament in 1840 and went to print it in Cape Town. It was there that he met his son-in-law to be, the famous missionary doctor,

David Livingston. He printed 2,500 copies of the New Testament. This implies that the number of people who could read Setswana had been growing (Schaaf 1994:99). The first draft of the whole Bible was completed in 1857. However, the Setswana Bible was not printed until 1872. The Moffats spent 46 years among the Bechuana, teaching and preaching in Setswana. He spread literacy through Bible translation, formal schooling, and informal schooling. In addition, he put his agricultural knowledge to work, teaching people irrigation techniques and how to grow vegetables in an inhospitable climate. He also built a printing press in Kuruman, which allowed him to print large quantities of his teaching materials in Setswana.

9.6.4 Saker's legacy on Duala literacy

The strategies used by Moffat and Saker were quite similar, even though there is no evidence that they knew of each other. Alfred Saker (1814–1880) was a mechanic, not a theologically trained missionary. According to Schaaf (1994:97), Moffat found himself in a situation where he had to broker peace between the Matabele and Bechuana. Saker also found himself in the unenviable position of peacemaker between two warring factions of Duala kings (Schaaf 1994:66). Like Moffat, Saker combined evangelism with business to advance literacy among the Duala of Cameroon. He and his wife arrived in Cameroon from England on February 16, 1844, when he was barely 30 years old. They had been commissioned by the Baptist Missionary Society (BMS). A few short years after they arrived, tragedy struck. One of the two Jamaican missionaries on whom they depended for support, Joseph Merrick, died on his way to England on furlough. The Sakers' four children died from malaria and other tropical diseases. Evangelism was stalling. The Sakers' request for missionary reinforcement was denied by BMS. Eleven years of ministry produced only 50 Duala converts (Schaaf 1994: 67). The Sakers faced other daunting obstacles. Their small Christian community ran into opposition from many fronts. Local chiefs and sorcerers began persecuting Christians because conversion to Christianity caused them to lose money. European slave traders also made life difficult for him because he accused them of immorality. On the face of mounting antagonism, Saker made a very strange move which Schaaf (1994: 67) describes as follows:

> Saker's response seemed at first strange. He founded a technical school; he taught the Duala to bake bricks of river clay, and grow new crops. These activities gave the Duala new sources of income, which were urgently needed

because intermediate trade between the interior and the Europeans on the coast was in the process of losing its most important product, slaves.

Fellow missionaries wrote nasty letters about Saker to the BMS leadership alleging that "he was too concerned with the work of civilization and that he had lost his spiritual vocation" (Schaaf 1994:66–8). In the midst of all this turmoil, Saker was learning Duala from Thomas Horton Johnson, a Duala speaker, who turned out to be a godsend. As soon as his Duala was good enough to translate the Bible, Saker realized that his Greek was not good and that he needed theological training. He ordered books from England, taught himself theology and Greek, and began translating. Eighteen years after his arrival, he completed the translation of the New Testament. Ten years later, that is, in 1872, he finished his work on the Old Testament. Saker's literacy strategies were effective. The Bible that he translated helped spread literacy in Duala. The curriculum of the technical school modernized the language by coining new words to describe various techniques and brick making materials.

9.6.5 Westermann's legacy on Ewe literacy

Diedrich Westermann (see 4.4.1) and his fellow German missionaries in Togoland achieved similar results in corpus planning and acquisition planning for the Ewe language. As noted in 4.4.2, many German missionaries spoke Ewe fluently. As a result, their achievements in corpus planning were the most spectacular of all missionary-linguists. They were prolific in their treatment of the phonetics and phonology of Ewe. They produced eight important grammar books and scores of Language Arts books in all the main academic disciplines. In addition to their eight German-Ewe bilingual dictionaries, they wrote a trilingual dictionary, Ewe-English-German as early as 1891. Afeli (2003) devotes seven pages (pp. 160–7) to listing the publications in Ewe produced by German missionaries. He also notes (p. 181) that until 1913, two thirds of all schools in southern Togo used Ewe as a medium of instruction, i.e., the FIM model. More impressive was the number of schools built by German missionaries. By 1912, there were 352 schools and 348 of them were run by missionaries. A total of 14,246 students were enrolled in these schools (Afeli, p. 184). Since schools were more commonly found in the Ewe-speaking areas of Togo, an overwhelming number of educated Togolese became literate in Ewe. German literacy strategies were the most pervasive and the most sophisticated for spreading literacy in colonial Africa. However, these achievements were short lived because a large portion of Togoland was ceded to France after the Treaty of Versailles. From then on, the French did everything they could to eradicate literacy in Ewe and replace it with literacy in French (see 4.4.4).

9.7 A comparison of the past and the present

The information presented so far leads to the following observation: the previous generations of missionary language planners were very successful in spreading literacy among the autochthonous populations because a number of them mixed together three indispensable ingredients: Bible translation, schools, and a newspaper in the local language. Let's contrast their strategies with those of contemporary missionary language planners in Africa and see why the former were more successful in spreading literacy than the latter.

9.7.1 Bible translation: Past and present

Wegener (1958) has carefully documented the correlation between Bible translation and the spread of literacy in European languages. The influence of the Bible in the standardization of written German and the subsequent spread of literacy is well attested. The year 2011 is the 400th anniversary of the King James Version (KJV) in English. Scholars of various traditions, Christian and non-Christian, alike have praised the literary influence of the KJV on English. In the cases reviewed in this chapter, except for Hebrew, the spread of literacy has been linked directly to Bible translation. Missionary-linguists translated the Bible into local African languages because they subscribed explicitly to the belief that the best way to win converts was to translate the Bible into the "heart languages" of the people. This was what motivated their tireless language planning efforts. By the end of 1885, they had translated the New Testament into 23 languages and the entire Bible into five languages. Now, let's compare their achievements with those of contemporary Bible translators. According to 2009 figures released by the United Bible Societies (UBS), 335 New Testaments and 173 Bibles have been translated into African languages.[68] So, since around 1900,

---

68 Retrieved from http://www.bsni.co.uk/system/uploads/files/Scripture_Language_Report_2009_original.pdf?1272967584 on July 5, 2011.

missionaries have translated 312 more New Testaments and 158 more Bibles. It is clear that contemporary missionary-linguists have had more success in Bible translation than their predecessors of a century or so ago.

9.7.2 The spread of local literacy: Past and present

One would expect that the upsurge in Bible translation activities would correlate highly with the spread of literacy in indigenous languages. Sadly, this is not the case. There are several reasons why 19th century missionary-linguists were more successful than contemporary ones. For one, there has been a shift in missionary strategy in spreading literacy. Most missionary agencies have relinquished Bible translation and related activities entirely to two dozen organizations that make up the Forum of Bible Agencies.[69] Rare are missionary organizations that still send out missionaries to do holistic ministries as was done in the past. Eighteenth and nineteenth century missionaries were Jacks-of-all-Trades. They planted churches, evangelized, ran schools and hospitals, translated the Bible, and taught literacy. Now Bible translation has been practically outsourced to Bible translation agencies. Two among them, SIL International and UBS, have emerged and now control most Bible translation projects in the developing world. Unfortunately, they focus most of their attention on Bible translation and pay little attention to literacy. As a result, warehouses are full of New Testaments and Bibles in local languages that are not selling because the locals do not know how to read in their own languages. Language planners of the past knew that Bible translation for the sake of Bible translation could not turn the speakers of local languages into literate individuals. This is the reason why Bible translation and literacy training were seen as inseparable. However, this perspective is not shared by contemporary Bible translators. Bible translation is glorified and literacy is relegated to a mere footnote because, presumably, far more money can be raised in the name of the former than in the name of the latter. This critical assessment of the performance of SIL International, UBS, and related organizations is supported by data. Take the case of Côte d'Ivoire discussed in 7.2.2. Figures reported by Ethnologue (2009) show that literacy rates are exceptionally low, even in languages where SIL International has completed a New Testament. The two Ivorian languages in which literacy is at 10% or higher are Baule and Adjoukrou.

---

69 The Forum of Bible Agencies lists member organizations at their website http://www.forum-intl.org/ . The information was retrieved on July 8, 2011.

Incidentally, the translations were done by Christian and Missionary Alliance and Methodist Church missionaries. In all the other languages which have been translated by SIL International or the UBS, literacy rates are below 5%. Even this low rate is to be taken with a grain of salt. Contemporary missionaries spend roughly three decades on translating the New Testament into a language that had not been previously reduced to writing. More often than not, during all that time, literacy in the local language does not spread to more than 100 individuals. The people who become literate in the language are those who are directly associated with the project as informants or reviewers. Translators translate until they are done. Several thousand copies of New Testaments or Bibles are then printed. A big dedication ceremony is organized and speeches are made. A few hundred copies are distributed. The rest is stockpiled in warehouses somewhere collecting dust. The reason is that Bible translation is now conceived of as an autonomous activity that is distinct from literacy. The missionary-linguists of the past centuries did not erect a wall of separation between Bible translation and literacy. They saw both as one and the same. St. Stefan translated the liturgy into Komi and built schools where he taught people how to read the language. Nineteenth century missionaries translated Scriptures and found creative ways to spread literacy among the local populations. When formal education was not enough, Saker founded a brick-making school and Moffat built a farming school where the languages of instruction were respectively Duala and Setswana. Mackay's literacy program in Luganda was very successful because being able to read and write the language was a prerequisite for baptism and confirmation. These missionaries and many more of their generation knew that Bible translation and literacy are in a tight symbiotic relationship. Today, literacy figures prominently in the mission statements of many organizations, but in reality it ranks a distant third behind Bible translation, and linguistic documentation (i.e., data collection and analysis).

9.7.3 Newspapers and the spread of local literacy: Past and present

Nineteenth century missionary language planners used the medium of the newspaper to spread literacy in local languages. We do not have evidence that all mission agencies used this medium, but we know that the ones that used it were very successful in spreading literacy. The Yoruba missionary team had a newspaper and literacy is still going strong in the language. Henry Townsend published the first Yoruba newspaper in 1859. Ben

Yehuda used the newspaper as a formidable instrument for spreading literacy in Hebrew. Swahili alone had three publications in the 19th century: a daily paper, a weekly paper, and a monthly paper. The newspaper is a powerful language planning tool that is seldom used by contemporary language planners. I do not know of a single SIL International or UBS Bible translation project in francophone Africa that has an indigenous newspaper. In 2008 and 2009 an incidental event reminded me that the Anyi Literacy Project must include a newspaper among its literacy strategies. I wrote the eulogies for my parents in Anyi and read them during the funerals. The 100 copies that I made were snatched away quickly. The only regret I had was that I had not printed enough copies. In the few months following the funerals, I received electronic mails from people that I did not even know thanking me for the publications. The unsolicited comments and congratulations made me realize that a newspaper in the local language can still be an instrument for spreading literacy.

9.7.4 Overcoming unorthodox strategies

Language planning is a game in the sense of the Game Theory. As such, one should expect that both orthodox and unorthodox strategies may be used by the players (see 2.3.6). Language planning can be construed as a two-person, non-zero-sum cooperative game. The community whose language is being planned constitutes one player. The other player is the applied linguist. In the best possible world, one would expect that both sets of players would work cooperatively to ensure the best possible outcome for the community. However, I know from personal experience and from the accounts of the struggles of the language planning heroes discussed in this chapter that that is not always the case. Ferguson (1968:254) writes that St. Stefan met considerable resistance from a man called Pam. He was the chief shaman of the area. He organized a resistance movement to oppose St. Stefan's literacy efforts. Ben Yehuda was vehemently opposed by a group of Israeli Jews described as "Orthodox fanatics." Not only did they oppose him, but they also conspired to have him jailed in 1904. Alfred Saker was opposed by a vast array of people: witchdoctors, European slave traders, and fellow missionaries. The latter wrote nasty letters about him because he was spending too much time on the brick-making school that he founded (Schaaf 1994:66–8). Bishop Crowther was the subject of malicious attacks by Rev. Henry Townsend after the Anglican Church appointed him bishop. They were both part of the original Yourba missionary team that had been assembled in Freetown. However, when

Rev. Townsend heard of Rev. Crowther's impending nomination as bishop, he wrote several letters to prevent the appointment from taking place. Olsen (2003:13) writes that "Henry Townsend would go down in history less for his mission work (he was reportedly an excellent linguist, devoted to Abeokuta) than for his opposition to Crowther." Townsend did not relent and continually brought charges or organized rabbles to bring charges against him. Subsequently, Bishop Crowther was dragged in front of a Commission of Inquiry to look into allegations of misconduct by his subordinates, not by himself, because he was a man of such outstanding integrity that they could not find fault with him per se. Instead, they got to him by firing 15 of the 18 leaders of the Niger Mission who worked for him. When Crowther protested their dismissal because the hearings had not been not properly conducted, "he was charged with violating his code of office. He died shortly thereafter, and a white bishop was put in his place. The continent would not see another African Bishop until 1952, sixty years after Crowther's death (Olsen, p. 15)." As altruistic as planning indigenous language may sound, it is still a game played by some with orthodox strategies and by others with unorthodox strategies.

9.8 Summary

Throughout history, individuals have taken the initiative for a variety of reasons to change the destiny of language. Usually, but not always, this entails reducing an oral language to writing, modernizing its lexicon, and cultivating it stylistically to adapt it to the requirements of a print medium. This is the burden that St. Stefan bore gladly but painfully when he set out to plan Komi in the 14th century. In those days, he had to rely on his common sense in the decisions that he made because there were no theories to guide him. Yet he achieved spectacular results because commonsense taught him that corpus planning had to go hand in hand with acquisition planning. The same commonsensical approach coupled with an invincible resolve to revive Hebrew, helped Ben Yehuda accomplish a language revitalization feat that no one has been able to emulate. With him we discover that an individual can truly make a difference in language planning. Such a person does not need to be necessarily well schooled in linguistics. Like Ben Yehuda, he or she must simply possess the following qualities:

> Through his charismatic personality, he instilled into those who showed some initial receptiveness to his projects the determination to go forth and complete the tasks on which he had embarked whether these persons later

acknowledged his influence or no. He was, moreover, possessed of the strength of character and singled-mindedness of purpose to continue what he had begun even in the face of what seemed insurmountable obstacles and even among those who were apathetic, antagonistic, or not interested in his projects... (Fellman 1974:455).

These attributes were found also in Bishop Samuel Crowther who rose from slavery to the pinnacle of ecclesiastic power in the 19th century. Shipwreck and other obstacles did not deter him from planning the Yoruba language from the ground up. The 19th century European missionaries who ministered in Belgian, British, and German colonies were endowed with the same attributes. They labored long and hard, more often than not at the expense of their personal safety and health, to plan Duala, Ewe, Luganda, Setswana, Swahili, and many other languages. They achieved language planning successes that have been for the most part unrivaled because they combined Bible translation with literacy education. In some instances, they pushed the frontiers of innovation and creativity by publishing newspapers to modernize the language and spread literacy further. Contemporary missionary language planners have not achieved similar successes though they are more numerous and better equipped. They have unnecessarily separated corpus planning from literacy planning. The examples offered by St. Stefan, Ben Yehuda, Bishop Crowther, Alfred Saker, Alexander Mackay, Diedrich Westermann, Johann Ludwig Krapf, Johannes Rebmann, and Robert Moffat, suggest that a better strategy is to return to the simpler methodology of the past. In those days, corpus planning and acquisition planning went hand in hand. Scripture translation, literacy instruction, and newspapers were interrelated strategies that some missionary-linguists in Belgian, British, and German colonies successfully used to the plan African languages in which they were ministering. Contemporary languages planners should use the same triad strategy instead of behaving as though the ingredients for successful language planning were in complementary distribution.

References

Adegbija, E.
2009 Language Attitudes in West Africa. *International Journal of Sociolinguistics,* 141, pp. 75–100.

Adeniran, W.
2009 Multilingualism and Language Use in Porto Novo. *The Languages of Urban Africa,* ed. by F. McLaughlin, 131–51. New York: Continuum.

Afeli, A.
2003 *Politique et Amébagement Linguistiues au Togo: Bilan et Perspectives. Thèse de Doctorat d'Etat.* Université de Lomé: Lomé, Togo. Online: http://www.orthographyclearinghouse.org/pub-papers.html

Ager, D.
1999 *Identity, Insecurity and Image: France and Language.* Philadelphia: Multilingual Matters.

Ajayi, J.
2011 *On Yoruba Literature.* Online: http://234next.com/csp/cms/sites/Next/ArtsandCulture/Books/5655127-147/story.csp.

Akinwumi, E. O.
2002 *Samuel Ajayi Crowther.* Online: http://www.transparencyng.com/index.php?option=com_content&view=article&id=1755:samuel-ajayi-crowther-by-reverend-dr-elijah-olu-akinwumi&catid=59:guest&Itemid=37

Alexander, N.
2009 The Impact of the Hegemony of English on Access to and Quality of Education with Special Reference to South Africa. *Language and Poverty,* ed. by W. Harbert et al., 53–66. Buffalo, NY: Multilingual Matters.

Alexander, N.
2008 Creating the Condition for a Counter-Hegemonic Strategy: African Languages in the Twenty-First Century. *Globalization and Language Vitality: Perspectives from Africa,* ed. by C. B. Vigoureux & S. S. Mufwene, 255–71. New York: Continuum.

Anyidoho, A. & M. E. Kropp Dakubu
2008 Ghana: Indigenous Languages, English, and the Emerging National Identity. *Language and National Identity in Africa,* ed. by A. Simpson, 141–57. New York: Oxford University Press.

Appleyard, D. & M. Orwin
2008 The Horn of Africa: Ethiopia, Eritrea, Djibouti, and Somalia. *Language and National Identity in Africa,* ed. by A. Simpson, 267–90. New York: Oxford University Press.

Bado, N.
2009 *Bilingual Education in Burkina Faso: Where do Parent and Teachers Stand?* MA Thesis: Ohio University: Athens, OH. Online: http://www.orthographyclearinghouse.org/pub-papers.html.

Bamgbose, A.
2004 *Language of Instruction Policy and Practice in Africa.* Online: http://www.unesco.org/education/languages_2004/languagein struction_africa.pdf.

Bamgbose, A.
1991 *Language and the Nation: The Language Question in Sub-Saharan Africa.* Edinburgh: Edinburgh University Press.

Batibo, H.
2009 Poverty as a Crucial Factor in language Maintenance and Language Death: Case Studies from Africa. *Language and Poverty,* ed. by W. Harbert et al., 23–36. Buffalo, NY: Multilingual Matters.

Batibo, H.
2008 The Circumstances of Language Shift and Death in Southern Africa. *Globalization and Language Vitality: Perspectives from Africa,* ed. by C. B. Vigoureux & S. S. Mufwene, 51–69. New York: Continuum.

Bender, M.
2002 From "Easy Phonetics" to the Syllabary: An Orthographic Division of Labor in Cherokee Language Education. *Anthropology & Education Quaterly,* Vol. 33, No. 1, pp. 90–117.

Bhola, H. S.
1984 *Campaigning for Literacy. Eight National Experiences of the Twentieth Century, with a Memorandum to Decision-makers.* Paris: Unesco.

Bhola, H. S.
2006 *Approaches to Monitoring and Evaluation in Literacy Programmes.* Online: http://unesdoc.unesco.org/images/0014/001459/145947e.pdf.

Binmore, K.
2007 *Game Theory: A Very Short Introduction.* New York: Oxford University Press.

Biola, E. & G. Echu
2008 Cameroon: Official Bilingualism in a Multilingual State. *Language and National Identity in Africa,* ed. by A. Simpson, 199–213. New York: Oxford University Press.

Bird, S.
1998 *When Tone Marking Reduces Fluency: An Orthography Experiment in Cameroon.* Online: http://www.orthographyclearing house.org/pub-papers.html

Blench, R.
2007 Endangered Languages in West Africa. *Language Diversity*

Endangered, ed. by M. Brenzinger, 140–62. New York: Mouton de Gruyter.

Block, D.
2006 Identity in Applied Linguistics. *Sociolinguistics of Identity*, ed. by T. Omoniyi & G. White, 34–49. New York: Continuum.

Blommaert, J.
2008 Writing Locality in Globalized Swahili: Semiotizing Space in a Tanzanian Novel. *Globalization and Language Vitality: Perspectives from Africa*, ed. by C. B. Vigoureux & S. S. Mufwene, 210–28. New York: Continuum.

Bloomfield, L.
1933 *Language*. New York: Holt, Rinehart and Winston.

Bokamba, E. G.
2008a The Lives of Local and Regional Congolese Languages in Global Linguistic Markets. *Globalization and Language Vitality: Perspectives from Africa*, ed. by C. B. Vigoureux & S. S. Mufwene, 97–125. New York: Continuum.

Bokamba, E. G.
2008b D. R. Congo: Language and "Authentic Nationalism."*Language and National Identity in Africa,* ed. by A. Simpson, 214–34. New York: Oxford University Press.

Botau, A. B.
2004 *Integration and Autonomy of Minorities in Côte d'Ivoire.* Online: http://www2.ohchr.org/english/issues/minorities/docs/docstable.doc.

Brenzinger, M.
2009 Language Diversity and Poverty in Africa. *Language and Poverty,* ed. by W. Harbert et al., 37–49. Buffalo, NY: Multilingual Matters.

Brenzinger, M.
2007 Language Endangerment in Southern and Eastern Africa. *Language Diversity Endangered*, ed. by M. Brenzinger, 179–204. New York: Mouton de Gruyter.

Bühmann, D. & B. Trudell
2008 *Mother Tongue Matters: Local Language as Key to Effective Learning.* Online: http://unesdoc.unesco.org/images/0016/001611/161121e.pdf

Bwenge, C.
2009 Language Choice in Dar es Salaam's Billboards. *The Languages of Urban Africa*, ed. by F. McLaughlin, 152–77. New York: Continuum.

Calfee, R. C.
2005 Exploration of English Orthography, From Orthography to Pedagogy: Essays in Honor of Richard L. Venezky, ed. by T. Trabasso et al., 1–19. Nahwah, NJ: Lawrence Erlbaum Associates, Publishers.

Canut, C.
2009   Discourse, Community, Identity: Processes of Linguistic Homogenization in Bamako. *The Languages of Urban Africa*, ed. by F. McLaughlin, 86–102. New York: Continuum.

Carrera-Carrillo, L. & A. Rickert Smith
2006   *7 Steps to Success in Dual Language Immersion: A Brief Guide for Teachers and Administrators*. Portsmouth, NH: Heinemann.

Chaudenson, R.
2008   On the Futurology of Linguistic Development. *Globalization and Language Vitality: Perspectives from Africa*, ed. by C. B. Vigoureux & S. S. Mufwene, 171–90. New York: Continuum.

Cheru, F.
2005   *Globalization and uneven Urbanization in Africa: the Limits to Effective Urban Governance in the Provision of Basic Services*. Online: http://www.international.ucla.edu/africa/grca/publications/article.asp?parentid=107324

Chomsky, N. & M. Halle
1991   *The Sound Pattern of English*. Cambridge, MA: The MIT Press.

Cipro, M.
1980   *Some Observations on Literacy and Development*. Online: http://unesdoc.unesco.org/images/0003/000388/038807mb.pdf.

Cole, R. & H. J. De Blij
2007   *Survey of Subsharan Africa: A Regional Geography*. New York: Oxford University Press.

Connell, B.
2007   Endangered Languages in Central Africa. *Language Diversity Endangered*, ed. by M. Brenzinger, 163–78. New York: Mouton de Gruyter.

Cooper, R. L.
1996   *Language Planning and Social Change*. New York: Cambridge University Press.

Coulmas, F.
1989   *The Writing Systems of the World*. Cambridge, MA: Basil Blackwell, Inc.

Crystal, D.
2000   *Language Death*. New York: Cambridge University Press.

Dakubu, K. M. E.
2009   The Historical Dynamic of Multilingualism in Accra. *The Languages of Urban Africa*, ed. by F. McLaughlin, 19–31. New York: Continuum

Dally, F.
2000   Les Langues Nationales à l'Ecole: Le Projet Démarre avec 10 Langues. *Notre Voie*, No. 753, Mardi 21 Novembre.

Daniel, J.
2003   *Mother Tongue Dilemma. Education Today: The Newsletter of UNESCO's Education Sector*. Online: http://www.unesco.org/education/education_today/ed_today6.pdf

Davis, M. D.
1983 *Game Theory: A Nontechnical Introduction*. New York: Dover Publications, Inc.

De Kadt, E.
2000 "In With Heart and Soul": The German-speakers of Wartburg. *International Journal of Sociolinguistics,* 144, pp. 69–93.

DeLancey, V.
2007 The Economics of Africa. *Understanding Contemporary Africa*, Fourth Edition, ed. by. A. A. Gordon & D. L. Gordon, 109–54. Boulder, Colorado: Lynne Rienner Publishers, Inc.

De Mesquita, B. B.
2009 *The Predictioneer's Game: Using the Logic of Brazen Self-Interest to See and Shape the Future*. New York: Random House.

DeFrancis, J.
1972 Language and Script Reform in China. *Advances in the Sociology of Language,* Volume II, ed. By J. A. Fishman, 450–75. The Hague: Mouton.

DePalma, R.
2010 Language Use in the Two-way Classroom: Lessons from a Spanish-English Bilingual Kindergarten. Tonawanda, NY: Multilingual Matters.

Der-Houssikian, H.
2009 Innovations on the Fringes of Kiswahili-speaking World. *The Languages of Urban Africa*, ed. by F. McLaughlin, 178–90. New York: Continuum.

Dewees, J.
1977 Orthography and Identity: Movement Toward Inertia. *Language and Linguistic Problems in Africa: Proceedings of the VII Conference on African Linguistics*, ed. by P. F. A. Kotey & H. Der-Houssikian, 120–31. Columbia, South Carolina: Hornbeam Press.

Djite, P. G.
2008 *The Sociolinguistics of Development in Africa*. Tonawanda, NY: Multilingual Matters.

Dobrin, L. M.
2009 SIL International and the Disciplinary Culture of Linguistics. *Language*, Vol. 85, No. 3, pp. 618–29.

Donnacha, J. M.
2000 An Integrated Language Planning Model. *Language Problems and Language Planning*, Vol. 24, No. 1, pp. 11–35.

Dua, H. R.
1996 The Politics of Language Conflict: Implications for Language Planning and Political Theory. *Language Problems and Language Planning*, Vol. 20, No. 1, pp. 1–17.

Essegbey, J.
2009 On Assessing the Ethnolinguistic Vitality of Ga in Accra. *The Languages of Urban Africa*, ed. by F. McLaughlin, 115–130. New York: Continuum.

Ethnologue
2009   *Languages of the World,* Sixteenth Edition, ed. by M. Paul. Lewis Dallas: SIL International.

Fage, J. D.
1988   *A History of Africa*, 2nd edition. London: Hutchinson Education.

Fellman, J.
2010   *Eliezer Ben-Yehuda and the Revival of Hebrew.* Online: http://www.jewishvirtuallibrary.org/jsource/biography/ben_yehuda.html.

Fellman, J.
1974   The Role of Elizer Ben Yehuda in the Revival of the Hebrew Language: An Assessment. *Advances in Language Planning*, ed. By J. A. Fishman, 427–55. The Hague: Mouton.

Ferguson, C. A.
1968   St. Stefan of Perm and Applied Linguistics. *Language Problems of Developing Nations*, ed. by J. A. Fishman, C. A. Ferguson, and J. Das Gupta, 253–65. New York: John Wiley & Sons, Inc.

Fishman, J. A.
1974   Language Modernization and Planning. *Advances in Language Planning*, ed. By J. A. Fishman, 77–102. The Hague: Mouton.

Frazer, T. C.
2006   An Introduction to Midwest English. *American Voices: How Dialects Differ from Coast to Coast*, ed. by W. Wolfram & B. Ward, 101–105. Malden, MA: Blackwell Publishing.

Freire, P.
1972   *Pedagogy of the Oppressed.* New York: Herder and Herder

Fromkin, V., R. Rodman & N. Hyams
2011   *An Introduction to Language*, Ninth Edition. New York: Wadsworth, Cengage learning.

Gellar, S.
1995   The Colonial Era. *Africa,*Third Edition, ed. by P. M. Martin & P. O'Meara, 135–55. Bloomington, Indiana: Indiana University Press.

Gilbert, E. & J. T. Reynolds
2004   *Africa in World History: From Prehistory to the Present.* Upper Saddle River, NJ: Pearson Education.

Goody, J.
1987   *The Interface between the Written and the Oral.* New York: Cambridge University Press.

Gordon, A. A.
2007   Population, Urbanization, and AIDS. *Understanding Contemporary Africa*, Fourth Edition, ed. by. A. A. Gordon & D. L. Gordon, 203–34. Boulder, Colorado: Lynne Rienner Publishers, Inc.

Grenoble, L. A., K. D. Rice & N. Richards
2009   The Role of the Linguist in Language Maintenance and Revitalization: Documentation, Training and Materials Development. *Language and Poverty,* ed. by W. Harbert et al., 183–201. Buffalo, NY: Multilingual Matters.

Grenoble, L. A. & L. J. Whaley
2006   *Saving Languages: An Introduction to Language Revitalization.* New York: Cambridge University Press.
Grinevald, C.
2007   Endangered Languages of Mexico and Central America. *Language Diversity Endangered*, ed. by M. Brenzinger, 59–86. New York: Mouton de Gruyter.
Gudschinsky, S. C.
            More on Formulating Efficient Orthographies. *The Bible Translator*, Vol. 21, No. 1, pp. 21–5.
Hale, K.
1992   On Endangered Languages and the Safeguarding of Diversity. *Language*, Vol. 68, No. 1, pp. 1–3.
Hale, K.
1992   Language Endangerment and the Human Value of Linguistic Diversity. *Language*, Vol. 68, No. 1, pp. 35–42.
Handman, C.
2009   Language Ideologies, Endangered-Language Linguistics, and Christianization, pp. 635–9. *Language: Journal of the Linguistic Society of America*, Vol. 85, No. 3.
Hasselbring, S. A.
2006   *Cross-Dialectal Acceptance of Written Standards: Two Ghanaian Case Studies.* Ph.D. Dissertation: University of South Africa. Online: http://www.orthographyclearinghouse.org/phdma-PhD.html.
Institut National de la Statistique de la République de Côte d'Ivoire
2011   *Langues Officielles et Languaes Nationales.* Online: http://www.ins.ci/gene/LANGUES%20OFFICIELLES%20ET%20LANGUES%20NATIONALES.html
International African Institute
1930   *International Institute of African Languages and Cultures. Memorandum I, Revised Edition Practical Orthography of African Languages.* Online: http://www.bisharat.net/Documents/poal30.htm.
James, W.
2008   Sudan: Majorities, Minorities, and Language Interactions. *Language and National Identity in Africa,* ed. by A. Simpson, 61–78. New York: Oxford University Press.
Jegede, D.
1995   Popular Culture in Urban Africa. *Africa Third Edition*, ed. by P. M. Martin & P. O'Mera, 273–294. Bloomington, Indiana: Indiana University Press.
Kanwangamalu, N. M.
1997   Multilingualism and Education Policy in Post-Apartheid South Africa, *Language Problems and Language Planning*, Vol. 21, No. 3, pp. 234–53.

Kaplan, R. B.
1998 Applied Linguistics and Language Policy and Planning. *Linguistics at Work: A Reader of Applications*, ed. by D. D. Oaks, 420–43. New York: Harcourt Brace College Publishers.

Kaplan, R. B. & R. B. Baldauf, Jr.
1997 *Language Planning: From Practice to Theory*. Philadelphia: Multilingual Matters.

Keim, C.
1995 Africa and Europe before 1900. *Africa,* Third Edition, ed. by P. M. Martin & P. O'Meara, 115–34. Bloomington, Indiana: Indiana University Press.

Keller, E. J.
1995 Decolonization, Independence, and the Failure of Politics. *Africa,* Third Edition, ed. by P. M. Martin & P. O'Meara, 156–71. Bloomington, Indiana: Indiana University Press.

Khapoya, V. B.
1998 *The African Experience: An Introduction,* Second Edition. Upper Saddle River, New Jersey: Prentice Hall.

Kipré, P.
1992 *Histoire de la Côte d'Ivoire*. Abidjan, Côte d'Ivoire: Edition Ami.

Knutsen, A. Moseng
2008 Ivory Coast: The Supremacy of French. *Language and National Identity in Africa,* ed. by A. Simpson, 158–71. New York: Oxford University Press.

Koffi, E. N.
2010 *Applied English Syntax: Foundations for Word, Phrase, and Sentence Analysis*. Dubuque, IA: Kendall Hunt Publishing Company.

Koffi, E. N.
1997 *Language and Society in Biblical Times*. Bethesda, MD: International Scholars Publications.

Koffi, E. N.
1995 Indigenizing Punctuation Marks. *Notes on Literacy*, Vol. 21, No. 2, pp. 1–11.

Kouadio, J.
2009 *Classification des langues ivoiriennes dans le domaine linguistique africain*. Online: http://www.francophonie.ch/index.php?detailNews&pk_news=2342.

Krauss, M.
1992 The World's Languages in Crisis. *Language*, Vol. 68, No. 1, pp. 4–10.

Kube-Barth, S.
2009 The Multiple Facets of the Urban Language Form, Nouchi. *The Languages of Urban Africa*, ed. by F. McLaughlin, 103–114. New York: Continuum.

Ladefoged, P.
1992 Another View of Language Endangerment. *Language*, Vol. 68, No. 4, pp. 809–11.

Laitin, D. D.
1992 *Language Repertoires and State Construction in Africa.* New York: Cambridge University Press.

Lamphear, J. & T. Falola
1995 Aspects of Early African History. *Africa,*Third Edition, ed. by P. M. Martin & P. O'Meara, 73–96. Bloomington, Indiana: Indiana University Press.

Leclerc, J.
2010 *Côte d'Ivoire.* Online: http://www.tlfq.ulaval.ca/axl/afrique/cotiv.htm.

Lessow-Hurley, J.
2000 *The Foundations of Dual Language Instruction.* New York: Longman.

Lestage, A.
1982 *Literacy and Illiteracy.* Online: http://unesdoc.unesco.org/images/0004/000489/048977eo.pdf

Laubach, F. C.
1947 *Teaching the World to Read: A handbook for literacy campaigns.* New York: Friendship Press.

Lind, A.
2008 *Literacy for All: Making a Difference.* Online: http://unesdoc.unesco.org/images/0015/001597/159785e.pdf

Logan, R. K.
1986 *The Alphabetic Effect: The Impact of the Phonetic Alphabet on the Development of Western Civilization.* New York: St. Martin's Press.

Longacre, R. E.
1964 *Tone Orthography in Trique. Orthography Studies: Articles on New Writing Systems.* London: The United Bible Societies.

Loucou, J.-N. et al.
1987 *Mémorial de la Côte d'Ivoire: Du Nationalisme à la Nation*, 3ème Tome. Abidjan, Côte d'Ivoire: Edition Ami.

Lucht, R.
1978 Siane Tone Orthography. *Notes on Literacy*, Vol. 24, pp. 25–28.

Mabille, J. et al.
1987 *Mémorial de la Côte d'Ivoire: La Côte d'Ivoire Coloniale*, 2ème Tome. Abidjan, Côte d'Ivoire: Edition Ami.

Makouta-Mboukou, J.-P.
1973 *Le Français en Afrique Noire: Histoire et Méthodes de l'Enseignement du Français en Afrique Noire.* Paris: Bordas.

Marchese, L.
1989 Kru. *The Niger-Congo Languages,* ed. by J. Bendor-Samuel, 119–40. New York: University Press of America, Inc.

Marten, L. & N. C. Kula
2008 Zambia: "One Zambia, One Nation, Many Languages." *Language and National Identity in Africa,* ed. by A. Simpson, 291–312. New York: Oxford University Press.

Maathai, W.
2009 *The Challenge for Africa.* New York: Pantheon Books.

Mazrui, A.
2008 Globalization and the Sociolinguistics of the Internet: Between English and Kiswahili. *Globalization and Language Vitality: Perspectives from Africa,* ed. by C. B. Vigoureux & S. S. Mufwene, 191–209. New York: Continuum.

McLaughlin, F.
2009 Introduction to the Language of Urban Africa. *The Languages of Urban Africa,* ed. by F. McLaughlin, 1–18. New York: Continuum.

McLaughlin, F.
2009 Senegal's Early Cities and the Making of an Urban Language. *The Languages of Urban Africa,* ed. by F. McLaughlin, 71–85. New York: Continuum.

McLaughlin, F.
2008 The Ascent of Wolof as an Urban Vernacular and the National Lingua Franca in Senegal. *Globalization and Language Vitality: Perspectives from Africa,* ed. by C. B. Vigoureux & S. S. Mufwene, 142–70. New York: Continuum.

McLaughlin, F.
2008 Senegal: The Emergence of a National Lingual Franca. *Language and National Identity in Africa,* ed. by A. Simpson, 79–97. New York: Oxford University Press.

McNulty, M. L.
1995 Contemporary Map of Africa. *Africa,* Third Edition, ed. by P. M. Martin & P. O'Meara, 10–45. Bloomington, Indiana: Indiana University Press.

McWhorter, J.
2003 *The Power of Babel: A Natural History of Language.* New York: Perennial, An Imprint of HarperCollins Publishers.

Mesthrie, R.
2008 South Africa: The Rocky Road to Nation Building. *Language and National Identity in Africa,* ed. by A. Simpson, 314–38. New York: Oxford University Press.

Mohanty, A. K.
2009 Perpetuating Inequality: Language Disadvantage and Capability Deprivation of Tribal Mother Tongue Speakers in India. *Language and Poverty,* ed. by W. Harbert et al., 102–24. Buffalo, NY: Multilingual Matters.

Moyo, A.
2007 Religion in Africa. *Understanding Contemporary Africa,* Fourth

Edition, ed. by. A. A. Gordon & D. L. Gordon, 317–50. Boulder, Colorado: Lynne Rienner Publishers, Inc.

Mufwene, S. S.
2010   The Role of Mother-Tongue Schooling in Eradicating Poverty: A Response to Language and Poverty. *Language*, Vol. 86, No. 4, pp. 910–32.

Myers-Scotton, C.
2006   *Multiple Voices: An Introduction to Bilingualism*. Malden, MA: Blackwell Publishing.

O'Toole, T.
2007   The Historical Context. *Understanding Contemporary Africa*, Fourth Edition, ed. by. A. A. Gordon & D. L. Gordon, 23–56. Boulder, Colorado: Lynne Rienner Publishers, Inc.

Olsen, T.
2003   Bishop Before His Time. The African Apostles: The Untold Stories of the Black Evangelists who Converted their Continent. *Christian History* Issue 79, Vol. XXII, No. 3, pp. 10–5.

Olson, K.
2009   SIL International: An Emic View. *Language*, Vol. 85, No. 3, pp. 646–57.

Omoniyi, T.
2006   Hierarchy of Identities. *Sociolinguistics of Identity*, ed. by T. Omoniyi & G. White, 11–33. New York: Continuum.

Öney, B. & Y. Durgunoğlu
2005   Research and Theory Informing Instruction in Adult Literacy. *From Orthography to Pedagogy: Essays in Honor of Richard L. Venezky*, ed. by T. Trabasso et al., 127–47. Nahwah, NJ: Lawrence Erlbaum Associates, Publishers.

Ong, W. J.
1982   *Orality and Literacy: the Technologizing of the word*. New York: Methuen and Co. Ltd.

Osborne, M. J. & A. Rubinstein
1994   *A Course in the Game Theory*. Cambridge, MA: The MIT Press.

Picoche, J. & C. Marchello-Nizia
1994   *Histoire de la Langue Française*. Paris: Editions Nathan

Pike, K. L.
1946   *Phonemics: A Technique for Reducing Languages to Writing*. Vol. 1. Glendale: Summer Institute of Linguistics.

Pinker, S.
1994   *The Language Instinct: How the Mind Creates Language*. New York: William Morrow and Company, Inc.

Poundstone, W.
1992   *Prisoner's Dilemma*. New York: Anchor Books.

Robertson, C.
1995   Social Change in Contemporary Africa. *Africa*, Third Edition, ed. by P. M. Martin & P. O'Meara, 313–29. Bloomington, Indiana: Indiana University Press.

Ryan, E. B., H. Giles & R. J. Sebastian
1982 *Attitudes towards Language Variation: Social and Applied Contexts*, ed. by E. B. Ryan & H. Giles, 1–19. London: Edward Arnold.

Schaaf, Y.
1994 *L'histoire et le Role de La Bible en Afrique: Il Poursuivit sa Route avec Joie*. Lavigny, Suisse: Ed. Groupes Missionaires.

Scribner, S. & M. Cole
1973 Cognitive Consequences of Formal and Informal Education. *Science,* Vol. 182, pp. 553–9.

Scribner, S. & M. Cole
1981 *The Psychology of Literacy*. Cambridge, Mass: Harvard University Press.

Shellington, K.
2005 *History of Africa,* Second Edition. New York: Palgrave MacMillan.

Simpson, A.
2008 Introduction. *Language and National Identity in Africa,* ed. by A. Simpson, 1–25. New York: Oxford University Press.

Simpson, A. & B. A. Oyetade
2008 Nigeria: Ethno-linguistic Competition in the Giant of Africa. *Language and National Identity in Africa,* ed. by A. Simpson, 172–98. New York : Oxford University Press.

Skattum, I.
2008 Mali: In Defence of Cultural and Linguistic Pluralism. *Language and National Identity in Africa,* ed. by A. Simpson, 98–121. New York: Oxford University Press.

Smalley, W. A.
1964 *How Shall I Write This Language? Orthography Studies: Articles on New Writing Systems*. London: the United Bible Societies.

Spencer, J.
1974 Colonial Language Policies and their Legacies in Sub-Saharan Africa. *Advances in Language Planning*, ed. By J. A. Fishman, 163–89. The Hague: Mouton.

Stroud, C.
2008 African Modernity, Transnationalism and Language Vitality: Portuguese in Multilingual Mozambique. *Globalization and Language Vitality: Perspectives from Africa*, ed. by C. B. Vigoureux & S. S. Mufwene, 70–96. New York: Continuum.

Stryker, R. & S. N. Ndegwa
The African Development Crisis. *Africa, Third Edition*, ed. by P. M. Martin & P. O'Meara, 375–94. Bloomington, Indiana: Indiana University Press.

Suleiman, Y.
2006 Constructing Language, Constructing National Identities. *Sociolinguistics of Identity*, ed. by T. Omoniyi & G. White, 50–71. New York: Continuum.

Svelmoe, W.
2009 We do not Want to Masquerade as Linguists: A Short History of SIL and Academy. *Language*, Vol. 85, No. 3, pp. 629–35.

Thorburn, T.
1972 Cost-Benefit Analysis of Language Planning. *Advances in the Sociology of Language*, Volume II, ed. by J. A. Fishman, 511–9. The Hague: Mouton.

Tibaijuka, A. K.
2008 *The Challenge of Urbanization and the Role of UN-Habitat*. Online: http://www.unhabitat.org/downloads/docs/5683_16536_ ed_warsaw_version12_1804.pdf

Topan, F.
2008 Tanzania: The Development of Swahili as a National and Official Language. *Language and National Identity in Africa*, ed. by A. Simpson, 252–66. New York: Oxford University Press.

UNESCO
1953 *The Unesco Courier*. Vol. VI, No. 11. Online: http://unesdoc. unesco.org/images/0007/000708/070841eo.pdf.

Vaillancourt, F.
2009 Language and Poverty: Measurement, Determinants and Policy Responses. *Language and Poverty*, ed. by W. Harbert et al., 147–60. Buffalo, NY: Multilingual Matters.

Vaillancourt, F.
1983 The Economics of Language and Language Planning. *Language Problems Language and Language Planning*, Vol. 7, pp. 162–78.

Vigouroux, C. B.
2008 From Africa to Africa: Globalization, Migration and Language Vitality. *Globalization and Language Vitality: Perspectives from Africa*, ed. by C. B. Vigoureux & S. S. Mufwene, 229–54. New York: Continuum.

Wa Thiong'o, Ngugi.
1986 *Decolonizing the Mind: The Politics of Language in African Literature*. Portsmouth, New Hampshire: Heinemann.

Walker, W., R. A. Norris, D. W. Lotz & R. T. Handy
1985 *A History of the Christian Church*, Fourth Edition. New York: Charles Scribner's Sons.

Walls, A.
1978 *Crowther, Samuel Ajayi: 1807 to 1891: Anglican Nigeria*. Online: http://www.dacb.org/stories/nigeria/legacy_crowther.html.

Wardhaugh, R.
2010 *An Introduction to Sociolinguistics*. Sixth Edition. Malden, MA: Wiley-Blackwell.

Welmers, W. E.
1974 Christian Missions and Language Policies in Africa. *Advances in Language Planning*, ed. By J. A. Fishman, 191–203. The Hague: Mouton.

Wegener, G. S.
   1958   *6,000 Years of the Bible*. New York: Harper & Row Publishers.
Wiesemann, U.
   1989   Orthography Matters. *Notes on Literacy*, Vol. 1, No. 57, pp. 14–21.
Williamson, K. & R. Blench
   2000   Niger-Congo. *African Languages: An Introduction*, ed. by B. Heine & D. Nurse, 11–42. New York: Cambridge University Press.

Index

A Level 162, 173, 269, 271
Abidjan 156, 158, 160, 168, 177, 184–6, 188, 194, 200, 206–8, 239, 262, 269, 271, 276, 279
ACALAN 21, 26, 33
Accra 158, 184–6, 194, 200, 202, 204–5
Africa (East) 56, 121, 124, 183, 245
Africa (North) 6, 56, 78, 97
Africa (Southern) 6, 138–9, 149, 183
Africa (West) 6, 56, 87–8, 95, 97–8, 115–7, 119–22, 129, 139
Africa (Central) 56, 80, 88, 104, 121, 128, 132, 184
AIM 63–4, 73, 75, 92, 97, 103–4, 120, 144–6, 156, 171
ancestral language 9–10, 12, 23, 33, 53, 56, 57, 64, 87, 159, 165, 172, 179, 180
Anyi 11, 147, 149, 152–3, 160, 174, 191, 217, 221
Anyi-Baule 152, 179, 208
assimilation 64–5, 75, 84–6, 89–90, 98–100, 106, 109–10, 130–1, 146

BAC 162, 173
Baule 11, 149, 153, 160, 174–5, 194, 207–8, 217, 232, 248, 260, 281, 306
Belgians 23, 46, 64, 73, 98, 109, 110, 130–2, 145–6, 295
Belgian colonial administrators 135
Belgian colonies 61, 71, 130, 133, 135
Belgian missionaries 61, 69, 134
Belgian teachers 134
Belgium 71, 76, 79, 132, 137, 138
Ben Yehuda 285–6, 290–3, 308–9
Benin 11, 37, 88, 104, 158, 186, 192, 203, 207, 216, 228, 233, 234
Bété 151–2
Bible translation 83–4, 218, 294, 295, 300, 303, 305–6, 308, 310
BMS 303

Britain (Great) 75, 78, 110, 113, 115, 137–9
British colonial administrators 61, 69–70, 115, 119, 122
British colonies 23, 61–2, 64, 67, 87, 112–3, 119–23, 128, 130
British missionaries 116, 124, 299
British teachers 61, 69, 114–5, 119, 122, 125
Burundi 7, 130, 137, 140, 145, 194, 201–2, 234

Central Africa 56, 121, 123, 128, 132
Central African Republic 88, 104, 232, 234
CMS 113, 117, 138, 296, 299, 300
competitive game 48, 287
Congo DRC 115, 184, 187, 204, 235
cooperative game 46, 52, 287, 308
Côte d'Ivoire/Ivory Coast 86, 151, 186, 205–6, 233, 259
Cotonou 158, 186, 203, 205
Crowther 116–7, 285–6, 293, 295–300, 308–10

De Mesquita 35–6, 42, 44- 6, 58–9, 65–6, 68, 73–4, 76, 96, 131, 170
development island 185, 187–190, 200
DIM 63–4, 73, 106, 127, 171–2
Direct Rule 20, 87, 98, 109, 130
Diula 151, 153, 174, 194, 207–8, 217–8, 243
Duala 140, 206, 303, 307, 310

English (the language) 5, 7, 14, 16, 18, 23–4, 26, 29, 52, 66, 91, 103, 114, 118, 119, 112, 128, 129–30, 136, 141, 163, 171, 175, 177, 192, 201, 206, 207, 215, 224, 239, 253, 264, 281, 294, 296, 297, 305
Ethiopia 11, 181, 183, 184, 186, 194, 202, 235, 240

ethnicity 7–8, 37, 112, 252
ethnolinguistic dominance 181, 194, 196, 202–5
ethnolinguistic equilibrium 181, 194, 196, 205, 207
ethnolinguistic loyalty 1, 6, 8, 10–1, 107, 181, 190–3, 196, 198, 216, 243, 250, 256
Ethnologue 8, 21, 132, 145, 147, 150, 204, 217, 223, 305
Ewe 20, 118, 139, 141, 144–5, 205, 245, 249, 304, 305, 310

FFIM 23–4, 27, 63–73, 135, 141–4, 146, 171, 293, 299–300, 304
France 75, 78, 79, 84–5, 87–8, 90–3, 95, 110, 136, 137–8, 147, 156, 276, 295, 305
Francophone 24, 71, 75, 89, 92, 99, 104, 106, 107, 191, 205, 215–6, 254, 295, 300, 308
French colonial administrators 87, 90, 96
French colonies 75, 86, 88, 91–2, 96–7, 100, 104
French missionaries 88, 101
French (people) 64, 73, 75, 77, 79, 83, 85–7, 89–90, 92- 4, 98–9, 109–11, 132, 137, 140, 145, 174, 191, 300, 305
French (language) 11–2, 14, 17, 18, 24, 27, 36, 60, 87, 104, 131–2, 136, 155, 204, 256, 277

game 15, 36–7, 39, 42–51, 65, 67, 76, 98, 129, 134, 214, 250, 287, 293, 309
game (language) 15, 36, 48–9, 51, 60, 65–8, 76, 79, 82, 86, 88, 91, 92, 97, 99, 101, 103, 104, 106, 107, 109, 114, 116, 122, 124, 127, 134, 140, 142, 146, 147, 165, 171, 287
Game theory 10, 34–5, 36, 37, 39, 40–3, 46, 48, 50–1, 54–5, 58, 73–6, 106, 177, 280
German colonial administrators 61
German colonies 61–2, 66–7, 71–3, 109, 137–8, 300, 310
German missionaries 61, 69, 116, 118, 138–9, 141–3, 145, 249, 301, 304

German teacher 61, 69, 142–3
German (language) 5, 39, 141, 143–5, 173–6, 178, 194, 205, 268–71, 273–4, 283, 292, 304, 305
Germany 75, 79, 105, 132, 137, 142–3, 174, 293, 294, 301
Ghana 6, 11, 16, 24, 46–7, 55, 87, 91, 115, 118, 120, 130, 145, 150, 153, 158, 173, 175, 182, 184, 186, 202, 205, 207, 235, 245, 280

Hebrew 5, 38, 83, 222, 286, 290–3, 297, 305, 308, 309
hegemony 59, 111, 181, 217
Hereros 137

illiteracy 212–4, 218, 233–4, 249
illiterate 13, 26, 91, 133, 158, 212–3, 215, 218, 219, 222, 236, 238, 240
impediment, 1, 3–4, 8, 10, 28, 32–3, 101, 259
indigenous language 6–8, 10, 15, 18, 31–2, 51, 53, 55–6, 63, 65, 68, 75, 83, 95, 101, 103, 105, 106, 109, 112, 117–8, 120–2, 128, 130, 132–4, 137, 147, 151, 153–4, 156, 158, 161, 164, 168, 175, 179, 194, 197, 200, 204–5, 215, 222, 241, 250, 256, 270, 280, 300, 306
indigenous LWC 6, 10, 14, 209, 255
Indirect Rule 109–14
Influence (I) 36, 59, 60, 66–8, 77, 88, 90, 99, 114, 125, 134, 244

Kabye 195, 205
Kenya 7–8, 14, 17, 23–4, 51, 57, 94, 121, 124, 127, 129, 158, 184, 187, 195, 203, 204, 224, 235, 256
Komi 287–9, 307
Krapf 121, 138, 139, 285, 286, 301, 310
Kru 149, 151, 208, 276

Lagos 16, 30, 112, 184, 185, 200
Laitin 10–1, 14, 16, 24, 35, 36–7, 52, 56, 83, 100–1, 118–9, 130, 156–7, 174, 195–8, 206, 240, 269

linguistic equilibrium 35, 52, 68, 107, 181, 194, 196, 205–7
literacy 14–20, 64, 83, 98, 105, 113–7, 121–2, 133, 139, 165, 171, 178, 212–44, 280, 294, 300–8
literate 25, 52, 58, 105, 133, 177, 202, 204, 211, 239, 249, 280, 299, 304, 306–7
local language 8, 12, 16, 27, 52–3, 56–8, 86, 94, 101, 110, 118, 124, 130, 139, 141, 160, 175–6, 179, 205, 209, 214, 216–8, 241, 256, 259, 268, 270, 274, 279, 288, 295, 305–6, 308
LPAA 30, 32–3
Luganda 121, 203, 225, 301–2, 307, 310
lusophone 75, 104, 106–7, 295, 300
LWC 1–10, 14, 20, 22, 27, 32, 51, 53, 64, 114, 136, 140, 153, 171, 175, 201–22, 239, 242, 244, 251, 256, 257, 260, 264, 267, 270, 274–81

Mackay 121, 285–6, 301–2, 307, 310
Mali 8, 12, 25, 44, 88, 104, 150, 181, 195
Mande 149–51, 208, 276
marketability 1, 16–8, 29, 107, 129, 253, 256, 279, 283
media of instruction 23, 33, 64, 73, 95, 106, 124, 130, 135, 146, 160, 164, 172, 257, 267, 278
medium of instruction 12, 15, 19, 24, 26, 27, 34, 64, 92, 97, 101, 103, 115, 117, 119, 122, 124, 134, 136, 141, 156, 160, 170, 215, 242, 264, 274, 301, 304
megacity 13, 181, 190, 194, 197, 198, 200, 204, 205, 206, 209
Mina 158, 195, 203
mission civilisatrice 84
missionary-linguist 138, 300, 301, 304, 306, 307, 310
missionary-linguistics 83
MM 27, 29, 31, 44, 63, 73, 106, 127, 153, 170, 174–96, 205, 260, 268, 270–81
Moffat 121, 285–6, 302, 303, 307, 310
mother-tongue education 12, 15, 18–20, 23–4, 26, 36, 44, 64, 107, 146, 159, 165, 175, 194, 210, 251, 253, 259, 268, 274, 280

Nairobi 14, 158, 184, 187, 190, 194, 200
Nash equilibrium 49–50
newspaper 12, 139, 164, 207, 251, 264, 271, 280, 290, 292, 300, 301, 305, 307–8, 310
Nigeria 7–8, 12, 15, 24, 29, 110, 114, 120, 173, 182, 186, 205
NLWC 260, 264–6, 268, 274, 279
non-assimilation 109, 130–1, 135
non-zero-sum game 48–9, 51, 308

O Level 161–2, 269, 271
orthodox (strategy) 42, 46–7, 308–9
Outcome 9, 14–5, 24–5, 34–5, 41–6, 48–9, 51–3, 56, 58–9, 73–4, 77, 79, 81, 103–5, 107, 109, 174, 197, 203, 205, 208, 211, 275, 308

Payoff 43–8, 57, 73, 103, 165, 177, 180, 216, 233, 237–8, 248–9, 250, 277, 289
player 15, 37, 43–50, 57, 59, 60–62, 66, 68–74, 77, 82, 86, 88, 91–9, 101–3, 107, 114–5, 119, 120–2, 134–5, 142–6, 165–71, 214–50, 308
Porto Novo 200, 205
Portugal 60, 75, 79, 84–5, 98–9, 132, 295
Portuguese colonial administrators 61, 69, 102
Portuguese colonies 20, 60–72, 79, 83, 86, 99–109, 126
Portuguese missionaries 83
Portuguese (language) 76, 83, 100, 103, 105
Position (P) 58, 60, 62–3, 68–73, 92, 97, 102, 106, 115, 119, 120, 122–3, 125–7, 134–5, 142–4, 166–70, 243–7
Predictioneer's Model 44, 58, 61–3, 65–66, 68, 74, 127, 146–7, 165, 180, 211, 214, 236, 242, 244, 250, 260, 268
pre-literate 13, 213, 219
Prisoner's Dilemma 35, 49, 53–6

Rebmann 139, 285–6, 301, 310
Repertoire Model 35, 52, 56, 172, 174, 181, 202–3, 205, 208–9

RLWC 260, 264–8, 274, 276, 278–9
rural development 240
Rwanda 7, 137, 140, 145, 186, 194, 201–2, 235

Saker 285–6, 303–4, 307–8, 310
Salience (S) 58, 60, 65–6, 68–73, 96–7, 102–3, 115, 119–20, 125–7, 134–5, 142–4, 166–70, 244–8
school (high school) 29, 33, 53, 95, 157, 161, 163, 173–5, 239, 261, 290
school (lower elementary) 122, 124, 125, 130
school (upper elementary) 125, 160
school (primary) 13, 15, 24–5, 63–4, 93, 95, 97, 133, 135, 143, 147, 160–1, 163–4, 173, 300
school (secondary) 14, 115, 118, 133, 143, 161–2, 172–6, 178–9, 180–1, 194, 196, 205, 207–8, 210, 251, 268–83
Senoufo 150, 153, 160, 174–5, 208, 217
Setswana 121–2, 302–3, 307, 310
seventh grade 25, 162
SIL International 20–2, 214–6, 218, 230, 244, 306, 307, 308
social network 181, 196, 198–201
South Africa 13, 99, 124–5, 127, 129, 130, 137–8, 140, 145, 184, 186–7, 234, 236, 253, 277, 302
Spanish 15, 52, 78, 171, 173–6, 178–80, 194, 205, 209, 215, 268–74, 277, 283
St. Stefan 285–9, 293, 307–10
Strategy (Game) 39, 43, 46–8, 50–1, 73, 87, 99, 121, 137, 139, 241, 253, 255, 288, 292, 299, 300–1, 306, 310
Strategic (Game theory) 1, 56

Sudan 110, 112–3, 181, 186, 236
Swahili 3, 6, 17–8, 20, 33, 58, 138, 184, 194, 201–4, 245, 301, 308, 310

Tanzania 3, 51, 129, 130, 137, 139, 145, 184, 186, 189, 203–4, 236, 240, 256, 301
TIM 23–4, 26–7, 63–4, 73, 115, 120, 124, 128, 135, 143, 146–7, 160–1, 171, 260, 268, 270, 279
Togo 30, 87, 104, 137, 140–5, 155, 158, 187, 195, 203, 207, 216, 233, 236, 245, 304–5
Tragedy of the Commons 35, 55–6

United Bible Societies (UBS) 215, 305–8
UNESCO 15, 18, 24–7, 128, 211–5, 218, 238–40, 242–6, 248–50, 282
unorthodox strategies 46–7, 308–9
urban language 184, 193, 203–4
urbanization 181–4, 189–90, 1996–8, 206, 209

weighted mean 36, 58, 64, 68–74, 96–7, 101–6, 115, 119, 120–8, 134–5, 141–70, 180, 246–50, 260, 268, 277
Westermann 139, 141, 285–6, 304, 310
White Man's Burden 84–5

Yacouba 150, 160, 174, 208, 217
Yoruba 32, 112, 116, 118–9, 182, 194, 205, 291, 301, 307, 310

zero-sum game 48–9, 51, 75, 81
Zimbabwe 124, 130, 133, 183, 186, 236